Unfinished Agenda

Unfinished Agendas

NEW AND CONTINUING GENDER CHALLENGES
IN HIGHER EDUCATION

Edited by

JUDITH GLAZER-RAYMO

The Johns Hopkins University Press
Baltimore

© 2008 The Johns Hopkins University Press
All rights reserved. Published 2008
Printed in the United States of America on acid-free paper
2 4 6 8 9 7 5 3 1

The Johns Hopkins University Press
2715 North Charles Street
Baltimore, Maryland 21218-4363
www.press.jhu.edu

Library of Congress Cataloging-in-Publication Data

Unfinished agendas : new and continuing gender challenges in higher education /
edited by Judith Glazer-Raymo.
p.   cm.
Includes bibliographical references and index.
ISBN-13: 978-0-8018-8862-5 (hardcover : alk. paper)
ISBN-13: 978-0-8018-8863-2 (pbk. : alk. paper)
ISBN-10: 0-8018-8862-x (hardcover : alk. paper)
ISBN-10: 0-8018-8863-8 (pbk. : alk. paper)
1. Women—Education (Higher)—United States. 2. Women in higher education—
United States. 3. Feminism and education—United States. I. Glazer-Raymo, Judith.
LC1568.U54 2008
378.1′9822—dc22   2007043395

A catalog record for this book is available from the British Library.

Special discounts are available for bulk purchases of this book. For more information,
please contact Special Sales at 410-516-6936 or specialsales@press.jhu.edu.

The Johns Hopkins University Press uses environmentally friendly book materials,
including recycled text paper that is composed of at least 30 percent post-consumer
waste, whenever possible. All of our book papers are acid-free, and our jackets and
covers are printed on paper with recycled content.

In memory of Pauline Lager,
A woman of independence and spirit

CONTENTS

I thank the remarkable scholars who have contributed original chapters to this volume and who have been supportive of this project from its inception. Their insights have greatly enhanced a most rewarding collaborative effort. On their behalf, I also express appreciation to the anonymous reviewer of the manuscript, who provided valuable feedback and encouragement, and to our colleagues who participated in our symposia at the annual meetings of the Association for the Study of Higher Education (Anaheim) and the American Educational Research Association (Chicago). A special note of thanks is due to the women trustees and faculty who responded to my requests for information and willingly shared their wealth of knowledge. I also thank our editor, Jacqueline Wehmueller, who encouraged me to pursue this "sequel" to *Shattering the Myths* and who has been so helpful throughout its development. And to the editorial staff at the Johns Hopkins University Press—Deborah Bors, Andre Barnett, Julie McCarthy, and Ashleigh McKown—a heartfelt thank-you. For their review of various sections, their technical assistance, and their thoughtful advice and support, I am grateful to Rita Bornstein and Becky Ropers-Huilman, to my valued colleague Anna Neumann and to my resourceful graduate students, Kimberley Pereira and Jennifer Prudencio. As always, I acknowledge the strength and wisdom of my spouse, Bob Raymo.

The current millennium has been characterized by an intensification of issues confronting women both in and out of the academy. Moreover, almost ten years have elapsed since the publication of *Shattering the Myths: Women in Academe* (1999), in which I reviewed women's progress since the 1970s. In my analyses, I focused on the impact of institutional and external policy initiatives for women doctoral students, faculty, and academic leaders in the context of evolving feminist agendas. Through interviews, site visits, and analyses of campus documents, I recorded the voices of women as they described their experiences and reflected on the strategies and mechanisms that had been employed to promote substantive changes in their institutions and in the larger society.

Embedded in the discourse of *Shattering the Myths* was the recognition that much remained to be accomplished in promoting gender and racial equality, for although women had made significant progress in gaining access to programs, positions, and professions formerly closed to them, they continued to lag behind their male cohorts on most indicators—hiring, promotion, tenure, compensation, named chairs, grants, and senior-level appointments. They also held the majority of part-time and non-tenure-track appointments. These gender disparities ran counter to women's majority status as students. Since 1979, enrollments of women have grown proportionately until, by 2005, they comprised 57.4 percent of all college students (National Center for Educational Statistics 2007). Scholars of color also expressed frustration with the tokenism and outsider status they experienced as faculty and administrators. In my concluding comments, I expressed my conviction that the retreat from affirmative action, the corporatization of the university under the guise of educational leadership, and the backlash against women's rights called for a contrasting vision framed more broadly in the context of economic and social justice.

Given these political and economic uncertainties and altered priorities both in higher education and in the larger society, what can women in leadership positions do to build a more inclusive agenda? To respond to this question, in 2006 I invited feminist scholars engaged in the study of higher education issues and policies to contribute original chapters across a spectrum of content areas and methodologies. Ten women accepted this invitation to consider the impact of gender on women faculty and administrators from a variety of perspectives. In four of the chapters, the authors invited junior colleagues (male and female) to collaborate with them in the collection and analysis of qualitative and quantitative data around the rubric of "unfinished agendas" and "new gender challenges" in twenty-first-century American higher education. The resulting collection of essays, grounded in the authors' unique perspectives and experiences, has been conceptualized as an intergenerational and interdisciplinary discourse on women in academe. To some extent, this intergenerational approach is reminiscent of Judy Chicago's collaborative project *The Dinner Party*, in which she metaphorically invited outstanding women from different historical periods to join her at the dinner table, creating symbolic place settings for thirty-nine mythical and historical women, from ancient history to the twentieth century, engaging the imagination of those who worked on this artistic project and encouraging viewers to conduct a conversation across the generations.*

The intergenerational nature of these chapters can be seen in the co-authorship of senior and junior scholars, lending multiple perspectives to the empirical research, ethnographic interviews, and analyses of the issues. Each of these scholars is concerned with the intersections of gender, race, ethnicity, and social class in analyzing her findings. They are also cognizant of the radically altered political, economic, and social climate that now threatens to reverse many of women's hard-earned gains of the past thirty-six years.

An overarching framework for these chapters is contained in the book's title and explicated in the first chapter: (1) the feminist agenda is an unfinished work in progress; (2) mounting external and institutional challenges threaten women's advancement; and (3) active engagement with the issues is essential in addressing new and continuing challenges in support of their resolution. The chapters are conceptualized as a continuum that highlights how women faculty and administrators interpret their professional and work-life experiences in diverse institu-

---

*Judy Chicago's *The Dinner Party* (1974–79) is a large-scale collaborative work of art, executed with the help of 400 women and some men over a period of five years. Shown initially at the San Francisco Museum of Art in 1979, it has been on display in a permanent installation in the Elizabeth A. Sackler Center for Feminist Art at the Brooklyn Museum in New York City since April 2007. See also Judy Chicago, *The Dinner Party: From Creation to Preservation* (London and New York: Merrell, 2007); and Johanna Demetrakas's documentary, *Right Out of History: The Making of Judy Chicago's* Dinner Party.

tional and external contexts. They set forth the circumstances of women's entry into academia and the challenges they face as untenured and tenured faculty in their struggle with multiple and often conflicting demands for accountability, productivity, family-work responsibilities, and what Becky Ropers-Huilman refers to in chapter 2 as the subliminal but very real "dance of identities." In three of these chapters, the authors draw on extensive interviews to weave rich tapestries that relate the diverse experiences of women faculty and senior administrators.

Women research faculty at mid-career (chapter 3) provide the focus for Aimee LaPointe Terosky, Tamsyn Phifer, and Anna Neumann's analyses of the experiences of twenty women scholars seeking to balance good teaching, scholarly research, and institutional service requirements. The authors go beyond conventional analyses of the continuing challenges for women professors in research universities as they contextualize the irreconcilable forces that distance women faculty from their "core scholarly learning." The continuum from institutional to external contexts is dramatically displayed in a case study of a large multicampus research university (chapter 4) conducted by Amy Scott Metcalfe and Sheila Slaughter, who explore the nature of academic capitalism, the pursuit of market-like activities by women and men faculty, and the impact of "resource-driven behavior" on gender identities. In this study, they argue persuasively that in the past decade, the quest for external sources of support and the "cult of competition" have further destabilized the uneven playing field for women. Ana Martínez Alemán, in chapter 6, further problematizes state and institutional demands for productivity and accountability as they affect women faculty engaged in undergraduate teaching, and the role of gender in definitions and assessments of teaching effectiveness. In each of these three chapters, the authors show clearly that the gender implications of these challenges are palpable and that they undermine gender equity policies and practices. But what is it about the institutional and external culture that creates a hospitable climate for women seeking careers in science and engineering, supporting higher levels of degree productivity in science, technology, engineering, and mathematics (STEM)? Frances Stage and Steven Hubbard (chapter 5) disaggregate academic degree data in the STEM fields to determine with greater specificity which institutions produce high numbers of women baccalaureates who then go on to earn doctorates in science and mathematics.

The work lives of presidents, chancellors, and trustees are often constructed in relation to the institutions or systems they govern. Given the decentralized structure of these systems and the diversity of their missions and types of control, the purview of academic leaders may also be considered in the context of myriad external influences. In chapter 7, Rita Bornstein, a former college president, considers the career trajectory for women administrators seeking senior-level positions and the multiple challenges they encounter in achieving legitimacy in the current economic and political climate. Often overlooked in this process is the central role of governing boards in the appointment of presidents and chancellors. Consistent with the basic premise of this text, in chapter 8 I consider the evolving role of women trustees in the context of their increased presence in professional, political, and corporate contexts, and (in comparison to their male cohorts) their growing majority as degree recipients.

The prevailing institutional culture experienced by women faculty in community colleges, ranging from heavy workloads and scarce resources to adjunct appointments and inadequate facilities, as documented by Kathleen Shaw, Kate Callahan, and Kimberly LeChasseur (chapter 9) operates in stark contrast to that of the research university. And in chapter 10, Caroline Turner expresses the continuing significance of race, ethnicity, social class, and national origin for first-generation women faculty and senior administrators of color in their quest for affirmation of their professional status. In their professional lives, feminists have long grappled with the personal and the political aspects of their experiences. Kelly Ward and Lisa Wolf-Wendel (chapter 11) draw on interviews conducted with 120 women faculty, applying liberal and poststructural feminist lenses in balancing institutional expectations and responsible parenting. These three chapters also shed light on women's tenacity in determining their lifestyle choices in academic cultures that are not always responsive to their individual situations.

In the Epilogue, I reflect on new and continuing challenges that women face as articulated by the authors who have contributed their research insights to this text and also challenge those in positions of leadership to be resolute in their support of gender equality.

Unfinished Agendas

CHAPTER ONE

The Feminist Agenda

A Work in Progress

JUDITH GLAZER-RAYMO

Achieving Gender Equality in Academe

Multiple challenges confront women in higher education in the twenty-first century. Themes developed in this chapter foreshadow the ensuing chapters that illustrate the impact of changing demographics, marketization, and the ungendering of public policy on women in the professoriat and in positions of academic leadership.

In presenting national data on women's progress, I have sought evidence that the gender gap has diminished for women faculty and in senior-level administrative positions. Among my concerns in this regard has been the often-repeated but erroneous observation that women's majority status as undergraduate and graduate students means that gender equality has been achieved, and that as a result, women no longer require the protection afforded them through affirmative action and anti-bias legislation. A more problematic observation has been that women may even be responsible for what is euphemistically referred to as "the new gender gap" in which women's undergraduate numbers so far exceed their male cohorts at some institutions that college presidents and their governing boards approve measures that they predict will restore the appropriate gender balance in enrollments.

The term "gender gap" first appeared in the *Washington Post* in October 1981, reporting a gender gap of 8 percent in women's support for Jimmy Carter over Ronald Reagan in the 1980 presidential election. By mid-1982, the National Organization for Women began using the term "to describe gender-based differences in voting behavior" (Goethals et al. 2004, 544–46). This gap was attributed to Reagan's opposition to the Equal Rights Amendment (defeated in 1982) and to abortion rights. Since then, it has been applied not only in analyses of voter preferences but also in comparing male-female workforce participation and experiences, and many other issues of statistical interest. It is now being applied by opponents of women's rights regulations in their analyses of postsecondary enrollment data and the implications of women as the majority of college and university students. See also King (2006) for an analysis of the role of race, income, and social class in calculating the widening gender gap.

Rather than being applauded for their academic achievements, women have become victims of their success, beneficiaries of laws and regulations that are now being called into question. These disparities have led critics of affirmative action and Title IX to assert that gender programs should address the declines in male enrollments rather than support mechanisms for expanding women's participation. This has led some colleges to engage in more vigorous recruitment of males through expanding male-dominated intercollegiate athletics, changing brand recognition by shifting resources from feminized fields such as nursing and teaching to more gender-neutral fields of technology and engineering, or, ironically, giving gender preferences in admissions to males.

Data from the National Center for Educational Statistics (NCES), the American Association of University Professors (AAUP), the Survey of Earned Doctorates, and the Commission on Professionals in Science and Technology (CPST) show that although women are now in the majority of students, more needs to be done to increase women's status as faculty and in senior-level administrative positions.

As a remedy for past discrimination, college and university administrators have devised affirmative action policies and programs to increase the recruitment, promotion, retention, and workplace opportunities in employment for women and minorities as well as removing admissions barriers. Mechanisms for improving education and employment opportunities have focused on expanding the pool of eligible candidates through vigorous recruitment strategies and professional development programs, among other means. These programs have been instituted voluntarily or in response to state and federal laws, enforcement, or court decrees. The year 1972 was a high-water mark for women in higher education, with passage of the omnibus Higher Education Act extending equal employment opportunity, equal pay, and anti-bias laws to women at all covered colleges and universities. This Act extended Title VII of the Civil Rights Act of 1964 to higher education full-time faculty and professional staff, assigning investigative authority and oversight of affirmative action plans to the Equal Employment Opportunity Commission (EEOC), including workforce analyses of good faith efforts to employ women and minorities; it also extended coverage under the Equal Pay Act of 1963 to professional, executive, and administrative employees in higher education institutions (see Glazer-Raymo 1999, 16, for a full account of passage and implementation of the HEA of 1972). Title IX, also enacted in 1972 (and promulgated in 1975) gave added protection against employment discrimination based on sex, extending its coverage to recruitment, hiring, and promotion practices; to lines of progression or tenure based on sex; and to compensation, benefits, and working conditions. As a consequence, colleges and universities revised their employment policies and set goals and timetables for the recruitment, promotion, and equitable compensation of women faculty and professional staff.

Enrollments and Degrees

The positive impact of the 1972 legislation could be felt initially in the burgeoning enrollments of women in programs that had formerly been closed to them. By 1979 women were in the majority of college students (50.9%), and these numbers have continued to grow throughout the ensuing decades. Of the 17.5 million students enrolled in 2005, women comprised 57.2 percent of undergraduates, 49.6 percent of first-professional students, and 59.8 percent of graduate students (National Center for Education Statistics 2007). When disaggregated by race/ethnicity, in 2005 women students were also in the majority of African Americans (65%), Hispanics (58.8%), Native Americans (61.2%), and Asian/Pacific Islanders (53.9%). By 2005, women also earned an impressive percentage of academic degrees: 57.4 percent of baccalaureates, 59.3 percent of master's degrees, 49.7 percent of first-professional degrees, and 48.7 percent of doctorates.

Data from the Survey of Earned Doctorates for the past twenty-five years as shown in table 1.1 indicate an increasing share of Ph.D.s earned by women in all fields, with the greatest increases in the life sciences (50.9%) and in professional fields (48.7%).

By 2005, women earned the majority of doctorates in fourteen fields and subfields, primarily in education (66.8%), health sciences (70.8%), humanities (51%), psychology (71.2%), and social sciences (55.5%). At the first-professional level, for the past decade, women have earned the majority of degrees in optometry (61.4%), pharmacy (67%), and veterinary medicine (76.7%); they are near parity with men in law (48%) and medicine (46.8%). The proportion of women of color earning doctorates is also increasing (18.4%): African-American women (7.8%), Hispanic women (4.1%), Native American women (0.6%), and Asian women (5.9%). Women "non-resident aliens" also accounted for approximately 18 percent of all doctoral

TABLE 1.1

Doctoral Awards by Field, Year, and Sex (All Fields)

Field of Study	1980 Total	1980 Women	1980 % Women	1990 Total	1990 Women	1990 % Women	2000[a] Total	2000[a] Women	2000[a] % Women	2005[b] Total	2005[b] Women	2005[b] % Women
All fields	31,019	9,407	30.3	36,064	13,104	36.3	41,287	18,126	43.9	43,295	19,564	45.2
Physical science[c]	4,071	496	12.2	5,809	1,059	18.2	5,971	1,423	23.8	6,692	1,766	26.4
Engineering	2,479	90	3.6	4,894	415	8.5	5,297	838	15.8	6,389	1,174	18.4
Life sciences	5,501	1,420	25.8	6,655	2,492	37.4	8,613	4,044	47.0	9,294	4,727	50.9
Social sciences	5,855	2,045	34.9	6,092	2,826	46.4	7,100	3,874	54.6	6,833	3,790	55.5
Humanities	3,871	1,532	39.6	3,822	1,748	45.7	5,629	2,832	50.3	5,343	2,724	51.0
Education	7,586	3,383	44.6	6,509	3,751	57.6	6,429	4,174	64.9	6,219	4,154	66.8
Professional/ other fields	1,656	441	26.6	2,283	813	35.6	2,248	941	41.9	2,525	1,229	48.7

SOURCE: National Opinion Research Center, *Survey of Earned Doctorates* (Washington, DC: National Science Foundation et al., 2005).

[a]Group total for 2000 excludes 74 individuals for whom sex was not reported.
[b]Group total for 2005 excludes 59 individuals for whom sex was not reported.
[c]Includes mathematics and computer science.

TABLE 1.2

Full-Time Faculty by Academic Rank and Race/Ethnicity (Fall 2005)

Academic Rank	All Faculty Total	All Faculty % Women	White, Non-Hispanic Total	White, Non-Hispanic % Women	Black, Non-Hispanic Total	Black, Non-Hispanic % Women	Hispanic Total	Hispanic % Women	Asian/ Pacific Islander Total	Asian/ Pacific Islander % Women	American Indian/ Alaskan Native Total	American Indian/ Alaskan Native % Women	Unknown Race Total	Unknown Race % Women	Nonresident Alien Total	Nonresident Alien % Women
All ranks	675,624	40.6	527,900	40.6	35,458	52.0	22,818	45.3	48,457	34.6	3,231	47.5	9,703	41.6	28,057	31.5
Professors	169,192	25.1	145,936	25.2	5,484	36.2	3,793	29.3	11,060	17.0	519	32.9	1,014	24.7	1,386	14.1
Associate professors	138,444	38.8	112,507	39.2	7,402	46.7	4,319	40.9	10,144	30.0	564	47.5	1,296	35.6	2,212	24.4
Assistant professors	159,689	46.0	114,470	47.4	9,897	54.9	5,728	47.6	14,922	40.3	706	56.7	2,809	43.0	11,157	31.3
Instructors	98,555	52.8	76,359	52.8	7,462	60.0	5,261	50.9	4,740	51.1	905	47.8	1,853	47.2	1,975	43.8
Lecturers	27,215	52.3	20,982	52.8	1,286	53.7	1,233	59.9	1,714	51.1	109	53.2	480	45.0	1,411	40.9
Other faculty	82,529	46.3	57,646	48.0	3,927	60.7	2,484	52.7	5,877	42.7	428	47.7	2,251	45.5	9,916	31.8

SOURCE: U.S. Department of Education, National Center for Education Statistics, *Integrated Postsecondary Education Data System (IPEDS), Winter 2005–6*, Washington, DC, 2005.

recipients in 2005. As Stage and Hubbard's chapter on women baccalaureates shows, there continue to be disparities in the proportion of minorities and women who earn Ph.D.s in science, mathematics, and engineering.

Full-Time Faculty

As faculty, women have their highest representation in two-year public colleges (50%); they are less well-represented in four-year and master's level institutions (41%) and in research universities (33%). By institutional type, they account for 40 percent of faculty in denominational colleges, 38 percent in public institutions, and 36 percent in independent or private institutions (Curtis 2006, 1). As shown in table 1.2, in 2005, women comprised 40.6 percent of all full-time faculty compared to 59.4 percent of men, an increase of 8 percent since 1995. When analyzed by rank, the higher the rank, the fewer the women is still the case. Women full professors account for 25.1 percent of all faculty, 38.8 percent of associate professors, and 46 percent of assistant professors. They continue to be in the majority of lecturers (52.3%) and instructors (52.8%). The majority status of women of color doctoral recipients holds only for African-American women faculty (52%), although Hispanic women (45.3%) and Native American women (47.5%) faculty are almost at parity with their male counterparts.

In their analysis of the shifting demographics in appointments of full-time faculty, Schuster and Finkelstein (2006, 50, fig. 3.4) provide a breakdown by faculty at various stages in their careers, noting that in 1998, women comprised 44.2 percent of new entrants, compared to 34.1 percent of mid-career and senior faculty. However, they also note that "the *rate* of infusion of women into the full-time faculty, having mushroomed earlier in this period, has begun to slow" (2006, 51). CPST data also show that women are still more likely to have their greatest representation in education, library science, nursing, social work, and the humanities, and to be less well-represented in the physical sciences, computer science, mathematics, and engineering, where they account for "just over one in ten engineering faculty" (Bell et al. 2006, 287).

Faculty Employment Trends: The Contingent Workforce

The dual employment track that I described in 1999 is even more pronounced in 2007 due to a further decline in tenure-track faculty positions and an increase in part-time and non-tenure-track hiring (Glazer-Raymo 1999, 2003). This trend is having a disproportionate impact on the generation of younger women faculty

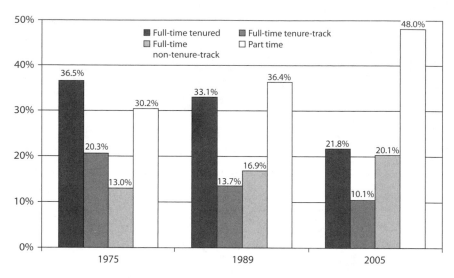

Figure 1.1. Trends in faculty status, 1975–2005. All degree-granting institutions, national totals. Source: U.S. Department of Education, *IPEDS Fall Staff Survey,* American Association of University Professors Office of Research and Public Policy, Washington, DC, 2006. Reprinted with permission from John Curtis.

who are graduating from doctoral programs in greater numbers, channeling them into postdoctoral adjunct teaching and research, and diminishing their chances for positive career trajectories (Glazer-Raymo 2003). The AAUP observes that unless significant changes occur in these employment patterns, a major challenge for women will be to reach parity with their male colleagues (West and Curtis 2006, 7). In their comprehensive account of the restructuring of faculty work and careers, Schuster and Finkelstein also take note of "hugely significant" changes occurring in the nature of new faculty appointments that are now likely to be off the tenure track (2006, 356). They hypothesize that "it may very well develop that this restructuring of appointments is highly consequential, rich with both intended and unintended effects, and from these insights might flow a reconsideration of institutional appointment policies" (357). Certainly, the market-like behavior that Metcalfe and Slaughter describe in chapter 4 will contribute to changing the patterns of faculty careers in research universities. The implications for women and minority faculty warrant close monitoring in this context.

An AAUP analysis of NCES *Trends in Faculty Status, 1975–2005,* as shown in figure 1.1, reveals that by 2005 contingent faculty, who may be part-time or full-time non-tenure-track, comprised more than two-thirds (68%) of all faculty in degree-granting institutions, an increase of 17.8 percent in part-time faculty and 7.1

percent in full-time non-tenure-track faculty in two decades (AAUP 2007). The concomitant decline in the proportion of full-time tenured (−14.7%) and tenure-track (−10.2%) faculty in only two decades is troubling. It is only in the community college sector that women are now in the majority of both tenure-track faculty (50.8%) and part-time faculty (51%).

Part-Time Faculty

Although part-time faculty are "demographically diverse," the AAUP Committee on the Economic Status of the Profession reports substantial differences in rates of pay based on per-credit-hour or per-course formulas, institutional type (two-year or four-year or doctoral), and institutional sector (public or private) (2006, 33, table D). Not surprisingly, part-time faculty teaching in private doctoral universities enjoy the highest per-course rates; their median pay is typically 50 percent higher than in public doctoral universities and 80 percent higher than in public two-year colleges, "which offer the lowest median rate of pay to part-time faculty members" (33). Shaw, Callahan, and LeChasseur (chapter 9) on women in community colleges provide further discussion.

One argument that the AAUP Committee rightfully rejects is that lower pay for part-time faculty can be justified based on purportedly fewer scholarship and service demands than for full-time faculty (2006, 33). A catch-22 situation is evident here: many part-time faculty have academic and professional credentials comparable to their full-time colleagues and pursue research to keep abreast of their disciplines and to be part of their professional community. Having been pigeonholed into part-time and non-tenure-track positions, they often find it difficult to move into equivalent full-time positions. Although the pressures on full-time and part-time faculty differ in many respects, both Terosky et al. (chapter 3) and Shaw et al. (chapter 9) find that the heavy and often erratic workload experienced by many women often takes them away from their original purpose in obtaining a doctorate—the pursuit of scholarly learning in their chosen field.

Non-Tenure-Track Faculty

In an analysis of indicators of gender equity, the AAUP reports that by 2005, women held 52 percent of non-tenure-track faculty appointments and 57 percent of full-time instructor and lecturer positions, leading the report's authors, Martha West and John Curtis, to observe that women are "significantly overrepresented in these non-tenure-track positions, the least secure, least remunerative, and least

TABLE 1.3

Salaries of Full-Time Instructional Faculty on Nine-Month Contracts: Women's Salaries as Percentage of Men's

	1974–75 (%)	1979–80 (%)	1984–85 (%)	1989–90 (%)	1994–95 (%)	1999–2000 (%)	2005–6 (%)
All faculty	82.6	82.1	80.6	79.9	80.8	81.5	82.0
Professors	88.3	90.4	89.0	88.8	88.3	87.7	86.0
Associate professors	95.1	95.3	93.8	93.4	93.5	93.1	92.9
Assistant professors	95.5	95.8	93.1	92.0	93.6	93.4	92.6
Instructors	87.9	96.0	91.5	93.8	95.2	95.5	94.3
Public institutions	84.1	83.6	82.4	81.0	82.1	82.6	83.0
4-year	81.8	81.3	80.4	79.6	80.7	80.9	81.0
2-year	91.1	90.5	90.6	89.8	90.4	92.6	95.1
Private institutions	77.9	77.6	75.5	77.2	77.7	79.4	80.4
4-year	78.4	78.2	76.1	77.5	78.8	79.6	80.5
2-year	91.6	90.0	90.3	95.2	77.1	85.3	101.5

SOURCE: U.S. Department of Education, National Center for Education Statistics, Higher Education General Information Survey (HEGIS), "Faculty Salaries, Tenure, and Fringe Benefits," surveys, 1970–71 through 1985–86; and 1987–88 through 2005–6; *Integrated Postsecondary Education Data System (IPEDS)*, "Salaries, Tenure, and Fringe Benefits of Full-Time Instructional Faculty Survey" (IPEDS-SA:87–99), and Winter 2001 through Winter 2005.

prestigious jobs among the full-time faculty" (West and Curtis 2006, 9). Their analysis of male-female tenure rates in 2005 also reveals that, regardless of institutional type, women are 10 to 15 percent less likely than men to be in tenure-eligible positions, leading them to conclude that the status of women faculty is "a series of accumulated disadvantages" emerging from women's underrepresentation in tenure-track positions and senior faculty ranks, and manifested in women's lower career earnings (West and Curtis 2006, 7).

Since the late 1970s, when the AAUP began to disaggregate data on tenure rates in its annual survey of the economic status of the professoriat, the gender gap has remained consistent—47 percent of women full-time faculty enjoy tenure as compared to 70 percent of men—and they predict that "with tenure-track appointments making up fewer than half of new full-time faculty positions, and the proportion of part-time positions continuing to rise," it is unlikely that the gender gap in tenure will diminish in the foreseeable future (Committee on the Economic Status of the Profession 2005, 28). Moreover, a survey conducted by the Center for Education of Women at the University of Michigan also found that by 2003 contingent faculty appointments in four-year colleges and universities accounted for three out of five faculty positions and for three out of four new hires (2006, 2). When confronted with these data, university deans and provosts often argue that caps on tenure-track appointments and higher bars for obtaining tenure can be justified on the basis of greater institutional flexibility in the allocation of resources; the high cost of pensions, health coverage, and other benefits, estimated at 25–30% for full-time instructional faculty, depending on institutional type (NCES 2007b, table 44-1b); and the purported lack of qualified candidates in the pipeline.

Salaries

Male faculty maintain a salary advantage over women faculty across all ranks and in all institutional types. In 2005, the average salary of women faculty across all ranks was 82 percent of their male colleagues', a comparison that has not changed since the NCES began disaggregating data for men and women faculty in 1974–75 as shown in table 1.3. Disparities are higher at the rank of full professor, and here again the data have changed only slightly in the past three decades. By institutional type, women faculty in two-year colleges (where there is a higher proportion of part-time and non-tenure-track faculty) enjoy salaries that are comparable to or even higher than men's, and those data show improvement over the past decade. The reason for 5 to 9 percent discrepancies in total salary data and by rank can be attributed in part to women's majority status at the lowest ranks (instructor and lecturer) and in part-time and non-tenure-track positions.

The College and University Personnel Association's 2007 faculty compensation survey shows wide variations by discipline for full-time faculty: law, business, and engineering, in which fewer women have tenure-track positions, continue to be the highest paying fields; while the increasingly feminized fields of education, English language and literature, history, and the visual and performing arts remain at the lower end of the salary scale.

Student and Faculty Activism

Social movement activism focusing on civil rights, women's rights, and opposition to militaristic policies was at its peak in the 1960s and 70s. And although various interest groups have continued to rally around disinvestment, globalization, affirmative action, and anti-militarism in the ensuing decades, the most striking resurgence of activism has emerged around unionization of part-time adjuncts and graduate students. Since 1990, unionized graduate employees have increased by 175 percent, and close to 40,000 graduate employees are now unionized (Rhoads and Rhoades 2005). Unions such as the United Automobile Workers (UAW) that had not been traditionally academic in origin perceive faculty and student adversity as an opportunity to organize adjuncts and graduate teaching assistants into collective bargaining units (see Jessup 2003 for a case study of the UAW and graduate student organizing at New York University). For the universities, this trend has been a wake-up call, forcing presidents and deans to revisit personnel policies, including benefit plans, teaching workloads, and compensation. The AAUP, the National Education Association (NEA), and the American Federation of Teachers (AFT) view the growth of a part-time teaching workforce as a threat to job security, working conditions, and the receipt of benefits for all faculty. The impact on women, who make up a sizable proportion of this marginalized workforce, has been substantial.

The AFT, which expressed its concern about the "vanishing professor" ten years ago, now takes a more activist stance in proposing federal and state legislation to reverse what it now characterizes as an "academic staffing crisis" (American Federation of Teachers 1998; McKenna 2007, 12). By 2007, AFT-sponsored bills were introduced in fifteen states to end the "economic exploitation of part-time/adjunct and other non-tenure-track faculty along with the shrinking ranks of full-time tenured or tenure-track faculty" (McKenna 2007, 13). The continued growth of adjunct and part-time faculty unions may empower their members, but there is little evidence that state legislatures see it in their self-interest to approve budgetary increases that will reverse this trend.

Ungendering Public Policy
Adjudicating Affirmative Action

Supreme Court rulings on affirmative action have been instrumental in restructuring the boundaries of higher education, providing access and opportunity for women and minorities at almost every level of the academy. In retrospect, the 1978 Supreme Court decision *Regents of University of California v. Bakke,* which allowed race to be considered as one of several factors used to admit minority students to medical schools, provided a template for tailoring undergraduate and graduate minority admissions policies and helped establish the practicality of a diversity rationale in states without a history of racial segregation and in response to the demands of historically underrepresented groups.

The conservative leadership that rose to power in the 1980s with the presidential election of Ronald Reagan ushered in a new era in the struggle for civil rights and women's rights. It was characterized by unrelenting attacks on affirmative action and Title IX as well as on social welfare and health policies. For women, the legacy of the Reagan-Bush years was highlighted by supply-side economics, attempts to scale back Title IX of the Education Amendments of 1972, and other domestic programs of particular interest to women. Its long-range impact occurred with the appointments to the Supreme Court of two conservative justices, Antonin Scalia and Clarence Thomas. That legacy has been further enhanced by the incumbent president, George W. Bush, who has overseen the selection of John Roberts as Chief Justice (replacing the late William Rehnquist) and Samuel Alito, replacing Justice Sandra Day O'Connor. These four appointments have tipped the judicial balance of power further away from women's rights, civil rights, and gay rights, and will influence the direction of judicial decisions (and the cases that reach the Court) for decades to come.

Justice O'Connor, the first woman to serve on the Supreme Court, was a "critical swing vote" on women's reproductive rights, affirmative action (in college admissions as well as in set-asides for minority contractors), religious school vouchers, and other key social issues (Greenhouse, 2005, A1). Her retirement (which she delayed until 2006), and the death of Chief Justice William Rehnquist, created the first vacancies in more than a decade and gave George W. Bush the opportunity to choose two conservative justices. Although a woman, Harriet Miers, the president's chief counsel, was nominated to replace O'Connor, her nomination was withdrawn and there is now only one woman remaining on the Court, Justice Ruth Bader Ginsburg.

During his years as president, Bill Clinton took a centrist position on affirmative action, while privately funded think tanks stepped up their offensive against this policy as well as related anti-bias laws and regulations. Although the impact of affirmative action extended to all public agencies in every state, public flagship universities became the combat zone for a well-oiled conservative campaign to invalidate policies that weighed "racial preferences" in admissions, employment, and contracting. Gender was rarely mentioned in the diatribes against affirmative action, but it was implicit in the rhetoric of color-blind, gender-neutral orthodoxy (see Thernstrom and Thernstrom 1997). Support for this campaign has also come from neoconservatives, who liken affirmative action to quota systems and reverse discrimination, asserting that it has historically denied access to members of ethnic or religious groups and that it continues to single out white applicants. The diversity rationale that had formed the basis for the *Bakke* decision acquired greater immediacy as presidents and chancellors sought justification for the criteria they used to admit students, hire faculty and staff, fund scholarships, and award government contracts. Legal actions raised the stakes for compliance, and in the process, affirmative action for women got lost in the ensuing discourse. As an incremental process, the redirection of policy based on the diversity rationale fragmented advocates of affirmative action into many competing interest and identity groups.

In 1994, when Republicans gained control of the U.S. Congress, conservative think tanks such as the Heritage Foundation and the Center for Individual Rights (CIR) charted a more aggressive course in their attacks on affirmative action. In 1995, Governor Pete Wilson and Ward Connerly, members of the University of California Board of Regents, gained support with a vote of 14–10 for a resolution ending affirmative action on its ten campuses. The following year, a referendum on Proposition 209, erroneously portrayed as a "civil rights initiative," extended this ban to all public agencies in California by a margin of 55–45. In 1995, the CIR also successfully challenged the constitutionality of admissions policies at the flagship University of Texas, charging that "racial preferences" had violated the Fourteenth Amendment rights of a woman applicant in the case of *Hopwood v. University of Texas Law School.* And in 1998, the CIR stage-managed a successful voter initiative in Washington State, where 90 percent of the voters are white, gaining passage of Proposition 200 to ban affirmative action in all public agencies, including higher education.

These statewide campaigns have been effective wedge issues, dividing women and minorities, a strategy heightened by the deliberate selection of white working-class women as plaintiffs in court cases in Texas and Michigan, pointedly contrasting their academic qualifications with those of minority men and women. The CIR, which brought these suits, has maintained, as do other legal observers, that the Supreme Court will eventually determine the future viability of affirmative action policy. This strategy, which proved effective for Cheryl Hopwood in Texas, was also applied in selecting Barbara Grutter and Jennifer Gratz as the plaintiffs in *Grutter v. Bollinger,* challenging the Michigan Law School's admission policy and *Gratz v. Bollinger,* which targeted admissions criteria of the University of Michigan's undergraduate College of Literature, Science, and the Arts.[1]

These cases are also noteworthy attempts by the CIR and other opponents of affirmative action to elevate their legal attacks on affirmative action from state referenda to federal court action, thereby eradicating this policy in one stroke. As in *Bakke,* the Court rendered a split decision. In the key judgment, *Grutter v. Bollinger,* it upheld 5–4 the Law School's affirmative action program, stating that there is a "compelling interest in a diverse student body . . . at the heart of the Law School's proper institutional mission" and that "the law school's educational judgment that such diversity is essential to its educational mission is one to which we defer" (O'Connor 2003). In the related case, *Gratz v. Bollinger,* the Court rejected Michigan's undergraduate admission policy for assigning a point system in their review of all minority applications and, in the view of the majority, violating the Equal Protection clause of the Constitution. In her majority opinion, Justice O'Connor acknowledged the importance of the briefs filed by other universities, professional associations, corporations, and the military, asserting that "context matters when reviewing race-based governmental action under the Equal Protection Clause." However, she put a time limit of twenty-five years for achieving race equity in American institutions.

Swift responses followed the Supreme Court decision. Having failed to accomplish their goal through the federal courts, opponents of affirmative action, led by Ward Connerly and his American Civil Rights Coalition, have returned to a state-by-state strategy. In November 2006, the Michigan Civil Rights Initiative (MCRI) Committee gained passage of Proposition 2, a constitutional amendment banning affirmative action in all public agencies in the state and extending this ban to public employment and contracting. Its passage by a sizable margin of 58–42 has energized its supporters to extend their campaign to other states, using the ballot box as well as the courts to achieve their aim. The wording of this proposition is the most inclusive to date, asking voters to check *yes* or *no* to:

A proposal to amend the state constitution to ban affirmative action programs that give preferential treatment to groups or individuals based on their race, *gender*, color, ethnicity or national origin for public employment, education or contracting purposes. (emphasis added)

The proposed constitutional amendment would:

- Ban public institutions from using affirmative action programs that give preferential treatment to groups or individuals based on their race, *gender*, color, ethnicity, or national origin for public employment, education or contracting purposes. Public institutions affected by this proposal include state government, local governments, *public colleges and universities, community colleges and school districts* (emphasis added).

- Prohibit public institutions from discriminating against groups or individuals due to their *gender*, race, color, or national origin. (A separate provision of the state constitution already prohibits discrimination on the basis of race, color, or national origin.)

In an excellent analysis of the potential impact of MCRI on women in the state of Michigan, Susan Kaufmann observes that in the decade since passage of California's Proposition 209, women have experienced a leveling-off in faculty hiring, with the annual rate only now approaching pre-1995 levels; declines in funding of minority health professionals; the elimination of scholarships, fellowships, and grants at all levels of education that consider gender, race, ethnicity, or national origin; and weakening of affirmative action in public contracting, including bidding opportunities for women and minority-owned businesses (Kaufmann and Davis 2006, 2). She also notes that Proposition 209's impact has been to erode "legal, court-sanctioned efforts by state and local governments to reach out to women and minorities" in reversing historic discrimination and exclusion from education, employment and business opportunities (1).

In 2005, a self-styled National Coalition of Free Men, also led by Ward Connerly, filed suit against the state of California regarding more than thirty programs that target women (Kaufmann 2006, 13 n. 17). In seeking state-by-state bans on affirmative action, this coalition's motives are quite transparent: to sever the protection afforded women and minorities under current laws and regulations. Having gained momentum in the MCRI vote, Connerly, now chairman of the American Civil Rights Institute, and his "Civil Rights Initiative" adherents have announced their intention "to get bans on racial and ethnic preferences on the ballots in four [now five] states—Arizona, Colorado, Missouri, and Oklahoma [and Nebraska]— as part of a plan to thrust the issue into the national spotlight in the November

2008 presidential election" (Schmidt 2007). Civil rights organizations have vowed to oppose the proposed ballot measures, indicating that affirmative action may well be used to promote partisan support for political candidates on both sides of the debate. Once again, higher education is the battleground on which this state-by-state strategy will be fought.

One outcome among university leaders has been to reaffirm their commitment to demographic and income diversity in admissions (Bowen, Kurzweil, and Tobin 2005). It is not clear whether gender will be part of this equation, particularly with the majority status of women students being framed as "the new gender gap." A CNN exit poll revealed that 70 percent of white males and 59 percent of white females voted for the Michigan ban; 70 percent of non-white males and 82 percent of non-white females registered their opposition, evidence of the divisive nature of this proposition and raising questions about public understanding of the consequences. Undoubtedly, civil rights and women's rights do not generate the same level of activism and support as they did in the 1960s and 70s. Whether or not the diversity rationale will be upheld remains to be determined. Michigan's first woman governor, who opposed passage of MCRI, has stated that the real success of affirmative action is to level the playing field for women, open the doors to male-dominated professions, allow women to become more economically and socially independent and more productive citizens, and "motivate their children and others to strive for higher and different goals in life . . . having a greater impact on our culture, economy, and society in general" (Granholm and Archer 2006, 10).

Walter Allen, who headed the team of expert witnesses in the Michigan cases, predicts that the Supreme Court rulings "will likely determine the future direction of U.S. higher education" (2006, 203). He argues that "as a student of inequality" for the past thirty years, he is persuaded that "racial and ethnic inequality operate at intersection with other hierarchical systems," including gender, social class, and cultural differences (205), and that suggestions that racial and gender discrimination no longer exist pose a danger for "affirmative action and other programs to promote fairness and equality" (213).

In his balanced analysis of affirmative action policy, Edward Kellough contends that regardless of the opposition being expressed to this policy, support is "unlikely to end completely until sufficient progress has been made in the battle against discrimination—and minorities and women are no longer disadvantaged in their efforts to achieve employment or educational opportunities because of race, ethnicity, or sex" (2006, 150). The truth, he states, is that we have not yet reached that goal, and that although advances have been made, much remains to be achieved. The reality is that without affirmative action, women and minorities would not have gained these opportunities, and that oversight will be required to assure continued progress.

Adjudicating Title VII

On May 29, 2007, the Supreme Court showed its determination to turn back the clock on women's and civil rights legislation when it ruled 5–4 in the case of *Lilly M. Ledbetter v. Goodyear Tire and Rubber Co.* that under Title VII of the Civil Rights Act of 1964, a litigant must file a federal claim of illegal gender-based pay discrimination within 180 days of when the discriminatory act first arises. The case involved a female supervisor at a Goodyear Tire plant in Alabama, "the only woman among 16 men at the same management level, who was paid [15–40%] less than any of her colleagues, including those with less seniority," something she learned late in her twenty-year career (Greenhouse 2007b). Upon her early retirement in 1998, she filed a complaint with the Equal Employment Opportunity Commission that supported her claim. Although she won a jury verdict in the lower court, the 11th Circuit Court of Appeals ruled against her, throwing out the jury verdict. The Bush administration joined Goodyear in arguing that "the 180-day clock generally starts when the discriminatory pay decision is made and not when each subsequent check arrives" (Lash 2007, 2). Justice Ruth Bader Ginsburg stated her dissent orally from the bench, arguing: "The court does not comprehend, or is indifferent to, the insidious way in which women can be victims of pay discrimination" (as cited by Lash 2007, 1).

Since passage of the omnibus Higher Education Act of 1972, Title VII has protected the rights of women in higher education to pay equity; indeed, numerous class action suits and complaints have been filed with the EEOC in the past thirty-five years by women faculty and professional staff to reverse gender-based inequities in compensation. As Ginsburg pointed out in her written dissent, Congressional intent was not only to prohibit discriminatory policies based on sex but to prevent the lingering effects of gender bias that would expand exponentially over an employee's work life (Greenhouse 2007a). Women legal scholars who commented on her dissent concurred that, given Justice Ginsburg's inability to persuade her colleagues otherwise, she was "sounding the alarm" to heighten public awareness of its impact (Greenhouse 2007b). It undoubtedly represents a new challenge to women in the workforce, a signal from the newly constituted majority on the Supreme Court that they intend to roll back many of the gains made in the past forty years. In a lead editorial on May 31, 2007, the *New York Times* indicated the symbolic importance of the *Ledbetter* decision, characterizing it as "Injustice 5, Justice 4," and stating that the Court "struck a blow for discrimination this week by stripping a key civil rights law of much of its potency."

Deregulating Title IX

Title IX's impact in the past three decades has been remarkable. Since its inception in 1972 (and promulgation in 1975), it has opened the doors to institutions, programs, and activities for girls and women at all levels of the educational system. In athletics alone, Title IX has been responsible for a 400 percent increase in women's participation in college sports and an 800 percent increase in participation of high school girls (AAUW Action Network 2007). However, since the mid-1980s periodic efforts have been made by the Department of Education (DOE) to chip away at Title IX, with varying results. As the only law that specifically targets sex discrimination in education, it states succinctly: *No person in the United States, on the basis of sex, can be excluded from participation in, be denied the benefits of, or be subjected to discrimination under any education program or activity receiving Federal financial assistance.* In the thirty-five years since its passage, its meaning has been extended and redefined, primarily through case law but also through the regulatory process, to include employment discrimination, sexual harassment and hostile environment, pregnant and parenting students, and academic and non-academic programs and services across a range of institutional types and levels (K–12 and postsecondary). Further extending its meaning, the regulations define affirmative action in Title IX as follows: "In the absence of a finding of discrimination on the basis of sex in an education program or activity, a recipient may take *affirmative action* to overcome the effects of conditions which resulted in limited participation therein by persons of a particular sex."

According to Nelly Stromquist (2006, 3), state compliance with Title IX has been minimal, particularly since 1998, when Congress terminated funding for gender equity programs under the Carl Perkins Vocational Education Act.[2] Efforts have been underway since 2001 by the Bush administration to deregulate sections of Title IX, challenging its viability on a number of levels. The National Coalition for Women and Girls in Education (NCWGE), which monitors gender-related federal actions, has been critical of the laxity in institutional compliance reviews, noting that in 2002 the Office of Civil Rights, the DOE's enforcement division, initiated only eleven reviews, the lowest number since 1989 (NCWGE 2004, 4). It also questioned the failure of the DOE to include funding for the Women's Educational Equity Act each year since 2001 and the issuance of new regulations permitting single-sex education.

Concerned about the lack of enforcement of Title IX's provisions among government agencies, in 2004 a Senate subcommittee commissioned a review by the General Accountability Office (GAO) of Title IX compliance in the sciences (GAO 2004). It found that four federal agencies made efforts to ensure that grantees comply with Title IX by performing several compliance activities, such as investigating complaints and providing technical assistance. However, most agencies have not conducted required monitoring activities, and three agencies—the Department of Energy, NASA, and NSF—referred complaints to either the DOE or the EEOC. As a result of this report, in March 2006 the DOE indicated its intention to conduct an in-depth investigation of whether selected colleges and universities were in compliance in mathematics and science. In December 2006, the National Women's Law Center (NWLC) conducted an examination of athletics complaints and compliance reviews related to Title IX conducted by the Office of Civil Rights (OCR) between 2002 and 2006. In its report, *Barriers to Fair Play,* issued in June 2007, it described continuing discrimination against girls and women in sports, schools' second-class treatment of women athletes, fear of retaliation by coaches of girls' and women's sports, and most importantly, laxity in OCR enforcement efforts, with only one compliance review of a school's athletics program conducted in the past five years (NWLC 2007, 12).

In what follows, I focus on three areas: (1) the Virginia Military Academy (VMI) decision on the use of public funds for male-only colleges, (2) the deregulation of single-sex education provisions, and (3) the proportionality rule in funding college sports. These areas are central to the public discourse of female-male participation and degree attainment in undergraduate education, the persistence of gendered career paths, and the policy process in allocating resources for college programs and activities under Title IX.

A recent op-ed article in the *New York Times* quoted the dean of admissions at Kenyon College, bemoaning the imbalance in female-male applications, suggesting that gender balance is the "large elephant in the middle of the room" and that less-qualified men may be receiving preference in admissions to higher-achieving women (Britz 2006). Her comments generated an outpouring of letters, media coverage, and corridor conversations about the need for "Affirmative Action for Men" (*Inside Higher Ed* 2006). This contretemps coincides with a directive to public institutions from the OCR that minority fellowships designed to promote affirmative action may be subject to legal challenges as a result of the *Grutter* decision. Evidence is accumulating that the notion of "affirmative action for men" is a genuine proposal, not just a catchy concept. A series of articles on "the new gender divide" in higher education discusses the changing college landscape in which "many small liberal arts colleges and huge public universities" with a 60–40 ratio of women to men undergraduates are rethinking their admissions policies (Lewin 2006, A1). Shenandoah University is featured as one institution that has narrowed the gender gap through the addition of Division III football with a roster of about one hundred players each year (Pennington 2006, A1). Problematizing the majority status of women students gives credence to a new form of gender bias that may also fuel the anti–affirmative action rhetoric of individuals and groups with little or no stake in the outcomes or intent of higher education policies.

The VMI Decision

In 1997 the Supreme Court held that the Virginia Military Institute (VMI), a public men-only college, violated the Fourteenth Amendment's equal protection clause when it denied admission to women, and that establishing the Virginia Women's Institute for Leadership (VWIL) at Mary Baldwin College, a private liberal arts college for women, did not remedy that violation. In her majority opinion, Justice Ruth Bader Ginsburg stated that gender classifications must have "an exceedingly persuasive justification" such as "to advance the full development of the talent and capacities of our Nation's people," but not "to create or perpetuate the legal, social, and economic inferiority of women."[3] Ginsburg also drew an analogy to cases of race discrimination, which are held to a standard of "strict scrutiny" by the Court, stating that the VMI ruling raised the bar in cases of gender discrimination, elevating the gender standard from "intermediate" to "heightened intermediate scrutiny." Although Title IX was not cited in this ruling, the implications for cases alleging gender discrimination would now be subject to a stricter standard than heretofore.

Single-Sex Education

Another perspective on the VMI decision relates to the use of public funds for single-sex education in the public schools and the DOE's unilateral decision to terminate a provision of Title IX that has been in effect since 1975. The original regulations permitted some sex-segregated education, such as single-sex schools or classes, solely as a remedy for gender discrimination and based on empirical research. In March 2004, the DOE proposed loosening the single-sex school provision, ostensibly to offer additional choices to parents and to make it easier for school districts to allocate resources for single-sex classes and single-sex schools. Although 5,000 comments opposing this action were registered, the DOE (based on a legal endorsement from the Attorney General, Alberto Gonzales) issued the new regulations in October 2006. The revised regulations will permit nonvocational single-sex schools, classes, and extracurricular activities in elementary and secondary schools for a variety of general purposes. These are construed rather broadly to foster "the achievement of an important governmental or educational objective."[4]

Women's organizations that monitor Title IX have expressed their opposition to the use of a back-door approach to deregulate provisions of the one piece of legislation specifically designed to expand women's participation in all education programs and activities. Instead, they view this change as an abrogation of federal commitment to such goals and an effort to promote gender neutrality for ideological purposes that include privatization of public education, faith-based initiatives, charter schools, and special-purpose academies. Above all, this cherry-picking further erodes Title IX and sends the message that rules can be changed by unelected officials for ideological rather than educational reasons and without benefit of empirical research findings. The 2006 regulations will permit single-sex facilities or classes as long as the gender that is not targeted for single-sex education also receives a "substantially equal" educational opportunity in a coeducational setting. "Substantially equal" is not defined in the regulation, and there are no instructions on how to learn if the single-sex activities contribute to increased sex stereotyping and sex discrimination or if they contribute to achieving any important governmental objectives such as increased academic achievement. The National Women's Law Center asserts that the new regulations "will allow school districts to exclude girls or boys from classrooms based on classic stereotypes, for example, that girls cannot learn in a fast-paced competitive environment or need to be isolated as the only way to protect them from sexual harassment or bullying," also noting the irony of this proposal from "an administration that has consistently undermined affirmative action and challenged programs that advance desegregation efforts and help disadvantaged students [and] is now issuing rules allowing segregation throughout our nation's public schools" (NWLC 2006, 2). Above all, there is no expectation that a single-sex program or school will have to show that it is any better than high-quality instruction designed to meet the same needs in coeducational environments.

Women and Athletics

One of the most highly publicized aspects of Title IX has been intercollegiate athletics. It applies to three broad areas: financial assistance to athletes, that is, scholarships; treatment, benefits, and opportunities for athletes, that is, playing facilities, coaching, other resources; and equal opportunity in accommodating their interests and abilities (Anderson and Cheslock 2004, 307). The most controversial provision refers to the "three-prong test" that considers an institution to be in compliance when "the female share of athletes is 'substantially proportionate' to the female share of undergraduates," an institution has a history of expanding athletic opportunities for women, *or* it "effectively accommodates the interests and abilities of prospective women athletes" (307). Title IX's impact on women's participation in athletics has been substantial, with the female share increasing from 15 percent in 1972 to 42 percent in 2001–2. In this rubric, compliance refers most frequently to the proportionality rule that seeks the alignment of enrollments by gender and participants in athletic programs.

Key Supreme Court decisions that have also extended the meaning of Title IX were *Franklin v. Gwinnett County Public Schools* (1992), in which the Court ruled that monetary damages may be awarded if the violation of Title IX was intentional, and *Cohen v. Brown University* (1997), in which the First Circuit Court of Appeals required Brown to adhere to strict criteria in demonstrating gender equity in intercollegiate athletics (Glazer-Raymo 1999, 26–27). In 1988, the Civil Rights Restoration Act also reversed *Grove City College v. Bell* (1984), which had ruled that only programs receiving federal aid were required to comply with Title IX, thereby exempting athletics from the law. The reauthorization of the Civil Rights Act of 1991 extended compensatory damages for victims of intentional discrimination based on race or national origin to include *sex,* disability, and religion, permitting punitive damages against organizations of more than four hundred employees. And in 1994, Congress also passed the Equity in Athletics Disclosure Act, mandating that schools and colleges release data on the participation of men and women in athletics programs.

The proportionality test has now been upheld by six circuit courts that have ruled that its enforcement does not impose a quota system. Anderson and Cheslock's analysis of data provided by the National Collegiate Athletic Association (NCAA) for 700 institutions for six years (1995–2001) reveals that "institutions were more likely to add female teams or participants than to cut male teams or participants in order to move closer to compliance" (2004, 310). They conclude that losses for men's sports may be attributed to the costs and benefits of maintaining teams, changing interests among undergraduate athletes, and the "arms race" in expenditures in the dominant big-money sports of football and basketball (310).[5]

In the past five years, the DOE has acted to deregulate the proportionality provision of Title IX. In 2002 the Secretary of Education, Rod Paige, formed a Commission on Opportunity in Athletics. Impetus arose from a suit brought by the

National Wrestling Coaches Association, which sued the DOE in 2002 on the grounds that departmental guidelines for enforcing Title IX constituted an illegal quota system discriminating against male athletes. Charges that the purpose of this DOE commission was to weaken the Title IX regulations on athletics came from many women's organizations, including the NWLC, the NCWGE, and the AAUW. Ultimately, the lawsuit brought by the coaches was dismissed and the commission's recommendations rejected.

The DOE then issued *Further Clarification of Intercollegiate Athletics Policy Guidance Regarding Title IX Compliance* (2003), which reaffirmed the validity of existing policies; and in February 2003, the Secretary of Education's Commission on Opportunity in Athletics issued a report to improve enforcement of athletics policies under Title IX, expressing its concern that some colleges and universities were cutting back on men's athletics to meet compliance regulations. The DOE dropped the other shoe in March 2005 when, without any advance notice, it posted *Additional Clarification: Three-Part Test—Part Three* on its Web site, stating that on campuses where the proportion of women athletes falls notably below the proportion of women students and sports programs for women are not expanding, colleges may use an e-mail survey to show they are obeying the law and women have no unmet sports interests and neither "sufficient ability to sustain a varsity team" nor "reasonable expectation of intercollegiate competition" (Department of Education 2005, 4). The implications were clear: schools could show compliance based solely on a survey of women students; a lack of response could be interpreted as a lack of interest, thus shifting the burden of proof from the institution to the female athletes. The president of the NCAA expressed disappointment that the DOE modified a Title IX regulation "without benefit of public discussion or input" and predicted that this change would "likely stymie the growth of women's athletics and could reverse the progress made over the last three decades" (Brand 2005). The NCAA's executive committee adopted a resolution discouraging member colleges from using the procedures set forth in the new guidelines and urging federal policymakers to rescind them, prompting a series of newspaper editorials in support of the NCAA's concerns. The *Baltimore Sun* asked rhetorically, "What message is the Bush administration trying to send to women in sports?" (18 April 2005, 8A), and the *New York Times* asserted that "the Bush administration has mounted a surreptitious new attack on Title IX, the 33-year-old law that has exponentially expanded the participation of girls and women in sports" (13 April 2005, A20).

The Resurgence of Feminist Activism in Postsecondary Education

Given that opponents of affirmative action have targeted public flagship universities and that research universities (both public and private) account for the principal share of federal research support (64%), I have been particularly interested in measuring women's progress in the nation's research universities (Glazer-Raymo 1999, 2007). I have also continued to track support given to women's and gender studies in baccalaureate and master's level universities and colleges (Glazer-Raymo 1999, 2005, 95–98).

One key source has emerged from a review of institutional commissions and task forces on the status of women faculty, staff, and students within and across public and private colleges, universities, and multicampus systems. In the case of public colleges and universities, statewide commissions on the status of women have provided oversight on compensation, benefits, and working conditions for public institutions. My analysis of the origin and development of campus commissions from 1969 to 1995 showed how they had been conceptualized within a liberal feminist framework of equal rights for women, driven by the demands of interest-group politics on campus, and prompted by changes in the policy environment (Glazer-Raymo 1999).

The blue-ribbon commission is a long-established governmental and organizational strategy for defusing potential sources of conflict and maintaining a semblance of democratic decision making, enabling those in positions of power and authority to distance themselves from controversial issues but, at the same time, to control the policy agenda by proposing incremental changes in the self-interest of the institution (Glazer-Raymo 1999, 168). First-stage commissions enabled feminist activists in professional schools, liberal arts colleges, and public and private universities to address gender bias on their campuses as it affected women students, faculty, and professional staff. These commissions, which served at the pleasure of the president of their universities, were largely grassroots in origin and dotted the higher education landscape in the late 1960s and throughout the 1970s. A hiatus in commission growth occurred in the 1980s following the defeat of the Equal Rights Amendment in 1982 as a new generation of women academics focused its energies on creating new scholarship in the liberal arts and sciences and building women's studies programs (Boxer 1998; Messer-Davidow 2002). In the process of creating new knowledge, feminists critiqued enlightenment perspectives based on principles of gender equality, moving instead toward more critical perspectives in their disciplines. Implicit in these critiques was a rejection of reports that focused mainly on gender variables rather than on the underlying assumptions that perpetuated outmoded bureaucratic structures and policies unresponsive to the changing demographics of student and faculty diversity.

In the 1990s, increased concerns among women and minority faculty about the lack of attention being given to their status within the larger university or system, led presidents to reconstitute, or create de novo, commissions and task forces that produced diversity action plans focusing on the intersection of gender and race/ethnicity, sexual orientation, age, and disabilities. Meanwhile, feminist epistemologies became even more diffuse, as postmodern, poststructuralist, and postcolonial critiques replaced liberal, Marxist, and radical feminist thinking. Women's studies programs were recast as gender, ethnic, cultural, or gay-lesbian-bisexual and transgender (GLBT) studies. Poststructuralist critiques of commissions questioned women's ability and willingness to challenge authority, given the risks of asserting contradictory views and the consequences of policy discourses that constructed women as outsider supplicants, passive victims, or deficient in professional skills or training (Allan 2003).

Overcoming the challenges of latent sexism, racism, or other "isms" and gaining more than cosmetic changes in longstanding policies and practices accentuated the powerlessness of women faculty and middle managers and the need to form coalitions across the borderlines of schools, departments, and institutions (in the case of multicampus systems). To a large extent, women's commissions and task forces often seemed to be on the defensive in trying to make the case for gender equality as a viable goal.

The Cambridge Controversies

Between 1999 and 2007, several events occurred that elevated the discourse to a higher level and that, in the case of Harvard University, managed to topple a president. In the mid-1990s, nine women senior scientists at the Massachusetts Institute of Technology (MIT) launched a new phase of feminist analysis of compensation and work conditions when they documented gender bias in the MIT School of Science for women seeking tenure, laboratory assignments, grants, and other perquisites of privilege as tenured research scientists (Committee on Women in the School of Science 1999). It took four years for their findings to be made public, but the online publication of this report on the university's Web site had far-reaching effects. It led to another series of reports by the newly formed and officially recognized MIT Committees on the Status of Women Faculty, revealing comparable gender inequities in the schools of architecture, engineering, humanities, and management (Council on Faculty Diversity 2002).

MIT's president, Charles Vest, trying to get ahead of the curve, convened a meeting of nine presidents and chancellors, and twenty-five women faculty from prestigious research universities—California Institute of Technology, Harvard, Princeton, Stanford, and Yale Universities, the Universities of Michigan and Pennsylvania, and the University of California at Berkeley. The presidents, now known as the "MIT Nine," issued a statement in which they acknowledged that gender barriers remained for women in science and engineering, and agreed to pursue gender equality in compensation and working conditions for their women faculty and to collect and share annual data (MIT News Office 2001).

Meanwhile, at neighboring Harvard University, another storm was brewing. On January 14, 2005, at a closed-session conference on increasing diversity in science and engineering sponsored by the National Bureau of Economic Research, a nonprofit economic research organization in Cambridge, President Lawrence Summers suggested in a 7000-word speech about diversifying the workforce in science and engineering: "My best guess, to provoke you, of what's behind all of this is that the largest phenomenon by far is the general clash between people's (women's) legitimate family desires and employers' current desire for high power and high intensity; that in the special case of science and engineering, there are issues of intrinsic aptitude, and particularly the variability of aptitude; and that those considerations are reinforced by what are in fact lesser factors involving socialization and continuing discrimination" (Summers 2005, 4).[6] Adding insult to injury, he likened the low numbers of women in science and engineering to the purportedly low number of Catholics in investment banking, whites in the National Basketball Association, and Jews in agriculture (1). These insensitive remarks struck many women as further evidence that those in positions of leadership continue to adhere to age-old stereotypes and fail to understand the complexities of the socialization process in academia and in the corporate world. Much like the reaction to "the shot heard round the world," which also occurred near Boston, calls for Summers' resignation were immediate and widespread, and the blogosphere responded with alacrity to his ill-considered hypotheses. The nature-nurture debate had surfaced once again, and from an unlikely source, the president of Harvard University. And so the question became—Are women any less motivated than men to be productive in their chosen field? Do unmarried women and women without children succeed simply because they are childless? Is one's religion or race a factor in making career decisions? Are socialization and discrimination less important than "intrinsic aptitude," and is that the primary reason for women's underrepresentation in science and engineering programs?

To defuse the controversy, less than one month after making his comments, Summers said that he had been misunderstood and convened two committees—a Task Force on Women Faculty (WF) and a Task Force on Women in Science and Engineering (WISE).[7] Nevertheless, in March 2005, the Faculty of Arts and Sciences voted "no confidence" in the president by a margin of 218 to 185, also voting 253–137 (both with 18 abstentions) to censure Summers for his comments about women's innate abilities as well as for his leadership style (Fogg 2005, A1). The receipt of the task force reports in May 2005 prompted another presidential announcement that $50 million would be spent over the next decade to "recruit, support, and promote women and members of underrepresented minority groups on its faculty" (Finder 2005, 1). By December 2005, the women's task forces reported the appointment of Harvard's first senior vice provost for faculty development and diversity (in July 2005), the creation of an ongoing committee on faculty diversity, a women's center for undergraduates, a campus climate survey for tenure-track ladder faculty, and the development of a New England consortium to facilitate dual-career recruitment (Task Forces on Women 2005). The nine university presidents of research universities, including Summers, also pledged support for women's advancement as academic leaders (Jaschik 2005). Nevertheless, in February 2006, immediately prior to a second planned vote of no confidence by the Arts and Science faculty, Summers announced his resignation effective June 30, 2006, having "reluctantly concluded that the rifts between me and segments of the Arts and Science faculty make it infeasible for me to advance the agenda of renewal that I see as crucial for Harvard's future."[8]

In early June, Harvard's newly created Office for Faculty Development and Diversity released a report on the enhancement of work-life programs "to holistically support scholars and faculty in balancing the demands of work and family" through new family leave policies, childcare facilities and scholarships, and funds to support research and professional travel for junior faculty with family responsibilities (Office for Faculty Development and Diversity 2006, 2). Although these moves quelled some of the criticism, women at Harvard are still only 8 percent of tenured natural science faculty compared to 39 percent in education and 21 percent in the social sciences (Finder 2006). The appointment of an inside candidate, Drew Gilpin Faust, founding Dean of the Radcliffe Institute for Advanced Study and a leader of the women's task force efforts, as Harvard's first woman president effective July 1, 2007, concluded a one-year search and consultation with faculty, students, staff, alumni, and others nationwide.

In 2004, MIT's Board of Trustees announced the appointment of its first woman president and first non-engineer, Susan Hockfield, a neuroscientist and provost at Yale University. Following Summers' remarks, Hockfield commented publicly on MIT's commitment to women through appointing them to key academic and administrative positions including her cabinet, the formation of a university-wide Council on Faculty Diversity, and committees on gender equity in each of MIT's five schools (MIT News Office 2005).

Duke University also launched a Women's Initiative in May 2002 "to more fully understand the experiences and needs of women at Duke and to develop strategies to address the challenges women face" (Women's Initiative 2003). Somewhat to the chagrin of the university, women undergraduates described "a social atmosphere that enforces stringent rules about acceptable behavior . . . the expectation that one would be smart, accomplished, fit, beautiful, and popular," while graduate and professional students raised questions about the campus environment for "students who are diverse in terms of race, ethnicity, sexual orientation, culture, or family situation" (2003, 1). Faculty concerns about the low representation of women among "regular rank faculty" were also revealed in this report, prompting Duke's president, Nannerl Keohane to establish the President's Commission on the Status of Women in 2003 for the purpose of monitoring implementation of the Initiative's recommendations.

Between 2002 and 2005, Johns Hopkins, Princeton, Rutgers, and Stanford Universities also issued reports on the status of women faculty at their institutions. Not surprisingly, they found that although gender disparities in hiring, promotion, tenure, and compensation were not as glaring as in previous decades, they nonetheless persisted. Diversity data also showed considerable disparity and very little movement over the years. And work-life issues, particularly for junior faculty, had not been alleviated, despite the many reports and public statements about the need to achieve a balance between professional and personal responsibilities. Their findings illustrate the subtleties of discriminatory practices in organizations that continue to privilege those in positions of power to the disadvantage of those who are seeking equity in resource allocation, prestige, and status.

The Graduate Employees and Students Organization at Yale University (GESO), one of several organizations to issue reports in response to Summers' remarks, commented on the slow pace of change in Ivy League universities, asserting that their workforces are "starkly stratified by race and gender," that the "academic ladder is broken," and that "the relatively few women who climb the academic ladder are (still) paid less than their male colleagues" (GESO 2005, 2). The disconnect between presidential rhetoric and statistical reality can be seen in data on Blacks and Hispanics in Ivy League universities: between 1993 and 2003, the numbers of untenured Black and Hispanic faculty "inched up from 5 percent to 6 percent, and for tenured faculty from 3 percent to 4 percent."[9]

At Princeton University, its president, Shirley Tilghman, appointed two task forces on the status of women faculty in the natural sciences and engineering (2003) and in the humanities and social sciences (2005). Among the issues raised in these reports were the slow progress being made to recruit and promote women into positions of authority and leadership, the low or moderate utilization of available pools of women Ph.D.s, and gender disparities in endowed chairs, senior faculty, and department chair appointments (Girgus 2005). Tilghman appointed a woman provost, dean of faculty, and dean of admissions, leading some alumni to comment initially on the feminization of Princeton's senior administration. Her provost, Amy Gutmann, gained the presidency of the University of Pennsylvania the following year, succeeding Judith Rodin, who is now president of the Rockefeller Foundation. Is it possible that an "old girls' network" is forming now that four women head Ivy League universities?[10]

Stanford University's Advisory Committee on the Status of Women Faculty followed by more than a decade a highly critical report made by the Provost's Committee on the Recruitment and Retention of Women Faculty (Glazer-Raymo 1999, 183–84). It adopted a different tone, surveying both women and men faculty and using collateral data to show the extent of disparities in faculty recruitment, compensation, resources, and recognition, including non-salary forms of compensation and support for research (Provost's Advisory Committee 2004). It found that women faculty, including women of color, had far greater workload pressures related to advising and mentoring, and higher stress levels related to the high cost and scarcity of quality childcare. These issues appeared to be pervasive among women of color and women at the highest faculty ranks. The committee recommended that Stanford's schools adopt "best practice" policies that included outreach and targeted funding to recruit women in underrepresented fields and divisions; hiring and retention packages that incorporated childcare, spousal hiring, paid family leaves, and stop-the-clock tenure policies; periodic evaluation of compensation packages; initiatives addressing sexual harassment and hostile environment claims that do not result in formal complaints; and appointment of an administrator to focus on gender equity who would collect data on a regular basis and collaborate with other institutions about gender equity challenges and corrective actions (Provost's Advisory Committee 2004, 9, 10).

Unlike prior women's commissions that were apt to be more acquiescent in their demands, these women had established professional reputations and were not willing to settle for platitudes and empty promises. The Internet has proven to be another critical factor in disseminating the findings of women's (and other) commissions and in motivating proponents and opponents alike to respond with alacrity. Indeed, the Internet has created a public forum for documents that were previously difficult to obtain and easily tossed into the outboxes of those in positions of power. Press releases, blogs, online newsletters, and organizational Web sites not only respond to these reports but propagate subsidiary reports that extend and sometimes redefine the discourse.

Conclusions

In a recent analysis of gender equity in higher education, the American Council on Education takes a second look at whether undergraduate male students in public and private colleges and universities are at a disadvantage in higher education, disaggregating indicators by institutional type, race, ethnicity, age, and socioeconomic status (King 2006). Having reviewed a number of conjectures made by educators, journalists, and social commentators, the ACE report observes that there is no consensus on its causes and very little comprehensive research on whether women's success is occurring at the expense of men (2006, v). In showing the rapidly increasing share of undergraduate degrees being earned by low- and middle-income Hispanic women, it illustrates the impact of affirmative action in strengthening the link between gender and ethnic diversity in admissions policy. The implications of the gender gap argument extend beyond undergraduate women students to all levels of the academy, perpetuating a myth that affirmative action, Title IX, and other remedies have outlived their original purpose and may even be discriminatory toward men.

Of immediate concern to both women and men faculty is the increased casualization of faculty in all fields and all institutional types. This decline in the number of full-time faculty and concomitant growth in the contingent faculty workforce has implications for the students they teach as well as for the future of the professoriat. The evolving dual track system is getting a major boost from the growing for-profit sector of universities and from professional and entrepreneurial units of universities under the guise of flexibility, adaptability, and cost savings. It will continue to have widespread ramifications for women as a growing proportion of newly minted doctorates seeking tenure-track positions, one of the major concerns of commissions on the status of women faculty.

One bright light is the recent increase in the appointment of women scholars as presidents and provosts of the nation's public and private research universities, signifying that greater attention is being given by governing boards and their search committees to the importance of women in leadership roles. However, the latest report on the presidency issued by ACE indicates that although the percentage of women presidents has increased from 10 percent to 23 percent in the past two decades, "women's progress has slowed in recent years" (Center for Policy Analysis 2007, viii). Furthermore, the representation of minority presidents has had a much smaller increase, from 8 percent in 1986 to 14 percent in 2006. (See Rita Bornstein [chapter 7] and Caroline Turner [chapter 10] for further discussion of these trends.)

The nurture/nature, public/private, and other either/or debates framed in terms of male/female differences serve as continued barriers to women's advancement, affecting the teaching and learning environment and the personal and professional well-being of both men and women. As Becky Ropers-Huilman (chapter 2) and Kelly Ward and Lisa Wolf-Wendel (chapter 11) illustrate so eloquently, multiple identities and the choices women make in their professional and personal lives also affect their diverse experience in the academy—race, ethnicity, socioeconomic status, age, and sexual orientation among them. Authors of the ensuing chapters address these new and continuing challenges, bringing to bear their research and scholarship on women, gender, and higher education.

NOTES

1. Barbara Grutter, Petitioner v. Lee Bollinger et al (02-241) 539 U.S. 306 (2003). Jennifer Gratz & Patrick Hamacher, Petitioners v. Lee Bollinger et al. (02-516). June 23, 2003. Retrieved on 3/27/2006 from *www.law.cornell.edu/supct/html/02–241.ZO.html*.

2. The Carl Perkins Vocational Education Act enacted in 1984 initially authorized a 10.5 percent set-aside in funds to eliminate sex bias and stereotyping in vocational programs, specifying that funds be used for gender equity coordinators and related statewide activities. The Technology Education Amendment of 1998 eliminated that provision, moving states away from gender equity considerations and oversight of compliance with Title IX (Stromquist 2006, 5).

3. Ginsburg, 7; see *United States v. Virginia et al.* (94-1941), 518 U.S. 515 (June 26, 1996). Retrieved from www.law.cornell.edu/supct.html/94-1941.ZS.html.

4. DOE regulation as cited in Federal Register 34 CFR Part 106: Nondiscrimination on the Basis of Sex in Education Programs and Activities Receiving Federal Assistance: Final Rule. www.ed.gov/legislation/FedRegister/finrule/2006–4/102506a.

5. See also Anderson, Cheslock, and Ehrenberg (2006) for a technical analysis of noncompliance with Title IX in Division I, II, and III schools between 1995/6 and 2001/2 as measured by the proportionality gap.

6. For a full transcript of this speech, see Summers (January 14, 2005), www.president .harvard.edu/speeches/2005/nber.html.

7. The task force reports contain numerous proposals for increasing the recruitment and retention of women faculty and for improving work-life policies for women, also drawing on policies adopted at Princeton, Stanford, MIT, and other institutions. See *Report of the Task Force*

on Women Faculty and Report of the Task Force on Women in Science and Engineering (May 2005). Retrieved on 7/1/2005 from www. news.harvard.edu/reports.php.

8. See Letter to the Harvard community, President Lawrence H. Summers, February 21, 2006. Retrieved on 3/18/2007 from www.president.harvard.edu/speeches/2006/0221_summers .html.

9. See the Graduate Employees and Students Organization at Yale (GESO) Web site for an example of how the Internet is being used to disseminate information about "casualization" at Yale University. It incorporates audios, videos, and text to promote its platform. Retrieved on 7/26/2007 from www.yaleunions.org/geso/

10. In addition to Presidents Faust, Gutmann, and Tilghman, Ruth Simmons has served as president of Brown University since 2001.

REFERENCES

AAUW Action Network. 2007. Support Title IX high school data reporting in the Senate. *Action Alert Online.* Retrieved on 2/13/2007 from www.aauw.org.

Allan, E. J. Spring 2003. Constructing women's status: Policy discourses of University women's commission reports. *Harvard Educational Review* 73 (1): 44–72.

Allen, W. R. 2006. Sticks, stones, and broken bones: Rhetoric and reality in the University of Michigan affirmative action cases. In *Higher education in a global society: Achieving diversity, equity and excellence,* ed. W. R. Allen, 203–26. Vol. 5 of *Advances in Education in Diverse Communities: Research, Policy and Praxis.* Amsterdam: Elsevier.

American Association of University Professors (AAUP). 2007. *Trends in faculty status, 1975– 2005. All degree-granting institutions, national totals.* Retrieved on 2/19/2007 from www .aaup.org/NR/FacStatustrend7505.pdf.

American Federation of Teachers. 1998. *The vanishing professor: An AFT higher education report.* Washington, DC: American Federation of Teachers.

Anderson, D. J., and J. J. Cheslock. 2004. Institutional strategies to achieve gender equity in intercollegiate athletics: Does Title IX harm male athletes? *Gender in policy and the labor market. AEA Papers and Proceedings* 94, 2 (May): 307–11.

Anderson, D. J., J. J. Cheslock, and R. G. Ehrenberg. 2006. Gender equity in intercollegiate athletics: Determinants of Title IX compliance. *Journal of Higher Education* 77, 2 (March/ April): 225–50.

Bell, N. E., N. M. Di Fabio, and L. M. Frehill, eds. 2006. *Professional women and minorities: A total human resources data compendium,* 16th ed. Washington, DC: Commission on Professionals in Science and Technology.

Bowen, W., M. A. Kurzweil, and E. M. Tobin. 2005. *Equity and excellence in American higher education.* Princeton, NJ: Princeton University Press.

Boxer, M. J. 1998. *When women ask the questions: Creating women's studies in America.* Baltimore: Johns Hopkins University Press.

Brand, M. 2005. NCAA urges U.S. to rescind title IX guidance. *Inside Higher Ed,* 29 April, 1.

Britz, J. D. 2006. To all the girls I've rejected. *New York Times,* 23 March, A21.

Center for Policy Analysis. February 2007. *The American college president,* 20th anniversary edition. Washington, DC: American Council on Education.

Center for the Education of Women. November 2006. Non-tenure track faculty: The landscape at U.S. institutions of higher education. Ann Arbor, MI: Retrieved on 3/2/2007 from www.cew.umich.edu.

Committee on the Economic Status of the Profession. 2005. Inequities persist for women and non-tenure track faculty. The annual report on the economic status of the profession, 2004–05. *Academe* 91, 2 (March-April): 21–30.

———. 2006. The devaluing of higher education. The annual report on the economic status of the profession, 2005–06. *Academe* 92, 2 (March-April): 25–34.

Committee on Women in the School of Science (MIT). 1999. A study of the status of women faculty in science at MIT. *The MIT Faculty Newsletter*, XI (4). Retrieved on 3/3/2006 from http://web.mit.edu/fnl/women/women.html/#The%20Study.

Council on Faculty Diversity (MIT). 2002. *The status of women faculty at MIT: An overview of reports from the schools of architecture and planning; engineering, humanities, arts, and social sciences; and the Sloan school of management.* Retrieved on 3/3/2006 from http://web.mit .edu/faculty/reports/overview.html.

Curtis, J. W. 2006. Faculty salary and faculty distribution fact sheet 2003–04. AAUP Committee on Women in the Academic Profession. Retrieved on 2/28/2007 from www.aaup.org/ AAUP/pubsres/research/2003–04factsheet.htm.

Department of Education. 2005. Users guide. Additional clarification of intercollegiate athletic policy: Three-part test—Part Three. U.S. Department of Education, Office for Civil Rights. www.ed.gov/about/offices/list/ocr/docs/title9guidanceadditional.pdf.

Finder, A. 2005. Harvard will spend $50 million to make faculty more diverse. *New York Times*, 17 May, A1.

———. 2006. Women on faculty still lag at Harvard, report finds. *New York Times*, June 14, A18.

Fogg, P. 2005. Board backs Harvard chief after a faculty thumbs down. *Chronicle of Higher Education*, 25 March, A1, 12.

General Accountability Office. July 2004. *Gender issues: Women's participation in the sciences has increased, but Agencies need to do more to ensure compliance with Title IX.* Washington, DC: Author.

GESO. February 2005. The (un)changing face of the Ivy League. Retrieved on 3/1/2005 from www.aauw.org.

Girgus, J. S. July 2005. *The status of women faculty in the humanities and social sciences at Princeton University.* Retrieved on 3/20/2007 from www.pr.edu/dof/policies_procedures/reports/ taskforce_human_socsci/GTF_Report_HumanSocSc.rev.pdf.

Glazer-Raymo, J. 1999. *Shattering the myths: Women in academe.* Baltimore: Johns Hopkins University Press.

———. 2003. Women faculty and part-time employment: The impact of public policy. In *Gendered futures in higher education: Critical perspectives for change*, ed. B. Ropers-Huilman, 97–110. Albany: State University of New York Press.

———. 2005. *Professionalizing graduate education: The master's degree in the marketplace.* ASHE Higher Education Report Series, 31 (4). San Francisco: Jossey-Bass.

———. 2007. Women in the American research university: Reaffirming the agenda for women's rights. In *Women, universities, and change: European Union and the United States*, ed. M. A. D. Sagaria, 161–78. London: Palgrave Macmillan.

Goethals, G. R., G. J. Sorenson, and J. M. Burns, eds. 2004. *Encyclopedia of leadership*, vol. 1. Thousand Oaks, CA: Sage Publications.

Granholm, R., and D. Archer. 2006. Proposal 2 hurts women, minorities. *Arab American News*, 10 November, 22: 10.

Greenhouse, L. 2005. O'Connor to retire, touching off battle over court. *New York Times*, 2 July, A1.

———. 2007a. Justices' ruling limits suits on pay disparity. *New York Times*, 30 May. Retrieved 5/30/2007 from www.nytimes.com/2007/05/30/washington/30scotus.html.

———. 2007b. Oral dissents give Ginsburg a new voice on court. *New York Times*, 31 May. Retrieved 5/31/2007 from www.nytimes.com/2007/05/31/washington/31scotus.html.

Inside Higher Ed. 2006. Affirmative action for men. Retrieved on 3/27/2006 from www .insidehighered.com/news/2006/03/27/admit.

Jaschik, S. 2005. 9 university presidents issue statement on gender equity. *Inside Higher Ed.*, 7 December. Retrieved on 4/5/2006 from www.insidehighered.com/news/2005/12/07/gender.

Jessup, L. 2003. The campaign for union rights at NYU. In *Steal this university: The rise of the corporate university and the academic labor movement*, ed. B. Johnson, P. Kavanagh, and K. Mattson, 145–70. New York and London: Routledge.

Kaufmann, S. W. 2006. *The potential impact of the Michigan Civil Rights Initiative on employment, education, and contracting.* Ann Arbor: Center for Education of Women, University of Michigan.

Kaufmann, S. W., and A. K. Davis. 2006. *The gender impact of the proposed Michigan Civil Rights Initiative.* Ann Arbor: Center for Education of Women, University of Michigan.

Kellough, J. E. 2006. *Understanding affirmative action: Politics, discrimination, and the search for justice.* Washington, DC: Georgetown University Press.

King, J. 2006. *Gender equity in higher education.* Washington, DC: American Council on Education, Center for Policy Analysis.

Lash, S. 2007. Justices bring quick end to pay-bias claim. *Chicago Daily Law Bulletin*, 29 May. Retrieved on 5/31/2007 from Lexis-Nexis Academic. Documents.

Lewin, T. 2006. At colleges, women are leaving men in the dust; THE NEW GENDER DIVIDE: Boys who coast. *New York Times*, 9 July, A1, 17.

Manning, J. 2005. Additional clarification of intercollegiate athletics policy: Three-part test— Part three. Office of Civil Rights, 17 March. Retrieved on 2/2/2006 from www.ed.gov/about/ offices/list/ocr/docs/title9guidanceadditional.html.

McKenna, B. 2007. The myth of the tenured faculty. *On Campus* 26, 6 (March-April): 12–14.

Messer-Davidow, E. 2002. *Disciplining feminism: From social activism to academic discourse.* Raleigh, NC: Duke University Press.

MIT News Office. January 30, 2001. Leaders of 9 universities and 25 women faculty meet at MIT; Agree to equity reviews. Retrieved on 6/1/2005 from http://web.mit.edu/newsoffice/2001/ gender.html.

———. January 27, 2005. President Hockfield speaks out on issue of women in science and engineering. Retrieved on 11/11/2005 from http://web.mit.edu/newsoffice/2005/gender-equity .html.

National Center for Education Statistics. 2007a. *Digest of Education Statistics: 2006.* Retrieved on 10/3/2007 from www.ed.gov/programs/digest/d06/tables/dt)06.asp.

———. 2007b. *The Condition of Education 2007.* Washington, D.C.: U.S. Department of Education. Institute of Education Sciences. NCES 2007–064.

National Coalition for Women and Girls in Education (NCWGE). December 28, 2004. Questions for Margaret Spellings. Retrieved on 2/1/2005 from www.ncwge.org.

National Women's Law Center. 2005. Bush administration covertly attacks Title IX by weakening athletics policies. *E-Update,* 5 April. Retrieved on 4/6/2005 from www.nwlc.org.

———. 2006. Administration's single-sex regulations violate Constitution and Title IX. Press release, October 24. Retrieved on 10/25/2006 from www.nwlc.org

———. June 2007. Barriers to fair play. Retrieved on 6/15/2007 from www.nwlc.org.

O'Connor, S. D. 2003. Excerpts from justices' opinions on Michigan affirmative action cases; From the decision of Justice O'Connor. *New York Times,* 24 June, A24.

Office for Faculty Development and Diversity. 2006. Office for Faculty Development and Diversity releases report. *Harvard University Gazette,* 15 June. Retrieved on 7/11/2006 from www.news.harvard.edu/gazette/2006/06.15/01-worklife.html.

Pennington, B. 2006. Small colleges, short of men, embrace football; THE NEW GENDER DIVIDE: Appealing to athletes. *New York Times,* 10 July, A1, 14.

Provost's Advisory Committee on the Status of Women Faculty. 2004. Report on the status of women faculty at Stanford University. Retrieved 7/3/2007 from http://universitywomen .stanford.edu/pacswf/pacsw.main.html.

Rhoads, R. A., and G. Rhoades. 2005. Graduate employee unionization as symbol of and challenge to the corporatization of U.S. research universities. *Journal of Higher Education* 76, 3 (May/June): 243–75.

Schmidt, P. 2007. 4 states named as new targets in affirmative-action fight. *Chronicle of Higher Education,* 4 May, 35.

Schuster, J. H., and M. J. Finkelstein. 2006. *The American faculty: The restructuring of academic work and careers.* Baltimore: Johns Hopkins University Press.

Stromquist, N. P. 2006. The dismantling of tools by the master: Evaluating gender equity by the state. Presented at the American Educational Research Association, San Francisco, April.

Summers, L. H. 2005. Remarks at NBER conference on diversifying the science & engineering workforce, January 14. Retrieved on 3/18/2007 from www.president.harvard.edu/speeches/ 2005/nber.html.

Task Force on Women Faculty. May 2005. Report of the task force on women faculty (Harvard University). Retrieved on 11/6/2005 from www.news.harvard.edu/gazette/daily/2005/05/ women-faculty.pdf.

Task Forces on Women. December 2005. Update on progress. Retrieved on 10/3/2006 from www.womenstaskforces.harvard.edu/whats_happening.php.

Thernstrom, S., and A. Thernstrom. 1997. *America in black and white: One nation, indivisible.* New York: Simon and Schuster.

West, M. S., and J. W. Curtis. 2006. *AAUP faculty gender equity indicators 2006.* Washington, DC: AAUP. Retrieved on 12/1/2006 from www.aaup.org/AAUP/pubsres/research/geneq.2006 .htm.

Women's Initiative. 2003. The findings. *Report of the Women's Initiative at Duke University.* Retrieved on 10/10/2007 from http://www.duke.edu/womens_initiative/docs/Womens_ initiative_Report.pdf.

CHAPTER TWO

Women Faculty and the Dance of Identities

Constructing Self and Privilege within Community

BECKY ROPERS-HUILMAN

In the early 1970s, women across the United States raised urgent questions about their participation as thinkers and leaders in American society. As a result, Women's Studies programs were born, and associated scholars insisted that greater attention be paid to the social institutions of higher education as they framed women's participation in all facets of life. Women came together and raised their consciousness about how their lives had been circumscribed by gendered norms in society. Scholarship emphasized gender oppression and the need to work together to overcome such oppression. This was a critical time in the development of higher education and marked a turning point for women's equitable participation both in education and in other social institutions.

In the past three decades, however, it has become clear that any movement seeking to identify its participants merely "as women" is shortsighted. All women are grounded in communities and life experiences that affect how their identities as women are constructed. Women faculty construct their identities in ways that incorporate the complex and contradictory expectations of all their roles, oftentimes leading to a finely tuned, yet at least partially subconscious, dance of identities. Women negotiate their identities as leaders, family members, ethnic community members, members of various disciplines, and academic citizens. These multiple identities both facilitate and impede the "productivity" that is typically associated with faculty roles and also affect one's affiliation with feminism in the academy.

In this chapter, I approach the issue of new and continuing challenges for women in higher education by discussing the various complexities associated with composing an identity as a woman faculty member in today's higher education institutions. While I draw on the reflections and experiences of others, I present scenes from my own dance of identities in order to illustrate choices and challenges that are made in response to sociocultural and contextual situations. Of course, each person's dance is individual and unique. Yet each person's dance is also performed with myriad others who share a larger cultural context and whose performances are influenced by that context.

I then turn my attention to the development of women faculty members, arguing that their unique intersections of identity warrant attention for the following reasons: First, the ways in which women construct themselves in their roles as faculty members provide models for others in academe, both students and faculty, of the multifaceted contributions that diverse women make to society. Through their involvement with students, women faculty teach other ways of living and learning and increase the range of beliefs and practices that are considered by those involved. Second, critical race feminist literature suggests that the negotiation of multiple identities, particularly by people who have multiple nondominant identities, exacts a painful toll on those doing the negotiating. This toll takes time and energy away from women faculty members' abilities to contribute their scholarly expertise in ways that would benefit the institution and the larger society. Third, as we increasingly become a global society in which borders and differences are constantly shifting, we benefit from the knowledge of those individuals and communities who have negotiated their identity performances at the borders of established communities and cultures.

Constructions of Self

The process of identity construction lasts a lifetime, but it takes particular forms during different stages of development. For example, while young children work to establish autonomy and interdependence (Harris 1991), young adults engage with cognitive development that often moves them from dichotomous thinking to cognitive complexity (Astin 1993). Throughout one's life, these developmental experiences shape the ways in which people see both themselves and each other. In this section, I discuss how women faculty members construct themselves through their choices as academics and community members. I assert that they are both members of particular academic institutions or disciplines and members of other communities that deeply influence their choices, perspectives, and academic constructions.

All people construct themselves—or, as Judith Butler (1990) asserts, perform their salient identities—in complex ways. We choose from among the various options that are available to us in our performances. For example, some women faculty members may decide to establish their authority by requiring students to address them as "Dr."; whereas others may choose to ask students to use their first names in order to break down hierarchies that they believe may negatively affect learning. Some women faculty may decide to keep a firm distinction between friends and colleagues; whereas others may decide that they can be unproblematically synonymous. Women faculty may dress in multiple ways, including changing their attire to be most effective—and educational—with various audiences (Ropers-Huilman 1998). Our constructions of self become apparent in our manner of dress, choice of interactions, and expression of our various community or cultural affiliations.

These constructions require both conscious and unconscious choices about which facets of ourselves we want to express. As Margaret E. Montoya (2003) points out, the masking and unmasking of oneself is particularly difficult for those whose cultural homes and associated practices are not well represented in the larger dominant society:

> Being masked may be a universal condition, in that all of us control how we present ourselves to others. There is, however, a fundamental difference when one feels masked because one is a member of one or more oppressed groups within the society. When members of the dominant culture mask themselves to control the impressions they make, such behavior is not inherently self-loathing. But when we attempt to mask immutable characteristics of skin color, eye shape, or hair texture because they historically have been loathsome to the dominant culture, then the masks of acculturation can be experienced as self-hate. (73)

In other words, while we each mask ourselves based on our readings of the sociocultural context and what we think is expected of us in that context, the degree to which this process alienates us from ourselves depends in large part on the degree to which we feel a "fit" within that context. If my core immutable characteristics are devalued and I choose to mask those characteristics, then it could be argued that I am masking myself rather than merely performing a different facet of myself. In essence, it is a form of silencing oneself in the interests of others. The extent to which one's identity performances are valued in the academy shapes one's abilities to contribute to it as well as one's desire and intentions to continue being a part of it.

As Anna Neumann and Penelope Peterson's *Learning from Our Lives: Women, Research, and Autobiography in Education* (1997) and Laurel Richardson's *Fields of Play: Constructing an Academic Life* (1997) so eloquently point out, women faculty are deeply affected by their cultural and "home" communities. Their manner of participating in the academic "conversations" associated with research, teaching, and service is constructed through their expectations as learned in their cultural communities and familial situations as well as by the resistances they encounter when they believe that they are proceeding logically within their home community's frame of logic.

The "self" of the woman faculty member is thus a multifaceted self, one who decides when and how to compromise or negotiate her various roles in constructing her dance. In the end, if this negotiation is too difficult, women faculty may choose to remain silent or leave particular positions, institutions, or the academic profession entirely. Again, Montoya's words are instructive of the loss that is incurred during this process:

> A significant aspect of subordination is the persistence with which we mimic the styles, preferences, and mannerisms of those who dominate us, even when we have become aware of the mimicry. Lost to the Outsider are those identities that would have developed but for our real and perceived needs to camouflage ourselves in the masks of the Master. Lost to all are the variety of choices, the multiplicity of identities that would be available if we were not trapped by the dynamics of subordination, of privilege. (2003, 73–74)

Women faculty members' dances of identities have the potential to contribute to the richness of our collective educational institutions. The situations in which particular groups and individuals are compelled to mask facets of themselves illustrate cracks in our higher education system's ability to serve our important social role to all members of society.

Privilege as Part of the Dance

The mask that Montoya describes is one that is put on by those in nondominant groups to disguise aspects of themselves that are not valued within a dominant culture. In postsecondary educational institutions, this mask might lead faculty members to limit the time they spend with students in order to protect research time, even if their preferences, values, and commitments would urge the opposite (Park 1996). The mask may induce silence in professional settings where people with similar identity characteristics have been systematically excluded (Gilmore 1991; Guinier 1991). In other words, even if one has clear ideas and contributions, she may choose not to contribute those ideas to the group because she is unsure if they will be accepted, since institutional history—as indicated by identities and ideas of leaders and honored faculty—suggests that they have been systematically excluded

in the past. The mask may mean agreeing to serve on many institutional committees in order to ensure that one's cultural community is represented, even when a
faculty member may prefer to allocate her time elsewhere (Tierney and Bensimon
1996). People who are "outsiders within" (Collins 1991) negotiate masks and opportunities regularly. In sum, access to higher education as students, faculty, and
administrators for those with identities that are associated with nondominant
groups does not necessarily lead to the same privileges as it does for those in dominant groups. The choices, opportunities, and experiences are shaped by those
identities.

Within this negotiation of identities, there are points of privilege. As Montoya
(2003) asserts, though, that privilege can trap those affiliated with it and limit the
potential of what we can collectively contribute to our institutions and the larger
society. Privilege and oppression are two sides of the same coin, and both limit
choices and modes of expression. Many women faculty members recognize,
whether consciously or subconsciously, the power of masks, and some of us are
able to convincingly wear them. Simultaneously, we recognize the value of being
true to ourselves in the various ways that is individually interpreted. Women faculty members who are also part of the current dominant racial group in the United
States may experience their dance of identities as being about both masking and
unmasking, about both oppression and privilege. For many, this dance becomes an
interpretive one, with many stops and starts. For those interested in equity in education and society, it also becomes a complex choreography of using one's power
ethically to destabilize both power and oppression.

Turning the Mirror

Peggy McIntosh (1990) asserts the imperative that white women examine their
racial privilege in addition to working against gender oppression. She articulates:

> After I realized . . . the extent to which men work from a base of unacknowledged
> privilege, I understood that much of their oppressiveness was unconscious. Then I
> remembered the frequent charges from women of color that white women whom
> they encounter are oppressive. I began to understand why we are justly seen as op-
> pressive, even when we don't see ourselves that way. At the very least, obliviousness of
> one's privileged state can make a person or group irritating to be with. (32)

As McIntosh points out, it is often much easier to notice how oppression affects
one's life than to become aware of how one experiences privilege and perpetuates
a social system that oppresses others.

In writing this chapter, I turned to McIntosh's work to reflect on the extent to which the list of privileges that she experiences as a white person could be understood within a higher education context. Some of these are remarkably present nearly two decades after McIntosh's initial writing and continue to have obvious manifestations in current higher education institutions. For example:

— I can, if I wish, arrange to be in the company of people of my race most of the time.
— I can be fairly sure of having my voice heard in a group in which I am the only member of my race.
— I can do well in a challenging situation without being called a credit to my race.
— I can be reasonably sure that if I ask to talk to "the person in charge," I will be facing a person of my race.
— I can choose to ignore developments in minority writing and minority activist programs, or disparage them, or learn from them, but in any case, I can find ways to be more or less protected from negative consequences of any of these choices.
— I can worry about racism without being seen as self-interested or self-seeking.

(McIntosh 1990, 32–33)

While I have personally experienced and seen others experience each of the privileges listed above, there are others that are particularly salient in my experience. Points of racial privilege that also find expression in higher education settings include:

• It will not be assumed by my peers that I am an expert on the history, theory, and current practices of members of my racial/cultural group.
• It will not be assumed that I was hired, at least in part, because of my racial/ethnic identity, rather than solely based on my academic qualifications.
• I will not be asked to serve on more than my share of service committees because of the need to diversify those committees.
• When I go to a university-wide meeting, I am confident that I will not be the only white person in attendance.
• When people debate about how much higher education institutions should invest in diversity, I can choose to position myself either as directly or indirectly involved by those debates or as not at all affected by them. Regardless, I will not suffer negative consequences because of my choice.
• When something negative or out of the ordinary happens to me, I am fairly certain that it is not because of my race or cultural norms.

- When I use language or a manner of speaking that I was taught growing up, I feel confident that my colleagues will be able to understand me and that my speech will not raise questions about my intelligence.
- I do not have to feel uncomfortable in discussions when colleagues discuss the difficulty of finding high-quality candidates of color and then complain that those who are qualified demand too much in compensation.
- As a white woman, I am never asked which "comes first" for me—my gender or my race. In the same vein, I am not asked to choose allegiance to *either* my race *or* my gender.

Privilege and oppression are both manifest in postsecondary institutions. Yet they are experienced differently by participants because we are positioned differently in relation to them. As evidenced throughout this book and others (Glazer-Raymo 1999; Kolodny 1998; Martin 2000; Ropers-Huilman 2003), gender continues to matter in higher education institutions. But the nature of gendered expressions and the ways those expressions are perceived are not somehow unraced. We each have unique experiences. And yet that acknowledgment does not mean that we do not need to interrogate the ways in which race and gender continue to play a part in our lives as participants in the social institution of higher education.

Performing the Dance

I have learned that in my current historic and cultural location, whether it is acknowledged or not, whiteness is cultural capital that I cash in on every day. The intersections of this privilege with my position as a faculty member and my experiences as a woman make my dance complex. In developing this chapter, I thought about italicizing this section to show that I am writing in a different voice. But that may be interpreted to mean that this voice is more or less authentic than the previous "academic" text. It is not. Like Carolyn Ellis's (1997) and Margery Wolf's (1992) efforts to tell their stories in multiple ways—to explain their research in ways that are both true to their hearts and true to the communities they wished to reach—these are but a series of acts in a lifelong performance, none more real than the next. It is my intention through the following stories to demonstrate various dances that I have performed while negotiating privilege and oppression as a white woman faculty member. It is also my intention to consider through these stories the potential of white women faculty members to dismantle racial and gender privilege from within their positions of power and oppression.

Dance 1: Encultured "(A)culturality"

In graduate school, I conducted research with feminist teachers who engaged with me both inside and outside of their classrooms. In one situation, the faculty member told me that in order to really understand her teaching, I would need to sign up for her class and do all associated coursework. In other words, I needed to be a "real student" in addition to being a researcher. The readings and discussions in this course were new to me, since they focused heavily on the experiences of non-white persons in educational systems. While I was silent for most of the class, feeling more comfortable in my note-taking researcher role, I made a comment at one point that particular readings demonstrated to me the rich cultures associated with nonwhite communities. The rich descriptions of these cultures, I told the class, made me feel as though I had no culture.

Nearly fifteen years later, I remember the face and name of the person who spoke next. He abruptly told me that my culture was everywhere, and that it was a privilege for me that I did not notice it. My practices, celebrations, behaviors, and aspirations were just "normal," while those from other backgrounds and cultures were unique, special, or even "exotic." His public reminder of my privilege was very uncomfortable. Yet my fellow student's willingness to interrupt my ignorance of privilege proved to be an important aspect of my professional identity. This is not to say that I recognize all of the privileges that whiteness brings to me, but I am willing to look for those instances and to bring them to the attention of others when I see them. Racial privilege became a "real," lived concept for me at that moment. No longer could I believe that racial privilege was an abstract concept that affected educational experience at the systemic level but only indirectly affected me.

Dance 2: The Neighborhood

Women faculty members do not live and work only at the academy. They return home to communities that they are a part of to varying degrees. My home is located a few miles from campus in a neighborhood that is largely segregated. Within a half-mile, there is a predominantly black neighborhood that we drive through regularly. However, this neighborhood is separated by a street and economic conditions that serve as clear markers of the racial divide.

My involvement in my neighborhood has been somewhat minimal, even though I am a firm believer in the importance of civic engagement and local community building. This has been partially because I have chosen to dedicate my time and energy elsewhere. However, my limited engagement has also been because of several instances in which I have been surprised by the beliefs of those who live close to me. In one case, a neighbor who had worked in public education for more than two decades told me that black people "just don't care about education." She relied on her experience as a teacher and teacher educator to make that assertion. Given that I have worked with African-American doctoral students in education who clearly care a great deal about it, and that I know many black families whose children's education is their top priority, I was confused. In fact, I asked her to repeat her comment, because I didn't believe I had heard her correctly.

In another case, following the horrors of Hurricanes Katrina and Rita in 2005, another neighbor warned me to be careful and protect myself because of the "monsters" who were now walking through our neighborhood. The people to whom she was referring had come from New Orleans after losing their homes and in many cases all their possessions. When I questioned her use of that term, she described an incident that she had nearly twenty years earlier that was intended to solidify her use of that term as accurate. She acknowledged that racial dynamics in Louisiana were complex, intertwined with poverty and years of social segregation. Yet the assumptions undergirding her statements were clear. It was "us" against "them," and "we" needed to protect ourselves. This collective and essentializing view of those individuals in the "other" group is the same view that led these neighbors to believe that I, as a white person, would understand and relate to their fears and assumptions. The dance I perform requires that I regularly come out as a "race traitor," to borrow Mab Segrest's (1994) characterization, as well as a feminist in both personal and professional contexts.

In these cases, what I worry about most is that I am hearing these stories and beliefs, while people who are being unfairly characterized are not. I am "privileged" in that assumptions are made about my willingness to hear these types of statements because I am a part of "we." Those who are being unfairly characterized do not get a chance to defend themselves or explain their choices or simply to say, "That's not me." Significantly, those making the characterizations are not isolated individuals whose beliefs and actions do not matter. Instead, they are raising children, serving in schools, teaching others how to teach. Most worrisome, they are interacting with children who do not share their racial background or identification, and they are likely conveying in subtle or direct ways to those children that they may grow up to be "monsters." Perhaps they are teaching those children that their parents don't care about their education. They are certainly teaching others in their immediate (white) circles what it means to live as a racially privileged person.

Dance 3: Choosing "Insignificant Research": "The Feminist Crap"

Women faculty who choose to do feminist research often experience critique of their scholarship, not necessarily on the basis of its quality, but on the merits of its sheer existence (Ropers-Huilman 2003). At a departmental gathering meant to welcome a new junior colleague, one of the most senior members of the department laughingly and heartily offered a welcome that was, I suspect, meant to be humorous. He said that he was happy to have a new person to do some "real" scholarly work, instead of "all that feminist crap." As I was the only one in the department at the time who did feminist scholarship, it was clear his characterization was of my work. His comment was made to the junior colleague (who was to work directly with me) in front of various graduate students, faculty colleagues, and me. No one—including me—challenged the characterization of my work. Since I was just approaching my promotion and tenure review, I did not know how to respond and chose not to. Later, when discussing my tenure review angst with this new colleague, he said that he didn't think I was going to get tenure at the institution. We discussed how, with comments like the one described here, the "writing was on the wall." Thankfully, the review went well, and I was granted promotion and tenure.

In a job interview situation shortly thereafter, I recognized the complexity of my position as a white woman faculty member who found it difficult to balance privilege and oppression. We had invited a promising junior scholar to interview for a faculty position. Her area of scholarship had to do with race relations in academic settings. I was intrigued by her thinking and looked forward to engaging in a lively discussion with her about her work. At what was intended to be an informal gathering shortly after she arrived, I began asking her questions about her scholarship. Another senior colleague who was in the room took the opportunity to tell her that looking at race relations in higher education was unimportant and that her current conceptual approach to research was not useful to our collective knowledge. I sat there somewhat stunned and tried to bring the conversation to a more informal place. I wanted to validate this junior African-American scholar's important work without directly challenging my senior colleague's views. I failed. I later learned that this interviewee considered leaving campus after the first day and not continuing with the interview process. I also learned that she believed I was culpable in the direction and tone of that conversation.

This experience taught me many things. I now am much more likely to think concretely about how another person may be experiencing a given interaction. For example, when a comment about an African-American person is made in a room where only one person identifying as African-American is present, I attempt to consider how that person may be experiencing that comment and ensuing discussion. I often encourage students I work with to "flip it around." By this I mean, if I am wondering how another person might feel in a given situation, I can imagine that I am in a similar situation. For example, how would I feel if the same comment were made about a white person and I was the only white person in the room? Clearly, this approach is complicated by different social forces and locations that make us never able to fully understand someone's position. Yet it is one place to start that does not require asking someone to serve as a representative for her or his race, ethnicity, or cultural background. It also recognizes that at some level human decency and respect is a common expectation and should be the norm in our educational practices.

This experience reminded me, though, that I cannot control the actions of everyone around me. Nor can I control the interpretations that people have of complex situations. However, I can speak my truth and try to open spaces for others to speak theirs. I can also continue, through my research, teaching, and service, to remind people how increasing our collective knowledge about particular nondominant populations and the interactions among all groups allows us to further the social mission of higher education.

Dance 4: Parenting

As described elsewhere in this volume, one's position in academic settings is also affected by one's family status. The informal dialogue that I have heard from professors who are new parents often goes something like this: Men talk about the lack of sleep, the intensity of the experience, and the difficulty in being away from their new family member because of the demands of the academic profession. Women talk about the lack of sleep; the intensity of the experience; the difficulty of finding time to work, given their new responsibilities; and the anxiety over finding child care that is nurturing, appropriate, and affordable. Only infrequently, as in a recent *Chronicle of Higher Education* essay (Latessa 2005), do men discuss the complexities they face as they make decisions associated with the work-family balance that is a given for most women. Parenting is a gendered experience that is intertwined with other identities and that takes shape in academic settings in particular ways.

Parenting has shaped my performance of identity. At first, my attempts to mask the effects of my new status as a parent brought me back to campus much earlier than my doctor had advised. Later, I reveled in the pure pleasure of being an active parent, while simultaneously longing for the time before children when I sincerely enjoyed the obsessive lifestyle that many academics choose. For a time I tried to do both, while realizing at sharp moments that such a life was—for me—impossible.

One such moment was when my child, at two years old, became increasingly sick. My partner and I juggled the care to some extent, but I monitored the situation by calling the doctor and staying at home except to teach class. When we finally learned that my two-year-old had to be hospitalized for several days, there was no question about my identity. When my little, energetic, full-of-life child lacked the strength to stand on his own, I knew exactly who I was. I was that child's mother. That is a crucial piece of my identity.

Looking back, I see the privilege inherent in my ability to choose to foreground a particular identity at that moment. And I believe that our society should allow all persons to make that choice. Race, gender, and socioeconomic class played a part in that privilege. That week, I was able to be there without fear of losing my job, without concern about medical attention, without question of whether I belonged there or not. In a parish (county) where 61 percent of the children live in poverty, I knew that my child would have whatever economic resources he needed to get well. I knew that the majority of doctors and nurses would be of my race—even in a state where a third of the population is black. I felt confident that my cultural values would be both understood and respected.

At the same time, my partner did not experience the same privilege that I did. Instead, he felt that although people were concerned, they nevertheless expected him to be at work. While he also works at a university, he was in a staff position that was demanding. He is also a man, and therefore is assumed by some to play a less-involved role in our family. While I recognize that his male privilege is real within the larger system of higher education and society, I also recognize that privilege is not unidimensional. Gendered assumptions limit choices. In essence, they restrict the dances that are possible for both men and women to perform.

Implications for Higher Education Practice and Research

The situations described here present only four ways in which I have chosen to craft my identity within the sociocultural contexts in which I find myself. Nevertheless, they are meant to illustrate some of the complexities associated with being a privileged member of the academy and society, while simultaneously wrestling with the oppression that limits the choices and experiences of women. As a white woman faculty member who is also a parent and ally for those trying to work against racist and sexist oppression, my particular dance is, of course, unique. Yet, through my dances, I have learned a great deal about the ways in which women faculty are positioned in higher education and how that positioning is complicated by racial and gendered identities.

What does this analysis mean for practice and research related to women's roles in higher education? My experiences lead me to consider the following specific practices that tend to reveal points of oppression and privilege that need active examination.

Hiring Practices

In hiring situations, the opportunity to enact one's privilege to perpetuate others' oppression is significant. Those in the position to hire new faculty or administrators can make judgments based on the candidates' manner of speech and dress, ways of constructing themselves that are often directly related to their cultural expression. These forms of expression, of course, may have nothing to do with intellectual abilities and may, in fact, be an asset in forging relationships with various groups of students and community members. However, at the time of hiring, they may be interpreted as a "lack of professionalism" or as an indicator that a person "doesn't want to fit in." Those who do not want to own the discrimination inherent in such judgments can nevertheless justify them by stating that while they don't have a problem with diverse "performances," they are uneasy with how others (students, parents, administrators, community members, etc.) will interpret those performances and how that might reflect on the department or unit.

The interpretation of one's research focus can also be a point where privilege and oppression are expressed. This can happen in multiple ways. As it did for me in the situation above when my research was described as "feminist crap," research on nondominant groups or based on social justice-oriented paradigms can be dismissed as unimportant and "unreal." While scholars of color can have this same experience, they also can be caught in a double bind, regardless of their research focus. On one hand, scholars of color who do research either focused on or situated in the paradigms of their home communities are asked about their ability to be objective or at least unbiased. While I have been questioned about my bias in my feminist work with women, I have never been questioned about my ability to fairly represent the white participants in my research. For those scholars of color who do not include in their research a focus on race, ethnicity, or cultural communities, they are nevertheless expected to be experts in that area. For women scholars of color, they must choose which mask will be palatable to those in a hiring situation.

Finally, in a hiring situation, some research has suggested that men are often chosen for leadership experiences based on their perceived potential, whereas women are chosen based on their proven productivity (Ridgeway 2001). In other words, once women have proven that they have "made it," they are seen as hirable in other situations. Men, on the other hand, need to show signs of potential, including having advocates who are able to convey that potential to future employers. If this is also true in the case of faculty members, men may be given career opportunities earlier than women. It would be important to ascertain the extent to which this is also the case with scholars of color, especially with women faculty members of color.

Interactions with Students

Privilege and oppression can be seen in interactions with students as well as in the evaluation of those interactions. Students notice the identity of the person who is facilitating their educational experiences. While this may seem obvious, their noticing may in fact be at a subconscious level, or it may be resisted because of the paradoxes inherent in their assumptions related to power and identities such as race and gender (Schein 2001; Wallace, Ropers-Huilman, and Abel 2004). In other words, they may be unable to reconcile a woman of color with their perceptions of scholarly authority. Power and privilege, as feminist scholars point out, are not inherent for all people in faculty positions. Attempting to access that power, then, will not be equally possible for women faculty of color, and their choice of performances will be differently negotiated.

We know that women faculty members tend to do the majority of teaching and service in higher education settings. In her provocative article "Why Shouldn't Women's Work Count?" Shelly Park (1996) questions why women and men are positioned differently in relation to the core functions of the academy and why those positions are differently valued. The academy's recent response has been twofold. Some institutions have attempted to elevate the status of teaching and community engagement. Others, however, have asserted that the playing field is fair. If women want the rewards associated with high research productivity, then they merely need to perform more research. While admittedly an oversimplification, this approach suggests that to fix the problem (if there is one), more women just need to be like more men.

This argument fails to understand the ways in which universities depend on the work of those who are willing to do that which is less valued. In this sense, the university replicates the structure of a traditional heterosexual family, in which both the man and woman perform tasks that are essential to the family's well-being. Yet a man's role as "breadwinner" is increasingly valued in society (i.e., through pay raises, an established career trajectory, and professional stability), whereas a woman's role as "caretaker" is decreasingly valued. When her arguably most demanding role as mother no longer demands her full attention, her contributions to society become unclear. Still, children and a home must be taken care of. Similarly, service and teaching are essential to the functioning of a university. Yet they often do not lead to national awards or even institutional accolades. Named professorships are reserved for those who have established outstanding records of scholarly achievement—meaning national prominence and external recognition, rather than the admiration and devotion of one's students. Retirement parties are not often given for women who work solely in their homes.

In the future, the academy must seek better ways to recognize the true value of the service and teaching that is disproportionately conducted by women faculty. Asking people to do one thing while rewarding them for doing something else is a sign of dysfunction (Checkoway 2001). In this sense, too many women faculty currently experience their work and institutions as dysfunctional.

Conclusion

What needs to happen in our institutions to accommodate women's multiple identities? Some ideas are noted in the discussion above. However, the question remains: Can we really change our social institutions and the people who seem to dominate in them? Will the dances that we perform become easier, with fewer situations that require the masking of ourselves? Many with whom I have discussed these topics express frustration and seem to answer these questions with a resounding "no." Often their resulting behavioral choice is to isolate themselves or to find another place to dedicate their efforts. The concerns I articulate here will undoubtedly continue to be struggles for the next several decades. However, despite much evidence to the contrary, I believe that there is hope for change. As a teacher, I have to believe that people can learn to see others with a greater sense of respect and authenticity. I have to believe that, as humans, we are interested in the greater good of our collective and that we can see our individual paths as intersecting with others' paths. I hold these beliefs because I am on that journey myself. I have grown and changed and will continue to do so. I also hold these beliefs because I have the honor to work with others who challenge the status quo, who believe that their efforts will make a difference in the world.

It is important for those of us choosing to be allies with others working for equity in society to be continually reflective about the ways in which privilege and oppression take shape in the environments around us. Students, nearly three million of whom will graduate this year (Chronicle Almanac 2006) and become our engineers, teachers, administrators, social workers, lawyers, and business people, learn from how we construct our dances in complex situations. Each of the dances that we perform as women faculty members has the potential to meaningfully shape the experiences of students we encounter. Reflecting on our own positions of oppression (or diminished choices) as well as our own points of privilege models for our students how to consciously be a part of the larger, more diverse society to which we all belong. It also is an opportunity to teach students—most of whom also walk the line between privilege and oppression—how to create their own dances.

We also dance for others in our communities and for ourselves. These dances re-establish our connections with communities that sustain us and serve as a source of strength as we construct our professional and personal lives. To the extent that we allow ourselves and others to become "unmasked," as Montoya (2003) describes it, we will work toward equitable and nurturing practices that expand higher education's potential to be a leader in shaping a nonracist and nonsexist society.

REFERENCES

Astin, Alexander W. 1993. *What matters in college? Four critical years revisited.* San Francisco: Jossey-Bass.

Butler, Judith. 1990. *Gender trouble: Feminism and the subversion of identity.* New York: Routledge.

Checkoway, Barry. 2001. Renewing the civic mission of the American research university. *Journal of Higher Education* 72 (2): 125–47.

Chronicle Almanac. 2006. *Projections of college enrollment, degrees conferred, and high-school graduates, 2006 to 2014.* Retrieved September 3, 2006 from http://chronicle.com/weekly/almanac/2006/nation/0101601.htm.

Collins, Patricia Hill. 1991. *Black feminist thought: Knowledge, consciousness, and the politics of empowerment.* New York: Routledge.

Ellis, Carolyn. 1997. Evocative autoethnography: Writing emotionally about our lives. In *Representation and the text: Reframing the narrative voice,* ed. William G. Tierney and Yvonna S. Lincoln, 115–39. Albany: State University of New York Press.

Gilmore, Angela D. 1991. It is better to speak. *Berkeley Women's Law Journal* 6 (1): 81–92.

Glazer-Raymo, Judith. 1999. *Shattering the myths: Women in academe.* Baltimore: Johns Hopkins University Press.

Guinier, Lani. 1991. Of gentlemen and role models. *Berkeley Women's Law Journal* 6 (1): 93–106.

Harris, Paul L. 1991. *Children and emotion: The development of psychological understanding.* Oxford: Basic Blackwell.

Kolodny, Annette. 1998. *Failing the future: A dean looks at higher education in the twenty-first century.* Durham, NC: Duke University Press.

Latessa, David. 2005. If you're happy and you know it. *Chronicle of Higher Education,* 21 October. Retrieved at http://chronicle.com/jobs/news/2006/08/2006083001c/careers.html.

Martin, Judith Roland. 2000. *Coming of age in academe: Rekindling women's hope and reforming the academy.* New York: Routledge.

McIntosh, Peggy. 1990. White privilege and male privilege: A personal account of coming to see correspondences through work in women's studies. *Independent School* 49 (2): 31–36.

Montoya, Margaret E. 2003. Mascaras, Trenza, y Grenas: Un/masking the self while un/braiding Latina stories and legal discourse. In *Critical race feminism: A reader,* ed. Adrienne Katherine Wing, 70–77. New York: New York University Press.

Neumann, Anna, and Penelope Peterson. 1997. *Learning from our lives: Women, research and autobiography in education.* New York: Teachers College Press.

Park, Shelly. 1996. Research, teaching, and service: Why shouldn't women's work count? *Journal of Higher Education* 67 (1): 46–84.

Richardson, Laurel. 1997. *Fields of play: Constructing an academic life.* New Brunswick, NJ: Rutgers University Press.

Ridgeway, Cecilia. 2001. Gender, status, and leadership. *Journal of Social Issues* 57 (4): 637–55.

Ropers-Huilman, Becky. 1998. *Feminist teaching in theory and practice: Power and knowledge in poststructural classrooms.* New York: Teachers College Press.

———. 2003. Negotiating identities and making change: Feminist faculty in higher education. In *Gendered futures in higher education: Critical perspectives for change,* 135–47. Albany: State University of New York Press.

Schein, Virginia E. 2001. A global look at psychological barriers to women's progress in management. *Journal of Social Issues* 57 (4): 675–89.

Segrest, Mab. 1994. *Memoir of a race traitor.* Cambridge, MA: South End Press.

Tierney, William G., and Estela M. Bensimon. 1996. *Promotion and tenure: Community and socialization in academe.* Albany: State University of New York Press.

Wallace, Dawn D., Becky Ropers-Huilman, and Ron Abel. 2004. Working in the margins: A study of university professionals serving marginalized student populations. *National Association of Student Personnel Administrators Journal* 41 (4): 569–87.

Wolf, Margery. 1992. *A thrice-told tale: Feminism, postmodernism, and ethnographic responsibility.* Stanford, CA: Stanford University Press.

CHAPTER THREE

Shattering Plexiglas

Continuing Challenges for Women Professors in Research Universities

AIMEE LAPOINTE TEROSKY, TAMSYN PHIFER, AND ANNA NEUMANN

In *Shattering the Myths*, published in 1999, Judith Glazer-Raymo commented on the remarkable increases in women's representation and status in American higher education. By the end of the twentieth century, American women were well in the doorway of academe—as faculty, administrators, and trustees—and were looking upward, pushing hard against multiple glass ceilings, reaching unprecedented career heights. The sounds of shattering glass had become part of the culture of American higher education.

However, the time for celebration had not yet arrived. As Glazer-Raymo also wrote in *Shattering the Myths*, despite these notable increases, American academic women still "lag[ged] behind men on all measures . . . salary, tenure, academic rank, interpersonal relationships with male colleagues and supervisors, working conditions" (1999, 198). How might we explain this conundrum?

Focusing on a portion of the population of faculty women in higher education, we suggest the following: at the turn of the twenty-first century, women in tenure-track faculty positions in major American research universities are finding their advancement obstructed by ceilings made not merely of glass, but increasingly of durable Plexiglas. What explains these ceilings? And what will it take to break through them?

We have come to view *Unfinished Agendas* as pointing out these Plexiglas ceilings, for they are the professional targets of the next generation of academic women. Prior to confronting these barriers, however, we need to know that they exist. We also need to understand better what they are made of and what it will take to bring them down. But there is more than ceiling replacement for future women scholars to attend to as they reconstruct the academic home they increasingly call their own: there is also a Plexiglas room, strongly resistant to intrusion. Outsiders can look in, but gaining entry is another matter.

This is the room of academic knowledge construction, the room from within which "legitimate" knowledge is broadcast far and wide in academe and society. It sits at the center of what higher education theorists have termed the "academic core" of college and university organization.[1] The room is large and full of very busy people, working passionately at their scholarly learning: pursuits of knowledge to which they have committed their professional lives (see Neumann 2006). Though most of these people engage in an activity they call "research," many engage also in teaching, outreach, and service, all attuned to those individuals' intellectual passions in mathematics, physics, literature, history, sociology, psychology, engineering, and so on.

We open this chapter with the allegory of the Plexiglas room as a way into an illusive topic within the study of faculty careers in higher education: professors' intellectual development, their growth as scholars and as *learners* of particular subjects of study, and their development as creators of knowledge through research, teaching, and other forms of professorial work, notably in university settings (a complete discussion is in Neumann, forthcoming). Though largely unstudied (see Menges and Austin 2001), the implications of this topic for understanding the positioning of women faculty in higher education are noteworthy. Consider, for example, this question: Once in the door of the university professoriat, *what exactly do these faculty women do* professionally and intellectually? And is what they do, work-wise, the stuff that truly matters in the American research university—namely, the defining and the making of meaningful academic knowledge? How close can these women get to the knowledge-making that drew many of them to academe in the first place? Who among them may gain entry and take up at least partial residence in the Plexiglas room, especially after tenure? Finally, is the work they do inside that room their own—that is, reflective of what they know and strive to know?

These are not questions we address in this chapter. They are not questions that we can answer at this time, given the current state of research in higher education. Rather, these are questions for the future. They require new programs of research tuned more fully than those in the past have been to women's contributions to the academic knowledge that university professors teach and otherwise share with others. Our aim here is more basic: (1) to articulate these large questions as warranting attention, in part, by defining *scholarly learning* as a central feature of all professors' development and therefore as central to consideration of women's careers as university-based scholars and professors; (2) to draw on *current* data to identify some of the challenges that contemporary women scholars face in entering, more fully than they have in the past, that metaphorical Plexiglas-enclosed room that would grant them open and fair involvement in the construction of academic knowledge; and (3) to explore these challenges as they surface within a limited career stage—the university-based, early post-tenure career—though acknowledging that that stage may reflect larger career patterns worthy of further exploration.

To fulfill this aim, we frame the question that guides this chapter as follows: *Which features of their work lives, in major American research universities, do recently tenured academic women experience as drawing them away from their scholarly learning—that is, from the production of knowledge, through research and teaching, as that grows authentically from their lives as women, especially from their own needs, compulsions, and desires to know things in particular that matter to them?* What, then, do senior university women tell us about the university dynamics that keep them out of the Plexiglas room, as a space for scholarly creation, for at least some portions of their work lives and larger careers? What can we learn about those dynamics from within women's representations of their experiences, as scholars and learners, within them?

We respond to this question in light of the career narratives of twenty women participating in a three-year study of the early post-tenure career. The women work in four major American research universities, represent diverse disciplines and fields (the sciences, social sciences, arts and humanities, and applied and professional areas of study), and vary in age from 29 to 60 years. Given limited research on the topic, we are not in a position to assert that the opportunities for scholarly learning are scarce for women alone. Neither do we suggest that the problems we explore in the early post-tenure career and in major research universities are limited to these sites. Rather, we make a limited statement, emblematic of broader research possibilities worthy of pursuit on multiple levels, about men and women of diverse backgrounds and orientations who engage in varying forms of professorial work in multiple disciplines and fields and in different types of institutions. Furthermore, we neither strive to make conclusive statements about the full range of forces that keep women from meaningful pursuits of knowledge through research, teaching, and other forms of professorial work, nor do we try to rank severity of the challenge that any force poses. Clearly, there are more—and much tougher— forces than those we present here. Our analysis features the more silent and commonplace forces that are such a part of the "wallpaper" of academe that we often fail to acknowledge, see, and name them—much as persons, unaware of the qualities of air, might fail to see and name it, or, to borrow from the thought of renowned anthropologist Clyde Kluckhohn (1949), much as fish would fail to see and name the water that surrounds them. Given their pervasiveness and dailiness, these forces may have substantial power to derail women's scholarly learning and thereby their contributions to academic knowledge.

We proceed as follows: (1) We define the concept of *scholarly learning,* underlining its import to the study of higher education broadly and women's academic careers specifically. We also describe the study of university professors' learning and development in early mid-career that has sought to refine this concept and from which we draw data to substantiate our claims about the kinds of challenges to scholarly learning that academic women experience. (2) We outline three institutional and professional "pulls" away from scholarly learning to which university-based women professors are likely to be subject through the early post-tenure career and possibly beyond this period as well. (3) We offer several suggestions—to faculty women and university leaders and policymakers—aimed at enhancing women's opportunities to realize the promises of scholarly learning and thereby the academic knowledge construction for which they were tenured. (4) We offer suggestions for future research on the academic career and on professors' scholarly learning as its central concern, with attention to the situation of academic women.

Framing the View
How Do We Conceptualize Scholarly Learning?

We draw on the concept of professors' *scholarly learning* as developed through the course of a three-year study of recently tenured university professors' learning and development (Neumann forthcoming). The key premises of this concept are summarized below:

- To learn is to construct knowledge about something not known or not well known.
- Ideally, both students and professors are learners. In this sense, professors, though serving as teachers, are also master learners. To do their work, they must learn.
- Professors may learn a great deal throughout their careers, including the scholarly "stuff" (the subject-matter knowledge and ways of knowing) that they teach to their students or that they develop for society and their scholarly communities through research and scholarship.
- When it is personally chosen and pursued, subject-matter knowledge and subject-matter based ways of knowing can hold deep emotional meaning for professors.

- Scholarly learning, defined as the construction or reconstruction of subject matter that is personally meaningful to the learner, may occur in multiple academic locations, amid multiple academic activities (traditionally, research, but also teaching, mentoring, advising, institutional service, outreach, professional service).

- Despite the possibility that scholarly learning can flourish within diverse academic activities—like research, teaching, outreach, and service—sometimes it does not. For example, a scholar's subject-matter learning, in teaching and service, can at times be quite limited (as when the scholar's teaching and research do not bear on her intellectual interests). The same may be true, of course, of a scholar's learning in research (as when a scholar engages in a study of little true interest to her, or when she spends most of her time administering research rather than carrying it out herself). Thus, academic work of all kinds can become reduced in scholarly learning. But this in no way ends the conversation about professors' learning. Academic work may require still other kinds of learning that matter greatly to academe but that do not bear directly on a professor's particular intellectual passions and curiosities. For example, a professor with growing teaching and institutional responsibilities would do well to learn how to read budgets, work with people on committees, initiate outreach projects, manage very large classes if such teaching is in her future, and so on. For a professor, such learning does matter. However, it must be understood for what it is (important instrumental endeavor) and what it is not (substantive), and it must then be balanced with scholarly learning that gives it meaning. Learning, in this "meta" way— to balance the more instrumental learning (for example, reading budgets) with learning that is more clearly attuned to a professor's core subject-matter commitments (scholarly learning, for example, in chemistry, literature, sociology, and so on), without harm to either, and in useful proportion—is very important. Learning how to strike a balance among the diverse calls to learn to which a professor is subject is a major task of the early post-tenure career.[2]

Why Should We Study Academic Women's Involvement in Scholarly Learning?

Broadly speaking, scholarly learning, as defined above, matters because as Lee Shulman (2004a, b) notes, it is at the heart of the educating professions, especially in higher education: to be a professor one must have some thing(s) to profess.

Scholarly learning drives the "what" of what professors teach, what their students and colleagues learn, what as scholars they research or create, and what they claim as scholarly expertise. Looking across the university, scholarly learning—and its products of scholarly knowledge and scholarly knowing—is what the university offers, distinctively, to society (Neumann, forthcoming; see also Becher and Trowler 2001).

Scholarly learning, though broadly applicable to all faculty, holds special meaning for women's knowledge production. As Sandra Harding (1991) and others have noted, women are "strangers" to the academic order. They have been deeply challenged historically in their efforts to enter the front door of academe and to make their way through the academic ranks (Rossiter 1982). Yet the challenges do not stop there. Even after the high-stakes academic-career test of the tenure review, women encounter blocks to their progress: the proverbial glass ceilings to their advancement in academe as in society (Glazer-Raymo 1999; Moore and Sagaria 1991; Martin 2000; Rosser 2004; Zuckerman, Cole, and Bruer 1991).

Yet, as the allegory of the Plexiglas room suggests, there is more to tell: even for those women who do burst through those initial ceilings there remain additional—we suggest tougher—barriers of access to meaningful forms of work. What can be said about the nature of personally meaningful work? We offer two observations: First, it is about a great deal more than women acceding to positions of administrative and organizational leadership, though this is important. And second, it is about women achieving positions and crafting opportunities—for themselves and for other women—to create or re-create the academic knowledge that constitutes academe and that constitutes also the larger social worlds in which we live. This includes shaping or reshaping academic and broader social values, relationships, and identities. This kind of knowledge construction is indeed what scholarly learning is, and we suggest that without direct and central involvement in it, women remain on the sidelines of academe, regardless of how much organizational and professional glass they shatter. Without some entrée to the Plexiglas room, women faculty members are not likely to become academe's central players or to accede easily to central roles in society's efforts to define itself. To study women's relationship to scholarly learning is to study their involvement within the "heart" of the enterprise: the creation of scholarly knowledge.

Why Study Those Forces That Pull Women Away from Scholarly Learning?

In this chapter we use the phrase "the pulls away from scholarly learning" to denote interpersonal, organizational, and social forces and situations that may draw an academic woman away from her scholarly learning toward something else. At times, that "something else" is of lesser value than the woman's scholarly learning. At other times, that "something else" is indeed "a good thing" and worthy of the woman's time and energy investments, even if to do it she has to set aside her scholarly learning. (Consider the case of women who become immersed in student advisement and colleague mentoring, truly good causes that may come at the cost of their scholarship.) The pulls that a professor encounters away from her own intellectual interests, toward equally important matters unrelated to her core interests, can distract her from the subject-matter questions and projects that anchor her reasons for being in academe. Such pulls may draw her attention to others' needs in ways that separate her from her own, as opposed to encouraging her to take both into consideration. Service, as a site of professors' work, represents just such a pull on professors' attentions and energies, and its surprise appearance and incursions into scholarly learning may be especially poignant right after tenure (Neumann and Terosky 2007). At this career stage, university professors are likely to face increased calls to learn in non-substantive ways—and also in substantive ways that are nonetheless tangential to their interests—purely for the good of others (Neumann forthcoming). Professors who assume large quantities of institutional service without thinking through its potential to contribute to or detract from their own intellectual agendas use up valuable time and energy that they could devote to their scholarly learning.

What Is Important about This View?

We view scholarly learning as valuable to an individual professor's professional and personal identity and to her persistence in scholarly work throughout her career. Professors' scholarly learning is also valuable to the social institution of higher education and to the knowledge-generating society of which higher education is a part. Because writers on higher education have not fully explored scholarly learning as a faculty career issue, a gap in knowledge remains. Without attending to the subject-matter knowledge that constitutes professors' teaching, research, outreach, and service, higher education itself is diminished in meaning.

If we assume that professors' scholarly learning is central to the future of American higher education and also that getting women's knowledge more fully into the "core" of higher education is a good thing—for women, for higher education, and for society—then we must identify and understand those features of modern-day academe that pull academic women away from their core scholarly learning. We discuss below how we explored and identified what some of these "pulls" might be and follow with representations of the "pulls" as the women in the study experienced them.

Data Sources, Study Design, and Method

This chapter derives from a three-year longitudinal study of university professors' learning and development in the early post-tenure career.[3] Forty professors (20 women/20 men) working at four American major research universities (Research-Extensive and Research I, two public and two private) participated in two-hour, on-site interviews carried out in project year 1; thirty-nine (20 women/19 men) participated in interviews of the same length in project year 3. Affiliation by field was as follows: sciences[4] (11 total, of whom 5 were women), social sciences (9 total, of whom 3 were women), arts and humanities (9 total, of whom 6 were women), and professional/applied fields (11 total, of whom 6 were women). Participating professors had been tenured and promoted to associate professor within three years of the first interview (study year 1). Thus, by the second interview (study year 3), they were between three and five years post-tenure. By study year 3, a small proportion had been promoted to full professor and a sizable group were planning to "come up for promotion" within a year or two.

Though project data are extensive (interview transcripts for years 1 and 3, observational notes, professors' scholarly documents, campus information), we focused this analysis on year-3 interviews due to their in-depth attention to professors' research, teaching, outreach, and service experiences, and especially to the emergent study theme of scholarly learning. Data analysis privileged the women's interviews (n=20) for identification of key themes (i.e., the "pulls" we describe in the remainder of this chapter). Data from interviews with male professors were entered into analysis solely for comparative purposes.[5] Analysis proceeded inductively, borrowing heavily from traditions of grounded theory (Glaser and Strauss 1967), a research approach that purports to induce theory from a "ground" of untheorized data but as conditioned by existing perspectives on phenomena related to the subject of study (see Schatzman and Strauss 1973, for discussions of theoretical mediation in qualitative research).

What Pulls Women from Scholarly Learning?

What are some of the features of university work life that may draw academic women away from their scholarly learning yet which higher education researchers have not adequately explored as potential barriers to that learning?

Our review of twenty women's accounts of their research, teaching, service, and outreach obligations yielded a broad array of "felt pulls" that they portrayed as distractions from their scholarly learning. We heard these "pulls" in these interviewees' expressed desires to build meaningful personal and family lives, to respond to academic structures that promoted gender equity in compensation and work support, to rectify administrative practices and policies that positioned women as "tokens" and "symbols" rather than as meaningful participants in institutional decision making, among others. These have long been the banners of campaigns to rebalance academe so as to "open doors" to women's full participation. It is important to note that virtually all of these campaigns deal with the structural and organizational features of higher education—clearly, higher education researchers of organization, governance, and administration, also attuned to gender inequities in academe, have much to work with.

However, with only some exceptions (e.g., Gumport 1990), higher education scholars have rarely gone inside those organizational structures to study professors' learning and development within them: to explore what happens to women scholars intellectually within academic organizational spaces that constrain opportunities for their thoughts to develop without limitations. Another way to say this is as follows: higher education research has, to date, sought to identify gender inequities in the obvious (formal) organizational structures of academe more than in the more amorphous processes of knowledge making and intellectual development—hence, scholarly learning—to which higher education researchers have historically had less access. In light of this observation, our aim in this chapter is to enlarge understanding of newly tenured women scholars' positioning, in the American research university, relative to their opportunities to engage in the kind of subject-matter knowledge construction that we call scholarly learning.

We turn now to three challenges—three "pulls"—that tenured academic women encounter as they strive to give due attention to their scholarly learning: first, a pull to increasing work that precludes the kind of scholarly learning we discussed above (e.g., non-substantive service, management of research rather than its conduct); second, a pull to unstrategized work, including tasks for which scholars are largely unprepared and unsupported; and third, a value-driven pull to work that seeks to right gender-based "professional wrongs," yet often with hidden costs attached.

A Pull to Increasing Work That Precludes Scholarly Learning

Prior analysis of the data collected through the study of university professors' learning and development, on which this chapter is based, showed that after tenure, non-substantive responsibilities increase, especially in the branch of professors' work commonly referred to as faculty service (Neumann and Terosky 2007; see also Baldwin et al. 2005). This may be especially true for professors in major research universities whose time often is "protected" for research prior to tenure, given the demands of the impending tenure review. But more must be noted: to do the range of new work that confronts university professors right after tenure, they have to learn how to do it. As such, their new work responsibilities increase—but so do their needs to learn what those responsibilities are, why they matter, and not least, how to carry them out. Both the learning and the doing of the new post-tenure work take time and effort, and if not well strategized, may get in the way of professors' scholarly learning (see Neumann, forthcoming). We discuss in this section two forms of this new work that materialize and expand through the early post-tenure career: (1) institutional service, and (2) research organization and administration. Though both forms of this faculty effort can, on occasion, include scholarly learning (see Neumann and Terosky 2007), we refer here only to versions that do not.

FACING INCREASES IN INSTITUTIONAL SERVICE

Following the award of tenure, sixteen of the twenty (80%) female study participants—in comparison to five of the nineteen (26%) male participants—noted increases in forms of institutional (i.e., university) service responsibilities that precluded their scholarly learning. However, the intensification of service-related work after tenure involved more than doing "extra work"; it also included carrying out increasingly important work. No longer were professors asked to sit on committees purely for symbolic reasons or to carry out easy or low-profile service. Usually, the work they took on was more challenging and visible. For example, many became academic program coordinators, joined committees with significant departmental leadership responsibility, or were appointed to key institutional policy committees as members or as chairs. For example, two women's responses to increases in service-related work show how they experienced its effects on their scholarly learning.

Shortly after the award of tenure and promotion to associate professor, Lina Jackson, a professor of literature, became coordinator of one of the academic programs to which she was appointed. In the first interview, she described her deep attachment to the subject of study to which she had committed her career. Two years later, in the final interview, she said her scholarship was languishing. Though challenged consistently throughout her career to stick by her scholarship and to manage a complicated personal life, after tenure Jackson felt more sharply than ever the intrusion of new administrative work. She defined this work as time-consuming and as having little bearing on her subject of study and teaching. She went on to say that she does not "get as much done [now] as [she] used to in the past," emphasizing that she was "not getting very much written." In the final interview, Jackson elaborated on the clash she felt between her desire to engage in the scholarly learning to which she was deeply committed and the new institutional responsibilities she now faces. In self-critique, she said she struggles to make her continuing scholarly learning and new service responsibilities fit into a workday:

> I am not really able to compartmentalize [my multiple responsibilities] well enough. It's true that I spend most of my time . . . doing teaching-related or administrative-related things. But I have to take some of them home that won't get done. . . . I have to occasionally turn off the lights [in my office], and pretend I'm not here to get some research done. So there's a lot of back and forth. I don't want to make the problem sound more dramatic than it is, but . . . it's a constant low-level worry.

In striving "to compartmentalize," as she said, Jackson tried to carve out space for scholarly learning, which she attached to research, and that others sharing her work space often intruded upon. Such intrusions were heightened due to the new post-tenure responsibilities she took on in administration and university service. She was challenged to draw a line—between time for research and time for service, time for self and time for responsiveness to others—that, in the past, she did not need to draw. To draw this line, Jackson had to reconfigure her life at work and at home; this took time and effort. Thus, as she learned her new service responsibilities, Jackson had to learn also how to carry out the larger task of finding and maintaining a balance in her life. As is evident, she was doing her work (the teaching and service) even as she was learning it, and struggling also to learn how to manage and balance it.

Nelda Casey, a professor in an applied/professional field, also faced dramatic increases in her administrative work when, like Lina Jackson, she became coordinator of her academic program shortly after the award of tenure and promotion to associate professor. Casey spoke in detail about the frustration and concern she felt in having to set her scholarly learning aside so as to carry out the new administrative responsibilities she had inherited. In both interviews, she claimed that her scholarly identity—her sense of self as a learner of her subject of study—was eroding in the face of the time and attention she was devoting to work other than that at the core of her learning interests: "This isn't very positive," she said, "but I have to say—I was just telling my husband this the other night, actually—that I feel like my sense, my identity as a scholar has eroded . . . in th[is] period of time of doing more of the administration and less of the research. And the research is what makes me happy."

Casey provides a poignant example of the deep tension faced by a number of female study participants: She felt pulled away from the substantive interests she had pursued through research pre-tenure. In her post-tenure career, she felt engulfed in less inspiring (though admittedly necessary) administrative work. As her administrative term neared its end at the point of the final interview, Casey looked forward to reinvigorating her scholarship:

> And so right now, I'm kind of excited because I'm in a period of knowing I've got 'til [date] to wrap up the rest of my . . . [administrative] work, but really to start ramping up the research. And so I have written a couple of proposals, really started thinking about what I want to do and really conceptualizing that all over again. . . . It's like . . . standing back and saying, "Okay, now, what do I want to do?" So, I guess that's it in a nutshell. . . . [T]here's just such tension between doing a lot of the . . . administrative work and doing research, for me at least.

Though Casey spoke with optimism about returning to her scholarship at the conclusion of her administrative work, she was clear about the effects that the multiyear program coordination assignment had had on her scholarly identity and career. She noted that her reduced research output over the past several years had rendered her "not as visible" in scholarship as she had been prior to taking on the coordinator role. She also realized—as did her dean, she said—that her administrative work, though important to her colleagues and department, had set her back "a number of years in terms of promotion" to full professor.

Though a number of the women participating in this study portrayed the tension they felt between their scholarly learning and new institutional work as reflective of a larger standoff between research and service, some portrayed that tension as a clash between teaching and service. These scholars represented their non-substantive institutional service responsibilities as pulling them away from the scholarly learning they experienced in course preparation and teaching. Asked if she had changed as a teacher over the past year or two since acquiring tenure, a professor of anthropology said, "This last semester, I . . . felt so swamped by the various administrative things that I probably didn't put as much time into [course] preparation as I would ideally have." The new learning and new work of the early post-tenure career created a clash for the anthropologist, and for multiple others, between the scholarly learning they experienced as they prepared to teach and the new service responsibilities that came their way. Their research might feel the brunt of the clash, but so might their teaching.

To summarize, upon gaining tenure, the majority of the women professors participating in this study experienced increases in institutional service that they portrayed as unrelated to the content of their scholarly learning. What did these professors' "new work" entail? The women in the study took on a variety of new roles in program and departmental administration and also in departmental, college-level, and university leadership. Though clearly of value to the university and to their colleagues and students, these women's participation in large-scale, non-substantive service efforts decreased the amount of time and energy they could devote to their scholarly learning.

FACING INCREASES IN RESEARCH MANAGEMENT

In addition to increases in university service, four of the twenty (20%) academic women participating in this study faced another pull away from their scholarly learning in the form of increased research administration. All four were classified as scientists within the study. Interestingly, these four women also reported increases in university service that drew them away from their scholarly learning. In contrast, none of the male study participants (including the six male professors in the sciences) referred to research management that detracted in tangible ways from their scholarly learning.

The four women in the sciences who said that increasing research administration got in the way of their scholarly learning laid out the following story line: they had been heavily engaged in research pre-tenure. However, as they advanced in rank, they became consumed with managing the logistics of the research enterprise (facility and budgeting reporting, bureaucratic politicking, personnel oversight, etc.). They said that rather than engaging directly in the substantive research they love, as they did before tenure, that now others, working in their labs or in the field, did this on their behalf. Although research is traditionally associated with scholarly learning, research management, its more invisible side, may well distract scholars from engagement with its substance. The case of Angela Brint summarizes their situations.

Angela Brint, a recently tenured scientist, plays a significant leadership role on a complex instrumentation project. In her leadership role, Brint devotes extended time and effort to coordination of other people's (students', post-docs', other colleagues') research efforts and projects. Though acknowledging her natural flair for such work, Brint describes its down sides: "It's sometimes frustrating," she said, "because it's [the work she oversees] often things that I actually personally could do a lot better myself." She offered jokingly that she ought to be appointed to the university's business school rather than to her science program since she devotes more time and energy to managing people and resources than to carrying out research. She added that given opportunity, resources, and time, she would prefer to work on substantive problems in her field rather than on the management of their pursuit by others. In sum, Brint portrays a career narrative of incompleteness and tension between personal interest and intellectual-professional realization.

Although Angela Brint prides herself on being a good manager, she worries what her future as a researcher will look like:

> I actually got into . . . managing [large projects, large groups of people] earlier than I probably should have. So I actually have not had as much experience . . . personally doing the science [substantive work] as most people. I've gotten used to . . . helping the post-docs and things like that. It would be interesting to go back and actually do science myself. I don't know if I'm going to have the chance to do that. . . . It's been so long since I've done it [that] I don't know if I miss it any more. . . . I do a lot of checking of other people's work. . . . Me, sitting down in the laboratory, figuring something out from scratch really does not happen very often, and I've got to be realistic with myself and realize it probably ain't gonna happen.

Brint feels immersed in research management, and she worries that this blocks her from substantive engagement in science.

In exploring the opportunities that the management of large-scale scientific work may offer, Brint becomes aware of another set of blocks: she learns that her authority as a university-based research manager is likely to be circumscribed by the idiosyncratic structure of academe, perhaps more so than were she working for a nonacademic research organization. She said, for example, that her administrative leadership of a university-based scientific enterprise does not entail "management in the normal [bureaucratic] employment structure," for among academics there is no clear "chain of command." In the university, one must learn to work across complex political and symbolic structures and processes where authority is broadly diffused, and where leadership is less about commanding than nudging or symbolic play (Birnbaum 1991). In describing her work as a research manager in academe, Brint referred often to her efforts to influence colleagues who might "get interested" in work that must be done, and in guiding researchers "in the right direction" while "giv[ing] them the resources they need to do what they're interested in." Though she had expected to manage activities and resources more directly, in her role as a manager of the scientific research enterprise, she learned after tenure that the role requires support of others' efforts and direction that is exercised, paradoxically, through indirection. Though she appreciates that this is what it takes to get organizational work done in academic science, Brint realizes too that she does so at cost to her scholarly learning. Such leadership takes time, effort, energy, strategy, and powers of orchestration; it can be a consuming job.

To summarize, women professors—all in the sciences—said that as they moved forward in their careers, their substantive work in the scientific enterprise was often displaced by research management. To manage research is not the same as to do it, and a number of the women scientists in this study stated, much as Brint did, that their growing managerial load was coming to displace the science to which they had devoted their careers.

SUMMARY: PULL TO INCREASING WORK THAT PRECLUDES SCHOLARLY LEARNING

Upon receiving tenure, a substantial majority of women participating in this study experienced increases in non-substantive institutional service, research management responsibilities, or both. Several worried openly that this change kept them from the work to which they were committed—their scholarly learning. Some also said that this change in their work slowed down their clock toward promotion in rank. The women in the sciences seemed especially at risk of experiencing clashes between their scholarly learning and research management.

A Pull to Unstrategized Work, Including Tasks for Which Scholars Are Unprepared and Unsupported

In the views of the women participating in the study, the pulls of institutional service and sometimes of research management on their scholarly learning surfaced largely by surprise. Eleven of the twenty (55%) women participants said that they were unprepared for this rise in service and administration and that they felt unsupported in learning how to respond to it. These women said further that they were unprepared for the "hit" that their scholarly learning would take in light of this surprising escalation of their service/management responsibilities. In contrast, only three of the nineteen (16%) men voiced feelings of unpreparedness and lack of support in the face of rising responsibilities that they cast as unrelated to their scholarly work. We present below the case of a professor of music faced with large-scale increases in service and administrative responsibilities for which she was unprepared.

Carmen Elias-Jones, a professor of music, took on extensive program coordination responsibilities after tenure. A serious and dedicated musician, Elias-Jones had given very little thought in the past to what administration and service might entail. When she took on her new post-tenure program coordination responsibilities, she felt unprepared for the disorder and the demands that engulfed her, choking off time that otherwise she would have devoted to her work with music, her version of scholarly learning. She described her experience:

> . . . I had a harder time—somewhere in the middle of the past two or three years—I had a harder time trying to juggle my time. Trying to find the good time for my practicing, and [for my] thinking about me. I found myself being spread very thin. I found myself being extremely frantic. And so I would say that that in some ways was a low point. It was partly because of all the administrative duties and my not being shrewd enough and savvy enough, having really come from the fearful days of saying "Yes" to everything and at whatever the cost to myself or to my time. So that was . . . a low point, a very hectic point.

Despite the "low point, a very hectic point," Elias-Jones quickly moved into action: she realized that to make time for herself and for her scholarly learning, she would have to learn first how to create an environment in which she and the others with whom she worked could get things done and simply learn. This would involve major workspace revision with attention to how colleagues and students in the program worked together. Elias-Jones focused heavily on clarifying communication among all: making program functions public, improving means of sharing information, and rethinking collaborative work. She also learned to speak out about what she could and could not do, given the realities she faced; what her responsibilities included and where they ended and others' responsibilities picked up. Learning to do all this while developing supportive norms and activities took time and energy that she would have devoted to her music. At times, her new administrative work progressed smoothly, but at other times, it did not:

> . . . when something was not done, and I ended up having to pick up the pieces, 45 minutes before the onset of a class, while a colleague came in and said he had to have lunch and sorry, he couldn't do it. When actually it was supposed to be his task. I handed the whole thing over to him so it wouldn't come back to me. But it did come back to me. Partly because [the person] didn't take the responsibility.

As this statement shows, Elias-Jones sought to activate a system of personal responsibility, some of which was her own but some of which was not. At times this parceling out of responsibility worked well, but as the excerpt suggests, at other times, it did not. When "things went bad," as in the instance above, Elias-Jones had to rethink—in effect, relearn—how to address the challenges at issue: a work-sharing system that did not work, a flawed communication system, a colleague with a habit of not following through, graduate student turnover, and so on.

In addition to adopting a software system that helped her announce, track, and otherwise coordinate program activities and resources, Elias-Jones developed a number of personal strategies for safeguarding her time for her own scholarly learning in music:

> I get here very early. I protect my schedule jealously, fiendishly. And to tell you the truth, I don't think that I'm considered to be . . . lazy, or that I'm trying to get out of certain things. I think students have a way of valuing your time if you tell them that it really is not at their disposal. . . . I've really become much more savvy. I've gotten really quite good at saying, "Try asking so and so for this," and, oh, very, very good at passing the buck. And saying, "No" to certain things, and really being quite firm. Because if I just keep coming up with the ready-made result, even though I have suffered or scrambled, the way I see it is there really is no incentive for behavior modification. So I just say, "I can't do this. Gotta give me 8 weeks lead time. Sorry to be so awful. Do appreciate the opportunities for my student. Can't do it." So back comes another thing, and it's two weeks from now—"Can't do that. I suggest we cancel it. But this is an excellent time to get dates for next quarter. Thank you so much, and really I'm so sorry to be awful."

Thus Elias-Jones developed, on the job, several strategies for carrying out her new responsibilities and also for managing her work life. Such strategizing was a major task of her early post-tenure career. The task came to her as a surprise; she was unprepared for it. She had to learn it. Elias-Jones also learned to improvise: immersed at times in non-substantive tangles of work, she learned how to find "ways out" from within them. Not all women participating in the study rose, as she did, above their circumstances by devising ways to manage activities and events, problems and opportunities; turning them to their favor; and allowing space and time for scholarly learning. Yet it seems fair to ask how much less energy-draining—if not more productive—her experience might have been had she been prepared, supported, mentored, or otherwise guided in the kinds of career- and job-crafting skills she would need through her early post-tenure career.

SUMMARY: PULL TO UNSTRATEGIZED WORK

The increase in post-tenure service and administration might be less burdensome if professors were able to strategize their service much as many do their research. But service is rarely a planned part of the professorial career; much like teaching, service is a form of work for which professors are not prepared (Neumann and Terosky 2007). Half the women participating in the study felt unequipped to address their rising service and management responsibilities in ways that allowed them to engage smoothly and productively in their scholarly learning. Though many "kept their heads above water"—largely by inventing survival strategies "in the thick of things" as they persisted in their new work tasks—they often did so on time and energy that they "bought" from their scholarly learning. They were pulled, then, to learn instrumentally about job and career management largely "on the job" and with little support. This instrumental learning differed greatly from their scholarly learning and absorbed time and energy that they otherwise would have devoted to more substantive and scholarly matters, the stuff for which, in fact, they were tenured.

A Pull to Work That Seeks to Right Gender-Based "Professional Wrongs" but at a Cost

Seven of the twenty women (35%) participating in this study experienced another pull on their scholarly learning that none of the men in the study reported. That pull grew from their efforts to right gender-based inequities that they witnessed or felt in the academic workplace, usually on their own campus. We briefly review some of these participants' day-to-day experiences in environments that they viewed as misusing women, or as being unreceptive to and unappreciative of women's contributions. We then discuss how experiences such as these moved some of the women to active response—which could, quite paradoxically, be costly to the advancement of their scholarly learning.

A woman scientist working in an area where few other women worked spoke clearly of the burden she felt as she served on many university committees that sought her membership in order to promote a vision of campus-wide gender equity:

> Until very recently, the demand for women to serve on all sorts of committees in my age group is just humongous. And you can't really say "No" to these things because they really have no alternative, so I've had a lot of obligations. . . . It's been a real opportunity, but there's a whole bunch of women coming along after me, and I'm hoping that we can share the load a little more.

Another woman, in a different scientific field but also with few female colleagues, elaborated:

> I think probably you get [on] a couple [of] committees, people realize that . . . you're responsible and you're easy to get along with, and you can do these things. So you get asked to do more of them. And there aren't very many women in [my sector of the

sciences] . . . there aren't very many associate professor women in [this sector]. And there's a couple of senior women who nobody wants to deal with. So I'm also kind of a token. Unusual. I get asked to do a lot of [time-intensive university committee service] . . . [because] they need a woman from the sciences . . . and they want to leave the untenured women alone.

Together, these two scientists make an important point that is rarely explored: being a woman in academe can be very challenging, especially so when gender, age, career stage, and density of women already in a field are taken into consideration. For example, these two women's hypotheses about the relevance of age and career stage paired with density/distribution of women in a field to women's well-being in science bears a far closer look than has been carried out to date (see Rosser 2004). The "pull" in these two cases may be summarized as follows: the two women scientists are asked to do more than they believe is their share of non-substantive work.

Other women in the study take still deeper looks into issues of gender inequity, commenting on differences in the work conditions and in access to rewards for diverse groupings in their fields. A social scientist concerned about steep inequities in reward systems among men and women, stratified further by age and career stage, spoke of needs to counter "the sheer sexism" that she believes infuses academe. But this scholar worried too that women need to "pick their battles with care" to avoid diffusing their power, in both real and symbolic terms. For example, she struggles with whether, when, and how to address salary differentials she has recently observed: she feels entitled to speak out but worries about the symbolic cost of doing so:

> How do I describe this? If I raise a really big fuss about something, I can sometimes get my way. . . . But you know, if women raise a really big fuss about anything, we're, you know, bitches. So, I think . . . what has become more apparent to me since I last spoke to you is just the sheer sexism of this profession I think is staggering . . . . I have realized that I'm just gonna have to deal with that for the rest of my life so . . . maybe the sheer sexism of the world is more apparent to me. But I'm not in the world. I'm just in academia mostly.

Like the two scientists previously cited, this social scientist is aware of large-scale gender inequities. She knows, as they do, that her job and career are entangled in these inequities. Yet the three women say very little about the effects of their own work environment on their experiences of scholarly learning. That personal and local connection is missing in the words they spoke in the interviews. Yet we must consider these women's silence on this matter at more than face value: the possibility remains that their awareness of inequity shapes the mindsets they bring to their studies, for research and teaching, and to the other work in which they engage. In any case, the work climates these women describe appear as anything but conducive to their professional advancement. We suggest the possibility that such environments exert a cost—yet one not clearly documented to date—on academic women's scholarly learning.

Such cost may be especially steep for women as they pick worthy battles to fight, for these are battles that take time and energy away from their scholarly learning. Women scientists in our sample were especially articulate about this matter. One of them related the following incident: as a member of a committee desiring to improve the conditions of women's work on campus, she had devoted extended time and energy to bring a particular feminist speaker to her campus. The task at hand was arduous: she and others had to make a case, to a difficult committee, to bring in the speaker they wanted; they had to work through the committee to raise funds and so on. While the scientist worked hard at this effort—for the good of the women scientists on her campus—her male departmental colleagues engaged in important substantive work in which she did not participate. They learned something, in their shared science, in which she had no part because she was otherwise occupied—struggling to bring in a feminist speaker for women in the sciences:

> And I would get into these great debates [on the committee selecting the feminist speaker.] . . . What really annoyed me was that my male colleagues would be [engaged in tasks more closely related to their research than I was,] and they were, you know, finding out how to [decipher an interesting/important formula,] while I was arguing about who was more feminist than the other. . . . I must say that was probably the only committee I've ever served on where aside from learning some interesting things in [general education/liberal arts,] I basically didn't learn very much.

By working for the good of the order, this scientist missed out on an opportunity to advance her scholarly learning, while her male colleagues engaged more directly and continuously than she did in their scholarly learning. The scientist was clearly engaged in important work on behalf of other women scientists, but that work, however important, cost the scientist a bit of scholarly learning. Such instances, repeated, reflect an erosion of opportunities for women to learn in substantive and meaningful ways.

SUMMARY: A PULL TO WORK THAT SEEKS TO RIGHT
GENDER-BASED WRONGS

A third of the women participating in this study described inequitable work practices that they had witnessed or felt, usually on their own campuses. Their experiences led us to wonder how learning proceeds in environments rife with inequity—how experiences of inequity may shape what is learned and how it is learned, what is gained and, especially, what is lost. If scholarly learning requires being in touch with work and ideas that one loves (see Neumann 2006), it is hard to imagine how such environments would encourage such learning. We suspect that women's emotional engagement with inequity—in itself not a bad thing— may have the unanticipated effect of displacing the emotion that they would otherwise devote to their scholarly learning.

Though we strongly applaud women's agency in fighting gender-based inequity—and any kind of inequity—we underline the need to weigh the costs of such engagement with care. Consider the case of the scientist who closes this section: although her positive action to bring a feminist speaker to campus is praiseworthy (she is doing something to help women), that agency comes at a cost. In devoting herself to helping other women, she herself loses out on scientific learning—on core insights—that her male colleagues, who fight no gender battles, construct. This situation, of course, reflects a paradoxical twist for academic feminism: advocacy on their own behalf and on behalf of other women for gender equity can, in the long run, take a toll on individual women's scholarly learning. Their positioning within the intellectual core of higher education may be risked.

Conclusions, Implications, and Questions for the Unfinished Agenda

Women have made historic strides in academe. As scholars and professors, they have contributed valuable research, creative insight, teaching, and service to their fields of study and campuses. We laud their advances, even as we acknowledge the organizational, professional, and collegial barriers they still face. In this chapter, we have examined only one of the challenges that women academics may face: a class of "pulls," located prominently (though not exclusively) in the strand of work known as faculty service and including research administration. Though it is erroneous to portray all faculty service as detrimental (a good portion of it can reflect scholarly learning, see Neumann and Terosky 2007), some forms of service, if not thoughtfully selected and designed, may draw women away from their scholarly learning and from their knowledge construction in the university and society. In some settings, women may be positioned to shoulder an inequitable burden of service that is unrelated to their scholarly learning and that may detract from it. Our study cannot make the claim that this is in fact the case in all universities, yet it can offer this view: that given women's susceptibility to being positioned in this way, university leaders, policymakers, and researchers of higher education need to attend more closely than they have in the past to the institutional positioning of women's knowledge construction efforts.

We further summarize the findings of our analysis as follows: (1) After receiving tenure, the women in the study faced dramatic increases in service and administrative responsibilities that precluded attention to their scholarly learning. (2) This was work for which they were largely unprepared, but which they assumed, typically unsupported. They had to learn their new responsibilities and to invent career strategies to manage their time, often on their own. Learning the new work that they faced, carrying it out, and strategizing their careers around these tasks took time and effort, pulling them away from the scholarly learning they sought to pursue. (3) A number of the women in the study confronted and advocated against inequitable work practices; this was challenging work that, if substantively unrelated to their areas of study, came at cost to their scholarly agendas. (4) Though the service load of males also went up, far fewer indicated the concomitant loss to their scholarly learning.

These findings lead us to two statements of concern: first, about the loss of women's potential contributions to academic knowledge production for the larger human good, defined as academe's core social contribution; and second, about the illusory quality of service engagement and administrative promotion as opportunities for reward and professional advancement.

The Loss of Women's Scholarly Learning

At the heart of its social mission is the university's promise to create, distribute, and otherwise share new knowledge for the social good, a goal often referred to formally as knowledge production and dissemination. We portray professors' scholarly learning as core to these processes (Neumann forthcoming) and believe that women professors should be positioned to contribute to them through their scholarly learning as fully as men historically have. In this chapter we asked whether the post-tenure workload changes that university women experienced, specifically in service and administration, had subtractive effects on their scholarly learning, and whether their male colleagues experienced similar pulls on their scholarly learning.

The data indicate that although women and men experienced similar increases in their service/administrative responsibilities, more women then men voiced concerns that the increases absorbed time and energy that otherwise would have been devoted to their scholarly learning. In other words, more women then men felt that their scholarly learning—their efforts to contribute to the university's central task of knowledge construction—suffered as a result of rising service/administrative work, even though both men's and women's service/administrative responsibilities increased. This pattern held with regard to study participants' involvement in institutional service. On other features of service and administration (research management, service and administrative responsibility for which one is unprepared, and work in support of gender equity in the university), women also reported higher workloads, detracting from their scholarly learning.

What can we make of this? We suggest the following possible scenario: that as women were drawn away from their scholarly learning, they had fewer opportunities to contribute authentically to the knowledge of their disciplines and fields and to academe at large than, it appears, did their male colleagues. We further suggest that pulls such as those described above touch both women's lives (reducing the possibility that they will realize their scholarly learning aims, cutting short their professional advancement) and the larger life of higher education and society— that is, in constraining women's abilities to contribute through their scholarly learning, we narrow, quite simply, what we can know for the greater good.

The Illusion of Reward and Career Advancement

The established cultures of the major American research university and normative reward structures and career advancement paths assume that professors will contribute to knowledge production and knowledge dissemination through their research, teaching, and public service. In recent years, this vision of what it means to be a professor has seeped into other types of institutions—private liberal arts colleges, state colleges, and community colleges—that have historically emphasized the teaching and public service missions of American postsecondary enterprise. This augers the worrisome possibility that women's university-based challenges, to participate meaningfully in academic knowledge construction through their scholarly learning, may seep into these other institutions as well.

Though numerous efforts are now afoot to rebalance the faculty reward structure (for example, by elevating teaching and service, thereby attracting faculty to these activities as avidly as to research), we do worry about the implications, for women's scholarly learning and for their careers, of their overly enthusiastic departure from research if their male colleagues do not do the same and in equal numbers. We hope that adjustments to reward and professional advancement structures will do more—for women, for teaching, and for service—than merely crystallize their value within a portion of the academic enterprise. Moreover, assuming that research continues as a viable and vital form of academic work—and we do clearly support this mission—then we need to be sure that women continue to enter the research side of the academic house as well and that their scholarly learning be valued in it. Alternatively, we realize that women's continuance in research careers that constrain their knowledge growth is problematic (for example, when they carry out research on topics that mean little to them). Faced with this situation, a professor's intentional move of her scholarly learning into her teaching, outreach, or service may be defensible if, that is, the teaching, outreach, and service allow her to pursue her scholarly learning in free and generative ways, and if that scholarly learning can be valued for its contribution to academic knowledge, that is, as equivalent to "research." The bottom line is this: "Rewards" for research, teaching, service, administration, and outreach that take away from opportunities for women's scholarly learning are illusory and require careful stock-taking, both by academic women and by university leaders and policymakers who support (or simply fail to question) them.

Implications for Practice and for Research on Higher Education Practices

The two preceding concerns may be viewed as starting points for thought about how to move forward.

CHANGING PROFESSIONAL DEVELOPMENT IN THE UNIVERSITY "AS IT IS"

The women—and men too—participating in our study were often "caught off guard" by post-tenure increases in service and administration. With this surprising change in workload, the women, in particular, experienced a "hit" on their scholarly learning that many of the men did not. As the preceding data indicate, many of the women described how unprepared and unsupported they were for the new work they were asked to take on. The combination of rising work responsibilities, inadequate preparation, and absence of support suppressed many women's abilities to maintain the intensity of the scholarly learning they had experienced pre-tenure (or hoped for post-tenure). Given this state of affairs and the concern that the university is not likely to change as quickly as we might want, we suggest a two-part plan of action and study in pursuit of improved practices of professional development for post-tenure professors.

First, higher education leaders and scholars should do a better job of studying and supporting professors as they advance from junior to senior professorial positions. Currently, scholars and leaders in higher education work at supporting junior faculty or revitalizing senior faculty, thereby overlooking mid-career, the period when "seasoned faculty" may be at the height of their intellectual and professional strength and vitality. Yet as the study data indicate, this career phase is anything but unproblematic (see Neumann forthcoming). We need to know far more about this career stage than we now do, and we need to put that knowledge to work for women and men alike. Practitioners, and practice-oriented researchers as well, need to ask themselves repeatedly: Why must the new post-tenure workload come as such a surprise to both men and women? And why must so many women feel the impact, bluntly, on their scholarly learning when, as the data suggest, not as many men do?

Second, though it is so much easier said than done, newly tenured professors should themselves explore, and if possible articulate and exercise, agency in and for their own careers, and their scholarly learning especially. To ignite such agency, professors might seek out career mentors and colleagues who are doing so themselves; create communities of practice and peer networks aimed at talking about and encouraging such agential action; and not least, attend to and craft the service and administrative portions of their own careers as carefully, fully, and substantively as many do their research and teaching careers. Not to do so is to leave the important task of career construction to others who may be limited in their abilities to fashion scholarly work lives that bear meaning for professors. Professors themselves must do this.

HEIGHTENING ATTENTION TO SCHOLARLY LEARNING THROUGHOUT THE ACADEMIC CAREER

One of us (Neumann forthcoming) has offered that scholarly learning is a key value in American higher education—clearly not the only such value, yet one that anchors many others. However, professors' scholarly learning is largely overlooked in higher education policy discourses that focus largely on professors' teaching and on other forms of knowledge sharing, though usually through the overly narrow rubric of faculty time use. We do need to continue talking and thinking, together and alone, about teaching, service, and the betterment of our campuses; but we need to do this from a base of appreciation for and open support of professors' scholarly learning, and not from a view of teaching and professorial work as, literally, subject-less. Scholarly learning assumes, and in fact demands, a *subject* of study—conceptualized, reconceptualized, and otherwise advanced by people of diverse backgrounds and equally diverse ways of knowing and understanding the world. We worry that without attention to professors' scholarly learning, Plexiglas ceilings, in academe and society, may remain in place for too long, and the Plexiglas rooms of knowledge construction in the university may remain inaccessible to new and talented thinkers, and thus to generative thought.

ACKNOWLEDGMENT

The research reported in this chapter was made possible by a grant from the Spencer Foundation. The data presented, the statements made, and the views expressed are solely the responsibility of the authors.

NOTES

1. For related theoretical discussion, see Birnbaum 1991, 1992.

2. For extended discussion of these premises and their derivation through two interrelated studies of the early post-tenure career as well as other related writings, see Neumann forthcoming; Neumann 2006; Neumann, 2005a, b; as well as Neumann and Pallas 2005; Neumann and Peterson 1997; Neumann, Terosky, and Schell 2006; Neumann and Terosky 2007.

3. To comply with pledges of confidentiality, we name no institution or person, and we omit or mask potentially identifying data. Some professors requested that instead of indicating their specific disciplines or fields of study, we use broader descriptors (e.g., a biologist wishing to be called a scientist or a political scientist wishing to be described as a social scientist).

4. Unless otherwise noted, the terms "scientist" or "professor" in one of the sciences (and the like) refer to scholars of pure scientific disciplines or interdisciplinary areas (e.g., biology, chemistry, biochemistry) and mathematics, but not scholars in the applied sciences (e.g., engineering), who are classified here as working in professional/applied fields.

5. Data analysis initially spanned both men's and women's interviews fully. However, since we sought to understand "pulls on women's scholarly learning" specifically, we redirected our attention toward pulls on the women specifically. In doing so, we sought to avoid conflation with other "pulls" that males may feel. We also sought to minimize diffusion of themes in the women's data with those in the full sample. We suspect, furthermore, that more than differences in "pull" exist between men and women. Differences in scholarly learning itself, though as shaped by pull, may be a feature of such data. Our reasoning is as follows: For women, especially, scholarly learning may include their distinctive responses to their "pulls" away from it.

Their experiences of those pulls may become embedded in their scholarly learning in ways they do not for men to whom many of the women's pulls appear not to apply. This is likely to happen because both scholarly learning and pulls on it are, by definition, linked experiences. To get a complete vision of gender-based differences across different parts of the linkage (scholarly learning/pulls on it) requires different kinds of data and a more complex analytic approach than we are able to leverage through this study: one that takes account of what scholarly learning means to a professor in relation to "pulls" she or he may experience on that learning.

REFERENCES

Baldwin, Roger, Christina Lunceford, and Kim Vanderlinden. 2005. Faculty in the middle years: Illuminating an overlooked phase of academic life. *Review of Higher Education* 29 (1): 97–118.

Becher, Tony, and P. R. Trowler. 2001. *Academic tribes and territories: Intellectual enquiry and the cultures of disciplines.* Bristol: Society for Research into Higher Education and Open University Press.

Birnbaum, Robert. 1991. *How colleges work: The cybernetics of academic organizations and leadership.* San Francisco: Jossey-Bass.

———. 1992. *How academic leadership works: Understanding success and failure in the college presidency.* San Francisco: Jossey-Bass.

Glaser, Barney, and Anselm Strauss. 1967. *The discovery of grounded theory: Strategies for qualitative research.* Chicago: Aldine Publishing Company.

Glazer-Raymo, Judith. 1999. *Shattering the myths: Women in academe.* Baltimore: Johns Hopkins University Press.

Gumport, Patricia. 1990. Feminist scholarship as a vocation. *Higher Education* 20 (3): 231–43.

Harding, Sandra G. 1991. *Whose science? Whose knowledge? Thinking from women's lives.* Ithaca, NY: Cornell University Press.

Kluckhohn, Clyde. 1949. *Mirror for man: The relation of anthropology to modern life.* New York: Whittlesey House.

Martin, Jane Roland. 2000. *Coming of age in academe: Rekindling women's hopes and reforming the academy.* New York: Routledge.

Menges, Robert J., and Ann E. Austin. 2001. Teaching in higher education. In *Handbook of research on teaching,* 4th ed., ed. Virginia Richardson, 1122–56. Washington, DC: American Educational Research Association.

Moore, Kathryn M., and Mary Ann D. Sagaria. 1991. The situation of women in research universities in the United States: Within the inner circles of academic power. In *Women's higher education in comparative perspective,* ed. Gail P. Kelly and Sheila Slaughter, 185–200. Boston: Kluwer Academic Publishers.

Neumann, A. 1999. Inventing a labor of love: Scholarship as a woman's work. In *Women's untold stories: Breaking silence, talking back, voicing complexity,* ed. Mary Romero, 243–55. New York: Routledge.

———. 2005a. To glimpse beauty and awaken meaning: Scholarly learning as aesthetic experience. *Journal of Aesthetic Education* 39 (4): 68–88.

———. 2005b. Observations: Taking seriously the topic of learning in studies of faculty work and careers. *New Directions for Teaching and Learning,* no. 102: 63–83.

———. 2006. Professing passion: Emotion in the scholarship of professors in research universities. *American Educational Research Journal* 43 (3): 381–424.

———. Forthcoming. *Professing to learn: Creating tenured lives and careers in the American research university.* Baltimore: Johns Hopkins University Press.

Neumann, Anna, and Aaron M. Pallas. 2005. Windows of possibility: Perspectives on the construction of educational researchers. In *The SAGE handbook for research in education: Engaging ideas and enriching inquiry,* ed. Clifton Conrad and Ronald C. Serlin, 429–49. Thousand Oaks, CA: Sage.

Neumann, Anna, and Penelope Peterson. 1997. *Learning from our lives: Women, research, and autobiography in education.* New York: Teachers College Press.

Neumann, Anna, and Aimee LaPointe Terosky. 2003. *Toward images of reciprocity in faculty service: Insights from a study of the early post-tenure career.* Presented at annual meeting of the American Educational Research Association, Chicago, April.

———. 2007. To give and to receive: Recently tenured professors' experiences of service in major research universities. *Journal of Higher Education* 78 (3): 282–310.

Neumann, Anna, Aimee LaPointe Terosky, and Julie Schell. 2006. Agents of learning: Strategies for assuming agency, for learning, in tenured faculty careers. In *The balancing act: Gendered perspectives in faculty roles and work lives,* ed. Susan J. Bracken, Jeanie K. Allen, and Diane R. Dean. American Association for Higher Education, 91–121. Sterling, VA: Stylus Publishing.

Rosser, Sue V. 2004. *The science glass ceiling: Academic women scientists and the struggle to succeed.* New York and London: Routledge/Taylor and Francis Group.

Rossiter, Margaret W. 1982. *Women scientists in America: Struggles and strategies to 1940.* Baltimore: Johns Hopkins University Press.

Schatzman, Leonard, and Anselm Strauss. 1973. *Field research: Strategies for a natural sociology.* Englewood Cliffs, NJ: Prentice-Hall.

Shulman, Lee S. 2004a. *The wisdom of practice: Essays on teaching, learning, and learning to teach.* San Francisco: Jossey-Bass.

———. 2004b. *Teaching as community property: Essays on higher education.* San Francisco: Jossey-Bass.

Zuckerman, Harriet, Jonathan R. Cole, and John T. Bruer, eds. 1991. *The outer circle: Women in the scientific community.* New York: W. W. Norton.

CHAPTER FOUR

The Differential Effects of Academic Capitalism on Women in the Academy

AMY SCOTT METCALFE AND SHEILA SLAUGHTER

> The urgency of feminism to establish a universal status for patriarchy in order to strengthen the appearance of feminism's own claims to be representative has occasionally motivated the shortcut to a categorical or fictive universality of the structure of domination, held to produce women's common subjugated experiences.
>
> —*Judith Butler,* Gender Trouble

As a concept, academic capitalism (Slaughter and Leslie 1997; Slaughter and Rhoades 2004) describes the ways colleges and universities are shifting from a "public good knowledge/learning regime" to a knowledge regime attuned to the market. In the public good knowledge/learning regime, the academic production process is removed from the market, buffered from the state, and occurs in a space that is neither market nor government. Its purposes—whether teaching, research, or service—are directed toward activity not primarily concerned with the generation of external revenues.[1] In contrast to the public good knowledge/learning regime, the "academic capitalist knowledge/learning regime" prefers students able to pay high tuition, departments and colleges close to high-end markets, and research that features partnerships with industry, start-up companies, and intellectual property licensing potential. The public good is redefined as what is good for economic development.

Academic capitalism as a theory seeks to explain how and why institutions of higher education and the people working within them engage in market and market-like behaviors. Slaughter and Rhoades (2004) theorize that the shift from the public good knowledge/learning regime to academic capitalism is accomplished through actors both inside and outside of postsecondary education. These actors forge new circuits of knowledge, develop interstitial units[2] to take advantage of these new circuits of knowledge, work with partners to construct intermediating organizations[3] with market potential, and participate in the rapid buildup of managerial capacity that enables universities to intersect with markets. Together, these complex and strategic networks link higher education to preferred markets.

Although the theory of academic capitalism has become an important lens for research in higher education, it has not been widely used to understand the effects of the market on academic women. The purpose of this chapter is to examine the ways in which academic capitalism intersects with the lives and careers of women in higher education.

Feminist theory plays a part equal in importance to the theory of academic capitalism in our analysis. Particularly useful are third-wave feminist theories that see gender as fluid and relational. Such theories problematize patriarchy, making it more complex than a monolithic structure of domination and therefore illuminating women's experiences as being more multifaceted than simple subjugation (Baumgardner and Richards 2000; Butler 1990; Haywood and Drake 1997; Walker 1995). According to Braithwaite (2002, 339), the desire to explore the "politics of contradiction, incorporation, and negotiation" marks third-wave feminist scholarship. In the current era, social relations are significantly complicated so that "traditional" binary positionalities (male/female, majority/minority, proletariat/bourgeois) become problematic. In short, we expect that women's experiences in higher education will be marked as much by their relationships with other women as by their relationships with men and that their experiences will depend on the class position of these men and women as well as their positionality with regard to markets. In other words, we must move beyond aggregated national or institutional measures of numerical representation and toward a more nuanced discussion of the intersections between gender, organizational location, and market hegemonies. This type of research relies on disaggregated data, primarily at the college level, occasionally augmented by departmental data as well as by data dealing with various administrative strata.

Our basic argument is that academic capitalism creates conditions within colleges and universities that allow men to recapture some of the historic privilege they have derived from higher education. In other words, men have sought ways to shift from one prestige system (the traditional academy with its expert-based power) to another (the entrepreneurial academy with its market-based power), recasting the value systems of higher education in the process. As women gained ground in the academy, albeit slowly and with great difficulty due to the gendered nature of the system, males in the academic profession faced a "crisis of hegemony,"[4] which de Sousa Santos (2006) sees in terms of the academy as a whole, but we see in terms of gender relations. In order to maintain academe's power and prestige relative to other male occupational arenas, an alternative internal hierarchy was created primarily by men. This internal hierarchy is the academic capitalist knowledge/learning regime, where the merit of one's knowledge product is no longer solely determined by peer review or the public good (which are suspect due to the increasing inclusion of women) but by preferred markets.[5] Because the marketplace is itself gendered (Beneria 1999; Ferber and Nelson 1993; Levin 2001), the rules and criteria for advancement in higher education merely shift from being normed on *homo academicus* (Bourdieu 1984) to *homo economicus* (Bowles and Gintis 1993). To the extent that they can succeed within these rational, individualistic, and competitive market-based criteria, women may have access to the rewards of higher education. Thus, academic capitalism may serve as a vehicle for the advancement of some women, but its very premise (competition) precludes the concept of equity.

Men and Women of the Academy

Traditionally, higher education served middle- and especially upper-middle-class men as a form of credentialism that allowed them to occupy professional, scholarly, and managerial positions in society. Until the 1970s, women were excluded from many professional schools or else professional schools had quotas that severely limited their numbers (e.g., law and medicine). Even at women's colleges, male professors often outnumbered female professors. Only a small number of professors were women in the 1950s and 1960s (Solomon 1985; May 1999).[6]

As women's social movements opened up space for them in the academy, men were forced to share their historic privilege. The entrance of women into scholarly, professional, and managerial positions was not an easy matter, and gender parity has remained elusive.[7] The total number of academic positions—from which women had previously been excluded—would have had to expand by 100 percent to provide enough spaces for women to be on par with men if the number of men in these positions remained constant. The rate of expansion of the American academy, however, has not been consistent across employment categories, allowing for differential access for women along the spectrum of support services, administration, and faculty positions. In recent years, the percentage of female employees at postsecondary institutions has increased from 51.7 percent in 1993 to 53 percent in 2003 (Li 2006). Yet the largest increases for women have been in the professional support/service category (45.4% change) and the executive/administrative/managerial category (53.1% change), occupational categories that have grown the most from 1993 to 2003. In these two employment classifications (and the historically female clerical/secretarial category), women outnumbered men in 2003. Thus, women have indeed moved into the academy, but they have been the most successful in areas that have had the most expansion. In areas of slower expansion, such as faculty positions, women have not made the same degree of progress toward parity (or over-representation). We see this differential success as reason to more fully examine the placement of women within the contemporary (largely entrepreneurial) academy.

Like men, some women faculty and administrators have become actors in new circuits of knowledge, interstitial and intermediating organizations, and an expanded managerial sector through which academic capitalism has become incorporated in colleges and universities. Indeed, a growing number of women are highly successful in the academic capitalist knowledge/learning regime. Although these highly successful women earn salaries that put them in the top 10 percent of all earners, they make up a significantly smaller portion of the earners than do men and often earn less than their male counterparts. Nevertheless colleges and universities, especially institutions that are not at the very top of the standard indicators of prestige—for example, community colleges and public doctoral granting universities—have a definite stratum of entrepreneurial women faculty and administrators. They usually earn more than women in gender-balanced fields, certainly more than women in female-dominated departments and colleges. These women participate actively in the construction of academic capitalism, problematizing theories that question the agency of women in higher education. To trivialize their success is to deny substantive gains made by the women's movement; to celebrate their success overlooks the majority of women who have not made similar gains. Further complicating feminist analysis, a number of these successful academic women structurally contribute to the dismantling of the liberal state[8] by working in academic or managerial units that redefine the boundary between the public and private sectors in ways that privilege the private sector. This is theoretically opaque because the private sector has generally been less supportive of women than the public sector in terms of faculty employment, regardless of institutional type, except for private (nonprofit) doctoral-granting universities (Glover and Parsad 2003).

In this chapter we explore the moves and counter-moves made by women and men to better understand how changes occur in the gender composition of postsecondary education. We expect to see greater gender disparity in marketized areas of colleges and universities. Focusing on markets will also direct our attention to the ascendancy of the neoliberal state that makes academic capitalism possible

(Slaughter and Leslie 1997). While we understand that generally women in academeme do not fare as well as men in terms of full-time status, rank, working conditions, salary, benefits, and opportunities (see chapters 1, 7, and 8 in this volume), we believe that enough women in higher education have done well in these regards that it is no longer useful to analyze gender *only* in terms of comparing men and women. The successes of second-wave feminism have brought us to the point where we have to move beyond treating successful women as exceptions or as somehow selling out. Instead, we have to analyze differences among women, while still keeping their relational position with regard to men in focus.

Method

To grapple with academic capitalism requires that we use an approach different than those used when analyzing large statistical data sets. To date, higher education institutions and agencies at the national level have not yet standardized categories for data that address the questions raised by academic capitalism, nor do they collect items related to a critical social analysis. Thus, we have information on technology transfer revenues gathered by the Association of University Technology Managers (AUTM), but little knowledge of the class, race, or gender of the students, faculty, and staff involved in this type of revenue generation. Similarly, we know that the number of administrators in postsecondary institutions now approximates the number of faculty and that a large number of women are administrators, yet the category "administration" is so broad as to be uninformative. For example, high-level administrators making over $100,000 are often not distinguished from mid-level administrators making half that amount. The National Science Foundation reports on fields of science but not on centers and institutes. In other words, most national data-gathering efforts were developed under the public good knowledge/learning regime and are not sensitive to the segmentation and stratification occurring within and among institutions as the academic capitalist knowledge/learning regime consolidates. Furthermore, questions of class, race, ethnicity, and gender were not broadly considered in the creation of these national-level studies.

Most importantly, national-level data, drawn from aggregated institutional-level data, obscure the specific sites in which women and men are located and how they move in relation to each other. Most large salary gaps are now at the inter-departmental or inter-college level rather than intradepartmental or intra-college. For example, majority-male engineering colleges are near the top of the pay scale, while majority-female nursing colleges are near the bottom. The differences in pay between men and women at the same rank in similar colleges may be negligible, but the differences between the colleges for faculty at similar rank are quite large. By concentrating on national analyses of aggregated institutional data, we find that women faculty earn approximately 85 cents for every dollar male faculty make (Curtis 2005). What this obscures is that a number of women within disciplines have succeeded in attaining rough parity with their male colleagues. Concentration on national and institutional averages turns women's attention to competition with male colleagues for relatively small amounts of money rather than directing women's attention to glaring inter-college gender disparities.

To better understand the unfinished agenda of women in higher education, we decided to look carefully at a single institution, Arizona State University.[9] Because we had access to institutional-level data, we were able to examine the relative locations and salaries of male and female faculty and administrators. This data allowed us to analyze where women and men are in terms of rank and field as well as how they position themselves with regard to the academic capitalist knowledge/learning regime. We focused on the position of men and women in fields close to the market: in new circuits of knowledge that bridge private and public sectors, in interstitial organizations focused on market activity, in intermediating organizations that bring corporate activity into universities, and in managerial capacities that address markets in intellectual property and services. In our final analysis, we paid particular attention to whether and how men are moving away from women, what markets women choose, stratification among women, institutional preference for particular markets, and on what side of the public/private divide women's work falls.

Arizona State University

Arizona State University (ASU) was founded in 1885 as Tempe Normal School, Arizona's teachers college. Like a number of colleges and universities, Tempe Normal went through successive transformations. It was in turn a state teachers college, a state college, a comprehensive university, and a doctoral granting institution. At present, ASU enrolls more than half of the university students in Arizona. It enrolled over 61,000 students at the undergraduate and graduate levels in 2005.

ASU is a doctoral university, specifically a Research University/Very High (RU/VH), formerly known as a Research I (Carnegie Foundation 2006). Despite its RU/VH standing, ASU is not among the top one hundred university recipients of federal research and development monies (National Science Foundation 2006, tables 11 and 15), an index that serves as both a prestige and an academic capitalism indicator. In addition, ASU is not a member of the Association of American Universities (AAU), another marker of research prestige. However, ASU has a dynamic research presence that is especially notable given that it has neither an agriculture college nor a medical school, both of which usually figure powerfully in research and entrepreneurial activity. In fact, the current president of ASU has a vision of transforming the institution into a "New American University," which according to their Web site is one that "breaks from traditional disciplinary and organizational constraints" to become a center of "knowledge entrepreneurship" and regional economic development.

ASU has a campus at Tempe and a number of other campuses in the Phoenix metropolitan area. Although we consider the other campuses in our analysis, we concentrate on the Tempe campus. We present our findings in two sections: the first pertains to faculty, and the second relates to entrepreneurial units that employ administrators and managerial staff. Our analysis of ASU reveals that substantial numbers of women faculty are located in a wide variety of previously male-dominated colleges and that they have nearly achieved salary equity. However, male faculty have retained very heavy dominance in a small number of professional colleges close to the market in which they, as well as the relatively small number of women in these colleges, receive substantially higher salaries than do faculty in the more gender-balanced colleges. Women administrators made substantial gains at the executive level, achieving rough parity in terms of numbers. However, analysis of selected salaries shows that the men who administer areas that deal with the cutting edge of academic capitalism do substantially better than women engaged in the management of more routinized areas. In other words, there is marked inter-college and inter-administrative stratification that seems to be determined by the relationship of professional colleges and administrative areas to high-end knowledge economy markets.

Faculty Salaries and Gender Balance

The percentage of ASU's full-time faculty who are women (40%) is higher than the national average (33%) at doctoral universities (AAUP 2004). On all campuses, whether men or women, ASU faculty in general earn more than faculty at similar universities (see table 4.1).

At the Tempe campus, for example, women earn very close to the national average for female faculty salaries (slightly above or slight below, depending on rank), which makes ASU one of the better institutions when we consider how female faculty fare nationally. But when we compare female faculty with their male counter-

TABLE 4.1
Arizona State University Faculty Salaries, by gender
(in thousands)

	Average Salaries—Males				Average Salaries—Females			
	PR	AO	AI	IN	PR	AO	AI	IN
ASU (Tempe)	109.0	74.7	67.2	43.7	97.4	67.0	61.2	39.5
All public cat I	103.4	72.8	62.7	41.8	93.8	67.6	57.5	39.9
ASU-East	88.8	75.1	63.8	NA	83.8	65.0	56.3	NA
ASU-West	90.6	71.7	60.7	NA	83.1	68.6	57.1	NA
All public cat IIA	79.8	63.7	54.0	39.8	76.6	61.1	51.6	39.1

SOURCE: American Association of University Professors, 2006.
NOTE: cat I = category I (doctoral), cat IIA = category IIA (master's), PR = professor, AO = associate professor, AI = assistant professor, IN = instructor.

parts, we see that male faculty at the Tempe campus earn more than the national averages for men at similar institutions. At the research-focused Tempe campus, men earn substantially more on average than women, with the average male full professor's salary at $109,000 and the average female full professor's salary at $97,400. As will be discussed below, there are disciplinary and time-in-service effects to consider, but on average, the male faculty at ASU are earning more than the women.

Our analysis of separate colleges[10] and departments reveals the further differences in salaries by gender (see table 4.2). Within colleges, women at the same rank are usually close in salary to men, and in a few instances they have even higher salaries than men. In other words, the disparities between men and women are inter-college rather than intra-college. The largest salary differences are between faculty in colleges close to the market and those who are in colleges further away from the market.

The Tempe campus has three male-majority[11] colleges—Business, Engineering, and Law. According to *U.S. News and World Report* (2006) the ASU Business college is ranked twenty-third in the nation, several graduate engineering programs rank in the top 20, and Law is fifty-third. From 2001 to 2005, women business faculty have experienced a slight increase; the female-male ratio has gone from 16 percent to 20 percent, a gain of four women at the associate level and of five women full professors. Overall, women had a net gain of five, and men had a decline of 12 as the college went from 154 to 147 faculty. Despite these gains in the number of women, Business remains a male-majority college. In Law, the number of women remained constant from 2001 to 2005, at 18 percent of law faculty. Even though the college is named after a path-breaking female Supreme Court justice (who hailed from Arizona), only five of the Sandra Day O'Connor Law School's twenty-nine faculty are women. As in Business, Law has had a slight decline in the number of

TABLE 4.2
ASU-Tempe Campus Median Salary and Years in Rank by College, Tenure, and Tenure-Track Faculty

| | 2001 | | | | | | 2005 | | | | | |
| | Female | | | Male | | | Female | | | Male | | |
Rank	No.	Salary	Years in Rank	No.	Salary	Years in Rank	No.	Salary	Years in Rank	No.	Salary	Years in Rank
Business												
Prof	5	109,150	4	69	116,300	10	10	141,962	3	67	141,460	11
Assc	12	91,259	8	37	85,380	13	8	106,325	5	30	105,555	13
Asst	7	87,076	1	24	94,735	2	11	118,430	3	21	117,455	4
Design												
Prof	2	69,763	2	10	87,859	10	3	87,122	5	6	96,553	10
Assc	9	53,258	3	12	57,271	5	10	62,742	5	11	64,501	14
Asst	8	44,877	2	12	47,000	2	4	50,632	4	10	52,600	1
Education												
Prof	11	74,686	3	35	79,746	9	14	92,912	7	31	94,401	11
Assc	10	58,715	11	13	58,007	5	12	67,698	5	10	69,495	6
Asst	13	49,968	2	2	48,401	3	12	58,159	3	7	61,631	1
Engineering												
Prof	5	108,129	4	71	101,877	7	7	110,528	5	81	115,841	7
Assc	6	70,977	6	66	73,673	5	9	84,788	3	48	87,164	6
Asst	9	63,135	2	31	65,023	1	5	82,886	4	35	76,275	3
Fine arts												
Prof	16	64,631	7	57	66,345	8	21	74,420	9	50	74,692	11
Assc	18	51,748	7	18	54,171	7	19	56,352	3	15	56,394	8
Asst	16	42,500	1	10	41,750	0	16	48,485	4	20	49,384	2
Honors College												
Prof										1	115,816	24
Assc												
Asst												

Journalism[a]											
Prof	5	103,000	7	21	117,335	20	4	66,082	12	6	81,071	11
Assc				2	67,875	2	2	51,056	3	3	60,611	8
Asst										2	52,602	2
Law											
Prof							3	110,320	7	19	136,177	21
Assc							2	88,174	2	5	86,445	1
Asst												
Liberal arts and sciences											
Prof	51	79,899	10	242	82,211	11	64	92,127	6	249	96,336	10
Assc	64	54,813	4	107	56,857	5	84	62,390	4	102	62,539	8
Asst	54	44,845	3	52	49,000	2	69	56,952	2	75	59,090	2
Nursing											
Prof	5	74,000	1				5	82,500	3			
Assc	9	56,289	4	1	54,788	6	13	70,457	3	1	59,483	10
Asst	8	51,744	3				9	60,166	1	1	59,554	3
Public programs											
Prof	14	80,036	4	35	80,181	8	4	105,127	10	12	106,255	11
Assc	17	58,215	3	17	57,597	6	14	67,095	6	6	70,280	11
Asst	21	48,946	2	11	46,000	1	6	55,080	3	11	53,901	2

SOURCE: ASU Office of Institutional Analysis.

NOTE: Some reviewers of this chapter suggested that we delete cells with fewer than three individuals so that individuals could not be identified. However, if we did this, we would lose data that illustrate where incremental changes in the location of men and women are occurring—for example, Design, Journalism, Nursing—which is the focus of our analysis. Given that the data are public, we decided to retain the small cells. Prof = professor, Assc = associate, Asst = assistant.

[a]Data are incomplete due to changes in college structures.

male full professors. Yet, although the college increased its number of female associate faculty (from zero to two), the number of male associate faculty also increased (from two to five), leaving the female faculty consistently outnumbered.

However, women in these fields do quite well in terms of earnings. The three male-dominated fields have by far the highest salaries at the ASU's Tempe campus. With the exception of Law, in which women earn 81 percent of men's wages at the full professor level[12] (w=$110,320; m=$136,177),[13] the salaries for men and women are comparable. Indeed, in Business, women full professors earn slightly more than men. In engineering, women full professors make 95 percent of men's salaries (w=$110,582; m=$115,841), which is above average in terms of the national pay gap between male and female faculty. While there are 55 women full professors in the three male-dominated fields, compared to 306 men across the three colleges (ratio 1:5.6 in 2005), these women are paid approximately the same amount as men, especially when time in rank is taken into consideration (Perna 2001).

A second group of colleges at ASU's Tempe campus—Public Programs, Liberal Arts and Sciences, Design, and Education—has nearly equal proportions of men and women, who earn comparable salaries (see table 4.2).[14] Generally, across these colleges, the salaries of men and women are near parity at the full professor level. For example, full professors in the Liberal Arts and Sciences make in the mid-$90,000s, with women earning 96 percent of men's salaries, even though the number of female full professors (64) is much less than of male full professors (249). Again, years in rank may explain the slight difference in salary between men and women at this level. Indeed, this college, which gained 73 faculty from 2001 to 2005, is making strides in hiring women by adding 48 more female faculty over this period, many of whom are entering the faculty at the lower ranks. Yet the number of male faculty is also rising, which has kept the gender ratio fairly constant at one woman for close to every two men.

Given the increasing numbers of women at these colleges at the assistant and associate level, they probably joined the ASU faculty in the 1990s and early 2000s. At these ranks—except in Design—the numbers of women are roughly equivalent to men. This is a notable change for women at research universities, where they continue to be fewer than men in most fields (Curtis 2005), and indicates ASU's commitment to improving gender equity. Our data do not enable us to address why women at ASU were successful in entering these fields. Men may have moved away from these colleges because salaries, relative to the male-majority colleges, lagged behind. Alternatively (or concurrently), women may have gained more ground through successful individual action (i.e., strong preparation), collective action (i.e., women's faculty associations, women's commissions, and/or affirmative action—

strategies that were the result of women's social movements aimed at improving their employment situations).[15]

The only other college with dramatically disproportionate gender ratios at the main campus is Nursing, the only college with more women than men at the Tempe campus. The ratio of women to men was 22:1 in 2001, and 13.5:1 in 2005. In stark contrast to faculty in the male-majority colleges, Nursing faculty at the rank of full professors were almost at the bottom of the pay scale in 2005 ($82,500), with only Fine Arts below them. As is the case nationally at research universities, Nursing salaries illustrate the preference given to disciplines that are not just close to the market, as Nursing is, but are close to the market *and* majority male, as nursing certainly is not. As a field, Nursing prepares graduates for decent jobs: it has a high scientific/technical component; there are dramatic shortages of nurses; pay for BA nurses is rising (although still far below MDs); and the nursing faculty is aging, with few entrants in the professorial track (American Association of Colleges of Nursing 2004, 2006). Yet full professors in Nursing, which are almost exclusively women, earn only 58 percent of female full professors in Business, a college dominated by men. Again, at ASU and at research universities nationally, we find that the variation between women is as significant as the variation between men.[16] The disparities between women's representation and pay in Business and Nursing show the impact of preferred markets on "women's fields" in higher education and the differential gender effects of the academic capitalist knowledge/learning regime on women.

Another example of this pattern can be found in the comparison of Fine Arts and Business. Fine Arts is a college with more men than women, with the men concentrated at the full professor level. In 2005, women full professors (n=10) in Business, who are paid approximately the same as men in Business, earned twice the salary of women in Fine Arts (n=21), who earn approximately the same as men in Fine Arts. Quality cannot be the issue because ASU's Fine Arts College, which is 11th in the nation, according to *U.S. News and World Report* in 2005, is ranked higher than ASU's Business, Engineering, or Law schools. The dramatic differences in salaries between Business and Fine Arts, despite the high-quality ranking of Fine Arts, points to the power of market proximity that works for Business.

THE COLLEGE OF LIBERAL ARTS AND SCIENCES

We analyzed the College of Liberal Arts and Sciences because it is the largest of the colleges, has made great gains in terms of gender equity, and yet houses the traditionally male and highly paid disciplines of mathematics and science.[17] Between 2003 and 2005, women made gains in representation, shifting their overall ratio from 1 woman for every 2.4 men to 1 woman for 1.97 men. Five of twelve disciplinary areas are male-majority: mathematics and statistics, life sciences, philosophy and religious studies, physical sciences, and psychology.[18] Women have made modest inroads at the assistant and associate levels in mathematics and statistics and in life sciences, held their place in the physical sciences and psychology, and lost ground in philosophy and religion. With the exception of the gender-balanced justice studies area, the heavily male-majority fields are highly paid, with their full professors earning more than all others. However, women located in the male-majority departments earned the most compared to all faculty in the college. In 2005, women full professors earned at least $4,000 more than their male counterparts in all the male-majority fields other than mathematics and statistics.

Health professions and related clinical sciences, a relatively new area composed largely of audiology and speech faculty, are female-majority. This field gained women and lost men over time, but by 2005 it had no women full professors and its associate professors earned less than all other associates, possibly related to differences of time in rank.

Generally, women have moved into such traditional fields as foreign languages, English, social sciences, and history; these fields, with the exception of foreign languages, seem to be working at gender balance. Our data show movement within ranks, with the numbers of men and women remaining comparable over a period of three years. Although there have been modest gains in some heavily male-dominated fields, women have moved in greater numbers into relatively new[19] areas—for example, justice studies and the health professions.

LOCATION OF WOMEN IN MALE-MAJORITY SCHOOLS

Given that women at the ASU Tempe campus earn roughly as much as men in the male-majority colleges of Business and Engineering,[20] we wanted to see where women in these units were located to better understand their career strategies and/or opportunities. Did women enter subfields within Business and Engineering that were defined as "women's work"? If women are clustered in subfields, what consequences does that have? For example, the "tipping point" hypothesis suggests that when women exceed roughly one-third of the members of an organizational unit, average salaries plateau (Bellas 1997).[21] If isolated in their departments, did women in these fields reach out to other women through organizations such as the Commission on the Status of Women, the Association of Faculty Women, or Women's Studies?

In the School of Business,[22] women were relatively isolated, dispersed across departments, and, within departments, usually divided by rank. There were no more than three women in six of the eight departments. In none of these six departments did women hold a named chair, confirming the findings in the literature that women are less likely than men to hold these positions.[23] However, two units—Marketing and Management—had clusters of women where women also held named chairs or professorships. Management had twenty faculty, six of whom were women—four full professors (of 14), one associate (of 5) and one assistant (of 2). One full professor was the Motorola Professor of International Management. The women were slightly more than one-third of the faculty, just beyond the tipping point (Kanter 1977; Pfeffer and Davis-Blake 1987). The concentration of women at the top rank (4 of 14 full professors) and the relative paucity of women in lower ranks raise questions about the strategies of women and men within the department. Did senior women try to recruit more women into the junior ranks? Did their relatively small numbers of women make it difficult for them to do so? Research indicates that as the proportion of women in a department grows, turnover increases up to a threshold of about 35–40 percent, when turnover for women begins to decline (Tolbert, Simons, Andrews, and Rhee 1995). Did men argue against hiring more women, to defend the male majority? Did senior women accede to male strategies to protect their own interests? Given our method, we can only raise these questions, not answer them. However, we think these questions need to be addressed if we are to understand the gender dynamics of higher education.

Marketing had twenty-one faculty, eight of whom were women, again bringing the ratio of women to men almost to the tipping point. These women were more evenly dispersed across ranks: three were full professors (of 14); three were associates (of 5); and two (of 2) were assistants. All three of the women full professors held named chairs: PetSmart Chair in Service Leadership, State Farm Professor, and W. P. Carey Chair in Marketing. In contrast, only three of the eleven men held chairs. Have the three senior women, honored with named chairs, been able to make successful alliances with the more numerous senior men to recruit more junior women? Has the success of these women shifted the tipping point, making men more amenable to increased numbers of women in their department? If women continue to enter marketing, will average salaries for faculty (men and women) plateau?

The School of Engineering, more heavily male dominated than the Business School, recently appointed a woman dean who is an electrical engineer. According to ASU, her "appointment is part of a major effort by ASU to move the Fulton School to the top level of engineering schools nationally. ASU will provide [Dean Deirdre] Meldrum with additional resources to hire new faculty and to invest in start-up labs and research initiatives" (Arizona State University 2006). ASU has chosen to invest heavily in Engineering, its most male-dominated school, creating the potential for a relatively separate internal hierarchy of male power and prestige that is closely tied to success in external markets.[24] Ironically, a woman heads this effort, raising the question of whether having women leaders makes any difference in academia's gender balance, a question we will return to in the conclusion of this chapter.

As in Business, only more so, the Engineering College has only a handful of women in most of its eight departments. One department, Civil and Environmental Engineering, has a woman chair, but there were only two other women in the department of twenty-five. However, Industrial Engineering, a department of twenty, has five (25%) women relatively evenly distributed across ranks. There is no apparent reason to explain women's move into Industrial Engineering.

The women in Business and Engineering do not have any obvious collective strategies. The Commission on the Status of Women's Tempe campus representative was not from either the College of Business or the College of Engineering (ASU Commission on the Status of Women 2006). The current (2006–7) 16-member Executive Board of the Association of Faculty Women has no women from the College of Business and two from the College of Engineering (ASU Faculty Women's Association 2006). Of the 120 tenured or tenure-track faculty who are affiliates of the Women and Gender Studies Program, none was from the College of Business or the College of Engineering (ASU Women and Gender Studies 2006). Perhaps because they are part of a man's world and do about as well as the very highly paid men who are their colleagues, their strategies, like those of *homo economicus,* are individualized.

Administrators, Professionals, and Staff

A high percentage of administrators, professionals, and staff at ASU are women. Of the 354 people classified as Executive/Administrative employees, 46 percent are women (table 4.3). This category represents the upper-administrative group of employees, including the president, vice presidents, and other executives. In the Professional category (mid-level executives), women are 56 percent of the 3,349 employees. The Clerical/Crafts workers (2,169 employees) are more often women than men, with women at 60 percent of the total (Arizona State University 2005).

As with the above section on faculty, we hypothesized that although the aggregate numbers for ASU point to gender parity, in positions closer to the market there may be a different gender balance and differential pay. To better understand the

TABLE 4.3
ASU Employees by Occupational Group and Gender, 2005

Employee Group	Male	Female	Ratio M:F	% F	TOTAL
Faculty	1,439	980	1:0.68	40.5	2,419
Executive/administrative	192	162	1:0.84	46	354
Professionals	1,470	1,879	1:1.28	56	3,349
Clerical/crafts	866	1,303	1:1.5	60	2,169
Total	3,967	4,324	1:1.09	52	8,291

SOURCE: *ASU Fact Book 2005–2006.*

ways in which women might be affected by academic capitalism, we focus our attention on units that are close to the market.

ENTREPRENEURIAL UNITS

ASU's main campus entrepreneurial units show much sharper gender distinctions than colleges and departments. Entrepreneurial units demonstrate the ways in which the academic capitalist knowledge/learning regime creates conditions within universities that allow men to recapture some of the historic privilege they derived from higher education. By entering interstitial entrepreneurial units such as centers and institutes—for example, ASU's Biodesign Institute—men are able to construct new circuits of knowledge that connect them to the market. Faculty in these entrepreneurial units are supported by intermediating units and organizations such as AzTE, the technology office, and TGen, a public/private bioscience partnership that provides an array of resources ranging from financial to technical. ASU has developed an expanded managerial capacity to foster academic capitalism that includes incentives to patent and copyright, legal assistance, access to venture capital, and institutional investment in startup companies. The academic capitalist knowledge/learning regime is not closed to women, but relatively few women are engaged at ASU or nationally, in part because much of the activity takes place in male-dominated science and technology fields.

Even in heavily male-dominated fields, however, men appear to have moved out of traditional departments into resource-rich centers and institutes, where they focus heavily on patenting and industrial partnerships. While they may have moved into centers and institutes to engage in well-financed, cutting-edge interdisciplinary research, they have also, in effect, moved away from women. Nationally and at ASU, women scientists and engineers in academia are less likely to benefit from the resources invested in entrepreneurial science than are men. A recent study by Whittington and Smith-Doerr (2005) showed that female professors produce fewer patents and engage less in the commercialization process than their male counterparts. Although women participate and produce less, the quality and impact of their patents is equal to or better than that of male scientists, as demonstrated by patent citations. Similarly, Thursby and Thursby (2005), in a study of 4,500 faculty in science and engineering at eleven major universities, found that women represented only 8.5 percent of their sample of professors who disclosed inventions, were most likely to be in the biosciences, and were more likely to be younger faculty.[25]

ASU's president has invested heavily in entrepreneurial research, dedicating Proposition 301 funds, the fruits of a voter initiative to improve education, to market-related science and technology. ASU has blossomed with entrepreneurial centers and institutes and risen rapidly on the Association of University Technology Managers' list of success indicators. In a 2005 AUTM study, ASU ranked seventh in the category of U.S. patent applications filed per $1 million spent on research, seventh for number of startup companies formed per $10 million on research, and tenth on number of inventions disclosed per $1 million on research.[26] Between July and November 2005, ASU had 43 invention disclosures (31 in the life sciences and 12 in technology), 15 provisional patent applications (3 files in the life sciences and 12 in technology), and 8 patents issued. ASU is moving rapidly from the public knowledge/learning regime toward the academic capitalist knowledge/ learning regime.

ASU's entrepreneurial units are lodged in the Office of the Vice President for Research and Economic Affairs, currently headed by a male. There are two tracks in the office: research administration and economic affairs; the latter leads the entrepreneurial units. The office oversees eight research centers (Flexible Display Center, MacroTechnology Works, Stardust Center, InCISE, Biodesign Institute, Global Institute of Sustainability, Decision Theater, and Arizona Institute for Nanoelectronics), all headed by male directors.[27] The fact that ASU has combined its office of research with an office of economic affairs, which is traditionally a separate office, stresses the centrality of entrepreneurial research at ASU.[28]

The research administration side of the office, headed by a male associate vice president for research, oversees the Office of Research and Sponsored Projects Administration (ORSPA). This side of the office has approximately ninety staff, excluding student workers and secretaries, over half of whom are women. The director of research administration is a woman, as is one of her three assistant research administrators. Slightly more than half of her managers are women. The staff that work under these administrators are grants and contracts officers, sponsored project officers, account associates, and the like. Their major task is to manage the external revenues that have been secured by professors who win grants and contracts from a variety of sources. Although women feature prominently in middle management in this office, they are akin to handmaidens, working for those who bring in research monies, most of whom are male faculty.

The economic affairs side of the office is led by a male associate vice president for economic affairs and public policy and a female assistant vice president. The associate vice president oversees the director of corporate relations and the executive director of the Stardust Center for Affordable Homes and the Family. The one woman under him is the director of media relations. The assistant vice president is the head of the ASU Technopolis, which provides a series of programs that coach, mentor, and connect innovators and entrepreneurs—in other words, an educational program for aspiring entrepreneurs. Also under the assistant vice president is another entrepreneurial educational program, the Edson Student Entrepreneur Initiative, this time, headed by a man. Although women are involved in Economic Affairs, their roles seem subordinate to men and involve "women's work"—media and education.[29]

A number of units listed as "related" to the Office of Research and Economic Affairs on the Web site are highly resourced interstitial organizations close to the cutting edge of the knowledge economy and deeply involved in entrepreneurial activity: the Biodesign Institute, the Flexible Display Center, and the Institute for Computing and Information Sciences and Engineering, with the clever acronym (InCISE).[30] They are interstitial in that their members are drawn from more traditional departments into new interdisciplinary formations. They are also heavily male: all of the units have male directors, and most of the unit participants are male.

The Biodesign Institute has eleven research centers, ranging from Adaptive Neural Systems and Applied NanoBioscience to Neural Interface Design and Single Molecule Biophysics (ASU Biodesign Institute 2006). The Biodesign Institute's leadership team is comprised of twelve men and one woman. The Biodesign group has access to clinical partnerships for research trials, many of which pay summer salaries; industrial partnerships, many of which offer opportunities for consultancies; and research and educational partnerships, which offer a dense network of contacts for future partnerships and research resources (ASU Biodesign Institute 2006). The Biodesign Institute has spun out three companies: Nanobiomics, recently incorporated into the Product Division of the Molecular Profiling Institute, which is commercializing the MammaPrint diagnostic test for Breast Cancer; AdveNsys, a biomedical company that provides adaptive neural systems for restoring and advancing human mobility; and Arizona Engineered Therapeutics (AzEra), a company creating protein-based therapies that address subarachnoid hemorrhage induced stroke, asthma, and vein graft failure (ASU Biodesign Institute 2006).

The other ASU Centers—the Flexible Display Center and InCISE—reveal patterns similar to the Biodesign Institute. The Flexible Display Center has nine men as members. InCISE has seven centers, all but one of which are directed by men. The one led by a female program director, CABIT, is not a research unit, but rather an entity located in the Carey School of Business that brings together researchers and business leaders, and does not have a staff. The Center most likely to have women, given their distribution in the university, is the Arts Media and Engineering Center. Yet only two of its nine faculty are women. The remaining five centers that comprise InCISE have only male faculty.

Should these entrepreneurial centers develop intellectual property, the faculty who participate in them benefit economically in substantial ways. If technology is licensed, they share in royalties, usually receiving one-third to one-half of profits on each unit sold. They often receive "upstream" research funding from corporations that have licensed technology based on their discoveries. If there is a spinout company, faculty can serve as consultants, on advisory boards, and sometimes even as administrators of the corporation. These opportunities have the potential to greatly increase their income stream.

These entrepreneurial centers work with Arizona Technology Enterprises (AzTE), the technology licensing arm of ASU. AzTE is a classic example of an intermediating organization (Metcalfe 2004). It bridges public and private sectors, injecting private sector goals, practices, and values into public institutions. As a consequence of this injection, intermediating organizations often participate in shifting public resources toward private sector goals. In the case of AzTE, the unit shifts institutional funds and human resources toward economic innovation. The calculus for determining who benefits and who pays as a result of these transactions is not yet clearly established, although the university, as an institution, probably puts more into innovation than it receives in return.[31]

AzTE is affiliated with economic affairs but housed under the ASU Foundation, perhaps because the Foundation is an arms-length organization that is not subject to the same tax and accounting rules as the university. AzTE is another male enclave. Men comprise the twelve-person board of directors, headed by ASU's president. The eight-person "executive team" responsible for running AzTE has five men and three women (the general counsel, legal assistant, and director of finance and administration). The managing director and four other executives are all men. The centers previously discussed are affiliated with AzTE. The mission statement of AzTE is as follows:

Arizona Technology Enterprises at Arizona State University works with university inventors and industry to transform scientific progress into products and services. Arizona Technology Enterprises transfers technologies invented at ASU to the private sector by mining university research, prosecuting patents, negotiating licenses, and marketing inventions. Technology transfer benefits the public by contributing to new product creation and new economic opportunities. Technology transfer facilitates ASU's efforts to attract and retain superior faculty and graduate recruitment, while returning income to the inventor and the University to support ongoing research. (AzTE 2006)

AzTE is an intermediating organization that links ASU to the market, bridging private and public sectors and shifting resources from the public sector to the private. All research universities now have technology transfer offices that engage in many of the same practices.

The collective strategy of women with regard to the academic capitalist knowledge/learning regime is unclear. Women generally are not well situated to access the market. Nationally, there are relatively few women faculty in science, technology, engineering, and mathematics (STEM) fields, and they are concentrated at less-prestigious universities. The opportunities offered by the academic capitalist knowledge/learning regime may be less well developed at these universities. Even when opportunities are well developed, as is the case at ASU, women faculty in STEM fields may not understand that there is an alternative hierarchy in the making and may therefore miss chances to participate. Alternatively, male faculty and administrators may habitually prefer men in the new hierarchy, effectively shutting out women.

However, women faculty may reject the academic capitalist knowledge/learning regime. For example, STEM faculty women at less-prestigious colleges and universities routinely say they are happy where they are because their preference is teaching. Certainly, STEM women have the ability to patent. As Thursby and Thursby (2005) note, women STEM faculty are less likely to disclose inventions than men even though there are no significant differences in male and female publication patterns. Contrary to men, women STEM faculty may be committed to a public good knowledge/learning regime. They may intuitively understand that the academic capitalist knowledge/learning regime moves the boundary between public and private sectors in ways that generally serve to limit women's opportunities. They may be committed to open knowledge and education. Or they may want less time-intensive careers so they are able to make a place in their lives for families.

Entrepreneurial units are emblematic of the academic capitalist knowledge/

learning regime. They are part of an alternative hierarchy largely constructed by men that restores to some men the privilege that higher education historically provided. The entrepreneurial units at ASU create new circuits of knowledge that connect the academy to the knowledge economy and make universities an integral part of the innovation process. A number of men moved away from departments in which they were initially housed—although still holding base positions in those departments—and built interstitial organizations such as centers and institutes that resulted in their moving away from women. Even in fields such as engineering, in which there were relatively few women, this has been the case. The university, as an institution, partnered these efforts, developing intermediating organizations such as AzTE that bridged private and public sectors. At the same time, ASU's managerial capacity was greatly expanded, enabling it to execute the same kinds of commercial ventures as the for-profit sector.

Conclusions

Our analysis has focused on the dynamism of men and women's individual and collective action vis-à-vis each other by contrasting institutional and college-level or unit-level views of gender equity. Generally, we found that women faculty and administrators at ASU are doing well in terms of salary and rank compared to their male peers. Women faculty at ASU were able to gain ground in many departments, particularly at the Tempe Campus and in fields other than business, engineering, and law. However, as women gained ground at ASU, an alternative internal hierarchy was created primarily by males—an academic capitalist knowledge/learning regime in which the merit of professorial knowledge was no longer solely determined by peer review or the public good, but by preferred (male-dominated) markets. Academic administration at ASU shows the same bifurcation: women have made significant gains in areas associated with the public good knowledge/learning regime but do not fare as well in the resource-rich academic capitalist knowledge/learning regime.

We hypothesize that the movement of men and women is complex and uneven. Women gain ground in some areas and lose ground elsewhere both within and across sectors of higher education. Some groups of women use different strategies than others, as do some groups of men. Sometimes women support each other, and sometimes they do not. Sometimes they struggle with men; at other times men and women work together to improve their position. As Butler (1990) suggests, theories of a monolithic patriarchy and of a common subjugated experience for women no longer predominate.

Analysis of the gender dynamics in postsecondary education is essential if women want to position themselves strategically at a time when higher education is undergoing a "crisis of hegemony" (de Sousa Santos 2006). Regardless of their location within higher education, women, individually and collectively, will face choices about strategies, given that greater stratification among institutions and within fields is occurring and that institutions and fields better able to align themselves with the academic capitalist knowledge/learning regime seem to do better, if better is understood in the sense of accruing more resources. Although we have featured the academic capitalist knowledge/learning regime in our analysis, we do not necessarily advocate that women develop collective strategies to join it. Individually, women can succeed within the rationalistic, competitive market criteria that characterize the academic capitalist knowledge/learning regime, but the collective subject of the regime is "man," which means that joint action by women is not supported. Rather, women need to analyze these changes in depth, make decisions about what they think higher education as a sector should look like, and work to attain those goals.

As they engage in such analysis, women should keep in mind that the academic capitalist knowledge/learning regime depends on the growth and power of the neoliberal state. The neoliberal state shifts the boundaries between the public and private sector, using public sector resources to enhance and stimulate the private sector; shifts public subsidy from welfare functions to entrepreneurial activity; exhibits a preference for commercial solutions to public problems; empowers managers rather than workers; privileges the individual over collectivities when collectivities pursue activities that would constrain capital; and favors secrecy and various schemes of classification of information over public circulation of knowledge and civil liberties (Blyth 2002; Harvey 2005). As these characteristics indicate, the neoliberal state also structurally prefers men to women, although its spokespersons would emphasize that the policy efforts are directed toward all competent individuals. In contrast, women and a variety of minorities, acting collectively, were able to press the liberal state for what they could not wrest from the private sector, so that women and minorities occupied one in four public jobs (Carnoy and Levin 1985). If women choose the academic capitalist knowledge/learning regime, they are in effect choosing the neoliberal state and closing down the network of public policies and agencies that made possible women's entry into the academy.

Similarly, women need to analyze the actions of groups of men. Much of the parity gained by women was achieved in the 1980s, when women moved into men's fields (Jacobs 1995). We need to understand what happened after the 1980s—did women turn away from men's fields, or did men's fields become more difficult to enter because the men within them were able to more successfully protect their boundaries? Similarly, do men in roughly gender-balanced fields support women, or do they seek to re-establish dominance? Do women aid and abet male dominance, as did women in the 1950s who hired returning male vets to enhance the status of their fields, or do women struggle to achieve dominance?

Moreover, women need to think through their goals with regard to how they want to position themselves individually and collectively within the academy. Is gender balance the best strategy for both men and women, and if so, how is it possible to maintain it? Research on gender group composition and work group relations suggests a positive linear relationship between the proportion of women in a group and favorable psychological environments for women (Tolbert et al. 1999). However, increased numbers of women in work groups does not necessarily increase positive attitudes of men toward women (Swamy and Bhatnagar 1995). Rather, some research points to "a negative relation between the proportion of women in a work group and the amount of support men provide to women colleagues," or men's greater support for other men (Tolbert et al. 1995). What do such findings, coupled with research suggesting that men express greater satisfaction when the proportion of men is higher as well as greater group attachment, mean for gender balanced departments (Tolbert et al. 1999)? Should women strive for gender balance, or should they seek dominance? How will their strategies likely shape individual and collective mobility for women?

If women want to address the remaining disparities in higher education, they will have to address the market issue directly. As we have seen in the case of ASU, the majority of salary disparity is inter-college and interdepartmental. If women want to have the same average institutional level salaries as men, they have two choices: (1) they can move into male-dominated departments in large numbers; or (2) they can demand salary equity across colleges and departments. Both courses of action have formidable barriers. As we have seen, men have been able to protect their positions in the most highly paid colleges and departments, and many of them are engaged in defending their positions by constructing the academic capitalist knowledge/learning regime, which shores up their privilege. Women will have to break through these barriers to enter these disciplines and fields. When women faculty raise the question of equity, they will be met with the market justification for "merit"-based systems. Administrators make the case that faculty in male-dominated colleges and departments must be paid more because they can make more in external markets. If women faculty are to make headway against this justification, they will have to deconstruct the market so that its unjustly gendered preferences are clearly revealed. That is a difficult task in an era when the "market" is reified, normalized, and increasingly unquestioned.

More generally, women need to analyze in depth the structural changes occur-ring in higher education so they will be able to decide what they think the sector should look like and then work to attain their goals. Should women, for example, decide to reject the academic capitalist knowledge/learning regime, they would not only have to struggle to redirect resources—which entails an external battle with the neoliberal state—but they will have to redefine the public good knowledge/learning regime so that it makes sense for the twenty-first century. Simultaneously, faculty women will have to decide whether to act for all women in higher educa-tion—a strategy that has not characterized the past thirty years—or to concentrate on their own sector. Should faculty women direct their energy to deconstructing the market so that all faculty make as much as men in the highest paid colleges, or should they direct their attention to bringing up salaries for all women, including middle-level administrators and clerical staff?

In a worst-case scenario, enough women individually might work for the con-solidation of the academic capitalist knowledge/learning regime and enough women in roughly gender-balanced fields might collectively concentrate on push-ing salaries and perks in the direction of those attained by professors and admin-istrators in the academic capitalist knowledge/learning regime that higher educa-tion would become extremely stratified by sector. In other words, the majority of women at research universities would likely not contest the strengthening of the academic capitalist knowledge/learning regime in return for expanded salaries and privileges. While the salaries and privileges for the bulk of women would not ap-proximate those of faculty engaged in the academic capitalist knowledge/learning regime, they would continue to be four times those of the average woman worker, and perhaps even reach five or six times more. Unless resources for the sector as a whole were greatly increased, support or tacit support for the academic capitalist knowledge/learning regime would very likely mean that salaries at institutions in the comprehensive, four-year, and community college categories would remain static or fall further behind.

Of course, women in non-research universities face similar choices. Institutions in the comprehensive, four-year, and community college category are as a group probably more highly vocationalized than research universities, and vocations/pro-fessions located close to male-dominated markets that are the building blocks of the academic capitalist knowledge/learning regime are likely preferred. Women in gender-segmented departments and colleges of non-research universities would have to think through many of the same strategies as women in research universi-ties like ASU. Ironically, as women have made gains in postsecondary education—as indeed they have since 1972 when Nixon signed the executive order that initiated

Affirmative Action—higher education has become more stratified according to almost every indicator: faculty and administrative salaries, social class origins of students, tuition, entry-level salaries of graduates, admission into graduate school. Women across sectors have to ask how their individual and collective mobility strategies figured in that stratification and then readjust their strategies, depending on their goals.

We must also ask how the strategies of women managers have figured in the changes that have occurred. Generally, the literature on women's leadership in higher education does not indicate that women leaders do much to change the lot of women at their institutions. However, given the changing terrain in higher education and the small samples of women in the studies to date, a new look at the role of leaders is probably needed. Do women leaders make a difference for women—within sectors or across sectors? Should women faculty seek to increase the number of women managers if they desire to institute a new knowledge/learning regime, or is this a project best undertaken collectively?

Like so many studies, ours raises many more questions than it answers. Because we relied primarily on quantitative data, we were unable to understand the many aspects of the gender dynamics we presented. To gain a deeper understanding of individual and collective strategies of women and men, we would need to interview people, look at social networks within organizations, follow individuals and groups over the course of their careers, compare new entrants to fields with more established job holders, and analyze how men and women viewed each other, individually and collectively, and how they helped, hindered, or ignored each other. We would also have to look closely at the way women treated other women and how that played into their success or lack thereof vis-à-vis men.

We invite academic women who are concerned about the structural changes in higher education to participate in the analysis of the gender dynamics of individual and collective career strategies. We are committed to the idea that to change the future, we must understand the present. In the end, we call for more research on the differential effects of academic capitalism on women. We cannot allow rote recitation of the statistics on women's participation in higher education to continue without demanding more information about the placement of women within fields, employment categories, and pay scales. Additionally, we believe that the location of women in relation to the market is of vital importance to our understanding of how women are faring in relation to men. Furthermore, attention must be paid to the ways in which women are competing not only with men for economic, academic, and political status, but also with other women. Finally, we question that if women do achieve numerical equity in terms of positions and salaries, but the academic capitalist knowledge/learning regime persists in the process, what has been won?

NOTES

Initially, we had intended this chapter to cover institutions of higher education in the Phoenix metropolitan area, ranging from community colleges to for-profit institutions. However, constraints of space prevented us from employing and analyzing data from other institutions, and we focus here only on Arizona State University. ASU provided the data for this study with the understanding that it was a multi-institutional analysis rather than a single case study, and ASU officials disagree with the analysis. We are solely responsible for the interpretation of the data in this chapter.

1. Colleges and universities have always been involved with markets and concerned with the generation of external revenues. However the academic capitalist knowledge/learning regime has brought about changes in orders of magnitude to the point where prestige systems and revenue generation systems now overlap significantly.

2. Interstitial units are offices and departments within the academic setting that operate as boundary organizations between the public and private sectors. Notable examples are offices of technology transfer.

3. Unlike interstitial units, intermediary organizations are not located within the academy, but rather they are situated between the academy, the market, and the state (Metcalfe 2004). These organizations seek to bring the public sector and private sector together. Professional associations, foundations, or special interest groups might serve in this role.

4. The crisis of hegemony that de Sousa Santos refers to is the declining power of the university in contemporary society. Although de Sousa Santos contextualizes this crisis within the academy as a whole, we suspect that the crisis of hegemony is in actuality a "crisis of patriarchy." As women have entered the academy, its position within society has slipped, and thus getting a degree is no longer as meaningful as it once was (i.e., expert status has been diluted by massification of the system, which was driven by women). Feminist perspectives on patriarchy permit us to see the academy as a gendered space where the cultural hegemony of higher education is both challenged and influenced by the presence of academic women, who are not viewed by society as having as much power as men.

5. Because markets also exhibit gender segmentation, "market-relevance" for the entrepreneurial academy is really determined by the market for knowledge-intensive and highly specialized goods and services, creating a mutually supportive cycle of production and consumption between academia and the high-technology sector.

6. In the 1920s, women accounted for approximately one-quarter of all faculty, but they were generally located in normal schools or sex-segregated fields. In the 1950s, women were pushed out of colleges and universities during the postwar expansion that rewarded men for military service and celebrated the traditional family (Eisenmann 2006; May 1999).

7. For overviews of the current condition of women faculty and staff in higher education, see Glazer-Raymo, Bensimon, and Townsend 1993; Glazer-Raymo, Townsend, and Ropers-Huilman 2000; Glazer-Raymo 1999.

8. The liberal state (approximately 1945–80) or Keynesian welfare state was characterized by modified state management of the economy, i.e., strong state stimuli of the economy through defense spending as well as occasional wage and price controls, and strong public welfare programs. Workers, women, and a variety of minorities, acting collectively, were able to press the state for that which they could not wrest from the private sector. In public higher education that meant space opened up, beginning in the 1960s. In contrast, the neoliberal state alters the boundaries between public and private sector by shifting subsidy from welfare functions to entrepreneurial activity, exhibits a preference for commercial solutions to public problems, empowers managers rather than workers, privileges individuals over collectivities that would constrain capital (Carnoy and Levin 1985; Harvey 2005).

9. Choice of this institution stems from a larger project on which the authors are engaged, a geographic or situated sociology of women in the Phoenix metropolitan area, in which an array of institutions of higher education is featured. We also had data on Maricopa Community College District, which we had hoped to present in this chapter, but due to space constraints we focus solely on ASU.

10. The college is the unit of analysis for most of the data. As a unit of analysis, the college allows us to avoid dealing with departments that do not fit standard configurations. (Disciplines are not appropriate units because they are national rather than institutional organizations and do not always conform to department organization at the institutional level.) However, department-level data can prove illuminating in the case of large colleges, especially if the college contains departments likely to have gender-marked salary differences. Thus, we analyze the College of Liberal Arts by department.

11. By male majority we mean at least four men for every one woman.

12. We use full professor salaries for many comparisons because the literature shows that wage gaps increase over careers, with the greatest gaps between men and women within the same field occurring at the highest rank.

13. With the average years in service for female full professors in Law being just seven, compared to the average of twenty-one years for male full professors in that college, the salary gap may be explained as a result of time in rank. This gap may change over time, as we note that at the associate level, women in Law make slightly more than men, which may mean that the women will earn consistently more as they progress through the ranks.

14. We did not consider "tipping" ratios at the college level because most decisions are made at the departmental level. See the discussion of the departments in the College of Liberal Arts and Sciences for a discussion of "tipping."

15. See Hart 2005 for a discussion of women's activism in higher education.

16. In 2004–2005, the median salary for doctorally prepared nursing faculty at the associate professor level was $77,605 and at the 75th percentile of research universities was $84,893. In 2004–2005, the median salary for doctorally prepared nursing faculty at the assistant level was $68,440 and at the 75th percentile of research universities, $73,333. (American Association of Colleges of Nursing 2006). At ASU, the median associate professor nursing salary was $70,457, and the median assistant professor nursing salary $60,166.

17. Data were made available to us not by department but by discipline. For example, "Area, Ethnic, Cultural and Gender Studies" is not a department but a group of programs and departments made up of Women and Gender Studies, African and African American Studies, Department of Transborder Chicana/o and Latina/o Studies, Asian Pacific American Studies, and American Indian Studies. There are more than thirty schools, departments, programs, and centers in the College of Liberal Arts and Sciences at ASU's Tempe Campus.

18. Areas with fewer than three faculty were not reported.

19. "New," as we employ the term, means from the 1970s forward. The Health Professions are primarily speech and audiology.

20. We did not include Law because of the salary gap.

21. Bellas (1997) makes the point that average salaries plateau or go down relative to previous patterns of increase and sometimes absolutely, as when cuts are negotiated. However, in the short time span (2000–2005) with which we are dealing, we are unlikely to see salaries go down, either relatively or absolutely.

22. All data from this section are taken from http://wpcarey.asu.edu/directory/sesction .cfm; specifically, the Department section, directory. Accessed July 14, 2006.

23. As Mixon and Trevino (2005) note, named professorships are determined by both market and non-market forces such as discrimination. They studied economics departments in the South, using the Blinder-Oaxaca decomposition tests and found gender discrimination that resulted in a 7.6 percentage point disadvantage for females (relative to males) regarding the likelihood of holding a named professorship in economics. Reviewers raised the possibility that ASU is a relatively new school and may not have the same number of chairs as older, more established schools. However, it is not the number of endowed chairs but the number granted to women that is at issue. The Carey School Web site shows that the departments of Economics, Finance, Information Systems, Management, and Supply Chain Management, and the Schools of Accountancy and Health Management and Policy have 13 chairs and 25 named professorships. Of the 13 chairs, 12 were men and one was a woman. Of the 25 named professorships, 21 were men and 4 were women. Two of the men appear to hold more than one chair or named professorship.

24. Historically, the physical sciences, particularly physics, had the highest prestige. In the science and technology world, engineering was technology and not accorded the same status as science because of its applied nature. Under the academic capitalist knowledge/learning regime, the applied or entrepreneurial dimension of the sciences is moving to the fore, and engineering is accorded greater respect.

25. Disclosure is the first step to patenting. Many universities require faculty to disclose to technology transfer offices any intellectual property that has potential for commercialization. After disclosure, the university decided whether to apply for a patent.

26. Of course, one of the reasons ASU does so well is that it has less grant and contract monies than the top one hundred recipients of federal research funds (National Science Foundation 2006).

27. An organizational chart for the Office of Research and Economic Affairs can be found at http://ovprea.asu.edu/OVPREAorg1006.pdf. Accessed November 13, 2006.

28. Furthermore, the gender composition of this office is counter to the Office of the Executive Vice President and Provost of the University, the chief academic office of ASU, where

women hold significant leadership positions. The university provost (a woman) oversees four vice provosts at the Tempe campus, who are each women. These vice provosts are in charge of graduate studies, the University College, academic programs, and academic personnel. At the Tempe campus, there may be a centralization of women's authority in the traditional academic functions of the university, with men in charge of the peripheral units that are closely linked to external markets. At the West, Polytechnic, and Downtown campuses, however, men lead in their roles as vice presidents and provosts. More work needs to be done to analyze the gender dynamics of the academic administration at ASU's various campuses.

29. It is not only universities in which women are confined to women's work. Women are often confined to women's work in large firms. See Zweigenhaft and Domhoff 1999.

30. A number of "related units"—Animal Care and Technology, Decision Theater, Macro-Technology Works, Research and Sponsored Projects Administration (considered above)—and research publications were excluded from consideration as entrepreneurial units because they did not focus on research or generation of external revenues.

31. We recognize that the public good can and does benefit from the entrepreneurial efforts of universities. However, to date there is not a well-developed index to account for the ratio of public investment in these efforts to the *social* rate of return, as opposed to the economic rate of return.

REFERENCES

AAUP. 2004. Faculty salary and faculty distribution fact sheet, 2003–2004. Retrieved on 6/28/2006 from www.aaup.org/research/sal&distribution.htm.

——. 2006. The devaluing of higher education: The annual report on the economic status of the profession, 2005–2006. *Academe* 92 (2): 24–105.

American Association of Colleges of Nursing. 2004. Nursing faculty shortage fact sheet. Retrieved on 11/18/2006 from www.aacn.nche.edu/Media/Backgrounders/facultyshortage.htm.

——. 2006. Faculty shortages in baccalaureate and graduate nursing programs: Scope of the problem and strategies for expanding supply. Retrieved on 11/18/2006 from www.aacn.nche.edu/Publications/pdf/FSWPJune05.pdf.

Arizona State University. 2005. ASU Fact Book, 2005–2006. Available at: www.asu.edu/uoia/fact.html.

——. 2006. Retrieved 7/24/2006 from the Ira J. Fulton School of Engineering Web site: www.asu.edu/news/stories/200602/20060207_meldrumdean.htm.

ASU Commission on the Status of Women. 2006. Retrieved on 7/12/2006 from http://aspin.asu.edu/csw/.

ASU Faculty Women's Association. 2006. Retrieved on 11/18/2006 from www.asu.edu/assn/fwa/board.html.

ASU. The Biodesign Institute at ASU. 2006. Retrieved on 8/2/2006 from www.biodesign.asu.edu.

ASU Women and Gender Studies. 2006. Retrieved 7/19/2006 from www.asu.edu/cls/womens
_studies/pages/AffiliateDirS06.htm.

AzTE 2006. AzTE Technology Enterprises Mission Statement. Retrieved 8/2/2006 from www
.azte.com/about_mission.html.

Baumgardner, J., and A. Richards. 2000. *Manifesta: Young women, feminism and the future.* New
York: Farrar, Straus & Giroux.

Bellas, M. L. 1997. Disciplinary differences in faculty salaries: Does gender bias play a role? *Journal of Higher Education* 68 (3): 299–321.

Beneria, L. 1999. Globalization, gender and the Davos man. *Feminist Economics* 5 (3): 61–83.

Blyth, M. 2002. *Great transformations: Economic ideas and institutional change in the twentieth
century.* Cambridge, UK: Cambridge University Press.

Bourdieu, P. 1984. *Homo academicus.* Paris: Les Éditions de Minuit.

Bowles, S., and H. Gintis. 1993. The revenge of homo economicus: Contested exchange and the
revival of political economy. *Journal of Economic Perspectives* 7 (1): 83–102.

Braithwaite, A. 2002. The personal, the political, third-wave, and postfeminisms. *Feminist Theory* 3:335–44.

Butler, J. 1990. *Gender trouble: Feminism and the subversion of identity.* New York: Routledge.

Carnegie Foundation. 2006. Classification. Available at www.carnegiefoundation.org. Accessed
July 5, 2006.

Carnoy, M., and H. Levin. 1985. *Schooling and work in the democratic state.* Palo Alto, CA: Stanford University Press.

Curtis, J. W. 2005. Inequities persist for women and non-tenure-track faculty. *Academe* 91 (2):
20–98.

de Sousa Santos, B. 2006. The university in the 21st century: Toward a democratic and emanci-
patory university reform. In *The university, state, and market: The political economy of globalization in the Americas,* ed. R. Rhoads and C. A. Torres, 60–100. Palo Alto, CA: Stanford
University Press.

Eisenmann, L. 2006. *Higher education for women in postwar America, 1945–1965.* Baltimore:
Johns Hopkins University Press.

Ferber, M., and J. Nelson, eds. 1993. *Beyond economic man: Feminist theory and economics.*
Chicago: University of Chicago Press.

Glazer-Raymo, J. 1999. *Shattering the myths: Women in academe.* Baltimore: Johns Hopkins University Press.

Glazer-Raymo, J. S., E. M. Bensimon, and B. K. Townsend, eds. 1993. *Women in higher education:
A feminist perspective.* Needham Heights, MA: Ginn Press.

Glazer-Raymo, J. S., B. K. Townsend, and R. Ropers-Huilman, eds. 2000. *Women in higher education: A feminist perspective.* Boston: Pearson Custom Publishing.

Glover, D., and B. Parsad. 2003. The gender and racial/ethnic composition of postsecondary
instructional faculty and staff, 1992–1998. *Education Statistics Quarterly* 4–3. Available online
at http://nces.ed.gov/programs/quarterly/vol_4/4_3/4_6.asp.

Hart, J. 2005. Activism among feminist academics: Professionalized activism and activist professionals. *Advancing Women in Leadership* 18. Retrieved 8/5/2006 from www.advancing
women.com/awl/social_justice1/Hart.html.

Harvey, D. 2005. *A brief history of neoliberalism.* Oxford: Oxford University Press.

Haywood, L., and J. Drake, eds. 1997. *Third wave agenda: Being feminist, doing feminism.* Minneapolis: University of Minnesota Press.

Jacobs, J. 1995. Gender and academic specialties: Trends among recipients of college degrees in the 1980s. *Sociology of Education* 68 (2): 81–98.

Kanter, R. M. 1977. *Men and women of the corporation.* New York: Basic Books.

Levin, P. 2001. Gendering the market: Temporality, work, and gender on a national futures exchange. *Work and Occupations* 28 (1): 112–30.

Li, X. 2006. Changes in staff distribution and salaries of full-time employees in postsecondary institutions: 1993–2003 (NCES 2006-152). U.S. Department of Education. Washington, DC: National Center for Education Statistics.

Massey, D. 1994. *Space, place, and gender.* Cambridge, UK: Polity Press.

May, E. T. 1999. *Homeward bound: American families in the cold war era.* New York: Basic Books.

Metcalfe, A. 2004. Intermediating associations and the university-industry relationship. Ph.D. diss., University of Arizona.

Mixon, F. G., and L. J. Trevino. 2005. Is there gender discrimination in named professorships? An econometric analysis of economics departments in the US South. *Applied Economics* 37 (8): 849–54.

National Center for Education Statistics. 2005. *Gender differences in participation and completion of undergraduate education and how they have changed over time.* Washington DC: U.S. Department of Education. Institute of Educational Sciences. NCES 2005-169: 18–19.

National Science Foundation, Division of Science Resources Statistics, Federal Science and Engineering. 2006. *Support to universities, colleges, and nonprofit institutions:* Fiscal NSF 06-309, Project Officer, Richard J. Bennof (Arlington, VA). Table 11. Federal obligations for science and engineering to the 100 universities and colleges receiving the largest amount, ranked by total amount received by type of activity, FY2003; Table 15. Federal obligations for science and engineering to universities and colleges, by location, institution and type of activity, FY2003.

Perna, L. W. 2001. Sex differences in faculty salaries: A cohort analysis. *Review of Higher Education* 24 (3): 283–307.

Pfeffer, J., and A. Davis-Blake. 1987. The effect of the proportion of women on salaries: The case of college administrators. *Administrative Science Quarterly* 33:588–606.

Slaughter, S., and L. L. Leslie. 1997. *Academic capitalism: Politics, policies, and the entrepreneurial university.* Baltimore: Johns Hopkins University Press.

Slaughter, S., and G. Rhoades. 2004. *Academic capitalism and the new economy: Markets, state, and higher education.* Baltimore: Johns Hopkins University Press.

Solomon, B. M. 1985. *In the company of educated women: A history of women and higher education in America.* New Haven: Yale University Press.

Swamy, R., and Bhatnagar, D. 1995. Attitudes toward women as managers: Does interaction make a difference? *Human Relations* 48 (11), 1285–1307.

Thursby, J. G., and M. C. Thursby. 2005. Gender patterns of research and licensing activity of science and engineering faculty. *Journal of Technology Transfer* 30 (4): 343–53.

Tolbert, P. S., M. E. Graham, and A. O. Andrews. 1999. Group gender composition and work group relations: Theories, evidence and issues. In *Handbook of gender and work,* ed. G. N. Powell, 179–202. Thousand Oaks, CA: Sage.

Tolbert, P. S., T. Simons, A. Andrews, and J. Rhee. 1995. The effects of gender composition in academic departments of faculty turnover. *Industrial and Labor Relations Review* 48 (3): 562–79.

U.S. Census Bureau. 2004. American Community Survey. Retrieved 7/5/2006 from www.census .gov/acs/www.

U.S. Department of Commerce, Bureau of Economic Analysis. 2006. Regional economic accounts. Retrieved 7/21/2006 from www.bea.gov/bea/regional/beafacts.

Walker, R., ed. 1995. *To be real: Telling the truth and changing the face of feminism.* New York: Anchor Books.

Whittington, K. B., and L. Smith-Doerr. 2005. Gender and commercial science: Women's patenting in the life sciences. *Journal of Technology Transfer* 30 (4): 355–70.

Zweigenhaft, R., and G. W. Domhoff. 1999. *Diversity and the power elite: Have women and minorities reached the top?* New Haven: Yale University Press.

CHAPTER FIVE

Developing Women Scientists

Baccalaureate Origins of Recent Mathematics and Science Doctorates

FRANCES K. STAGE AND STEVEN HUBBARD

Research on women and students of color in what is called the mathematics/ science pipeline[1] has expanded rapidly in the last two decades (Gilbert and Calvert 2003; Hubbard and Stage forthcoming; Kinzie, Stage, and Muller 1998; National Science Foundation 1998, 2002; Stage and Maple 1996; Widnall 1988). Education policymakers, government agencies, and philanthropic foundations support this research as well as programs to encourage students at the undergraduate and doctoral levels, and particularly women and minorities, to major and persist in science and mathematics (Benjamin 1991; NSF 1998, 2002). Nevertheless, the percentage of bachelor's degrees awarded in science, technology, engineering, and mathematics (STEM) majors continues to decline for all students (Drew 1996, NSF 2005) in addition to the shortage of underrepresented groups, specifically women and racial and ethnic minorities (Hanson 1996; NSF 2002; Sonnert 1995).

When one examines the numbers for students who ultimately go on to science careers, the situation is more dismal (Gilbert and Calvert 2003). African Americans and Latinos each comprise only 3 percent of all employed scientists and engineers (Rosser 1995). Even when using the National Science Foundation's practice of including graduates of psychology and the social sciences as scientists in its reporting, minorities earn doctoral degrees at a fraction of their proportion in the general population. For example, from 1995 to 1999, Blacks earned 3.5 percent and Hispanics 3.7 percent of all doctorates in the sciences. Native Americans earned 0.5 percent (NSF 2005), and their subsequent transition to the science and engineering labor force is even lower. Additionally, the reality of higher education is that relatively small numbers of aspiring scientists begin their careers at elite institutions (Stage and Hubbard 2005). If the numbers of scientists produced is to increase significantly, all colleges and universities will have to graduate students who aspire to be scientists and who move on to graduate work in the sciences.

In this chapter we focus on data from institutions that graduated baccalaureate students who earned doctorates in the sciences in a ten-year period, 1995–2004. Our purpose is to identify colleges and universities that produce large numbers, relative to comparable institutions, of women bachelor's graduates who ultimately earn doctorates in the STEM fields. First we identify expected institutions; these include women's colleges, Ivy League universities, and technical institutes that have been and remain important producers of women who move on to science careers. Next we identify a smaller number of colleges that were unexpected yet successful producers of bachelor's degree earners who went on to earn doctorates. We define unexpected institutions as those that have small numbers of students or a relatively small proportion of women students in their student body, yet produce relatively large numbers of women scientists. This list might also include nonselective or even open-enrollment institutions.

Unexpected producers might be overlooked but are equally important in attempts to expand women's roles as scientists. By identifying these unexpected institutions, state and institutional policymakers can identify peer institutions, that is, those that are comparable in enrollments, funding, and quality of students and that have seemingly solved the problem of fostering undergraduate students who are interested in the sciences. Additionally, future research can focus specifically on the internal environment, including espoused mission and faculty attitudes as well as practices and curricula, of those institutions. By 1995–99 women earned 33 percent of all science and engineering doctorates. Most of the increase resulted from increases in psychology, where women earned 67 percent of all doctorates (the only science field where they achieve 50 percent representation). In mathematics, the physical sciences, and engineering, women earn fewer than 25 percent of doctorates (NSF 2005; Thurgood, Golladay, and Hill 2006). Our data included women who were U.S. citizens and permanent residents and who earned their doctorates in the fields of mathematics, science, and engineering.[2] We excluded women in the social sciences (e.g., sociology and anthropology) and psychology as well as noncitizens.

While a broad examination like this has limitations, it can be useful in guiding scholarship as well as policy. Colleges and universities of all sizes and levels of quality and with varieties of missions produce women scientists, and the most successful of those can serve as examples for others. Research focused on explicit and implicit policies, faculty attitudes, and departmental practices can shed light on successful strategies for developing scientists. While doctoral completion does not mean ultimate success, it serves as a crucial marker in scientists' careers, particularly for women scientists.

Why Don't Women Succeed?

Several factors may explain why women don't succeed—sociological, demographic, and attitudinal. Women's ultimate success as mathematicians and scientists depends on a series of experiences, successes, and personal decisions that often begin in early childhood. Successful negotiation through the earliest weed-out courses of the undergraduate years is the easy part. Beyond the undergraduate years, without mentoring, a woman is unlikely to choose graduate coursework in science or math. When she does and is successful, she must still identify a supportive mentor, negotiate any serious personal relationships so that she has the flexibility to move into a tenure-track or scientist position, and then, over the course of five years (in academe), convince colleagues that she can teach, set up a laboratory, earn external funds to support it, publish in refereed journals, and be collegial in reportedly uncollegial settings. In addition, she may begin her family at this stage in her career. She must accomplish all this under the watchful eyes of skeptics like Lawrence Summers, the former president of Harvard (see Wilson and Fain 2006), who is unfortunately only the most notorious of some who share his doubt in women's ability to do science.

In the first stage of this process, at the undergraduate level, we know that women and minorities are more likely to change majors when their grades seem low—while men with lower grades are less likely to switch (Drew 1996). In her book *Has Feminism Changed Science?* Schiebinger (1999) observes that women are expected to be modest, which often correlates with low self-esteem. Men, on the other hand, tend to exaggerate more, which enhances their ability to succeed. She noted a study that found three-quarters of women and only half of the men named low self-esteem as the reason they left science.

The master's degree level can be a problem for an unsophisticated student who believes it to be a necessary step toward the doctorate. In some fields, the terminal master's degree is seen as preferable for those seeking positions in business and industry, particularly in chemistry, geosciences, and engineering (Glazer-Raymo 2005). Yet the master's degree is not emphasized or recruited.[3] Additionally, in her recent study of the master's degree, Glazer-Raymo (2005) found no student aid programs to support master's level students in the science, technology, engineering, and mathematics disciplines.

Women who choose science careers in postsecondary education face barriers to the retention and tenure of women in a university faculty (Johnsrud and DeJarlais 1994). Hamilton (2004) discusses the obstacles for women (particularly for women of color). For instance, women earned 44.4 percent of the doctorates in the biological sciences between 1993 and 2002 but got only 30.2 percent of the jobs. In contrast, white men earned 43.2 percent of the doctorates, but they got 55.4 percent of the jobs (Hamilton 2004). Johnsrud and Heck (1994) found that women faculty were more likely to leave their university positions than their male counterparts. Metcalfe and Slaughter (chapter 4 in this volume) describe funding shifts within institutions that favor major centers in fields dominated by men. Schiebinger (1999) cites NSF findings that women have a tendency to leave the sciences in their late thirties, the usual age when professionals assume leadership roles in their institutions. Perhaps women leave science rather than face the uphill battle of earning rewards and recognition.

Schiebinger applies Rossiter's description of several types of segregation (Hierarchical, Territorial, and Institutional) to her discussions of women scientists' experiences. Hierarchical segregation suggests that the higher one moves up the ladder of power, the fewer the females. Territorial segregation demonstrates that women tend to be concentrated in low-paying occupations. For instance, women scholars predominate in the social sciences, humanities, and education disciplines, which are typically lower paying than STEM fields. Finally, Rossiter's concept of Institutional segregation reveals that more prestigious institutions typically take longer to promote women. As Schiebinger notes, women have been admitted to the top-tier institutions as students, but they are rarely asked to join the faculty at these prestigious institutions (where they are often retained as perennial postdoctorates).

Women's colleges tend to do very well at helping women succeed in science. However, these institutions tend to be elite liberal arts institutions. These colleges are typically highly selective, but they do not have the research equipment and funding that are important for advancing the careers of faculty (Schiebinger 1999). Women's colleges are successful because they diminish competition, encourage cooperative learning, and support faculty mentoring. But these institutions prepare only a small number of the women who enter college expecting to earn a bachelor's degree in mathematics and science fields, and while their graduates do well in graduate school and beyond, they cannot be relied upon to meet the entire supply of women scientists.

Schiebinger (1999) cited evidence that practices of science systematically exclude women and favor men. The language, methods, and interpretations used tend to focus on patriarchal parameters. In the past, experiments often excluded females.

In particular, research in the health sciences typically focused on male problems. Because mathematics and science were male dominated, the male-oriented values held by scientists were not identified as biased. These values became identified as an "objective" view of the world. Schiebinger also identified a male-oriented view of mathematics and science in the classroom laboratory, discussed by other scholars as well (see Harding 1991). For example, researchers recently learned that educational computer software intended to improve math, spelling, and language skills were designed to appeal to boys (Schiebinger 1999).

For most STEM fields, access points to doctoral scientist research are earning a baccalaureate degree and then a Ph.D. The National Research Council (NRC) and the NSF collect and analyze data that can be used to identify schools according to their production of earned doctoral degrees in science. These data can be examined by discipline to identify undergraduate institutions that produce relatively large numbers of women bachelor's degree recipients who ultimately earn doctorates in the sciences. As one might expect, large, highly ranked research universities and the most selective women's colleges often appear on the lists (Tidball 1974; Tidball, Smith, Tidball, and Wolf-Wendel, 1999). Here we also use that data to identify a small number of colleges that are unexpected yet successful producers of women bachelor's graduates who ultimately earn mathematics and science doctoral degrees. By identifying these institutions, we propose that future research can focus specifically on the environment, practices, and curricula of those institutions.

The following research questions guided our study: Which institutions produced high numbers of women undergraduates who went on to earn doctorates in the STEM disciplines? Can we identify unexpected institutions, such as small-enrollment institutions, those that do not have a specific mission to serve women, or those that are nonselective and still produce relatively large numbers of these successful students?

Conceptual Framework

Institutions and faculty can serve to enhance or detract from students' views of themselves as scholars. Studies on self-efficacy by Bandura and others demonstrate that positive faculty beliefs about students' abilities as well as their own abilities to teach result in positive student achievement (Bandura 1986, 1999). For example, black students at Historically Black Colleges and Universities (HBCUs) such as Spelman or Morehouse are likely to experience more positive attitudes regarding their abilities. Black students at predominantly white institutions report skepticism on the part of faculty as well as classmates regarding their abilities to perform college level work (Brown 1994). Science faculty at research institutions are less likely to be interested in teaching when compared to their humanities counterparts (Blackburn and Lawrence 1995). Additionally, researchers have found differences in faculty attitudes toward students and toward teaching at schools differing in demographic composition (Hubbard and Stage forthcoming). Such attitudes can diminish enthusiasm on the part of learners at the least, and at worst embarrass or intimidate them. In a study comparing women and men over the undergraduate years, women's goals steadily diminished (Smith, Wolf, and Morrison 1995). In addition, Wolf-Wendel (1998) found that both white women and women of color experience alienation and exclusion in predominantly white coeducational colleges. By providing science and mathematics classroom experiences that foster participation and encouragement for a broad array of students, faculty can enhance student learning (Stage and Kinzie 1999; Stage, Muller, Kinzie, and Simmons 1998).

Some research shows that both male and female undergraduate science students demonstrate improved grades and boosted confidence when faculty altered their pedagogy to reflect inclusionary techniques (Rosser and Kelly 1994). Research has also established that role models play an important part in the development of individuals' aspirations (Hanson 1996). Some students who do not see others like themselves in certain fields will choose not to major in those fields. In an age where the media pervade our homes and classrooms, we see few images of women and minorities as scientists and engineers. By fostering role models and an institutional ethos of belief in the ability of all students to learn, students can feel welcomed into the academy and not be afraid to explore new learning challenges. It is likely that institutions that unexpectedly produce large numbers of graduates who go on to earn doctorates in mathematics and the sciences demonstrate evidence of positive institutional ethos.

Baccalaureate Origins

Baccalaureate origin studies view institutions as the unit of analysis, comparing institutions in terms of the success of their baccalaureate graduates. These studies identify a specific criterion for success and compare a population of institutions on that criterion, typically employing productivity ratios to control for institutional size (Wolf-Wendel, Baker, and Morphew 2000). The earliest baccalaureate origins studies examined lists from *Who's Who of American Women* to identify colleges that ultimately produced high achievers. Those studies found that women's schools, but also relatively small coeducational institutions with greater selectivity and those with high per student academic expenditures, were more likely to produce women achievers (Tidball et al. 1999). The original study (Tidball 1974) did not find demographic differences between students who attended high-producing institutions and students who attended lower-producing institutions. But given differences in productivity, Tidball concluded that there had been a loss of talent in the lower-producing institutions. In a later study, using data from the early 1970s, Tidball (1986) explored the relationship of numbers of women faculty to number of women achievers. She found a correlation of 0.953 between the two variables. Tidball and her colleagues (1999) recommend that any study on baccalaureate origins must pay attention to proportions, not sheer numbers. While very large schools may produce impressive numbers, those numbers may be the same as much smaller schools that do an excellent job of mentoring the few students they have.

More recent work on baccalaureate origins has been conducted by Wolf-Wendel and colleagues. Wolf-Wendel (1998) combined data from *Who's Who* references with doctoral records file data from the National Research Council to examine levels of success for European-American, African-American, and Latina women. She found distinct groups of institutions that promoted success for these women. Wolf-Wendel noted that selective, coeducational, predominantly white institutions did not appear on her lists. And women's institutions remained important in the development of successful graduates. Historically black women's colleges, historically black coeducational colleges, and predominantly white women's colleges were all important producers of successful African-American women. Formerly all-women's colleges and currently Hispanic-serving colleges were more likely to graduate successful Latinas. Predominantly white, coeducational institutions graduated the smallest proportion of successful Latinas.

In a study of the relationship of institutional selectivity and resources to doctoral productivity, Wolf-Wendel, Baker, and Morphew (2000) found differences for white, African-American, and Latina women. Institutional selectivity and resources played an important role in predicting the doctoral productivity ratio of white women. But for African-American and Latina women, only instructional expenditures was a significant predictor of institutional productivity. Institutional status as an HBCU or a Hispanic Serving Institution (HSI) was more important (Wolf-Wendel et al. 2000).

Women's Identities as Scientists

Earliest views of women scientists from the 1950s and 60s describe a narrow range of psychological characteristics less often associated with femininity. Some researchers believe that such descriptions as well as stereotypical images of the male scientist of that era were used in a way that discouraged women from the study of science (Gilbert and Calvert 2003). Still others promoted a form of science education that would have a wider appeal in producing greater numbers of scientists, but ultimately the curricula were viewed as diluted and not as rigorous as traditional scientific training. Currently, some researchers also decry the distinctions made by some scholars between masculine and feminine approaches to science, given the wide range of characteristics displayed by men and women scientists. These scholars advocate an approach that minimizes masculine-feminine distinctions.

Gilbert and Calvert (2003) explored women scientists' understanding of themselves and science. Most of the women interviewed reported that their scientific work actually required masculine modes of thinking—deductive and analytical, focused, linear, and not peripheral. They believed that they were scientists because they had the ability to think in a masculine way. Furthermore, they found it necessary to "keep their personal lives separate from [their] professional lives" (2003, 871). Some saw science as isolating, and others felt that they were the odd person among their colleagues. Alarmingly, these reports are from scientists who had succeeded through the major hurdles required to be a scientist. They bring to mind descriptions of the dual nature of the college experience for undergraduate students of color attending predominantly white institutions or for other women in atypical majors.

Methods

The dataset formulated for this study was accessed through the National Academy of Sciences Internet site that includes the National Science Foundation (NSF) Survey of Earned Doctorates via WebCASPAR. From there we accessed statistical data focused on mathematics, science, and engineering resources at U.S. colleges and universities. The database provides information from NSF Surveys as well as from the National Center for Education Statistics.

We searched within the institutional dataset option, then narrowed our dataset to the Survey of Earned Doctorates (SED) records file, a census of individuals earning research doctorates from U.S. institutions, to identify the baccalaureate origin of graduates who earned doctorates from 1995 to 2004. We collected data in six categories for each undergraduate institution: gender of doctoral recipients, academic institution of baccalaureate degree, enrollment of the institution by gender, academic year of doctorate, Carnegie classification of baccalaureate institution,[4] and total doctoral degrees in STEM disciplines. In addition, we included only U.S. citizens and permanent residents in our study. Using our criteria, we downloaded the

TABLE 5.1.
Research Institutions: Baccalaureate Origins of Women Scholars Earning Ph.D.s
in Engineering, Mathematics, and Science, 1995–2004

Research I	No. Ph.D.s	No. Engr	High Female Enrollment	No. Ph.D.s	Low Female Enrollment	No. Ph.D.s
University of California, Berkeley[a]	712	106	University of California, Berkeley[a]	712	Cornell University[a]	610
Cornell University[a]	610	74	University of Michigan, Ann Arbor[a]	509	MIT[a]	484
University of Michigan, Ann Arbor[a]	509	80	University of Illinois, Main	439	Harvard University[a]	353
MIT[a]	484	184	University of California, Davis[a]	428	University of California, San Diego[a]	347
University of Illinois, Main	439	77	University of Wisconsin–Madison	394	Stanford University[a]	306
University of California, Davis[a]	428	34	Pennsylvania State University, Main	386	University of Pennsylvania[a]	276
University of Wisconsin–Madison	394	26	University of California, Los Angeles[a]	323	Princeton University[a]	262
Pennsylvania State University, Main	386	55	University of Texas at Austin[a]	321	University of Virginia, Main	254
Harvard University[a]	353	17	Texas A&M University, Main[a]	315	Duke University	252
University of California, San Diego[a]	347	33	Purdue University, Main	315	Virginia Tech	245

Research II	No. Ph.D.s	No. Engr	High Female Enrollment	No. Ph.D.s	Low Female Enrollment	No. Ph.D.s
University of California, Santa Cruz[a]	185	4	University of Delaware[a]	169	University of California, Santa Cruz[a]	185
University of Delaware[a]	169	24	State University of New York at Buffalo[a]	130	Rice University[a]	164
Rice University[a]	164	32	Brigham Young University, Main[a]	114	University of Notre Dame	119
State University of New York at Buffalo[a]	130	26	Auburn University, Main[a]	101	Rensselaer Polytechnic Institute[a]	116
University of Notre Dame	119	23	University of South Florida[a]	93	State University of New York at Albany	115
Rensselaer Polytechnic Institute[a]	116	52	Washington State University	88	Clemson University	106
State University of New York at Albany	115	6	Kansas State University	83	University of Vermont	103
Brigham Young University	114	11	University of South Carolina at Columbia[a]	82	University of California, Riverside[a]	91
Clemson University	106	22	University of Oklahoma, Norman[a]	77	Lehigh University	77
University of Vermont	103	1	Southern Illinois University, Carbondale	72	University of Rhode Island	69

NOTE: Mean women's enrollment: Research I, 8,218, and Research II, 6,810.

[a]Major producer of students of color who earned doctorates in the sciences (Stage and Hubbard 2005).

number of science and engineering graduates for each academic year (AY), based on gender and academic institution, then summed the number of doctoral degree recipients (AY 1995–2004) for each institution.

From the database, we identified women's colleges, the Carnegie classification for each institution (see Appendix A), the number of undergraduate students enrolled in 1995–2004 and the number of women undergraduate students enrolled in 1995–2004. Within each Carnegie classification category (e.g., Research I, Research II, Doctoral I, Doctoral II, etc.), we ranked institutions by the number of women doctoral graduates in descending order. Displaying the rankings by classification helped identify unexpected producers—small and relatively nonselective institutions[5]—that might not be obvious in a list of all institutions grouped together. When analyzing the top ten producers of STEM doctorates, we expected that larger and more selective institutions would graduate more women scientists. To control for large enrollments, we also ranked institutions based on high/low enrollment of women undergraduates (using the classification's mean female enrollment as the cut-off). We hypothesized that unexpected producers provided unique environments that supported women to overcome obstacles and resulted in larger numbers of women scientists.

Results

From 1995 to 2004, more than 108,000 doctorate degrees in STEM fields were awarded in the United States. Approximately 34 percent of those doctorates were awarded to women. However, the percentage of women doctorates differed when analyzed by Carnegie classifications. Comparing the baccalaureate origins of STEM doctorates based on gender, Research I and II institutions had the lowest percentage of women baccalaureates who earned doctorates (31% and 29% respectively) when compared with men. Liberal Arts I and II institutions had the highest percentages of women baccalaureate graduates who earned their doctorates in STEM majors compared with men—(44% and 43% respectively for women). Tables 5.1 through 5.4 depict findings for the ten most productive institutions within each Carnegie classification. Table 5.1 lists the high producers of women scientists for all Research institutions. The upper half lists the top ten baccalaureate origins of women scientists from Research I institutions; the lower half, the top ten producers of women scientists from Research II institutions.

Each table is divided into three separate columns, each indicating the institutional name and the number of women Ph.D.s produced in the ten-year period from 1995 to 2004. The first column presents the top ten institutions and number of women doctorates for those institutions in that Carnegie classification. The first column also includes the number of women baccalaureates from each institution earning engineering doctorates from 1995 to 2004. We display this information because colleges with large engineering schools have an advantage over their peers in terms of numbers of women who ultimately earn doctorates. For example, for the Massachusetts Institute of Technology (MIT), 184 of the 484 undergraduates ultimately earned doctorates in engineering. The remainder, 300, earned other non-engineering STEM Ph.D.s. This can be compared with peers by subtracting percentages of engineering doctorates. For example, Pennsylvania State University's total of 386 included 55 who earned engineering doctorates. Their total for non-engineering doctorates, 331, exceeded MIT in non-engineering STEM majors. In the second and third columns, they are ranked again according to undergraduate female enrollments. The second column presents the top ten institutions from among those with high undergraduate female enrollments (an enrollment above the classification's average female enrollment). The third column presents the same information for institutions with low female enrollment (those that are below the Carnegie classification's average)—these are unexpected producers.

Finally, a letter *a* next to an institution's name indicates that it emerged in a similar study examining the same data for institutions that produced large numbers of baccalaureate graduates of color who went on to earn doctorates in the sciences (Stage and Hubbard 2005). A letter *b* by an institution's name in the tables indicates that the college or university is a women's institution (female enrollment above 80%).

Research Institutions

Table 5.1 lists the institutions that were the major producers of future research scholars for Research I and II classifications. A total of 19,981 scholars from the Research I (mean women's enrollment—8,218) and Research II (mean women's enrollment—6,810) institutions ultimately earned doctorates in the sciences between 1995 and 2004. The University of California at Berkeley, with 712 scholars in the ten-year period, was the most productive Research I institution. It is highly selective, with a higher-than-average female undergraduate enrollment during the ten years studied. Cornell University, second, with 610 women graduates who ultimately earned their doctorates, is also highly selective; however, it has a lower-than-average female undergraduate enrollment. MIT was the fourth-highest producer of women scientists and was second when compared to those institutions with low women's enrollment. When compared to other Research I institutions,

MIT was also unique with the highest percentage of women who earned their doctorates in engineering, 38 percent. Berkeley, Cornell, University of Michigan, MIT, UC-Davis, UCLA, University of Texas, Texas A&M, Stanford, and Princeton also were found to be major producers of scholars of color (Stage and Hubbard 2005). High achievement in both categories possibly indicates a high level of commitment to the success of their underrepresented scholars in STEM fields.

Table 5.1 also includes the analysis for Research II institutions. UC–Santa Cruz, when compared to all institutions in this classification, had the highest number of women baccalaureates ultimately earning doctorates (n=185) during the period studied. This institution also had a lower-than-average female enrollment and was an unexpected producer of women scientists. Our analysis identified six additional Research II institutions that were unexpected producers of women scientists: Rice, Notre Dame, Rensselaer Polytechnic Institute (RPI), SUNY Albany, Clemson, and the University of Vermont. Seven of the overall top ten producers in the entire Research II category had lower-than-average women's enrollment.

Several institutions from this analysis of women doctorates also appeared in our previous analysis of minority STEM producers (Stage and Hubbard 2005). These institutions included Auburn University, RPI, Stanford University, SUNY Buffalo, University of Delaware, UC-Riverside, UC–Santa Cruz, University of Oklahoma, University of South Carolina, and University of South Florida.

Doctoral Institutions

More than 4,000 women from all Doctoral I and Doctoral II institutions earned their doctorates in a STEM field between 1995 and 2004. As shown in table 5.2, William and Mary was the highest producer of women scientists (n=189) in the Doctoral I classification. In addition, several unexpected producers appeared in the top ten baccalaureate origins of women scientists for Doctoral Institutions. In the Doctoral I classification, five institutions with low female undergraduate enrollment (lower than the mean women's enrollment—5,336) were listed in the top ten baccalaureate origins of all Doctoral I institutions. These unexpected producers were: William and Mary, Boston College, SUNY Binghamton, Loyola University of Chicago, and Marquette University. All five of these institutions are selective institutions. From our previous study on the production of scientists of color, twenty-four institutions (over half) listed in the Doctoral I and II classifications as high producers of women scientists were also listed as high producers of minority scientists. For the Doctoral I classification, the institutions listed in both studies included: SUNY Binghamton, University of Alabama, Florida Institute of Technol-

TABLE 5.2

Doctoral Institutions: Baccalaureate Origins of Women Scholars Earning Ph.D.s in Engineering, Mathematics, and Science, 1995–2004

Doctoral I	No. Ph.D.s	No. Engr	High Female Enrollment	No. Ph.D.s	Low Female Enrollment	No. Ph.D.s
College of William & Mary[a]	189	6	Miami University of Ohio	116	College of William & Mary[a]	189
Miami University of Ohio	116	7	University of Alabama[a]	70	Boston College	100
Boston College	100	6	University of Akron[a]	70	State University of New York at Binghamton[a]	100
State University of New York at Binghamton[a]	100	7	Bowling Green State University	65	Loyola University of Chicago	81
Loyola University of Chicago[a]	81	3	Indiana University of Pennsylvania	64	Marquette University[a]	80
Marquette University[a]	80	10	University of Texas at Arlington[a]	59	University of Missouri, Rolla	53
University of Alabama[a]	70	13	Northern Illinois University	58	Drexel University	46
University of Akron[a]	70	8	University of Southern Mississippi[a]	53	Texas Woman's University[a,b]	45
Bowling Green State University	65	2	University of Toledo	52	Florida Institute of Technology[a]	42
Indiana University of Pennsylvania	64	1	Western Michigan University[a]	45	Adelphi University	35
University of Texas at Arlington	59	6	Old Dominion University[a]	42	Catholic University of America	35

Doctoral II	No. Ph.D.s	No. Engr	High Female Enrollment	No. Ph.D.s	Low Female Enrollment	No. Ph.D.s
Dartmouth College[a]	137	14	University of New Hampshire[a]	136	Dartmouth College[a]	137
University of New Hampshire[a]	136	16	Baylor University[a]	82	Wake Forest University	58
Baylor University[a]	82	1	San Diego State University[a]	75	Michigan Technological University	57
San Diego State University[a]	75	1	University of Maryland, Baltimore Cty.	63	University of Maine	52
University of Maryland, Baltimore Cty.[a]	63	25	University of Central Florida[a]	62	North Dakota State University	49
University of Central Florida[a]	62	13	Montana State University, Bozeman	53	Worcester Polytechnic Institute	48
Wake Forest University	58	0	University of Nevada, Reno	42	Duquesne University	36
Michigan Technological University	57	26	George Mason University[a]	41	Texas Christian University	34
Montana State University, Bozeman	53	9	Florida International University[a]	39	University of San Francisco	34
University of Maine	52	4	University of Southwestern Louisiana[a]	37	State University of New York College of Environmental Science & Forestry	30

NOTE: Mean women's enrollment: Doctoral I, 5,336, and Doctoral II, 4,398.

[a]Major producer of students of color who earned doctorates in the sciences (Stage and Hubbard 2005).

[b]Women's institution—female enrollment above 80%.

ogy, Marquette, Loyola, William and Mary, University of Southern Mississippi, University of Akron, Western Michigan University, University of Texas Arlington, Old Dominion University, Texas Women's University, University of Missouri (Rolla), Adelphi University, and Boston College. Again, the institutions listed in both studies likely embrace a commitment to advancing underrepresented scholars in mathematics, engineering, and the natural sciences.

Dartmouth was the top producer of women scientists in the Doctoral II classification. Dartmouth is a highly selective Ivy League institution; therefore, it is not surprising that it was listed in the top ten of this category. However, three additional institutions were listed as the top ten baccalaureate origins for the entire classification with lower-than-average female enrollment (mean women's enrollment—4,398)—Wake Forest, Michigan Tech, and University of Maine. All three institutions are selective to highly selective institutions. Michigan Tech focuses on engineering, science, and technology. North Dakota State rose to the top ten compared with other low-women's-enrollment institutions (less than 4,398). The Doctoral II institutions that appeared in both our study of minority scientists and this study include: Florida International University, San Diego State, University of Central Florida, George Mason University, Dartmouth, University of Maryland-Baltimore County (UMBC), University of Southwest Louisiana, Baylor, and University of New Hampshire.

The Doctoral I and Doctoral II institutions included several that did not have engineering schools and whose graduates include relatively small numbers (less than 10%) who earned doctorates in engineering: UMBC with 40 percent (25), University of Alabama with 18.6 percent (13), University of Central Florida with 21 percent (13), and Michigan Technological University with 45.6 percent (26). All had relatively high percentages of bachelor's graduates who earned engineering doctorates.

Comprehensive Institutions

The top ten Comprehensive institutions listed in table 5.3 present some interesting results because of their diversity. The Comprehensive classification is large, with more than 422 institutions categorized as Comprehensive I institutions and 84 institutions categorized as Comprehensive II. A total of 6,675 scholars from Comprehensive institutions earned doctorates in the sciences. The institutions in this classification vary, based on institutional control (private vs. public), size (undergraduate student enrollment: 175–23,000), and mission (e.g., denominational, public technical, and private non-religious colleges and universities). Cali-

TABLE 5.3

Comprehensive Institutions: Baccalaureate Origins of Women Scholars Earning Ph.D.s in Engineering, Mathematics, and Science, 1995–2004

Comprehensive I	No. Ph.D.s	No. Engr	High Female Enrollment	No. Ph.D.s	Low Female Enrollment	No. Ph.D.s
California State Polytechnic University, San Luis Obispo[a]	94	21	California State Polytechnic University, San Luis Obispo[a]	94	Trinity University[a]	74
City University of New York Hunter College[a]	75	0	City University of New York Hunter College[a]	75	Valparaiso University	41
Trinity University[a]	74	7	San Francisco State University	67	Bradley University	37
San Francisco State University	67	3	University of Dayton	67	Creighton University	37
University of Dayton	67	19	Humboldt State University	62	State University of New York College at Fredonia	36
Humboldt State University	62	4	State University of New York College at Geneseo	60	University of Scranton	36
State University of New York College at Geneseo	60	4	San Jose State University[a]	58	University of Richmond	36
San Jose State University[a]	58	3	Villanova University	57	Santa Clara University	35
Villanova University	57	9	Rochester Institute of Technology	54	Loyola College	30
Rochester Institute of Technology	54	6	James Madison University	53	Simmons College	30
			Truman State University	53		

Comprehensive II	No. Ph.D.s	No. Engr	High Female Enrollment	No. Ph.D.s	Low Female Enrollment	No. Ph.D.s
Mary Washington College	34	6	Mary Washington College	34	Long Island University Southampton[a]	27
Calvin College[a]	32	2	Calvin College[a]	32	Mount St Mary's College[a,b]	16
Long Island University Southampton[b]	27	1	College of St Catherine[b]	27	Gwynedd-Mercy College[b]	14
College of St Catherine[b]	27	1	University of Wisconsin–Green Bay	18	University of Tampa[b]	13
University of Wisconsin–Green Bay	18	0	Capital University	15	Chestnut Hill College[b]	12
Mount St Mary's College[a,b]	16	2	Drury College[a]	12	St Edward's University[a]	10
Capital University	15	0	Weber State University	10	Viterbo College	10
Gwynedd-Mercy College[b]	14	0	Linfield College[a]	9	Walla Walla College[a]	10
University of Tampa[b]	13	0	College of Notre Dame of Maryland[a]	8	Spring Hill College	10
Chestnut Hill College[b]	12	0	St John Fisher College	8	Point Loma Nazarene College	9
Drury College[a]	12	0	Lake Superior State University	8	Mount St Mary's College and Seminary[b]	9
					University of Mary Hardin Baylor[a]	9
					West Virginia Wesleyan College	9

NOTE: Mean women's enrollment: Comprehensive I, 2,723; and Comprehensive II, 1,563.
[a]Major producer of students of color who earned doctorates in the sciences (Stage and Hubbard 2005).
[b]Women's institution: female enrollment above 80%.

fornia State Polytechnic University in San Luis Obispo was the largest producer of women scientists for the Comprehensive I classification. It is a selective institution, which emphasizes "learning by doing" (Cal Poly Web site). However, 22.3 percent or 21 of its doctorates were in engineering, but only 73 in non-engineering STEM fields. This is slightly less than CUNY's Hunter College, the second-highest producer of women scientists in the category, with 75 and no engineering Ph.D.s. Both institutions had higher-than-average women's enrollment. The third institution listed in the top ten of this category was an unexpected producer. Trinity University is a selective liberal arts and science university located in San Antonio, Texas. Of the Comprehensive I institutions, it was the only one listed in the top ten for the entire classification with lower-than-average women's enrollment (lower than mean women's enrollment of 2,723). In our previous study of minority scientists (Stage and Hubbard 2005), we identified four Comprehensive I institutions as high producers of women as well as minority scientists: Hunter College, California Polytechnic, Trinity, and San Jose State. A future study of these institutions may provide some insight on how institutions create positive academic environments for minority and women scientists.

The highest producer for Comprehensive II institutions was Mary Washington College; Calvin College was a close second. Both are highly selective institutions with higher-than-average women's enrollments. Long Island University's (LIU) Southampton campus, now a branch campus of Stony Brook University, was an unexpected producer of women scientists. This institution was moderately selective but had a lower-than-average women's enrollment (lower than the mean women's enrollment of 1,563). In the Comprehensive II classification, we also found four women's colleges that were high producers of women scientists—Chestnut Hill College, College of St. Catherine, Gwynedd-Mercy College, and Mount St. Mary's College. Comprehensive II institutions analyzed as high producers of women and minority scientists include Calvin College, College of Notre Dame of Maryland, Drury College, LIU-Southampton, Mary Washington College, Mount St. Mary's, University of Mary Hardin Baylor, University of Tampa, St. Edward's, Linfield College, and Walla Walla College.

In this classification, several did not have engineering schools, and a total of six institutions had more than 10 percent of ultimate Ph.D. earners in engineering. California Polytech with 22.3 percent (21), University of Dayton with 28.41 percent (19), Villanova with 15.8 percent (9), Mary Washington with 17.6 percent (6), and Mount St. Mary's with 12.5 percent (2), each had relatively high percentages of bachelor's graduates who earned engineering doctorates.

TABLE 5.4.

Liberal Arts Institutions: Baccalaureate Origins of Women Scholars Earning Ph.D.s in Engineering, Mathematics, and Science, 1995–2004

All Liberal Arts I	No. Ph.D.s	No. Engr	High Female Enrollment	No. Ph.D.s	Low Female Enrollment	No. Ph.D.s
Wellesley College[a,b]	189	6	Wellesley College[a,b]	189	Swarthmore College[b]	118
Mount Holyoke College[a,b]	177	7	Mount Holyoke College[a,b]	177	Pomona College[b]	79
Smith College[a]	157	2	Smith College[a,b]	157	Reed College[b]	77
Oberlin College	142	2	Oberlin College	142	Amherst College[b]	69
Bryn Mawr College[a,b]	134	5	Bryn Mawr College[a,b]	134	Grinnell College[b]	64
Carleton College[b]	128	2	Carleton College[b]	128	Bates College	64
Swarthmore College[b]	118	7	St Olaf College	106	Bowdoin College[b]	59
St Olaf College	106	6	Barnard College[a,b]	87	Kalamazoo College[b]	57
Barnard College[a,b]	87	3	Bucknell University[b]	85	Franklin & Marshall College	56
Bucknell University[b]	85	6	Williams College[b]	84	Haverford College[b]	52

All Liberal Arts II	No. Ph.D.s	No. Engr	High Female Enrollment	No. Ph.D.s	Low Female Enrollment	No. Ph.D.s
Evergreen State College	32	1	Evergreen State College	32	Lebanon Valley College	22
Ohio Northern University	29	5	Ohio Northern University	29	Texas Lutheran University	20
St Mary's College[a] (Indiana)	28	1	St Mary's College[a] (Indiana)	28	Berea College	17
Mississippi University for Women[a]	23	1	Mississippi University for Women[a]	23	Fisk University[b]	17
Lebanon Valley College	22	0	Augustana College Sioux Falls	19	Susquehanna University	16
Texas Lutheran University	20	2	State University of New York Purchase College	18	Tougaloo College[b]	15
Augustana College Sioux Falls	19	0	Carlow College	18	Albertson College	15
State University of New York Purchase College	18	0	Cedar Crest College	18	Texas A&M University Galveston[b]	13
Carlow College	18	1	Metro State College of Denver	17	Seton Hall College	12
Cedar Crest College	18		St Norbert College	17	Mount Union College	12
			Regents College of New York	16	Marietta College	12
					Eastern Mennonite University	12

NOTE: Mean women's enrollment: Liberal Arts I, 871, and Liberal Arts II, 1040.

[a] Women's institution: female enrollment above 80%.

[b] Major producer of students of color who earned doctorates in the sciences (Stage and Hubbard 2005).

Liberal Arts Institutions

Table 5.4 lists the top ten producers of women scientists for Liberal Arts I and II institutions. A total of 6,646 women scientists (18%) who ultimately earned their doctorates had their baccalaureate origins from Liberal Arts institutions. As shown in table 5.4, several women's colleges are listed in the Liberal Arts I and II top ten producers. Three highly selective women colleges are listed at the top of the Liberal Arts I classification—Wellesley, Mount Holyoke, and Smith. Two more—Bryn Mawr and Barnard—appear in the top ten. Swarthmore—a highly selective private college—was the only Liberal Arts I institution listed in the top ten with a lower-than-average women's enrollment (mean women's enrollment 871).

In a previous study, several Liberal Arts I colleges also found to be high producers of minority scientists were Amherst, Bowdoin, Bryn Mawr, Bucknell, Carleton, Grinnell, Haverford, Kalamazoo, Mount Holyoke, Pomona, Reed, Wellesley, Williams, and Swarthmore (Stage and Hubbard 2005).

Evergreen State College was listed as the top producer of women scientists in the Liberal Arts II classification. It is a moderately selective public institution known for its interdisciplinary and collaborative academic programs. Only two women's colleges are listed in the Liberal Arts II classification—St. Mary's in Indiana and Mississippi University for Women. Like the Liberal Arts I classification, the Liberal Arts II classifications had few unexpected producers. Only two institutions had a lower-than-average female undergraduate enrollment (mean women's enrollment 1,040) and were still listed in the top ten of all Liberal Arts II institutions—Lebanon Valley College and Texas Lutheran University. Both Lebanon Valley and Texas Lutheran are moderately to highly selective institutions, and they both list biology and the biological sciences as popular majors. Three Liberal Arts II colleges were found to be high producers of both women and minority scientists (see Stage and Hubbard 2005)—Fisk University, Tougaloo College, and Texas A&M at Galveston.

Few Liberal Arts colleges include engineering curricula. Only two Liberal Arts II colleges in these two classifications had more than 10 percent of their ultimate science Ph.D. earners in engineering. Ohio Northern University had 17.2 percent (5) of its STEM doctorates in engineering. Similarly, 10.5 percent (2) of the baccalaureate graduates of Augustana College in Sioux Falls, South Dakota, who earned STEM doctorates, earned them in engineering.

Summary

We expected larger institutions as well as more selective women's colleges to produce relatively larger numbers of women scientists. At the top of the list of high producers of undergraduate bachelor's degree earners who went on to earn doctorates in STEM fields during the ten years in our study were the Ivy League colleges, other highly selective colleges and universities, and a handful of technical institutes. Those institutions undoubtedly recruit and admit women only at the highest levels of academic achievement. They are to be commended for producing large numbers of graduates who are successful in the sciences. For instance, five out of the eight Ivy League institutions are represented in the tables (Cornell, Harvard, Penn, and Princeton in the Research I table and Dartmouth in the Doctoral II table). Ivy League institutions accounted for a total of 1,637 out of 10,190 women baccalaureates produced by the top ten producers in all classifications who ultimately earned their doctoral degrees in the sciences.

In this study, women's colleges were also expected high producers of women scientists. The performance of women's colleges in the production of women who ultimately earn doctorates is well documented (Tidball 1989; Wolf-Wendel 1998). Here, thirteen women's colleges were represented as top producers in four of the six Carnegie classifications that included women's colleges. Women's institutions were found in the Doctoral I, Comprehensive II, Liberal Arts I, and Liberal Arts II classifications. The thirteen women's institutions listed in our results, despite relatively low average enrollments, produced 918 women graduates who went on to earn their doctorates in mathematics, engineering, or sciences during the ten-year period. In a study of the baccalaureate origins of scholars of color, HBCUs played a similar major role (Stage and Hubbard 2005).

Women's colleges offer a wealth of characteristics that promote women's education—in their institutional sagas, missions, and histories (Manning 2000; Tidball et al. 1999). They include large numbers of role models for intelligent, successful women from administrators through faculty and peers in the classroom. Women's colleges also tend to employ inclusionary pedagogy techniques (Rosser and Kelly 1994) in their classes. Schiebinger (1999) notes that women's colleges tend to encourage cooperative learning environments and interdisciplinary study and to discourage competition. However, women's colleges do not have the capacity to begin to supply the numbers of women needed in STEM fields. Also women's colleges tend to be small, private liberal arts colleges that do not have the resources of the large Research I institutions. In addition, some critics argue that women's colleges

TABLE 5.5

Unexpected High Producers: Baccalaureate Origins of Women Ph.D.s in Engineering, Mathematics, and Science, 1995–2004

Institutions	No. Ph.D.s	Carnegie Classification	Selectivity[a]	Unexpected Minority Institution[b]
Cornell University	610	Research I		X
MIT	484	Research I		X
Harvard University	353	Research I		X
University of California, Santa Cruz	185	Research II	X	X
Rice University	164	Research II		X
Rensselaer Polytechnic Institute	116	Research II		X
State University of New York at Albany	115	Research II	X	
University of Vermont	103	Research II	X	
College of William & Mary	189	Doc I		X
State University of New York at Binghamton	100	Doc I		X
Loyola University of Chicago	81	Doc I	X	X
Marquette University	80	Doc I	X	X
Dartmouth College	137	Doc II		X
University of Maine	52	Doc II	X	
Trinity University	74	Comp I	X	X
Long Island University Southampton	27	Comp II	X	
University of Tampa	13	Comp II	X	X
Chestnut Hill College	12	Comp II	X	
Swarthmore College	118	LA I		X
Evergreen State College	32	LA II	X	
Lebanon Valley College	22	LA II	X	
Texas Lutheran University	20	LA II	X	

[a] Institutions with moderate to low selectivity: average score below 1,200 (*Princeton Review* 2000).
[b] Institutions that were identified as unexpected producers of minority scholars earning Ph.D.s in Engineering, Mathematics, and Science (Hubbard and Stage 2005).

do not allow women to experience the skills needed to maneuver in a world dominated by men (Schiebinger 1999).

One of the purposes of this chapter was to identify institutions that might not be expected to produce large numbers of women graduates who go on to earn doctorates in the sciences and mathematics. We found several unexpected producers of women scientists. Additionally, we found that several of the unexpected institutions that were high producers of women who went on to become research scientists also appeared in the similar study of students of color who went on to become research scientists (Stage and Hubbard 2005).

Table 5.5 lists colleges and universities that graduated high numbers of women who went on to earn doctorates in STEM majors. Institutions listed had at least two of the following three characteristics: a high producer of doctoral women in this study, low selectivity, and unexpected high producer in the previous study of students of color (Stage and Hubbard 2005). The first three columns list the names of the institutions, the total number of women Ph.D.s in STEM fields from 1995 to 2004, and the institution's Carnegie classification. The next column indicates whether the institution was a moderate- to low-selectivity institution (defined by average SAT scores below 1200). The final column indicates whether the institution was an unexpected baccalaureate origin of minority scholars (Stage and Hubbard 2005).

In the Research I category, Cornell was the second highest overall producer of female STEM doctorates and was identified as an unexpected producer. Its undergraduate women's enrollment was below average, and it also emerged as a high producer of minority scientists (Stage and Hubbard 2005). For the Research II category, UC–Santa Cruz was also identified as an unexpected producer. It is a large research institution with science and engineering faculty recognized for their contributions to science and their professions. William and Mary, a highly selective institution also identified as an unexpected producer of women scientists, was the highest producer in the Doctoral I classification. It enrolls fewer women than the average Doctoral I institution and was identified as a high producer of minority scientists (Stage and Hubbard 2005). Dartmouth was also identified as an unexpected producer in the Doctoral II classification for the same reasons as William and Mary.

Trinity University, a selective private institution in San Antonio, Texas, was identified as an unexpected producer for the Comprehensive classification. It enrolls fewer women than the average Comprehensive I institution, but it was the third-highest producer of women scientists for the Carnegie classification. It is also recognized as a high producer of minority scientists (Stage and Hubbard 2005). Finally, Swarthmore and Evergreen State were identified as unexpected producers for Liberal Arts I and II institutions, respectively. Swarthmore is a highly selective liberal arts institution and one of the nation's first coeducational institutions. Interestingly, Evergreen, not a women's college but a college with relatively high women's enrollment, was the highest producer of the Liberal Arts II institutions. This institution also encourages inclusionary techniques as well as student-centered learning. It also has a reputation of being interdisciplinary and focused on social justice issues.

Finally, one institution that appeared on the list of high producers in the Comprehensive II category despite relatively low women's enrollment was Mount St. Mary's. Interestingly, the college also appeared along with very selective institutions that did not report SAT scores to the *Princeton Review*. According to the Web site, this college accepts students with SAT scores in the selective range and grade point averages between 3.27 and 3.97 but also accepts students for associate degree programs with lower SATs and grade point averages between 2.6 and 3.3. It is probably able to attract promising students to the associate degree program, some of whom will ultimately graduate with bachelor's degrees.

A limitation of this study is that we used basic information about each institution. Carnegie classifications have been used as a systematic way of grouping similar institutions to avoid losing important information about smaller or less-selective institutions in a gross comparison. A more detailed analysis of top producers within a particular classification might use document analysis and interviews to include institutional mission, resource allocation, admission criteria, popular majors, and department and classroom practices in a more focused analysis. An in-depth qualitative study of unexpected producers, particularly those who rose to the top in both the analysis of scholars of color and in this study is warranted.

Implications

Baccalaureate origin studies as described by Wolf-Wendel, Baker, and Morphew (2000) view institutions as the unit of analysis, compare institutions in terms of the success of their graduates, and compare a population of institutions on a specific criterion, typically controlling for institutional size. This study demonstrates the usefulness of baccalaureate origins research to understand underrepresented students' experiences in mathematics and science fields. With the results of our large-scale quantitative analysis, we are able to point to institutions that are more successful than their peers in promoting women and, in a second study, students of color in nontraditional fields. A next step is a more detailed focus on one or more of the notable exceptions who are successful in promoting budding scientists.

Despite the fact that the highly selective institutions mentioned above produced large numbers of successful women scientists, total numbers are still lacking (in all but a handful of STEM disciplines women earn doctoral degrees at a fraction of their proportion in the general population). Many more women scientists must be produced to begin to reach gender equity. The vast majority of women students begin their academic careers in relatively nonselective colleges and universities; more must be done to promote women's success in these schools. The results presented here cannot take into account the influence of family educational background and income. We know that students with greater family resources have a stronger sense of self and are also more likely to attend highly selective institutions. However, the appearance of the unexpected institutions in our study demonstrates that there is no room for complacency when it comes to the production of underrepresented scientists. Institutions not represented here can undoubtedly learn from their peer institutions. Nearly every type and level of quality are represented on these lists. Many of the institutions we listed as high and unexpected producers were highly selective institutions, but several were nonselective.

Undoubtedly, the weed-out phenomenon still has a major influence in mathematics and the sciences. This phenomenon is strongly connected to institutional and departmental ethos as well as to faculty attitudes. Faculty can take two opposing approaches in their undergraduate science classes. One approach views all students as potential scientists who must be fostered and guided as they learn the basic skills and science content needed to succeed. A second view embraces a more clerical function in which the instructor's role is to present a series of tests and trials in which few students succeed and move on to ultimately become scientists.

These views regarding the role of science faculty can be changed through institutional policies related to rewards for credit hour production, numbers of majors graduated, and ultimate success of graduates. In a national study of faculty data, Hubbard and Stage (in press) found differences among faculty attitudes and expectations of students based on characteristics of specific institutions, including institutional type, mission, and student-of-color enrollment characteristics. Additionally, they found that in institutions where faculty understood administrative priorities regarding teaching mission and success of students, they used those priorities to guide their behaviors (Hubbard and Stage in press). Clearly, greater emphasis should be put on the teaching role and success rate of students, particularly at institutions that are not highly selective.

New Challenges to Women Scientists

This decade is particularly critical for women in the sciences as federal programs promoting affirmative action for underrepresented students continue to disappear. Today the majority of students are women. Unfortunately, when looking at institutional data, many analysts take the short view and merely examine lists of declared majors. As administrators and faculty evaluate the numbers, they may conclude that the crisis of women's participation in the sciences is over. An examination of graduation rates by major and by gender is needed to tell the real story. Besides the perception of overrepresentation, several other issues for women are growing: shifts in the financing bases of higher education, increasing reliance on part-time faculty, family responsibilities unrelieved by institutional support, and public statements that fuel centuries-old beliefs about women's inability to perform science.

The past decade in higher education has seen *shifts in the bases of support* that can have negative effects for new faculty. Primary among those has been sharp decreases in the proportion of state support represented in operating budgets. The shortfall is made up by increasing tuition and enrollments, along with an increasing emphasis at all schools on garnering research dollars. These shifts have resulted in institutions of all types and at all levels competing for grant and contract monies at a time when federal policies have drastically reduced such funds. Added to that problem are internal funding shifts by institutions toward more technical and entrepreneurial research and development that might garner patent and industrial partnership funds and away from other liberal arts and basic sciences (Slaughter and Rhoades 2004). These shifts toward technological advances are driving changes in STEM fields, according to Glazer-Raymo (2005), which are now more interdisciplinary and problem-focused, for example, neurosciences, molecular biology, and computational chemistry. For women to be successful in these high-rolling environments, they need the time and flexibility to retool, connections with colleagues across disciplines, and a supportive departmental climate. Metcalfe and Slaughter (chapter 4 in this volume) discuss the political ramifications of academic capitalism in higher education.

Given the budget shifts and shortfalls described above, higher education institutions have shifted to reliance on increasing numbers of *part-time faculty* as an inexpensive way to cover demands caused by increases in enrollments. Ultimately, this means fewer faculty positions and greater competition for scholars graduating with doctorates in the sciences. Glazer-Raymo (2005) reports a high number of science postdoctorates who are unable to gain tenure-track positions and who are disillusioned about finding their way in academic careers. Dual-career families and combining *family responsibilities* with work are both increasing phenomena in higher education. In the past, couples were often able to find two tenure-track positions at the same university in order to continue their careers. Now, more frequently, one of the pair must give up his or her research, at least temporarily, in order to stay together. At best, the sacrificing partner wins a series of faculty lecture positions or part-time work in someone else's funded project. In addition to career dead ends, such sacrifices can cause personal tensions. Finally, budget cuts often mean that institutional supports for ancillary benefits such as preschools and university laboratory schools have long since disappeared.

In addition, we now see the expression of long-dormant bad attitudes and beliefs such as those spouted by Lawrence Summers, former president of Harvard (Wilson and Fain 2006). Public expression of such antediluvian beliefs are shocking to those of us who survived the "gender wars" of the 1970s, but they serve as a reminder of possible negative thinking of others who do not have a platform that "protects" them as they make such assertions. Although we are unlikely to hear expressions of doubt about women's intelligence in a faculty meeting, such beliefs can result in greater skepticism about the value of women faculty members' lines of original research, tempered letters of support, lack of opportunities, and negative tenure votes. Women of color are likely to face even greater challenges regarding their abilities to perform in science and mathematics fields (Hamilton 2004).

Finally, as women continue to move into the STEM fields in greater numbers, clearly, critical junctures must be attended to. The time between the first and second years of undergraduate study are crucial for women who change majors and opt out of sciences (Kinzie, Stage, and Muller 1998). Mentoring of students as they move toward baccalaureate completion to consider graduate study is also important. Mentoring of women during graduate study could be influenced by institutional policies that, instead of focusing on race and gender of admitted students, value their ultimate success. Master's level study might represent a new possibility for expanding participation in STEM careers. According to Glazer-Raymo (2005) the master's degree is not emphasized in the sciences, and few programs provide financial support for master's level study. Yet in business and industry, master's degrees in many sciences and mathematics are preferable. Recruiting promising students into STEM programs at the master's level can ultimately provide a second source of candidates for doctoral programs as well.

Clearly, responsibilities for overcoming the issues described above are national, institutional, and local. Creative approaches that move beyond traditional ways of doing things are needed. For example, movable postdoctoral positions could be funded by national agencies or foundations and awarded to outstanding underrepresented graduates who choose the site for the postdoctorate in order to move with their partners. Finally, a word is needed about counting scientists.

Overrepresenting the Representation

The National Science Foundation counts social scientists as research scientists in its published figures. Most of us know from our research that experiences of successful researchers in the sociology of education include interaction with a broader representation of women and minorities. Underrepresented scientists in most STEM fields do not have colleagues or even administrators like themselves to serve as role models and confidantes. (One of us left science after a master's in mathematics for some of the reasons described in the literature—lack of mentoring, feeling like the odd one of the group, seeing no sense of purpose in the endless mathematical puzzles performed, etc.).

Focus on women in science, engineering, and technology majors is important;

historically, women have been underrepresented among scientists and mathematicians, and their subsequent transition to the science and engineering labor force is even lower. Researchers have increasingly demonstrated the importance of role models for the development of individuals' aspirations (Hanson 1996; Tidball 1989; Wolf-Wendel 1998, 2000). Research on students' decisions to go on to college and choice of possible careers demonstrates that decisions are often made by children as young as elementary school (McDonough 1997; NSF 1998). Some students who do not see others like themselves in certain fields will limit their possibilities.

The number of women scientists and engineers has important implications for role modeling in elementary and secondary as well as higher education. Teachers who did not see women and persons of color in science roles when they attended college will be less likely to expect high achievement of girls and other students of color in their own science and mathematics classrooms. Research shows that women who initially choose mathematics and science majors are more likely to switch to a non-science major, even when the GPAs of those who switch are, on average, higher and not substantially different from students who do not switch.

Finally, because our society values technical skills, mathematics serves as a gatekeeper to careers that are provided economic advantages over other nontechnical ones. We hope to begin to understand ways that the undergraduate college experience might be more positive for aspiring scientists. The task is to understand what is happening nationally, institutionally, departmentally, and in the classroom. By focusing on institutions that are successful producers of scientists, we may begin to develop a model that will lead to increased effectiveness in recruitment and retention of women students into science, mathematics, and engineering training and development, as well as the fostering of their ultimate successes. This understanding could lead to more positive experiences for all mathematics and science majors, both male and female.

APPENDIX A: CARNEGIE CLASSIFICATIONS

The Carnegie classification includes all colleges and universities in the United States that are degree-granting and accredited by an agency recognized by the U.S. Secretary of Education.

Research Universities I (91 institutions) offer a full range of baccalaureate programs, are committed to graduate education through the doctorate, and give high priority to research. They award 50 or more doctoral degrees each year. In addition, they receive annually $40 million or more in federal support.

Research Universities II (38 institutions) offer a full range of baccalaureate programs, are committed to graduate education through the doctorate, and give high priority to research.

They award 50 or more doctoral degrees each year. In addition, they receive annually between $15.5 million and $40 million in federal support.

Doctoral Universities I (50 institutions) offer a full range of baccalaureate programs; the mission of these institutions includes a commitment to graduate education through the doctorate. They award at least 40 doctoral degrees annually in five or more disciplines.

Doctoral Universities II (57 institutions) offer a full range of baccalaureate programs; the mission of these institutions includes a commitment to graduate education through the doctorate. They award annually at least 10 doctoral degrees—in three or more disciplines—or 20 or more doctoral degrees in one or more disciplines.

Master's (Comprehensive) Universities and Colleges I (422 institutions) offer a full range of baccalaureate programs and are committed to graduate education through the master's degree. They award 40 or more master's degrees annually in three or more disciplines.

Master's (Comprehensive) Universities and Colleges II (84 institutions) offer a full range of baccalaureate programs and are committed to graduate education through the master's degree. They award 20 or more master's degrees annually in one or more disciplines.

Baccalaureate (Liberal Arts) Colleges I (160 institutions) are primarily undergraduate colleges with major emphasis on baccalaureate degree programs. They are selective in admissions and award 40 percent or more of their baccalaureate degrees in liberal arts fields.

Baccalaureate (Liberal Arts) Colleges II (361 institutions) are primarily undergraduate colleges with major emphasis on baccalaureate degree programs. They are less selective in admissions or they award less than 40 percent of their baccalaureate degrees in liberal arts fields.

From: NSF's Scientists and Engineering Statistical Data System, on a page concerning Information on Individual SESTAT Elements. http://sestat.nsf.gov/docs/carnegie.html.

NOTES

1. Mathematics/science pipeline—students' continued participation in mathematics, science, or engineering; achievement in those subjects; and the development of attitudes and interests that lead them to continue to pursue those subjects (Berryman 1983; Chipman and Thomas 1987; Maple and Stage 1991).

2. We included mathematics, all engineering fields, and all physical sciences, life sciences, and geological sciences.

3. In the biological and physical sciences, doctoral degrees earned outnumber master's degrees (Thurgood, Golladay, and Hill 2006).

4. We used the 1994 Carnegie classification that was encoded in the Survey of Earned Doctorates data file.

5. We defined *selective* by using the reported SAT averages from *The Princeton Review* (2005). Institutions with SAT combined averages below 1200 were identified moderate or low selectivity. SAT scores were unreported by Cornell, Harvard, Mount St. Mary's College, Rice, and Wake Forest.

REFERENCES

Bandura, Albert. 1986. *Social Foundations of Thought and Action: A Social Cognitive Theory.* Englewood Cliffs, NJ: Prentice-Hall.

———. 1999. *Self-Efficacy: The Exercise of Control.* New York: Freeman.

Benjamin, Marina. 1991. *Science and Sensibility: Gender and Scientific Enquiry, 1780–1945.* London: Basil Blackwell.

Berryman, Sue E. 1983. *Who Will Do Science? Minority and Female Attainment of Science and Mathematics Degrees: Trends and Causes.* New York: Rockefeller Foundation.

Blackburn, Robert T., and Janet H. Lawrence. 1995. *Faculty at Work: Motivation, Expectation, Satisfaction.* Baltimore: Johns Hopkins University Press.

Brown, O. Gilbert. 1994. *Debunking the Myth: Stories of African-American University Students.* Bloomington, IN: Phi Delta Kappa Educational Foundation.

Chipman, Susan F., and Veronica G. Thomas. 1987. The participation of women and minorities in the mathematical, scientific, and technical fields. *Review of Research in Higher Education* 14: 387–430.

Drew, David. 1996. *Aptitude Revisited: Rethinking Math and Science Education for America's Next Century.* Baltimore: Johns Hopkins University Press.

Gilbert, Jane, and Sarah Calvert. 2003. Challenging accepted wisdom: Looking at the gender and science education question through a different lens. *International Journal of Science* 25:861–878.

Glazer-Raymo, Judith. 2005. *Professionalizing Graduate Education: The Master's Degree in the Marketplace.* ASHE Higher Education Report, 31, #4. San Francisco: Jossey-Bass.

Hamilton, Kendra. 2004. Faculty science positions continue to elude women of color. *Black Issues in Higher Education* 21 (3): 36–39.

Hanson, Sandra L. 1996. *Lost Talent: Women in the Sciences.* Philadelphia: Temple University Press.

Harding, Sandra. 1991. *Whose Science? Whose Knowledge? Thinking from Women's Lives.* Ithaca, NY: Cornell University Press.

Hubbard, Steven, and Frances K. Stage. In press. Attitudes, perceptions, and preferences of faculty at Hispanic serving and predominantly black institutions. *Journal of Higher Education.*

Johnsrud, Linda, and Christine DeJarlais. 1994. Barriers to the retention and tenure of women and minorities. *Review of Higher Education* 17:335–53.

Johnsrud, Linda, and Ronald Heck. 1994. A university's faculty: Predicting those who will stay and those who will leave. *Journal of Higher Education Management* 10 (1): 71–84.

Kinzie, Jillian, Frances K. Stage, and Patricia Muller. 1998. Exploring choice of a science, mathematics, or engineering college major: Aspirations, psychological factors, and cultural capital. Paper presented at the annual meeting of the Association for the Study of Higher Education.

Manning, Kathleen. 2000. *Rituals, Ceremonies, and Cultural Meaning in Higher Education.* Westport, CT: Greenwood Press.

Maple, Sue A., and Frances K. Stage. 1991. Math/science major choice: The influence of family background and high school experience by gender and ethnicity. *American Educational Research Journal* 28 (1): 37–60.

McDonough, Patricia M. 1997. *Choosing Colleges: How Social Class and Schools Structure Opportunity.* Albany: State University of New York Press.

National Science Foundation (NSF). 1998. *Shaping the Future: Perspectives on Undergraduate Education in Science, Mathematics, Engineering, and Technology,* Vol. 2. Arlington, VA: National Science Foundation.

———. 2002. *Selected Data on Science and Engineering Doctorate Awards: 1995.* Arlington, VA: National Science Foundation.

———. 2005. *Women, Minorities, and Persons with Disabilities in Science and Engineering: 2002.* Arlington, VA: National Science Foundation.

Princeton Review. 2005. *The Princeton Review's Complete Book of Colleges 2006 Edition.* New York: Random House, Inc.

Rosser, Sue V., ed. 1995. *Teaching the Majority: Breaking the Gender Barrier in Science, Mathematics, and Engineering.* Athene Series. New York: Teachers College Press.

Rosser, Sue V., and B. Kelly. 1994. Who is helped by friendly inclusion? A transformation teaching model. *Journal of Women and Minorities in Science and Engineering* 13:175–92.

Schiebinger, Londa. 1999. *Has Feminism Changed Science?* Cambridge: Harvard University Press.

Slaughter, Sheila, and Gary Rhoades. 2004. *Academic Capitalism and the New Economy: Markets, State, and Higher Education.* Baltimore: Johns Hopkins University Press.

Smith, Daryl, Lisa E. Wolf, and D. Morrison. 1995. Paths to success: Factors related to the impact of women's colleges. *Journal of Higher Education* 66 (3):245–66.

Sonnert, Gerhard. 1995. *Who Succeeds in Science? The Gender Dimension.* New Brunswick, NJ: Rutgers University Press.

Stage Frances K., and Steven S. Hubbard. 2005. Developing scientists of color: Baccalaureate origins of recent math and science Ph.D.s. Presented at annual meeting of Association for the Study of Higher Education, Philadelphia, November.

Stage, Frances K., and Jillian Kinzie. 1999. Reform in undergraduate science, mathematics, engineering, and technology: The classroom context. Presented at the annual meeting of the Association for the Study of Higher Education, San Antonio, TX, November.

Stage, Frances K., and Sue Maple. 1996. Incompatible goals: Narratives of graduate women in the mathematics pipeline. *American Educational Research Journal* 33:23–51.

Stage, Frances K., Patricia Muller, Jillian Kinzie, and Ada Simmons. 1998. *Creating Learning Centered Classrooms: What Does Learning Theory Have to Say?* ASHE-ERIC Higher Education Report, vol. 26, no. 4. Washington, DC: George Washington University.

Thurgood, Lori, Mary Golladay, and Susan Hill. 2006. *U.S. Doctorates in the 20th Century.* Washington, DC: National Science Foundation.

Tidball, M. Elizabeth. 1974. The search for talented women. *Change* 6 (4): 51–52, 64.

———. 1986. Baccalaureate origins of recent natural science doctorates. *Journal of Higher Education* 57:606–20.

———. 1989. Women's colleges: Exceptional conditions, not exceptional talent, produce high achievers. In *Educating the Majority: Women Challenge Tradition in Higher Education,* ed.

C. S. Pearson, D. L. Shavlik, and J. G. Touchton, 157–72. New York: American Council on Education–Macmillan.

Tidball, M. Elizabeth, Daryl G. Smith, Charles S. Tidball, and Lisa E. Wolf-Wendel. 1999. *Taking Women Seriously: Lessons and Legacies for Educating the Majority.* Phoenix, AZ: Oryx Press.

Widnall, Sheila. 1988. AAAS Presidential Lecture: Voices from the pipeline. *Science* 241:1740–45.

Wilson, Robin, and Paul Fain. 2006. Lawrence Summers quits as Harvard president in advance of new no-confidence vote; Derek Bok to step in. *Chronicle of Higher Education,* 21 February.

Wolf-Wendel, Lisa E. 1998. Models of excellence: The baccalaureate origins of successful European American Women, African American Women, and Latinas. *Journal of Higher Education* 69 (2): 144–72.

———. 2000. Women-friendly campuses: What five institutions are doing right. *Review of Higher Education* 23 (3), 319–45.

Wolf-Wendel, Lisa E., Bruce Baker, and Christopher Morphew. 2000. Dollars & $ense: Institutional resources and the baccalaureate origins of women doctorates. *Journal of Higher Education* 71 (2): 165–86.

CHAPTER SIX

Faculty Productivity and the Gundos Question
Faculty Productivity and the Gender Question

ANA M. MARTÍNEZ ALEMÁN

Though advances by women in the academic profession over the last thirty years are notable—for example, the percentage of full-time faculty women has doubled in the three decades—women faculty continue to lean toward teaching rather than research more consistently than their male counterparts and still publish less than male colleagues according to Schuster and Finkelstein (2006, 86, 99). Even at research universities, where the research productivity stakes are higher for faculty, women faculty "are more likely than their male colleagues to be somewhat more engaged in teaching activity and less involved in research" (90, 91). Yet curiously, the amount of time academic women spend teaching has decreased considerably in the last three decades (90–91), suggesting that women in the academic profession have increased their activity in the market economy of research production. Taken together with the data that show that the gap in obtaining external research funds is narrowing between women and men faculty (104), we see a picture of the academic woman, especially those in research universities, that suggests that though women faculty still operate not so insignificantly in the "feminized" economy of teaching and learning, they, like their male colleagues, are active in the masculine economy of research production.

But the focus of this chapter is less to argue that women are particularly disadvantaged in the governing rubric of faculty productivity and more to assert that measures of faculty productivity are a phenomenon of gender itself. This chapter presents the case that gender as an organizing, conceptual, and functional principle has been absent from the deliberation of faculty productivity in American higher education, especially as American higher education has progressed toward entrepreneurial or corporate activities and values (Clark 1998; Slaughter and Rhoades 2006). Most striking in the faculty productivity efforts of the last two decades is the disregard for the relational or erotic[1] nature of undergraduate teaching and the concomitant indifference to the impact of gender *as an organizing construct* on university teaching. The privileging of research and publication in faculty productivity appraisals further fortifies and reinvigorates the attributes of masculinity in the profession while at the same time eroding the "feminization" (and not the "womanization") of the academic profession. Over the last thirty years the academic profession may indeed have become "more feminized" simply by the demographic increase of female faculty, or what I will call the "womanization" of the profession, and the value that some of these women faculty have given teaching and learning. But the rise of faculty accountability metrics that privilege publication and research over teaching and learning, coupled with the increase in research and publication by women suggesting that women, too, can operate in the masculine activities of the profession (Schuster and Finkelstein 2006), implies that the "feminization" of professional academic activities is a dubious contention. Favoring a masculine economy of gender in faculty productivity measures or overlooking gender as an organizing construct in faculty productivity efforts serves to reduce faculty to "fungible functionaries" (Minnich 2005, 9), a position historically unfavorable to anything feminine.

In what follows, I seek to answer the following questions: Does a "production" model of faculty economy effectively ignore gender because it cannot accommodate the relational nature of teaching and learning? When teaching is considered in faculty productivity metrics, does a "production" model by definition—for example, student contact hours, course evaluations—dismiss gender as a factor of consequence? Is the economics of faculty productivity incapable of operating an anthropology of gender that captures the reproductive character of teaching? In ways oppositional to the rational and self-sufficient character of a production model of teaching, the "reproductive" character of teaching invokes relational qualities such as emotion, intimacy, and connection (Martin 1985). In this chapter I argue that the unfinished agenda in the academy is the gendered economy of faculty productivity, or more specifically, gender itself.

Conceptual Frameworks
Gender and Knowledge

Though the term "gender" is now used in both casual and scholarly discourse to convey the conventionally held biological distinction of female and male as well as the cultural practice and performance of norms of "masculinity" and "femininity," in this examination of faculty productivity, the latter meaning of gender will be employed. Although it is undoubtedly tied to Western philosophical treatises

(Aristotelian ones in particular), gender will be used here to refer to those historic and social proscriptions placed on assumed biological sex difference. These sex roles have social, cultural, and psychological norms and scope imbued with meaning that determines their social, cultural, and economic merit, appeal, and importance across time and locality. As a continuum of characteristics and behaviors deemed "masculine" or "feminine," gender is the collection of attributes historically claimed and conferred upon men and women most often as categorically paradoxical; that is, men are "masculine" and women are "feminine," and these are mutually exclusive categories. Here, I will use gender to mean these traits and their symbolic meaning for faculty productivity standards and metrics, whether performed by women or by men.

Central to the construction of gender in Western cultures are the distinctions and correlated worth we give to knowledge. In the West, epistemological traditions have equated masculinity with rationality, objectivity, autonomy, and efficiency, while standards of femininity have been crafted as masculinity's contradictions: emotion, subjectivity, dependence, and imprecision. The specific association of knowledge with sex, and consequently with its corresponding gender norms, presents us with a knowledge paradigm in which the dualistic and binary construction of gender renders some knowledge certain and tangible, and other knowledge ambiguous and indeterminate.

The cornerstone of the gendered bifurcation of knowledge as a function of sex derives from early Western philosophers: Plato asserts in the *Republic* that women are but lesser men; Aristotle contends that as the primary physical distinction, sexual differentiation determines psychological differences; and eighteenth-century philosophers like Kant and Rousseau reinforce dichotomous sex differences to organize knowledge and arrange the social world. For example, Kant and Rousseau agree that the difference between women (the feminine) and men (the masculine) is essential and that their knowledge will be of different and complementary quality. Women's understanding will come from her senses and will be simplistic; men's cognition is reasoned and contemplative. This legacy of gender differentiation and privileging distinguishes intellectual history in the West, but it is the Cartesian project's emphasis on method and objectivity that is the indubitable foundation for the regulatory logos of an economy of gender that we find in faculty productivity measures today.

The importance placed on method and that which is credible or warranted in Cartesian philosophy constitutes the epistemological rubric of faculty productivity undeniably rooted in Aristotelian sex distinctions. Descartes' stipulation that the mind (a thinking, reasoning thing) and the body (a non-thinking, intuitive thing) are naturally distinctively different figures prominently in his treatise on the importance of certainty and objectivity and the mistrust of all else (Bordo 1987). Unlike the mind, the body—and by extension anything that is associated with it—is not governed by reason or rational thinking. Situated by sex and gendered social arrangements, the body's activities are outside the realm of reason and logic, and, given Aristotelian sex distinctions, become associated with the feminine. As a consequence, emotions, feelings, sentiment, and sensations—all functions of the body that cannot be trusted because they fluctuate and change from person to person—become the centerpiece of a gendered epistemology.

To achieve cognitive certainty or trust, we must stabilize the intuitions through the authority of method. Method enables us to make credible and reliable all claims that we may put forth, thereby dependably systematizing knowledge. Our knowledge claims require methodological trustworthiness and reliability in order to be credible, plausible, and convincing. Method enables us to differentiate truthful propositions from false ones, or those ideas and explanations that are tainted by our (bodied) senses, or "subjectivity." "Objectivity," the cognitive condition borne of method, is awarded epistemic authority; while "subjectivity," the condition borne of bodied, situated knowing and cognitively fragile without the full power of reason, replication, consistency, and neutrality, is imperfect, fallible, and unsatisfactory. Subjectivity, by nature a condition of specifically bodied or situated bias or prejudice, cannot induce sensible consensus. Because they are value-laden and influenced by epistemic relations, subjective claims leave us doubting their verity. Under the influence of Cartesian rationalism, we value most those knowledge claims that are verifiable through method untainted by the effects of the relational unpredictability of subjective experience. We seek a purity of knowledge that can be unified through method. As Susan Bordo maintains, this Cartesian rationalism reconstitutes knowledge as masculine and propels an intellectual "flight from the feminine" (1987, 5).

Revered knowledge, then, is a gendered scheme that eschews the feminine—or, as Lorraine Code suggests, "knowledge properly so-called must leave the particularity and seductiveness of sensory and affective experience behind to approach the ideals of objectivity, rationality, and impartiality" (1991, 242). Furthermore, because rationality and reason is the province of masculinity in the West, women's roles and the norms of femininity must be their epistemological antagonists. So as masculinity demarcates standards for knowledge—its ideal forms, its excellence, its representative function—femininity will come to characterize conceptions of knowledge that are imperfect and inferior. Experience in feminine spheres, those gendered activities associated with women, will not carry the same epistemological authority and stature as those performed in the domain of the masculine. Masculine domains will create or produce new knowledge that is empirically resilient and will factor in the verification or interpretation of universal principles. Such knowledge is scientific, systematic, methodical, disciplined, and capable of being controlled. It is a domain in which knowledge is organized to produce and/or verify ontological structures. It is a realm in which the aim of reason is to erect or sustain universal concepts, to reliably identify what in reality conforms to indisputable and undeniable comprehensive conclusions.

The domain and province of gendered knowledge in Western tradition has been partitioned dichotomously so that masculinity and femininity occupy different, oppositional, and at times complementary spaces. Owing much to the historic and philosophical sex/gender hierarchical distinctions that advantage masculinity, realms of knowledge reflect prevailing norms of gender. Masculinity—rational, deliberative, and authoritative—operates in the "public" because it is in the public where reason must prevail. It is in the public where rational knowledge is employed to make social arrangements consistent with tangible evidence. In the public sphere, emotion and all facets of subjectivity are incongruous with the truthful inquiry that creates reasonable harmony. It is in the "private" sphere, the location of subjectivity (affection, emotions, and intersubjectivity), that the feminine must reside. Bodied, practical, and individual, the private sphere is the province of femininity; and as a result, all knowledge constituted there and all functions carried out within the private will be subordinate to that of the public.

Work and Teaching

Jane Roland Martin's (1985) contention that education in the West has historically privileged the "productive processes" simultaneously ignoring society's "reproductive processes" to its own detriment employs the ideology of gender to understand modern education. Maintaining that education is "preparation solely for carrying on the productive processes of society," Martin captures the gendered nature of education—that because it inculcates the traits the broader culture considers masculine, its standards and measures of excellence will embody these same dispositions (1985, 194). It is Martin's examination of the absence of women and the role of gender in philosophical treatises on education that allows her to claim that society's "reproductive processes"—those operations historically relegated to and regulated in the feminine relational medium of the home or "private" sphere—are contradictory to the aims of patriarchal relations or "productive processes"—economic, political, and cultural public functions.

Though the distinction between the public and private spheres as explained by Martin is a contentious liberal feminist conception (Tong 1989), it is useful to this analysis of faculty productivity because it serves as a way to ascertain the effect of gender on faculty productivity standards. The sexual division of work in the private and public spheres is an account of women's inequality, specifically because women's activity in the home (the reproductive processes) is not intellectually or socially equal in prestige and value to men's productive work outside the home. Historically, the specialization of the processes and roles in the private sphere have not been recognized as a function of labor worthy of the status and cachet held by the production or work functions in the public sphere. The "feminine" activities of the private and symbolically relational have not been accorded the social and economic power and regard of the rational and contractual associations of public production. As a consequence, feminine labor—those "reproductive processes" characteristically relational and centered on the socialization of children—has been ideologically situated in what Martin (1985) calls the "ontological basement." As the metaphysical fountainhead for how we have apprehended and postulated the worth of teaching and learning (Goodman 2004), the feminine or reproductive activities of the home have been regarded as epistemologically and metaphysically insignificant. Historically, feminine or domestic acts have been interpreted as having little (if any) economic value. Consequently, we have assumed those processes ineligible for production value in the public sphere.

As a relational activity associated with the home and hence with the feminine, teaching carries a symbolic femininity that informs our social and cognitive structures. For example, in Madeleine Grumet's analysis of the feminization of teaching, *Bitter Milk,* we see teaching's symbolic power to compose "epistemological systems and curricular forms" (1988, 3). As a symbol for nurturance, caring, compassion, and mothering, teaching and all of its behaviors, activities, and performances is a sign of the relational, a symbol of femininity. It can be argued that teaching, whether performed in children's schooling or in universities, is a narrative of femininity, a tale of the meaning of relationships.

As a discourse rooted in women's experience with relational, reproductive, and nurturing processes in the home, teaching is "women's *work*"; and as feminine "work," it carries meaning that conveys its source and consequently its economic value. Work or action that has productive value (i.e., a price determined in a market economy), once performed by women and as a result feminized, is devalued in a marketplace permeated with patriarchal beliefs and principles. The value of reproductive processes like teaching, then, is inextricably tied to its symbolic meaning, in this case, its gender. While it is true that teaching as a "feminized profession" is related to historically specific conditions and events like the development of the "family wage"—itself a gendered concept (Apple 1986; Nicholson 1980)—it is the coupling of the patriarchal privileging of men's public practices with capitalism's market economy that advances the devaluation of women's *labor,* praxis unremunerated because it is outside of a market economy. As a consequence, a teacher's lower wages and occupational undervaluing in professional markets can be understood as a condition constituted by the symbolic value of the feminine or the *market* value of those reproductive, relational processes of the private sphere. The undervaluing of teaching in the marketplace, then, can be said to be an economy of gender, a system characterized by gendered attributes and dispositions and their corresponding public value.

The market value of the reproductive processes and relational activities that comprise teaching in all manner of public sites will be derivative of its symbolic worth, a reflection of the cultural significance of gender, and specifically, the intellectual and economic merits of the feminine. To have market value in the public (the only domain in which the market functions), then, activity must operate in a gendered economy of masculinity. In a gendered economy in which masculinity is advantaged, work is accorded value to the degree that it is consistent with or corresponds to masculine standards and ideals. The laws of such a gendered market will reflect principles of the symbolic meaning and economic merit of gender roles, composing corresponding systems of value and remuneration. "Men's work," those "productive processes" not bearing the symbolic and market impediments of femininity, will rightly claim economic advantage in any professional system in which it is employed. Productive processes, characterized by masculine traits of self-sufficiency, rationality, objectivity, empirical corroboration, and contractual obligation, will garner professional value and its concurrent capital rewards.

In light of these conceptual matters, claims made by sociologists Christopher Jencks and David Riesman (1968) about university teaching in the mid-twentieth century today sound like a reverberation of gender ideology and the economy of gender that propelled American higher education into the twenty-first century. In *The Academic Revolution* (1968), their classic text on the growth of the American university, they write that "teaching is not a profession in the way that research is," noting that "it seems easier to judge individuals [faculty] on the basis of papers they turn out than to judge them on the basis of their interaction with other people. A graduate student's performance in comprehensive examinations is said to provide 'hard' evidence of his competence, while visits to his classes provide only 'soft' evidence. A professor's book can be evaluated in 'objective' terms, whereas his course syllabi, lectures, and examination questions can be valued only 'subjectively'" (531). Without saying as much, Jencks and Riesman identify the economy of gender that operates in the American university. Notwithstanding their failure to explicitly characterize faculty productivity metrics that have transformed the American university in the last three decades of the twentieth century as a gendered phenomenon, Jencks and Riesman capture the gendered quality of research and teaching in the university: research is work of quantifiable, objective, and professional outputs, or "production processes." Teaching is relational, subjective, and quasi-professional activity, or "reproductive process." Research, the production of faculty, is quantifiable evidence of market value. It is "hard" evidence because it is factual, tangible, masculine, and very much unlike the qualitative, interactional, "soft," feminine substantiation of teaching.

University Teaching and the Academic Marketplace

As Eric Gould (2003) points out, the modern American university has a paradoxical culture that rewards knowledge production (or knowledge that has market or exchange value) while simultaneously operating as a resource of symbolic or intrinsic value (knowledge with no exchange value, that has no price) through teaching general or liberal education to undergraduates. It is not surprising to hear, then, that though faculty are publishing and producing more, their interest in undergraduate education is on the rise (Schuster and Finkelstein 2006). In other words, the modern American university operates as a market actor in an economy of exchange *and* as an agent in a symbolic economy powered by labor (teaching) that has no market value.

On the one hand, the modern American research university has evolved to function much like a corporation in the free market, using its resources or capital (faculty) to create specific commodities or products (knowledge) suitable for exchange. Operating in a free market, the modern university understandably must engage in processes and develop policies to maximize profits and minimize costs. The production of its commodity (knowledge having exchange value in the market) takes on the character of economic activity such that concerns about demand, quantity of commodities produced, and their rate of production become important. Universities as corporate entities are then likely to craft policies and procedures reflecting an ethos of production or market economics that will likely devalue symbolic knowledge and its associated processes. Yet on the other hand, the American university simultaneously operates in symbolic production through teaching and learning. As a source of wide-ranging symbolic knowledge that is transmitted through faculty teaching and student learning, the university functions in an economy of cultural and social worth as well. As an institution of symbolic production, its actors engage in processes with figurative intentions, with "soft," subjective, unquantifiable interactions that are incompatible with market exchange. Teaching and learning, effectively having no exchange value, appear at odds with the university's corporate bearings. And of course, faculty women report a greater interest in this economy that has no exchange value, an interest that exceeds male faculty's interest by some 10 percent (Schuster and Finkelstein 2006, 129).

In an era in which American higher education has become more managerial, the fact that women faculty report a greater interest in teaching than male faculty is not so surprising, however. The increasing presence of women in the academic profession in the last thirty to forty years has coincided with the advancement of interdisciplinary studies—Gender and Women's Studies, American Studies, Chicano and African American Studies, and so forth—and epistemologies that have disturbed and repositioned traditional curricula and, most importantly, privileged and given primacy to teaching. Thus the women in the academic profession may have brought the renewed value on teaching and on the science of teaching in higher education, especially because women have entered such teaching-intensive fields, typically interdisciplinary areas that have been influenced and informed by feminist and critical epistemologies that give epistemic importance to student knowledge claims. Reminiscent of Virginia Woolf's contribution of a second guinea presented to advance women in the professions—progress she supposed would "feminize" masculinity in the professions—academic women may have brought femininity to the profession and to the growing managerialism of the academy through the teaching and the worth many have given to this activity.

A similar observation of the American university is put forth by Slaughter and Leslie (1997) in their examination of the evolution and rise of the "entrepreneurial university" and the implementation and consequences of "academic capitalism." As Slaughter and Leslie point out, the university, though historically never wholly autonomous or fully free of market influences, has shifted its attention to the market value of knowledge, consequently aligning its ethos and operations toward a market economy. As a consequence of progressively diminished public funding in the last thirty years, the university (and the research university in particular) has entered a market economy in which its only product, knowledge in the form of research, has become its commodity. In a system of academic capitalism, the university has become increasingly obligated to knowledge production in the form of empirical research, effectively changing the historic culture and practice of academia. In the era of academic capitalism, "academic labor" has responded to incentives from the market and not to the organic interests of the scholar. As "capitalists," faculties have engaged in "market-like" behaviors or performed more market-production work (research with market value) than symbolic reproductive activities (teaching). Though Slaughter and Leslie don't explicitly make the distinction, in their phenomenology of academic capitalism, academic "labor" implicitly becomes academic "work." Faculty, now "market actors" competing for research funding, become increasingly committed to production work with market value. Logically, then, faculty will be evaluated as *workers*; their performance (their market-value functions) will be measured by production standards and the degree to which their work is cost-effective. Thus, though historically a profession with a "tacit social contract" for the production of symbolic knowledge (Slaughter and Leslie 1997), the American university faculty is now an entrepreneurial profession with capitalist concerns.

Though academic capitalists increasingly engage in productive work, the American faculty must still perform and be evaluated on reproductive processes, above all, the labor of teaching, or what Hopkins (1990, 12) calls "the multidimensional character of the [academic] production function." The problem, of course, is that teaching, as a consequence of its gendered ideology, functions in this economy as a contradictory process with intangible outputs by definition impossible to quantify and measure. Faculty work as "asynchronous production" (Layzell 1999), one part research and one part teaching, frustrates productivity measures with its internal incompatibility. The attempts to measure the effectiveness of teaching, or teaching as an output variable, is inconsistent with its gendered conceptualization. Teaching, as previously noted, has been theorized and actuated as feminine labor and as such is incongruous with production processes, or that work characterized by masculine ideals of knowledge. The quality of student learning and the quality of faculty instruction are "intangible inputs" that are by nature and design relational, individual, and variable. Productivity metrics can never really reflect the effectiveness of these reproductive processes, a fact confirmed by higher education scholars (e.g., Hopkins and Massey 1981; Fairweather 1999; Middaugh 2001).

The faculty "productivity problem" in the era of academic capitalism is really one of epistemological and ontological inconsistency. By including teaching as an input variable in faculty productivity measures, we engage in futile mathematization; that is, we can not reduce to mathematical form behaviors and processes that are not in agreement with long-established Cartesian standards. As human resources in academic capitalism, then, faculties are expected to work *and* to labor, to produce market-valued knowledge (research) and to labor to engender symbolic knowledge (teach), to be both masculine and feminine. But labor is not production; it is not a process measurable by tangible outputs over a period of time.

Labor can not "produce" concrete, material, or quantifiable commodities. Labor has no literal "marketplace" constituted by a demand for goods, no specified form of these goods, and no authentic site for their distribution. What university students are taught and what they learn (and this assumes an efficient, maximum output correlation between these two inputs, i.e., that students always learn everything that teachers teach) has symbolic use and worth but not use-value as do goods of production. Faculty labor (teaching), then, is not compensatory activity in the sense that what it gives rise to has no actual price and as such can't be bought or exchanged. Historically, we do not pay for reproductive processes, but if we do—when teaching becomes feminized, when children are cared for outside the home, when nursing becomes a profession—because it is "women's work," its market value is reduced.

Thus, if the American university has been transformed into a corporate entity and is populated by faculty who are academic capitalists, a few things stand to reason:

First, because "capitalists don't invest in things that they can't own" (Thurow 1996) and because symbolic knowledge cannot be owned, it seems reasonable that faculty will be more likely to engage in productive processes, to engage in more research activity, a condition highlighted by Slaughter and Leslie (1997). Incentive to produce goods is a distinctive element of capitalist markets; and as "academic capitalists," faculties have responded accordingly. Research productivity is understood by faculty as the valued commodity of their work (Diamond 1999). Faculty publication rates are known to have value in faculty reward systems (Fairweather 1996). In the last thirty plus years, university faculty, believing that research and not teaching will be given more weight in tenure and promotion determinations, have reacted as market actors by increasingly obtaining contractual funding from extra-university sources for research production (Schuster and Finkelstein 2006; Finkelstein, Seal, and Schuster 1998). Ironically, the market incentive of academic capitalists is nonetheless simultaneously tied to the symbolic worth of reward-driven incentives.

At the same time that academic production is awarded market value, rewards for success in the academic marketplace have also taken on the symbolic worth of status and prestige. The "cost-benefit taxonomy" of the academic marketplace has classified externally funded, market-value research as the most credible of academic products, granting faculty who perform it advantaged professional standing and reputational eminence (Slaughter and Leslie 1997). But such prestige cannot be solely symbolic and free of productive characteristics in this scheme because it is an ancillary of academic production. Here, prestige garnered through the delivery of products (research that has market value as a response to incentives) takes on market value. In this scheme, prestige can be exchanged repeatedly in the academic research marketplace. Though typically a professionally symbolic condition, because it has been brought into the public sphere of the marketplace as collateral and credibility for trustworthy production, prestige leaves the realm of the symbolic and becomes tangible. Once tangible and associated solely with the productive processes, production prestige cannot be accessible to, or associated with, reproductive activities. Because compensatory reward ("merit pay") will understandably be tied to effective production, it stands to reason that external funding will be privileged over teaching in faculty reward policies.

The gender implications of compensatory rewards tied to effective production (research with market value) are evident when we look at the data on women faculty and teaching. Though teaching loads for women faculty are declining, women faculty across academic fields are oriented to teaching more than to research. Though the number of women faculty at research universities is growing, even in the male-dominated research fields women faculty dedicate more of their time to and are more engaged in teaching activities than are their male counterparts (Schuster and Finkelstein 2006). Thus, because rewards in the form of merit pay and even promotion in rank are tied to market-value production, women faculty seem prone to be disadvantaged.

Second, the transformation of the American research university into a corporate entity has created standards and benchmarks for faculty performance that feature quantifiable products or "output" measures like the number of refereed publications within a specific period of time. As the best measure of faculty productivity (Fairweather 1999), "publishing productivity"—the tally of the goods of productive processes (research)—provides a dubiously fair-minded record that encourages standardization and problematic differentiation. Capturing faculty production rate gives rise to expectations and yardsticks for production that reinforce faculty's worker status. Production rates, in this case the number of standard-bearing publications (refereed), can be predicted or expected much like we can calculate any expected output in a total product curve. Thus, the output for faculty production is the number of publications possible as a function of faculty time and/or other input variables. These expectations in production unavoidably become standards, and comparisons between professors become inevitable. Standardization of academic work, a logical deduction of work's Cartesian masculinity, motivates an adherence and loyalty to its measures that as Minnich (2005, 171) asserts, will "valorize a dominant tradition." Here the tradition is one that operates in an economy of gender in which publication excellence, as in all Cartesian measures, will be an exclusive domain of masculinity. Though the publication gap between men and women has narrowed (Schuster and Finkelstein 2006, 102), indicating that women successfully operate in this economy, it is nonetheless an economy that is gendered masculine. Simply put, more women faculty may be producing in the gendered (masculine) economy of academic production.

Unlike the reproductive activities of teaching and instruction, the productive processes of the faculty present the corporate, capitalistic university with (presumed) neutral measures that can be readily tabulated and assessed. For example, faculty at research universities average approximately four refereed articles per two-year period (Cataldi and Fahimi 2005, 33). Education faculties publish about half as much as engineering faculty, and women publish less than men (Fairweather 1999). But because of its inherent gendered epistemology, the faculties' instructional efficacy expressed either as an individual or collective output cannot deliver productivity norms and standards. Though higher education researchers and scholars have attempted to capture the epistemologically oxymoronic "instructional productivity" through objective measures like student classroom contact hours, time spent on teaching, and even ratios of instructional approaches (e.g., Fairweather 1999; Fairweather and Rhodes 1995; Layzell 1999), all admit failure in solving the essential dilemma that assessing teaching and learning presents: "the problem of capturing the intangible inputs and outputs" (Layzell 1999, 23). For example, the Higher Education Quality Control Commission in the United Kingdom has largely been abandoned because of the difficulty in constructing a measure that accurately assesses the quality of university teaching.[2] Attempts at post-tenure review have also experienced this predicament. As the aspect of faculty activity that most confounds and challenges efforts to measure faculty performance, teaching and learning relationships are the focal point of "intangible" reproductive processes in the university. Teaching and learning escape capture by productivity standards because they are by nature elusive, subtle, immaterial, and subjective. These processes resist normalization and standardization because they are unidentical and heterogeneous and are governed by the variability of relational effectiveness.

Frustrated by the impediments used by a gendered economy to measure instructional effectiveness/productivity, researchers, scholars, policymakers and institutional administrators have put forth efforts to appraise the "quality" of university teaching and learning. As an end run around the gendered epistemological constraints of productivity mandates, the rhetoric of "quality" is invoked as a way to create market value for faculty labor. If we were to somehow quantify the *quality* of instruction, if we were to convert or translate a reproductive process like teaching and learning to a production function like the number of classroom contact hours, effectively measuring the *quality of the contact by hours expended,* we could determine the market value of faculty instruction. The problems with such a conversion are many, however.

The problems begin and end with the difficulty of constructing an operational definition for teaching and learning, a highly subjective, complex, and intricate relationship. An operational definition will require a precise explanation of how the value for the teaching and learning relationship was derived. The definition must be authoritative and uniform, having no ambiguity to ensure that the same measure can be used by others to effect comparisons and correlations in the academic market economy. As such, we must control for variability within the measure or control for any and all inconsistencies in the teaching and learning relationship. But how can we standardize a highly individualized, relational activity like teaching, a highly particularized process like learning, as well as their *inter*dependence? Our inability to translate and convert reproductive labor to production work seems predictably discouraging and hopeless. The paradigmatic incongruity between production and reproduction as processes carried out by university faculties appears to deem fruitless any attempt to *account* for teaching and learning. It seems to me that we are at an epistemological impasse. Perhaps we need a conceptual matrix or an economy of gender consonant with reproductive processes in order to attend to its quality.

Teaching and Learning as a Gift Economy

The gift economy that I offer here as a theoretical beginning for the reconceptualization of faculty productivity as it relates to teaching and learning is an anthropological view of university teaching and learning (Martínez Alemán 2007). At the very least, the gift economy can capture conceptually the anthropology of the teaching-learning relationship and can serve as a reconciliation of the contradictions in the postulates of the academic market economy. Conceptualizing teaching and learning as gift economy gives us a means to recognize and comprehend the internal gender logic of these relationships, helping us to make sense of and enabling us to *attend* to its performance. This proposition is an ethnographic one; it demands that we allow for the complex contexts and meanings of behaviors in the teaching and learning relationship and that we seek to understand how it is performed and what it means to have performed it. It is a proposal for a view of faculty productivity that recognizes the gendered economy of teaching and learning.

Unlike the market economy of faculty productivity, the gift economy is a flight *to* the feminine and not a flight to the objectivity and price-value market that characterizes Cartesian market economies. Idiosyncratic, subjective, and symbolic, the gift economy deals in erotic commerce; it is an inter-relational activity that cannot be commodified and carries only symbolic worth. This gift economy, like Mauss's (1990 [1950]) rendering, is a system that generates relational commitments that consequently communicate the principles of intellectual traditions. The gift economy that I propose as a framework for attending to the ethnography of university teaching and learning is consistent with a gendered ontology that captures the feminine. Attuned to the needs of the actors as relational beings, the gift economy is not profit-driven but rather bears the marks of reciprocity and generosity that have only symbolic worth.

For teaching and learning to be understood and thus attended to as a gift economy requires

- that the identity or the biography of the participants is given significance
- that knowledge and its transmission (teaching and learning) is the gift
- that the gift is not consumed or commodified, that it has no market value and cannot be exchanged
- that no two gifts are the same or given in the same way
- that the worth of the gift is symbolic; that is, the gift has life beyond itself
- that the economy joins self and other (teacher and student) in erotic commerce
- that the economy of gift-giving is one in which gifts (knowledge) are circulated and consequently have symbolic worth beyond the original giving relationship
- that gift economies are not economies of exchange and that they are not economies of obligation (Martínez Alemán 2007).

What is posited here is that if we understand or construct an ethnographic account of university teaching and learning as gift-giving, we will be better able to observe, distinguish, and report those behaviors that are effective. An ethnography of teaching and learning as gift-giving allows us to detect if change has taken place as a consequence of the economy. If the gift (knowledge) carries the identity or pedagogical characteristics of the faculty and is received by the student—that is, the student accepts or learns the ideas transmitted in the gift—then we can say that the relationship (to this point in time) has functioned effectively (Martínez Alemán 2007).

To judge teaching and learning's economy, then, requires us to make sense of the symbolic meaning of the gift (knowledge), something that is intentionally subjective and particularized and is need-specific. Functionally altruistic (Vaughan 1997), teaching and learning operate in an association that is by design other-oriented and sympathetic. Gifts are given freely in the relationship; teachers give knowledge without the expectation of tangible or commodity reciprocity. Students don't pay for knowledge; it is given as gift. If students "paid" for faculty knowledge within the teaching-learning relationship, faculty would have to claim ownership of ideas, and ideas would then become property. Of course, the notion of ideas as property is consonant with current academic market economy. "Intellectual property" and "patent" claims are illustrative of academic capitalism's impulse to make tangible, or to make commodities of the intangible. Once knowledge is owned, once ideas are property, faculty can really give them away; they must sell or exchange the commodity in the marketplace. But what "price" does the transmission of knowledge bear? In other words, if I "sell" my knowledge, if I circulate my ideas in an exchange economy, what do I expect in return? Who is the buyer, and what is her obligation? What is the student's "debt" to me? Though students and perhaps parents as their fiduciary agents pay the university (in the form of tuition), this is an association of productive exchange coupled to reproductive giving as a matter of historic and material causes. The twenty-first-century student may be a "consumer" of higher education with relevant product "demands," but gifts (ideas, knowledge) cannot be regulated for tangible, productive uniformity. Perhaps the current "consumption" is really about the quantifiable products of the university—number of courses offered, number of faculty-contact hours, average class size, range of student activities and services, average time to degree, rates of completion, and nothing else.

What does it mean, then, to have performed in an economy of intangibles? What does it mean to give the gift (to teach effectively) and to receive the gift (to learn)? How can university academic administrators and faculty themselves assess the gift economy of instruction? How can we rightly appraise and take stock of instructional performance?

To assess a reproductive economy like teaching and learning, I suggest that we consider the appropriateness of ethnography and feminist ethnography in particular. As an economy of gift that incorporates the relational activities of teaching and learning, a method that is consonant with teaching and learning's gendered character is necessary. University teaching and learning demands a method of evaluation that can capture the meaning of these reproductive processes in a language that is conceptually harmonious with the economy of gender in which it circulates. Feminist ethnography appears a suitable methodological choice for this task since its primary goal is to present an emic, careful, and exhaustive description of events.

A view of processes and their effects—or in this case, an examination of the reproductive process of teaching and its result, learning—feminist ethnographic practice holds promise as a method for assessing faculty teaching performance in that
it is not paradigmatically constrained by Cartesian logic. Collecting data through
targeted means such as open-ended questions of participants and "participatory
action" (Hesse-Biber and Nagy 2006; Behar 1993; Fals-Borda and Rahman 1991),
this type of ethnography allows for the subjective claims of reproductive processes,
most importantly, the relationship's symbolic worth. An ethnographic view of the
gift economy of teaching and learning will employ the participation of those who
may be affected by the outcomes of the assessment—faculty and students.

But like all feminist ethnographic endeavors, assessment of teaching and learning is extremely time-consuming and labor-intensive and cannot provide the comparative scales of experience that we are accustomed to in the academic market
economy. To be truly capable of describing and assessing the gendered economy of
teaching and learning; to explain the details specifically as well as broadly; to thickly
describe the teaching habits, behaviors, and strategies that faculty employ; to elu-
cidate and reveal the meanings that derive from the interactions between teacher
and student in the gift economy; to catalogue this day-by-day, course-by-course,
student-by-student, demands much more than higher education's corporate ethos
of efficiency can accept. Longitudinal, narrative-driven, "value-added," portfolio-
based, and case-specific, these ethnographies of feminine economies will be unlikely to appeal to the corporate university.

Conclusions

Recently, the Federal Commission on the Future of Higher Education released
a report that outlines its specific findings and recommendations on American postsecondary education. Though concerned primarily with issues of access and financing, the commission's report cites evidence that colleges and universities "make no
serious effort to examine their effectiveness on the most important measure of all:
how students learn" (U.S. Government 2006, 6). In the same report, the commission warns that colleges and universities do not "seek institutional effectiveness"
and have "disregard for improving productivity" (5) but suggests that institutions
through state policy boards should require "aggregate summary results of all postsecondary learning measures" (22). Test scores, certification, and licensure attainment, degree completion and graduation rates, along with "other relevant measures" (22) constitute the aggregate summaries.

In this report two things seem obvious to me. First, the economy of teaching and learning employed by the federal government via the Commission on the Future of Higher Education is a market-economy directive, a policy informed by a gendered economy of masculinity incapable of truly representing "the quality of instruction and learning" that the commission demands (22). Using measures scripted by a gendered economy of masculinity such as the Measure of Academic Proficiency and Progress (MAPP), the data gathered and measures calculated by institutions will say little, if anything, about how and why faculty teach and how and why students learn.[3] Second, in its recommendations the commission calls for an academic "bottom line" that will enable consumers (state governments and in-dividual tuition payers) to see institutional results in the areas of "academic qual-ity, productivity, and efficiency" (20). In a gendered academic economy, these three conditions are particularly incongruous with the call for an assessment of instruc-tion and student learning.

Judging by this report and its directives, the "unfinished agenda" in faculty pro-ductivity and accountability remains the specter of gender. Arguably, the more the university directs its efforts to operating like a corporation in a market economy, the more it makes every effort to function like a corporate entity, the more we will obscure and be unable to appraise the reproductive processes that best capture its educational mission. To invest in a gendered economy of femininity in order to attend to, and thus "account" for, teaching and learning is a costly one for institu-tions, fiscally and culturally. The costs of implementing ethnographies of teaching and learning effectiveness contradict institutional incentives to reduce the costs of instruction. More problematic is the cultural shift that an investment in ethnogra-phies of teaching and learning entails—the move away from a gendered economy of productivity toward an economy of reproduction. But because faculty produc-tivity is a function of two competing gendered economies, of two contradictory intellectual paradigms, remaking measures of faculty performance means that we must develop, appreciate, and support an accountability bilingualism of sorts, an impure separation of faculties' reproductive and productive processes, and trans-late their meanings accordingly. This is the challenge of the academic profession and the unfinished agenda of gender in the academy.

NOTES

1. The term "erotic" used in this discussion is related to the Platonic connotation of the love of ideas and knowledge carried by persons. Here "eros" is used to describe the quality of knowledge-seeking that faculty and students possess. Later in the chapter, I discuss "erotic com-

merce" in this very light.

2. See, for example, www.aua.ac.uk/publications/conferenceproceedings/2002southampton/rogerbrown.htm.

3. See Measure of Academic Proficiency and Progress (MAPP) online at www.ets.org.

REFERENCES

Apple, Michael. 1986. *Teachers and texts: A political economy of class and gender relations in education.* New York: Routledge and Kegan Paul.

Behar, Ruth. 1993. *Translated woman: Crossing the border with Esperanza's story.* Boston: Beacon Press.

Bordo, Susan. 1987. *The flight to objectivity: Essays on Cartesianism and culture.* Albany: State University of New York Press.

Cataldi, E. F., and M. Fahimi. 2005. *2004 National Study of Postsecondary Faculty (NSOPF:04). Background characteristics, work activities, and compensation of instructional faculty and staff: Fall 2003,* table 23. Washington, D.C.: National Center for Education Statistics. Retrieved on 10/5/2007 from http://nces.ed.gov/das/library/tables_listings/2006176.asp.

Clark, Burton. 1998. *Creating entrepreneurial universities: Organizational pathways of transformation.* Oxford: Pergamon.

Code, Lorraine. 1991. *What can she know? Feminist theory and the construction of knowledge.* Ithaca, NY: Cornell University Press.

Diamond, Robert M. 1999. *Aligning faculty awards with institutional mission: Statements, policies and guidelines.* Boston: Anker Publishing.

Fairweather, James S. 1996. *Faculty work and public trust: Restoring the value of teaching and public service in American academic life.* Boston: Allyn and Bacon.

———. 1999. The highly productive faculty member: Confronting the mythologies of faculty work. In *Faculty productivity: Facts, fictions, and issues,* ed. William G. Tierney, 55–98. New York: Falmer Press.

Fairweather, James S., and Robert A. Rhoads. 1995. Teaching and the faculty role: Enhancing the commitment to instruction in American colleges and universities. *Education Evaluation and Policy Analysis* 17:179–94.

Fals-Borda, Orlando, and Muhammad Anisur Rahman, eds. 1991. *Action and knowledge: Breaking the monopoly with participatory action research.* New York: Apex Press.

Finkelstein, Martin J., Robert K. Seal, and Jack Schuster. 1998. *The new academic generation: A profession in transition.* Baltimore: Johns Hopkins University Press.

Goodman, Robin Truth. 2004. *World, class, women: Global literature, education and literature.* New York: Routledge-Falmer Press.

Gould, Eric. 2003. *The university in a corporate culture.* New Haven: Yale University Press.

Grumet, Madeleine. 1988. *Bitter milk: Women and teaching.* Amherst: University of Massachusetts Press.

Hesse-Biber, Sharlene N., and Patricia L. Nagy, eds. 2006. *Emergent methods in social research.* Thousand Oaks, CA: Sage Publications.

Hopkins, David S. P. 1990. The higher education production function: Theoretical foundations and empirical findings. In *The economics of American universities: Management, operations, and fiscal environment,* ed. S. A. Hoenack and E. I. Collins, 11–32. Albany: State University of New York Press.

Hopkins, David S. P., and William F. Massey. 1981. *Planning models for colleges and universities.* Stanford, CA: Stanford University Press.

Jencks, Christopher, and David Riesman 1968. *The academic revolution.* Garden City, NY: Doubleday.

Layzell, Daniel T. 1999. Higher education's changing environment: Faculty productivity and the reward structure. In *Faculty productivity: Facts, fictions, and issues,* ed. William G. Tierney, 3–38. New York: Falmer Press.

Martin, Jane Roland. 1985. *Reclaiming a conversation: The ideal of the educated woman.* New Haven: Yale University Press.

Martínez Alemán, Ana M. 2007. The nature of the gift: Accountability and the professor-student relationship. *Educational Philosophy and Theory* 39 (6): 574–91.

Mauss, Marcel. 1990 [1950]. *The gift: The form and reason for exchange in archaic societies.* New York: W. W. Norton.

Middaugh, Michael F. 2001. *Understanding faculty productivity: Standards and benchmarks for faculty productivity.* San Francisco: Jossey-Bass.

Minnich, Elizabeth Kamarck. 2005. *Transforming knowledge,* 2nd ed. Philadelphia: Temple University Press.

Nicholson, Linda. 1980. Women and schooling. *Educational Theory* 30 (3): 225–34.

Schuster, Jack H., and Martin J. Finkelstein. 2006. *The American faculty: The restructuring of academic work and careers.* Baltimore: Johns Hopkins University Press.

Slaughter, Sheila, and Larry L. Leslie. 1997. *Academic capitalism: Politics, policies and the entrepreneurial university.* Baltimore: Johns Hopkins University Press.

Slaughter, Sheila, and Gary Rhoades. 2006. The neo-liberal university. *New Labor Forum* (spring/summer): 73–79.

Thurow, Lester C. 1996. *The future of capitalism: How today's economic forces shape tomorrow's world.* New York: William Morrow.

Tong, Rosemarie. 1989. *Feminist thought: A comprehensive introduction.* Boulder, CO: Westview Press.

U.S. Government, Department of Education. 2006. *Secretary of Education's Commission on the Future of Higher Education Draft Report.* Retrieved 7/29/2006 from www.ed.gov/about/bdscomm/list/hiedfuture/index.html.

Vaughan, Genevieve. 1997. *For-giving: Feminist criticism of exchange.* Austin, TX: Plain View Press.

CHAPTER SEVEN

Women and the College Presidency

RITA BORNSTEIN

Despite the gains of recent years, women remain significantly underrepresented in top government, corporate, and higher education leadership positions in the United States. Chile, Finland, Germany, Great Britain, India, Ireland, Israel, Liberia, Pakistan, and the Philippines have had women heads of state, while Americans still debate about "whether women have the right hormones, the right brains, the right motivation or the right abilities to take on the challenges of the modern world" (Barnett and Rivers 2006). Although women have made considerable progress in all domains, that progress is slow, tenuous, and limited by the intractability of gendered organizational structures, perspectives, and expectations.

This chapter assesses twenty-first-century challenges to the steady movement of women into the higher education presidency. These formidable challenges include pipeline inadequacies, barriers to the legitimacy of women presidents, and leading in a turbulent external environment. I conclude the chapter with recommendations for unclogging the pipeline to the presidency, de-gendering our expectations for the presidency, and redefining leadership appropriate to the twenty-first century.

As we move through this rapidly changing, diverse, global, market-driven, high-technology era, traditional hierarchical, bureaucratic, and segmented organizations are increasingly obsolete. Those using old management models are under pressure to become more flexible, nimble, responsive, and innovative. The global competition for new ideas, new products, new markets, new technologies, and new capital requires new types of organizations characterized by a high level of trust and reciprocity within the workforce: collaborative, team-centered, with permeable boundaries.

Higher-education institutions are typically less bureaucratic and more egalitarian than most corporations and are thus better positioned to serve as models of collaboration, teamwork, and consensus-based decision making. Such models, however, should also demonstrate inclusiveness, which would mean eradicating the organizational biases and structures that limit the options of women. (The options for gay women and women of color are especially limited.) Through the advent of feminist scholarship, women and men have begun to understand that the taken-for-granted ways of leading are gender-specific, based on a traditionally masculine organizational environment. As longtime outsiders in academe, women have used their marginality to see, understand, and describe the male-normed culture. Men have dominated social institutions for so long that, according to Duerst-Lahti and Kelly, "masculine assumptions underpin the norms that become normal in social relations. So, when women enter and act within the realm of leadership and governance, they do so within ideological terms of masculine norms" (1995, 20). By identifying, acknowledging, and eliminating the structural and cultural impediments to women's leadership, higher-education institutions can, indeed, serve as models of the new twenty-first-century organization.

New organizational systems require new approaches to leadership. Although men dominate the leadership of higher education, we are beginning to understand that women, whose experiences tend to make them adaptable, creative, and relational, offer skills especially well suited to leading within the new organizational structures. Indvik reviews numerous studies suggesting that women leaders' preferred style of cooperative leadership "provides a good fit with the evolving requirements for 21st-century global leadership" (2001, 222–23). Oakley believes that, given the trend toward flatter organizations and team-based management, women's "interactive" styles may represent an important new approach to leadership (2000, 327). It properly falls to the academy, given its values of equity, excellence, and innovation, to redefine leadership for this new era and to demonstrate new pathways for identifying, preparing, and supporting women and people of color for the presidency of postsecondary institutions.

Women have made progress over the past thirty-five years. According to a survey by the Center for Policy Analysis of the American Council on Education, by 2006, 23 percent of college presidents were women, up from less than 10 percent in 1986 (Center for Policy Analysis 2007, 15), and women now preside at several large and prestigious universities. However, the trends are mixed. The number of women leading two-year colleges has increased rapidly, up from 8 percent in 1986 to 29 percent in 2006, but progress has been slower at other types of institutions (15–16). The proportion of minority presidents, both women and men, increased from 8 percent of all presidents in 1986 to 14 percent in 2006, and a higher proportion of minority than non-minority presidents are women: more than one-third of Hispanic and nearly one-third of African-American presidents, compared with 22 percent of white presidents, are women. Overall, however, minority women comprise just 4 percent of all presidents (19–20).

Although the representation of women in the presidency is far short of the percentage of students, faculty, and administrators, it is an important advance over women's scant representation in higher education in the early 1970s when, with the exception of the Catholic women's colleges, women headed no four-year coeducational institutions and just eight nonsectarian women's colleges (Carnegie Commission 1973, 123).

So is the glass half full or half empty? Will the numbers of women presidents continue to grow, or will they remain static, even decline? Has the glass ceiling in higher education been penetrated permanently, or have women been given a temporary pass to the executive suite? Glazer-Raymo takes a negative stance: "Unfortunately, commonly held beliefs about the glass ceiling underestimate its impermeability" (1999, 197). Despite the gains women have made, we may well be at a crossroads where the momentum could go in either direction.

It is helpful to locate the question of women's advancement into the top jobs in academe in a wider context. Similar obstacles impede women in other sectors of the American workforce, and as I noted earlier, social anxiety and biases inhibit election of a woman to the U.S. presidency. Women face these biases in the corporate world, and thus many who bump up against the glass ceiling leave to form their own companies. Oakley reports that between 1975 and 1990 women entrepreneurs started businesses at twice the rate of men (2000, 330).

In the legal world, although women represent half of law school graduates and of new associates hired, they "disappear" before they reach the upper tiers of law firms. In 2005, women were just 17 percent of partners at major law firms, up slightly from 13 percent in 1995. The barriers to women's making partner include the lack of mentoring and networking, family responsibilities, and dissatisfaction with the "billable hours" regime (O'Brien 2006). In the religious sector, women now make up 51 percent of students in divinity schools, but after they are ordained their careers lag far behind those of their male counterparts. Protestant clergywomen hit a "stained-glass ceiling" that restricts them to small or dying congregations and allows just a minuscule number to lead large congregations. Parishioners simply cannot accept women as religious authority figures (Banerjee 2006). Barriers to women's advancement are similar in many occupations, including the higher-education presidency.

Pipeline Inadequacies

The overwhelming number of higher-education presidents and even association heads are still men, despite the fact that female presidents are now successfully leading all types of institutions. While the gains are impressive, there is no certainty that the numbers will be sustained or grow. The impediments to women's motivation and preparation for the presidency are unsurprising in a system that structurally and culturally privileges men.

In part, this is a pipeline issue. Women are underrepresented in senior faculty and administrative positions, resulting in far fewer women than men in candidate pools for presidencies. In its December 3, 2004, edition, the *Chronicle of Higher Education* reported that although women earn 51 percent of all Ph.D.s, they comprise only 38 percent of college and university faculties and just 28 percent of the faculties at research institutions. In America's elite universities, women comprise less than 30 percent of professors and 40 percent of assistant professors (Wilson 2004).

Not only are there fewer women eligible for presidencies, but many female candidates are passed over because of their nontraditional backgrounds. Family obligations take many women off the career track for a time, resulting in a professional disadvantage. Since women remain the primary caregivers in our society, it is not surprising that considerably more men than women presidents are married (89 to 63 percent) and more men have children (91 to 68 percent) (Center for Policy Analysis 2007, 72). Some qualified women, lacking mentoring and relevant experience, feel under-prepared and simply do not apply. In an interview, Alice Eagly, professor of psychology at Northwestern University comments: "The anticipation of gender prejudice causes many women to hesitate to apply for higher-level positions until their qualifications are exceedingly good—in fact, better than those of the men who apply" (*Harmony* 1998, 110). Many presidents, both women and men, feel they were under prepared for the position, exposing a need for more systematic training and mentoring (Bornstein 2005). Women in particular suffer from a lack of support, encouragement, mentoring, training, and visibility. Experienced mentors can help women overcome obstacles to advancement and decide when to seek a presidency. Women in every field lack mentors, but those who do have mentoring are more likely to achieve top positions. In a survey of 91 women presidents, Brown found that the majority had mentors, some as many as three or four, who "assisted their move up the administrative ladder" (2005, 663).

Because of their slower career trajectories and the desire to be perceived as extremely well qualified, women often seek their first presidencies at an older age than do men. This delay may inhibit their seeking a second presidency. Since 21 percent of presidencies are filled with sitting presidents (Center for Policy Analysis 2007, 10), the pool of experienced women candidates is further limited. Another pipeline problem limits the available pool of minority candidates for the presidency. George Vaughan, professor of higher education at North Carolina State University, who conducted a survey revealing stagnation in the percentage of minority community college presidents, is quoted as saying: "As long as you have 90 percent of presidents with doctorates and you don't have minorities in graduate schools, you're not going to fill the vacancies. They just aren't in the pipeline" (Ashburn 2006). Another factor constricting the pool of people of color is their concentration in dead-end staff positions such as affirmative action or human relations officer rather than in career track positions such as dean or vice president.

In a large-scale survey of presidents conducted by the *Chronicle of Higher Education,* more women presidents than men, 46.3 percent compared to 28.5 percent, had previously served as a provost or chief academic officer (*Chronicle* 2005). In the 2006 ACE survey, the percentage of women presidents who had been senior academic affairs officers had increased to 53 percent (Center for Policy Analysis 2007, 16). Because this is the traditional stepping-stone to a presidency, especially for women, it is of concern that women academic vice presidents are ambivalent about or even averse to the presidency. According to a survey of 657 women academic vice presidents conducted by Diane Dean (2003), 63 percent did not desire a presidency. Of this group, 73 percent felt they could secure a presidency if they wanted one. This finding indicates that although these highly accomplished women do not want the presidency, it is not because they lack self-confidence. It is worth noting, however, that some women chief academic officers indicated that, despite their resistance to the presidency, reassurance, confidence, and "encouragement from the right people might change their minds" (2003, 17–18).

Some women do not aspire to a presidency because they prefer to remain close to the academic heart of the institution, and according to Dean, they have an aversion to fundraising and external socializing, and they want "to have a life" (2003, 10, 14). Although we do not have comparable data about male provosts' aspirations for the presidency, we do know that many, if not most women provosts have already spent much of their professional lives trying to balance family and work responsibilities in organizations that tend not to value or support activities in the private sphere. Women provosts are keenly aware that women presidents often earn less and juggle more responsibilities than men in comparable positions.

For example, in her dissertation, Steinke reports that of the women presidents she interviewed, the one with young children had instructed her office that unless someone at the college was dying, she did not want to be disturbed at home. She also explained how she planned her family's weekly schedule:

> "I'm super highly organized. I have a family calendar, and I do it on Sundays and I have a nanny and a housekeeper and an ex-husband and two kids and tutors, and I just do the master calendar on Sunday and everybody gets a copy, and it stays on the counter in the kitchen, and if you got to change something, you change that and let me know. It's very detailed." (2006, 115, 164–65)

Another obstacle to women's achieving presidencies resides in the search process itself. Although search committees today are generally 50 percent male and 50 percent female, boards are male dominated. Many men and women feel more comfortable selecting male leaders, especially when few women are in the candidate pool and many of those have had nontraditional professional careers. While there is no clear trend, some search committees and boards may feel virtuous about having already had a woman as president and feel free to revert to men with whose personal characteristics, leadership style, and experiences they feel most comfortable.

Barriers to the Legitimacy of Women Presidents

The presidency presents formidable challenges to all incumbents, but women face special hurdles in gaining acceptance and legitimacy from their constituents (Bornstein forthcoming). According to Hollander and Julian, stakeholders accord legitimacy to a leader they view as a good fit with the institutional culture and competent "in helping the group achieve its goals" (1978, 118, 148). Constituents generally judge cultural fit and good leadership based on their experience with previous presidents and leaders. Even the most well-qualified and experienced women presidents are impeded by models, values, and expectations based on male norms.

In the essentially masculine work culture of higher education, women presidents and their constituents (boards, faculties, students, alumni, community leaders) have limited, if any, experience with women in top leadership positions. As a result, all parties have stereotyped expectations for their relationships. Nonetheless, women leaders who fit into the culture and exhibit technical competence in managing their institutions have a good chance of being accepted by constituents. In her study of women managers in fourteen federal agencies, Rusaw (1996) found that when these women demonstrated technical competency they earned legitimacy, overcame gender bias, and gained management positions.

Among other things, technical competence in the higher-education presidency involves four areas related to finances: managing the budget; raising philanthropic dollars; lobbying legislators for government support; and, when feasible, developing commercial ventures. The financial arena has traditionally been the purview of men, and even today there are few women chief financial officers. In the ACE survey of presidents, women reported themselves "insufficiently prepared" to deal with financial and fund-raising matters far more often than did their male counterparts (Center for Policy Analysis 2007, 81). Women presidents must remedy these handicaps and overcome the stereotypes that they are users, not managers of money, and consumers, not generators of resources. They must also demonstrate their competence in handling legal affairs, which bedevil presidents in all types of institutions. Because the president, along with the board, has the fiduciary and legal responsibility for the institution, judicious oversight of its financial and legal affairs is vital to presidential legitimacy.

Women of color face both gender- and race-normed expectations that give rise to even more complex challenges. After interviewing twelve African-American female college presidents, Waring wrote: "The majority reported that they felt they have to take more time talking with people and thinking about their presentation of self and ideas because of their race and their gender" (2003, 40). She concludes that understanding the "identity" of leaders, along with their skill sets, will help us understand how their personal histories influence their conceptions of leadership (42–43).

Ruth Simmons, the first African-American president of Brown University, serves as a good example of the impact of identity on leadership. Simmons's identity is based, in part, on her being the descendant of slaves, which inspired her to lead an inquiry into the university's involvement with slavery. She has also broken barriers for women: while president of Smith College, she established the first women's college engineering program and founded a magazine for minority women.

Gendered expectations present special challenges to those who are the first woman president in their institutions. Steinke (2006) interviewed six first-time women presidents for her dissertation on "firstness." For these women gender did not seem to be an impediment, but it was a "shadow" over their effectiveness: "Being the first person in any category often brings more scrutiny from constituents, raises questions about a woman's ability to perform well in a role that has always been done by men, and . . . points to the need for higher standards in order to hold any doubts at bay. Gender has a shadow-like effect on the presidency that is often unnoticed until an anomaly, or a difference for either good or ill, occurs" (2006, 181–82).

It is at the point of entry, notes Freeman, that women are blocked by "entrenched perceptions and cognitions associating leadership with maleness" (2001, 39). As

Hollander (1992, 72) observes, "Women begin with an initial hurdle to attaining legitimacy" resulting from "the effect of expectations about a prototype." Glazer-Raymo points out that those who are invited to participate in the system are expected to "adapt to existing institutional norms" (1999, 196–97). A case in point is Dr. Tessa Martinez Pollak, the first Hispanic president of Our Lady of the Lake University in San Antonio, Texas, who says: "When you're the first, there's enormous pressure to defy stereotypes. You have to overcome doubt that you'll be able to accomplish something. You always have to prove yourself and reverse doubt" (Gardner 2006, 15).

Women new to the presidency often behave and lead in ways congruent with male-normed expectations. According to Oakley: "In the almost all-male world of upper management . . . women are forced to change their linguistic style to a more command-oriented form in order to be perceived as strong, decisive and in control" and to behave with authority and decisiveness (2000, 325). Women are careful not to dress or speak in too feminine a style that might be construed as weak, ineffective, or even incompetent. In a study of the impact of gender and sexuality on leadership in Australia, Sinclair (2005, 178) notes that women "camouflage" their gender and sexuality by avoiding overt displays of femininity in their dress, speech, associations, and behavior. Women leaders also may downplay their interest in issues related to women and feminism. Nannerl O. Keohane did not make women's and family issues a priority when she became president of Duke University because she wanted "to be taken seriously as a major player." Aware of those who suspected that a woman could not "run the place," she waited until her last years when she had the "prestige and clout to turn to women's issues" (2006, 198–99).

By contrast, says Sinclair, men nourish their identities and validate their power and self-importance by trying to conform to an ideal of "heroic" leadership. They work Herculean schedules and avoid spending time at home with their family that they find "terrifying" (2005, 45). In fact, successful men often thank their wives publicly for supporting their careers by single-handedly running their households and raising their children. These men consider the public sphere to be masculine and the private sphere the domain of women. Sinclair notes that the behaviors of male and female executives flow from the continuing identification of executive leadership with "a tough stoicism, a rejection of the sentimental and the feminine" (2005, 177).

Without question, all leaders must exude confidence, assertiveness, and decisiveness in order to give constituents a sense of comfort and security. They also cannot publicly second-guess their decisions. Men are more likely than women to have been socialized into these behaviors. Stereotypically male behavior is associated with competence, and feminine behavior with weakness and incompetence (Oakley 2000, 326). In the words of one president who was the first woman in the role: "I think that people want to be assured that I'm not too soft—that I'm tough enough to do the job . . . make tough decisions and have fiscal discipline. And in actuality, I'm fine in all of those things, but I need to figure out how to convey that" (Steinke 2006, 81). In time, successful presidents learn which behaviors are appropriate in which situations. For example, a president may act unilaterally to dismiss a staff member based on evidence of criminal misconduct. On the other hand, a president must act collaboratively to develop an institutional strategic plan.

One first-time president who never had a chance to establish her legitimacy was Denice Denton, Chancellor of the University of California, Santa Cruz. Denton was one of the first openly lesbian presidents, and she endured constant criticism from the moment she was appointed. She was attacked for her sexual orientation, her appearance, her own and her partner's compensation; for improvements to the president's house; for being too liberal; and for being too conservative. Denton had little prior administrative experience and was unable to handle the unremitting criticism. In the second year of her presidency, she jumped to her death from the roof of a forty-four-story building. She seems to have been underprepared for the exceptional challenges she faced, and she lacked an adequate support system (Fain 2007).

Women who preside or aspire to preside over institutions with medical schools and Division I athletic programs face especially challenging legitimacy hurdles. These high-cost, high-maintenance programs have vocal boosters and detractors who require a great deal of a president's attention and tend to be uncomfortable dealing with women executives. The high-profile problems arising in both areas garner intense media and public scrutiny.

Male executives in the corporate world have few opportunities to work with executive women. As a result, the roughly 80 percent of higher-education governing board members who are men have difficulty in knowing how to interact with a woman president. The greater percentage of women on community college boards may help explain the growing number of women presidents in that sector. Male presidents are more likely than female presidents to build strong bonds with board members by joining them for golf and other recreational activities as well as for vacations. The lack of these natural opportunities for networking and relationship building requires that women use professionally and institutionally related interactions to build comfortable, trusting, and reciprocal relationships with male trustees. The same is true in developing relationships with senior male faculty.

The pathways women presidents find to creating these important relationships lack the spontaneity and authenticity inherent in relationships outside of the executive role. In fact, to be considered legitimate and effective, college and university presidents must actually relinquish some of their authenticity. Authenticity is what distinguishes each individual from others; it expresses a person's unique self. An individual's private (authentic) self may be somewhat different from her or his public persona, and the two may become blurred. Managing this double life is particularly challenging for many women and men, who seek to remain true to themselves without compromise. This commitment to authentic behavior is problematic because "the need to act as the embodiment of the institution diminishes the president's individualism" (Bornstein 2004). Says one female president: "In a sense, you're not even a person . . . many of your duties are not really about a person, they are about a construct or a role, and that's a big difference from anything else you do" (Steinke 2006, 140). The presidency imposes constraints on the incumbent's speech and action that are anathema to some otherwise high-potential candidates.

A number of scholars link authenticity with good leadership. Cashman (1997) considers authenticity the "foundation of leadership." Naddaff reports on research that provides evidence of "a real link between authenticity and increased leadership effectiveness" (2005, 302). Cashman believes that true leaders must share their "real thoughts and feelings" (1997), but the college presidency inhibits the incumbent's free expression of ideas and involvement in activities such as partisan politics. Goleman and colleagues assert that "the art of handling relationships well . . . begins with authenticity: acting from one's genuine feelings" (2002, 51). However, a president's relationships with constituents, unlike real friendships, may be considered inauthentic because they are freighted with the president's hidden agenda. With a prospect, it may be the need to solicit a gift; with a trustee, to secure approval for a policy change; with a faculty member, to win support for cost containment measures. Many successful presidents dislike what they perceive as the phoniness inherent in these relationships but maintain a strong personal sense of identity and integrity despite the compromises they make in enacting the presidency. Those who retain a hold on their authentic selves despite these compromises have a sense of humility about the presidency, value their private lives, and encourage honest feedback from their colleagues, friends, and spouses. They also cultivate a sense of humor, including the ability to laugh at themselves.

Once in a presidency, women are less likely to wrap their identities totally within their institutional role because they must balance the personal and professional aspects of their lives. This ongoing balancing act makes the lives of women multidimensional, thus preparing them for a graceful and timely exit from the presidency. Experience with multiple roles also suggests that women are more likely than men to be comfortable in returning to a professorship or accepting a non-leadership position. In their quest for acceptance and legitimacy, one area of authenticity that women administrators often ignore is the recognition of sisterhood across positions and rank as well as among colleagues from other institutions and sectors. Such relationships among women can be nourishing, instructive, and authentic. As one woman president said: "I'm in a group of executive women— women CEOs that do what I do—and that has been one of the best groups that I've been a part of, because they all have their own companies and they all have their own issues. They're my peers . . . the number one piece of advice that I would give that I didn't know—is that you've got to find peers fast to hold you up that have nothing to do with your college" (Steinke 2006, 112).

Leading in a Turbulent External Environment

Many studies find no difference in the leadership effectiveness of women and men (Freeman 2001, 33, 38; Hollander 1992, 72; Birnbaum 1992, 44, 46; Kabacoff 2000, 4). Other studies have found women leaders to be more generative, interactive, consultative, relational, empowering, and connected than male leaders (Rosener 1990, 120; Bensimon 1993, 472; Rusaw 1996; Jablonski 2000, 245). Birnbaum concedes: "If gender differences are critical to the ways in which we experience and make sense of the social world . . . there may be an important relationship between gender and leadership" (1992, 43). Rosener says that women's "interactive" leadership style encourages participation, shares power and information, enhances other people's self-worth, and gets others excited about their work (1990, 120). Women, however, have found that "feminine" leadership behaviors are both desired and denigrated by their constituents. Jablonski points out that both male and female faculty are conflicted about their desire for a "participatory" yet "strong, aggressive" style of leadership (2000, 249). This conflict disadvantages women presidents. When they exhibit a caring, consultative style, they are called weak and indecisive; when they adopt traditional authoritarian and directive behaviors, they are criticized for being too heavy-handed.

In her study of six female design engineers, Fletcher (1999) found that certain behaviors, characterized by empathy, mutuality, reciprocity, and sensitivity to emotional contexts, "get disappeared" because they are seen as feminine and are not associated with workplace competence. She reminds us that in today's environment these traditionally feminine, private-sphere behaviors are increasingly associated with organizational effectiveness, along with the traditional male, public-sphere attributes of technical competence, autonomous action, competitiveness, and linear thinking. Fletcher calls for an integration of feminine and masculine traits and practices. Such a change would involve the recognition that relational practices are important workplace competencies in an era when organizations are being encouraged "to reinvent themselves, push decision making to lower levels, encourage teamwork and collaboration, flatten the hierarchy, and think systemically" (1999, 3, 4, 29, 84, 113, 114).

There is growing evidence that while both men and women are perceived as effective leaders, women's leadership style tends to be more adaptive, relational, and committed to democratic participation, collaboration, teamwork, and consensus building. Many of these abilities emerge naturally from the complicated lives women lead as mothers, wives, and workers: juggling multiple responsibilities, adapting to interruptions in their careers, responding to emergencies, and developing sensitivity to emotional cues. Kabacoff, in a study of male and female corporate CEOs and senior vice presidents, found that men were seen as "more restrained in emotional expression" and women as more emotionally expressive, energetic, and intense, with a greater interpersonal orientation (2000, 4). Women may also have more "emotional intelligence," defined by Goleman (1995, 34) as the ability to control impulsiveness, persist in the face of frustrations, regulate one's moods, and empathize with others.

Bateson asserts that "women have always lived discontinuous and contingent lives" and that their traditional adaptations should be seen as a resource. They have the "ability to shift from one preoccupation to another, to divide [their] attention, [and] to improvise in new circumstances" (1990, 13). Helgesen (1990) offers a compelling metaphor for women's ways of leading. Based on her observational study of four successful women executives, she reports that they led from within an organizational "web of inclusion." These women created a model much like a spider's web, with themselves in the center of things—a model quite different from the traditional hierarchical, top-down model of leadership. The interrelated web-like structure enhanced the flow of information and communication and resulted in stronger relationships and better teamwork. It in no way diminished the leader's authority. Helgesen suggests that this way of leading is "more suited to the information age than the hierarchical structure," which was more appropriate in the industrial era (1990, 50–58).

One of the presidents in Steinke's study reported: "I think my style is different than any of my male predecessors . . . much more participatory, much more listening oriented, much more relational. All those things are associated with sort of stereotypical female ways of acting and interacting. People notice that difference" (2006, 86).

Another said: "I've grown in my understanding of how critical it is to nurture a team of leaders. I knew to some extent, but not nearly to the extent I now know the importance of cultivating and calling out and enabling a team of leaders for the institution. That is because [of] the kind of president I am. I mean, I'm not a single figurehead type of president" (2006, 144).

The relational emphasis that women bring to the higher-education workplace is essential for promoting social capital, a vital mix of trust and reciprocity that characterizes healthy and successful organizations. Rusaw (1996) considers trust "an essential leadership skill" necessary "for successful and effective task completion."

Leadership is often dichotomized as transformational (charismatic, visionary, authoritative) or transactional (collegial, interactive, and collaborative). Typically, men are identified with a strong, visionary, top-down transformational style and women with an inclusive, participative style, although many scholars believe these styles represent a continuum of behaviors that leaders can apply as appropriate to the situations in which they find themselves (Northouse 2001, 135; Hollander 1987, 7). In a 2000 survey of 377 presidents, almost 50 percent of respondents considered themselves transformational, but of those, 71 percent said that most presidents are transactional (Bornstein 2003, 98–99). Presidents, overwhelmingly male, tend to devalue transactional leadership.

Women presidents are more likely than men to take an adaptive and situational approach to leadership. When asked if they saw themselves as transformational or transactional in leadership style, 41 percent of female respondents to the survey indicated that they are both transformational *and* transactional as compared with just 25 percent of the male presidents (Bornstein 2007). These women did not consider transformational and transactional leadership as dichotomous, but rather as styles that can be employed as appropriate. I have called this adaptive, situational approach to leadership "transformative" and well suited to the demands of the presidency (Bornstein 2003, 97–100). According to Alice Eagly, there is no one generally effective leadership style. "Some situations," she says, "call for a more autocratic, directive style, and others call for a much greater component of communication, consensus building, and participation. . . . The ideal leader therefore would shift from one style to another, after an astute sizing up of the style that would be optimal in each situation" (*Harmony* 1998, 108).

The key leadership competencies of interaction, collaboration, and consensus building are necessary if a university or college is to be responsive to increasing economic pressures and changing student needs. Curricular and pedagogical change in academic institutions cannot be imposed from the boardroom or executive suite but requires substantial constituent involvement. A high level of involvement is also required to avoid rancor in the implementation of cost containment and reorganization initiatives. Presidents in this era, both women and men, must be resilient, adaptable, and creative leaders, able to inspire trust and collaboration while juggling a myriad of external as well as internal responsibilities. In addition to building the quality, reputation, and financial health of their institutions, presidents must participate in community and economic development initiatives and deal with the challenges of global competition, market forces, and ever-changing technologies.

The seemingly insatiable quest of presidents for new revenue and enhanced reputation is the inevitable result of competition, soaring costs, and the continuing decline in government financial support. The seductions of the global marketplace are beginning to eclipse traditional academic values. Several university presidents are generating revenue by allowing a for-profit corporation to digitize all of their library materials, eventually to make them available worldwide through the Web. Many presidents welcome pharmaceutical and other corporate financial support for research, the results of which are often restricted from circulation rather than submitted for peer review. Other market-driven sources of revenue include commercial projects and amenities such as lavish skyboxes in football stadiums to attract corporate sponsors and donors.

The high-technology environment continues to push the boundaries of what we consider to be teaching, learning, and publishing. After a slow start, new technologies have been embraced by and are transforming academic institutions. Presidents must be far-sighted and entrepreneurial but prudent in deciding how much and how often to invest in new technology. Presidents also have to be prepared for new forms of communication. Students, faculty, and alumni e-mail their presidents directly about problems, suggestions, and issues. They expect timely answers. Demand grows for remote computer access to coursework and material. Plagiarism escalates as the Internet expands its content. And, unexpectedly, the so-called "blogosphere" is having an impact on presidents. Actions taken on a campus generally attract little public notice; however, once a blogger takes on an issue it can escalate rapidly and cause serious problems for a president. Female and male presidents alike have had certain actions subjected to negative attacks by bloggers, leading to extensive coverage by the mainstream press and agitation among the institution's constituents. In several instances, this has resulted in serious consequences, such as disaffected alumni rallying support for their election to the governing board in order to promote a particular point of view. On the other hand, some presidents are developing their own blogs to express their ideas.

The traditionally female strength of relationship building is especially important in developing constituent, legislative, and public support for the institution and for higher education generally. This includes the generation of significant philanthropy, which has become increasingly important to institutions as government support has waned. Many presidents are impatient with the process, insensitive to nuances in behavior, better talkers than listeners, and uncomfortable creating relationships with prospects, legislators, and business and community leaders with whom they have little in common. The attributes typically associated with women—patience, emotional sensitivity, and good listening skills—are especially useful in developing these relationships. Women presidents who develop a positive attitude toward these necessary external activities find themselves enjoying the process. To a surprising degree, external support is contingent on the confidence people have in the president. This makes relationship building vital to the enterprise.

To a large extent, presidents are judged more by successful capital campaigns, new facilities, and additions to the endowment than by academic initiatives. Successful presidents approach fund-raising as a necessary means of securing external interest and financial support to fulfill their academic mission and to build institutional quality. Women need to overcome their aversion to this aspect of the presidency and apply their relational skills to increasing the resources available to underwrite their institutional aspirations.

Presidents are not alone in these endeavors. The role of governing boards in the coming era will be more important than ever, and presidents are learning that they must involve board members along with faculties in all aspects of strategic visioning, planning, and resource development. Presidents who come into the position ill-prepared to work productively with their boards can make serious errors. Women presidents need to focus on forging collegial relationships with board members and strengthening board effectiveness.

A number of very public presidential and governance failures have heightened expectations for transparency, accountability, and oversight. A successful president-board partnership requires systematic and regular processes of evaluation and feedback for both the president and the board. Some presidents, both female and male, have lost their legitimacy because of a heavy-handed leadership style, management incompetence, excessive expenditures, or serious misconduct. Some trustees have derived significant personal gain from business arrangements with the institutions they serve. In many cases, when boards have failed to respond to such behaviors, faculties have demanded that they take action. Legislative and public scrutiny has also made boards more vigilant about preventing presidential missteps and presidents more alert to potential conflicts of interest among trustees. Leadership failures make the presidency more vulnerable, trusteeship more demanding, and faculty activism more likely.

The turbulence of the twenty-first-century environment requires that both male and female presidents learn to apply a wide range of styles and skills to assure the health and growth of their institutions. At times, a president is called upon to act decisively and quickly; at other times, a more collegial, high-involvement process is necessary. The challenge for presidents is to act appropriately and effectively.

Looking to the Future

The presidents responding to the *Chronicle* survey affirmed that although the presidency is all-consuming and very difficult, they consider it a great honor and privilege to serve (*Chronicle* 2005). Despite the challenges, women and people of color increasingly respond to the call to serve and they serve well. More women hold higher-education presidencies than at any earlier time in American history. With a few exceptions, they have led competently and successfully, thus helping to shatter the gender stereotypes and biases inimical to equality of opportunity. However, the hurdles for women presidents remain formidable: limited numbers of women presidential aspirants in the pipeline, serious impediments to the acceptance and legitimacy of women presidents, and considerable leadership challenges in the rapidly changing higher-education environment.

Can we look forward to the day when women will be groomed for, selected, and supported in presidencies based on their individual strengths and talents? Will women's ways of leading be validated and valued as legitimate presidential behaviors? Will constituents learn to judge presidents on their effectiveness rather than on stereotyped expectations? Will women eventually represent 50 percent of college presidents?

Trustees, sitting presidents, and faculties must act now to assure that the numbers of women appointed to and successful in the presidency continue to grow, that gendered expectations for presidential behavior are eliminated, and that women's ways of leading as well as men's are valued as important workplace competencies and integrated into the leadership style of both women and men. Following are a series of recommendations to help meet those goals.

Unclogging the Pipeline

There are a number of ways to unclog the pipeline of women eligible for the higher-education presidency, thereby steadily increasing their numbers. Institutional leaders must intentionally establish and execute plans to increase the pool of women interested in and well prepared for presidencies. This means:

1. institutionalizing policies that enable women to manage both family and academic responsibilities (e.g., a flexible tenure clock, child care facilities, flexible work schedules);
2. increasing the numbers of women in senior faculty and promoting them earlier to line administrative roles;
3. recruiting women and people of color into doctoral programs;
4. providing appropriate opportunities for women to have mentors, training, experiences, and visibility;
5. developing support networks to increase women's interest in and preparation for the position;
6. assuring the inclusion of women on search teams and as serious candidates in the selection process.

Both male and female presidents must take responsibility in this effort to remedy the inherent institutional bias against the advancement of women and minorities by identifying promising leaders, encouraging their interest, augmenting their experience, and giving them visibility. Women presidents have a particular responsibility to mentor aspiring and new women presidents. Shirley Tilghman, the first woman president at Princeton University, encountered some grumbling among faculty and others when she appointed a number of women to top administrative posts. Historically, all-male administrations and faculties were unremarkable and taken for granted. Today, while a woman president may be accepted as a novelty, a woman-dominated administration is such a departure from custom that it can cause anxiety.

Presidents also need to hold their administrators accountable for identifying talent and providing opportunities at every level of the organization. Without such active leadership and modeling by all senior executives, we cannot expect steady progress. One example of a system-wide project to develop the leadership abilities and career opportunities of black women in a predominantly white university is "Sisters Mentoring Sisters." This project is geared not only to providing knowledge and skills to advance the careers of participants but also to helping combat "the

feelings of isolation and alienation that kept Black women at the university physi-
cally divided and emotionally estranged" (Green and King 2002, 157). Importantly,
this initiative grew out of a goal of the university's top administration for the institution to become more inclusive and diverse.

Women presidential aspirants must also assume responsibility for systematically
developing their own competencies and augmenting their experiences. They need
to (1) seek out mentors, both men and women; (2) fill the gaps in their preparation; and (3) acquire skills in managing, public speaking, networking, budgeting,
fund-raising, and implementing change through work in community and professional organizations as well as within higher education.

Degendering the Presidency

Although there are now many examples of successful women presidents, there
are also a number of failures. Many male presidents fail, but the interrelated issues
of gender, leadership, and legitimacy pose special problems for women, who face a
Catch 22: If higher-education leaders act now to eliminate sex-role stereotypes and
obstacles, the number of women in leadership positions will increase; but until
there is a critical mass of women in the senior ranks of faculty and administration,
the existing gendered leadership stereotypes will be difficult to eradicate. Individual women presidents can, however, demonstrate alternative leadership styles and
strategies that are successful and are perceived as legitimate. Corporate leaders may
prove to be allies in supporting women's alternative leadership styles because increasingly they view adaptive, creative, and relational practices as necessary in the
new organizational environment. What can be done?

1. In many institutional settings, women presidents still need to fit into the culture as they find it and then gradually change it to accept their own style, making
difference a virtue by legitimating alternative ways of leading. Often this means
that at first women need to demonstrate that they are strong, tough, and decisive.
As they become accepted, they can show their more collegial and consultative
dimensions.

2. Men presidents, who have been socialized into a command and control style
of leadership, need to better adapt to the professed egalitarian culture of the academy by learning to express stereotypically "feminine" behaviors such as listening,
expressing empathy, consulting, and empowering.

3. Boards, administrators, and faculties need to cease "disappearing" so-called
"feminine" behaviors and, instead, legitimate them as important workplace
competencies.

4. In the higher-education setting, where the president is less the boss of the workforce than first among equals, all parties need to enact new ways of behaving and new structures for interacting. If we cannot overcome embedded gendered stereotypes in the academy, we have little chance of doing so in other organizations.

Redefining Leadership

There are a number of good reasons why it is important to have women at the helm of colleges and universities. Certainly, women are entitled to full equality of opportunity and access to all positions in the academy. Moreover, students, faculty, and staff, both women and men, need female role models at every level of our institutions to help overcome gendered expectations for performance. Perhaps most important, women presidents can help redefine and demonstrate leadership that is particularly suitable for twenty-first-century organizations and a good fit with the culture of the academy.

To meet the needs of twenty-first-century organizations, especially in the evolving world of higher education, we need new leadership models for both women and men:

1. Presidents will have to learn to apply different styles of leadership in different situations.
2. The "transformative" approach encourages adaptability and creativity, allows presidents to act authoritatively or interactively as appropriate, and should become the norm for both women and men.
3. Operating conceptually from the middle of a web rather than the top of a ladder enhances the flow of information and teamwork without diminishing a president's authority.
4. Relational practice may well be the best way of enabling collaboration and enhancing social capital.

Women must embrace the relational attributes characterized as feminine to create strong bonds with external as well as internal constituents. And although many women are uncomfortable with legislative relations and fund-raising, they can develop new and positive ways of approaching these activities relationally and from a mission-driven perspective. Male presidents, no less than women presidents, must develop the ability to build strong relationships and articulate the institutional mission as a spur to state and private funding.

Notions of heroic leadership are inappropriate for higher-education presidents today. The idea that great leaders transform institutions has given way to the recognition that responsiveness to institutional needs can make a leader great. The leader and her constituents influence each other and share responsibility for leadership. Heroic leadership has been supplanted by enabling leadership.

Relationship building, engagement, and collaboration have become the gold standard for leadership, along with adaptability and the unabashed integration of the public and private spheres of life. Helgesen's view is that women's leadership qualities "will help reconcile the split between the ideals of being efficient and being humane" to produce a more collaborative kind of leadership that redefines what "strong leadership" means (1990, 249). Johnetta Cole, who broke barriers when she became the first African-American woman president of Spelman College, writes, "We can surely create and practice models of teaching and leading that reject the old boys' way of doing it by command and control and by encouraging competition between groups. . . . We women can and often do exercise a more collaborative style of pedagogy and administrative leadership" (2005, 17).

From the evidence, we can conclude that women are not by nature less suited for the college presidency. In fact, they are well suited to the demands of today's presidency. Individual presidents need a complex array of competencies, feminine and masculine, to respond successfully to the changing needs of their institutions. To overcome gender-based stereotypes: (1) notions about workplace competence must be broadened and reinforced; (2) leadership qualities that derive from the experiences of women must be identified and valued; (3) cultural and structural impediments to the advancement of women, gay people, and people of color must systematically be destroyed; and (4) boards, administrators, and faculties need to act now to make these changes in order to attract the best presidential leadership for the twenty-first-century higher-education environment.

Rosener says: "By valuing a diversity of leadership styles, organizations will find the strength and flexibility to survive in a highly competitive, increasingly diverse economic environment" (1990, 125). To ensure that women continue their advance to the presidency and to enhance the quality of all presidential leadership will require the following: assuring diversity in the pipeline to the presidency; eliminating gendered expectations for leadership; and accepting individuated leadership styles appropriate for nonhierarchical, collaborative, interactive organizations. The academy, with its commitment to equity, excellence, and innovation, is best positioned to take the lead in this re-visioning and transformation of organizations and their leaders.

ACKNOWLEDGMENTS

The author is grateful to Ellen Kimmel, Ann Die Hasselmo, and Frances Lucas for their insightful comments and suggestions on the manuscript.

REFERENCES

Ashburn, E. 2006. Survey finds few gains in diversity of community-college leadership over past 5 years. *Chronicle of Higher Education,* 24 April.

Banerjee, N. 2006. Clergywomen find hard path to bigger pulpit. *New York Times,* 26 August, A1.

Barnett, R. C., and C. Rivers. 2006. Behind international curve: Why are American women last to take lead? Orlando *Sentinel,* 7 May, A25.

Bateson, M. C. 1990. *Composing a Life.* New York: Penguin.

Bensimon, E. M. 1993. A feminist reinterpretation of president's definitions of leadership. In *Women in Higher Education: A Feminist Perspective,* ed. J. S. Glazer, E. M. Bensimon, and B. K. Townsend, 465–74. Needham Heights, MA: Ginn Press.

Birnbaum, R. 1992. *How Academic Leadership Works: Understanding Success and Failure in the College Presidency.* San Francisco: Jossey-Bass.

Bornstein, R. 2003. *Legitimacy in the Academic Presidency: From Entrance to Exit.* Westport, CT: ACE/Praeger.

———. 2004. The authentic, and effective, college president. *Chronicle of Higher Education,* Point of View, 30 July, B16.

———. 2005. The nature and nurture of presidents. *Chronicle of Higher Education,* 4 November, B10–11.

———. Forthcoming. Women and the quest for presidential legitimacy. In *Women in Academic Leadership: Professional Strategies, Personal Choices,* Vol. 2: *Women in Academe,* ed. D. R. Dean, S. J. Bracken, and J. K. Allen. Sterling, VA: Stylus Publishing LLC.

Brown, T. M. 2005. Mentorship and the female college president. *Sex Roles* 52 (9/10): 659–66.

Carnegie Commission on Higher Education. 1973. *Opportunities for Women in Higher Education: Their Current Participation, Prospects for the Future, and Recommendations for Action.* New York: McGraw-Hill.

Cashman, K. 1997. Authentic leadership. *Innovative Leader* 6 (11) # 305. Retrieved on 7/1/2007 from www.winstonbrill.com/bril001/html/article_index/articles301_350.html.

Center for Policy Analysis. 2007. *The American College President,* 20th anniversary edition. Washington, DC: American Council on Education.

Chronicle of Higher Education. 2005. What presidents think: About higher education, their jobs, and their lives. 4 November, A25–40.

Cole, J. 2005. Transcending boundaries to build a new academic leadership model. *The Presidency* (Winter): 14–17.

Dean, D. R. 2003. America's women chief academic officers and their presidential aspirations.

Paper presented at the annual conference of the Association for the Study of Higher Education, Portland, OR, November.

Duerst-Lahti, G., and R. M. Kelly. 1995. On governance, leadership, and gender. In *Gender Power, Leadership, and Governance,* ed. G. Duerst-Lahti and R. M. Kelly, 11–37. Ann Arbor: University of Michigan Press.

Fain, P. 2007. Too much, too fast. *Chronicle of Higher Education,* 19 January, A24–27.

Fletcher, J. K. 1999. *Disappearing Acts: Gender, Power, and Relational Power at Work.* Cambridge: MIT Press.

Freeman, S. J. M. 2001. Women at the top: 'You've come a long way, baby.' In *Women on Power: Leadership Redefined,* ed. S. J. M. Freeman, S. C. Bourque, and C. M. Shelton, 27–60. Boston: Northeastern University Press.

Gardner, S. 2006. Brains, courage, talent, perseverance, and sheer grit: 10 Latinas with the right moves. *Hispanic Outlook in Higher Education* 16 (10): 13–16.

Glazer-Raymo, J. 1999. *Shattering the Myths: Women in Academe.* Baltimore: Johns Hopkins University Press.

Goleman, D. 1995. *Emotional Intelligence.* New York: Bantam Books.

Goleman, D., R. Boyatzis, and A. McKee. 2002. *Primal Leadership: Learning to Lead with Emotional Intelligence.* Boston: Harvard Business School Press.

Green, C. E., and V. G. King. 2001. Sisters mentoring sisters: Africentric leadership development for black women in the academy. *Journal of Negro Education,* Black Women in the Academy: Challenges and Opportunities, 70 (3): 156–65.

Harmony: Forum of the Symphony Orchestra Institute. April 1998. Gender and leadership: A review of pertinent research, #6, 100–110. Evanston, IL: Symphony Orchestra Institute.

Helgesen, S. 1990. *The Female Advantage: Women's Ways of Leadership.* New York: Doubleday.

Hollander, E. P. 1987. College and university leadership from a social psychological perspective: A transactional view. Presented at the Invitational Interdisciplinary Colloquium on Leadership in Higher Education, Teacher's College, Columbia University.

———. 1992. The essential interdependence of leadership and followership. *Current Directions in Psychological Science* 61:71–75.

Hollander, E. P., and J. W. Julian. 1978. Studies in leader legitimacy, influence, and innovation. In *Group processes,* ed. L. Berkowitz, 115–51. New York: Academic Press.

Indvik, J. 2001. Women and leadership. In *Leadership: Theory and Practice,* 2nd ed., ed. Peter G. Northouse, 215–47. Thousand Oaks, CA: Sage.

Jablonski, M. 2000. The leadership challenge for women college presidents. In *Women in Higher Education: A Feminist Perspective,* 2nd ed., ed. J. Glazer-Raymo, B. K. Townsend, and B. Ropers-Huilman, 243–51. Boston: Pearson Custom Publishing.

Kabacoff, R. I. 2000. Gender and leadership in the corporate boardroom. Portland, ME: Management Research Group.

Keohane, N. O. 2006. *Higher Ground: Ethics and Leadership in the Modern University.* Durham, NC: Duke University Press.

Naddaff, T. 2005. Leading authentically. In *Enlightened Power: How Women Are Transforming the Practice of Leadership,* ed. L. Coughlin, E. Wingard, and K. Hollihan, 301–14. San Francisco: Jossey-Bass.

Northouse, P. G. 2001. *Leadership: Theory and Practice,* 2d ed. Thousand Oaks, CA: Sage.

Oakley, J. G. 2000. Gender-based barriers to senior management positions: Understanding the scarcity of female CEOs. *Journal of Business Ethics* 27 (4): 321–34.

O'Brien, T. L. 2006. Up the down staircase. *New York Times,* 19 March, sec. 3.

Rosener, J. B. 1990. Ways women lead. *Harvard Business Review* 68 (6): 119–25.

Rusaw, A. C. 1996. Achieving credibility: An analysis of women's experience. *Review of Public Personnel Administration* 16:19–30.

Sinclair, A. 2005. *Doing Leadership Differently: Gender, Power and Sexuality in a Changing Business Culture.* Melbourne: Melbourne University Press.

Steinke, K.. 2006. Madwoman, Queen, and Alien-being: The Experiences of First-time Women Presidents at Small Private Institutions. Ph.D. dissertation, Bowling Green State University.

Waring, A. L. 2003. African-American female college presidents: Self conceptions of leadership. *Journal of Leadership and Organizational Studies* 9 (3): 31–44.

Wilson, R. 2004. Where the elite teach, it's still a man's world. *Chronicle of Higher Education,* 3 December, A8–14.

CHAPTER EIGHT

Women on Governing Boards

Why Gender Matters

JUDITH GLAZER-RAYMO

Throughout this book, my co-authors have set forth persuasive arguments that gender matters for women as scholars, teachers, learners, and administrators. In this chapter, I take up that challenge, focusing my attention on women trustees of higher-education governing boards. At the outset of this exercise, I assert my belief that gender matters even when it is not articulated, that thinking in existential terms, one's gender, whether male or female, is part of and defines our identity. I place gender representation on governing boards in historical context, looking at the circuitous route women have taken in gaining access to boardrooms, the demographics of their participation on public and private boards, and the observations of women trustees regarding their experiences. Consistent with the overall theme of this book, I focus on how women trustees have constructed their identities and professional priorities on boards, the difference that gender made in establishing their legitimacy, and the new and continuing challenges or "unfinished agendas" that need to be dealt with in rethinking organizational governance.

Throughout this chapter, I take the position that diversity and equity as basic components of the cultural norms underlying governance structures have been only partially realized with respect to the inclusion of women trustees, including women of color. In the private sector, the pressures on trustees as potential donors to ever-expanding capital campaigns contradict the values embedded in equity and diversity statements. And in public systems, where political realities influence the selection process, token appointments of women and minorities provide only the veneer of compliance with diversity and equity rhetoric. I adopt a critical feminist perspective in this analysis of trusteeship within the context of changing conditions of governance in recent years. In tracing women's efforts to gain access to the corridors of power and reach the pinnacle of organizational structures, it is first necessary to understand how social relations shape our institutions and how existing constructs sustain the boundaries and borderlines that have kept women in subordinate roles. Deconstructing the gender-neutral discourse may be the first necessary step in rejecting acceptance of the status quo and working toward more transformative models that recognize women as full partners on boards as in other leadership positions.

Governance Critiques

In the past decade, renewed interest in the governance of American higher education has provoked a number of critiques about the quality of the academic enterprise, escalating costs to students and their families, and a lack of public accountability in the expenditures of public monies. Presidential selection and executive compensation have elicited widespread attention and criticism from faculty, students, and alumni (Chait 2006), and in the case of American University, from the U.S. Senate Finance Committee (Fain 2006).[1] Analytical studies propose elaborate strategies for improving board effectiveness and accountability and for assessing board performance (Chait, Holland, and Taylor 1996; Ingram and Weary 2000).

In an introduction to his compendium of essays on shared governance, William Tierney characterizes the contested terrain of university governance as "the perfect storm" in which traditional postsecondary institutions—and, by implication, their governing boards—are experiencing "turbulence" resulting from profound technological, fiscal, and structural change (Tierney 2004, xv). Two essays in his book question the ability of part-time lay boards to adequately address the complex issues confronting twenty-first-century higher education (Duderstadt 2004; Keller 2004). In another series of essays, Ehrenberg (2004) and his contributors also pose fundamental questions about higher education governance, revealing the ambiguity of trustees' power in relation to top-heavy managerial bureaucracies and the complexity of their interactions with presidents and faculty. Although an underlying assumption of the essays in these books is the central importance of who serves on boards and the extent of their service to the public good, neither gender nor racial diversity is part of the discourse about governance reform.

Presidential Leadership Studies

In reviewing studies of higher-education leadership, college and university presidents have been the primary focus, and, by extension, their working relationships with the university community, including their governing boards (Birnbaum 1992). In her memoir, Rita Bornstein (2003), former president of Rollins College (and a contributor to this volume), acknowledges the special challenges that women encounter in attaining and sustaining academic legitimacy. These challenges extend to the norms and expectations of their positions and the ability of women presidents to sustain effective working relationships with trustees in male-dominated cultures. Although more women are being appointed to senior leadership positions, they continue to face obstacles in their efforts to secure university presidencies.

Nannerl Keohane, former president of Duke University, criticizes governance structures that constrain presidential authority, pointing to the "game of tug-of-war" between the board, the faculty, and the president, the decline of shared governance, and the need to support the president's "effective power as the leader of the institution" (2006, 117). She raises questions about the complexity of governance in a politicized context, the encroachment of the external regulatory environment on institutional decision makers, and the intractability of entrenched organizational structures. Keohane is now a member of the Harvard Board of Overseers that has selected a woman, Drew Gilpin Faust, as the first female president of Harvard University in its 371-year history. While one can only speculate on Keohane's role in this appointment, her presence on the board indicates that a woman trustee can influence presidential selection in laudable ways.

The selection of seven prominent women scholars as presidents of major research universities in this decade will undoubtedly have a beneficial impact in heightening public recognition of women's leadership abilities. In addition to President Faust at Harvard University (2007), these presidents and the year of their appointments include Mary Sue Coleman, University of Michigan (2002); Amy Gutmann, University of Pennsylvania (2005); Susan Hockfield, MIT (2004); Ruth Simmons, Brown University (2001); Lou Anna Simon, Michigan State University (2005); and Shirley Tilghman, Princeton University (2004). These appointments present an opportunity to reject pervasive gender stereotypes and unconscious biases that serve as barriers to women's participation on governing boards and, as Deborah Rhode and others observed in a symposium on women and leadership, to consider the difference that gender makes in organizational governance. Among the issues that Rhode raises are the lack of awareness that gender inequalities even exist, the lack of mentors to provide access to social and professional networks, and the gap between policies and practices in workplace structures, which "compromise fundamental principles of equal opportunity and social justice" (2003, 17).

In a preface to thirteen interviews with women leaders from a range of professions, Mary Hartman also asserts the need to "reimagine leadership, and think in new ways about what it is and what it might be, and to articulate more forcefully why it matters that women in far larger numbers be supported in seeking and

securing decision-making positions" (1999, 7). One of the women leaders interviewed, Ruth Simmons, president of Brown University and former president of
Smith College, and the first African-American woman to head an Ivy League university, sets forth the underlying premise of this chapter when she states: "*Feminist
leadership is about advocating fair opportunities for women in everything you do and
demanding in every conceivable way the respect to which women's abilities and intel-
lect entitle them. . . . For better or worse, we have been born in a time when women
and minorities still do not have the full rights to which they are entitled*" (Simmons
1999, 254).

Women Trustees in Historical Context
The Absence of Women on Boards

Women were in absentia on governing boards and as presidents for the first 240
years in the history of American higher education. The instrumental role played by
the founders of women's colleges and women's organizations demonstrates their
strength, perseverance, and single-mindedness in reversing this trend. The earliest
lay board established in the mid-seventeenth century at Harvard College was a dual
governance model consisting of a Board of Overseers and an operating board of
the President and Fellows of the College. It was superseded in the eighteenth century by a single, self-perpetuating board of non-academic laymen and clergy as at
Yale, Princeton, and early public universities (Kerr and Gade 1989). Following the
Civil War and the founding of the land-grant universities, institutional boards were
secularized, and businessmen and alumni began to replace clergy on both public
and private boards. It was not until the late nineteenth century, when women's colleges, normal schools, and coeducational colleges were founded, that the door
opened slightly to give women alumnae initial access to governing boards. Women's
socioeconomic status as members of the prestige elite defined their position on
boards as in the larger society, but men remained in the majority of board appointments, very often as the fathers or husbands of women alumnae.

The Role of Women's Colleges and the AAUW

The prime mover in promoting women as faculty, presidents, and trustees, the
Association of Collegiate Alumnae (ACA), founded in 1882, was adamant in its endorsement of "well-trained and qualified women as trustees." In 1891 its Committee on Collegiate Administration undertook a study of board governance, resolving that as a condition of membership in ACA, universities and colleges should

incorporate into their bylaws a provision for "women in the student body, on the faculty, and on the boards of trustees" (Talbot and Rosenberry 1931, 80). A breakthrough occurred in 1889 with the establishment of Barnard College as a coordinate of Columbia College and the appointment of an equal number of eleven male and eleven female trustees to its founding board. In her memoir, its founder, Annie Nathan Myer, articulated the popular view that male trustees were essential, since they not only "held the purse-strings" but adhered to "the masculine viewpoint and method of attack [which] have inestimable value, and are essential complements to the special contributions of women" (Myer 1935, 83).

In 1914, spurred on by its advocacy for women's full suffrage, the ACA reorganized its Committee on Collegiate Administration as the Conference on Women Trustees. Its members, who represented women's colleges, affiliated colleges, and coeducational universities, approved a resolution that "it is our duty" to define the role of women trustees more broadly in promoting equity in the salaries, promotion, and representation of women faculty comparable to their male colleagues and to assure that women faculty do not end up with the "social and other nonacademic duties" not assigned to men (Talbot and Rosenberry 1931, 200). And in 1921, one year following enactment of the Nineteenth Amendment giving women the right to vote, the ACA and the Southern Association of College Women merged to form the American Association of University Women (AAUW 2006). Evidence of the slowness of women's progress was reported in a 1917 study of 143 colleges, identifying only 75 women trustees (3% of the total) and a 1947 study of 30 universities that identified only 3.4 percent women trustees (Chamberlain 1991, 338).

Impact of the Women's Movement

Following World War II, the growth of public higher education and the advent of public multicampus systems, state coordinating boards, and the conversion of formerly all-male colleges into coeducational institutions increased pressure to add women to male-dominated power structures, including institutional governing boards. This process typified what feminists refer to disparagingly as the "add women and stir" method, in which change occurs mainly at the margins with minimal impact on the institutional culture. This trend accelerated in the 1960s and 70s, particularly after passage of Title IX (enacted in 1972), when colleges and universities were being challenged in the courts on the underrepresentation of women faculty, administrators, and students in their educational programs and activities. The AAUW demonstrated its advocacy for gender diversity on boards, convening a conference of women trustees in 1964 (the first such event since 1912). A flood of commission reports and institutional surveys documented pervasive sex discrimination against women students, faculty, and staff in higher education (Glazer-Raymo 1999). Seventy women's organizations coalesced around passage of the ERA in the 1970s, prompting reassessments of gender and race equity policies among governing boards and presidents. After all, how could any self-respecting trustee or college president proclaim this new mission when he or she denied women a seat at the governance table?

State and institutional commissions on the status of women pressured governors and legislatures to appoint women to senior administrative positions, and since it was the board that selected the presidents and chancellors, board composition came to the forefront in these deliberations. This was particularly the case in the public sector, where demands were strong for the inclusion of women in leadership positions. Elizabeth Luce Moore, the first woman to be appointed chair of a state governing board—the State University of New York—in 1968, had also chaired the boards of Wellesley College, the Institute for International Education, and various nonprofit boards. A prominent member of the social and prestige elite, married to a banker, and the sister of the *Time-Life* publisher Henry Luce, she was hand-picked by Governor Nelson Rockefeller, a close family friend, to work with chancellor Samuel Gould in overseeing the development of a new master plan for SUNY and its transformation into the largest state multicampus system in the nation.[2]

Board Restructuring: 1960s–1990s

The rate of growth among state systems not only transformed the colleges and universities in multicampus systems but, by the mid-1970s, increased the power of state coordinating boards with concomitant shifts in the power bases of trustees from institutions to the state level. These shifts had an indirect impact on the participation of women trustees, particularly in the public sector, where politics played a more central role in board appointments and effectiveness. MacTaggart (2004) provides a useful taxonomy of governing boards that shows the complexity (and the potential for chaos) in higher-education governance in the current decade.[3] It also shows how board structures and, by implication, board responsibilities in the public sector continue to be bifurcated between (a) top-down consolidated boards that generally have voluntary or advisory powers over entire systems; (b) segmental systems that oversee presidential appointments, financial and capital budgets, program reviews and approvals, and contract negotiations for multiple state institutions; and (c) more localized (campus-level) models of governance that have authority for institutional missions, contract negotiations, faculty and student policies, development, and advocacy of operating and capital budgets (MacTaggart 2004).

In some states (New Jersey and Florida among them), devolution is now occurring in which coordinating and system-wide boards are being eliminated, downsized, or restructured and are being replaced by institutional boards. One consequence is increased inter-institutional competition for scarce resources as "states oscillate between governing and coordinating structures" (MacTaggart 2004, 107). In Florida, for example, where the Board of Regents was abolished by the legislature in 2001, the governor now appoints 50 percent of the trustees of its eleven universities and twenty-eight community colleges. A constitutional amendment approved by the voters in 2002 intended that a reconstituted Board of Governors would play a dominant role in setting priorities and shielding local boards from political interference (Schmidt 2003). Although women have gained new opportunities to participate on local university and college boards as a result of devolution, it may be that the relative prestige of these semi-autonomous boards will diminish as the governor (working through his Board of Governors) vies with the legislature for greater control over public higher education.

Shared Governance

Concern about the erosion of faculty influence in institutional governance led the American Association of University Professors (AAUP), the American Council on Education (ACE), and the Association of Governing Boards (AGB) to issue a joint statement in 1966, defining the concept of shared governance. Implicit in this concept, faculty were to gain legitimate power over curriculum, pedagogy, research, faculty status, and aspects of student life relating to the educational process (AAUP 2001). Endorsed by the AAUP in April 1967, it was later amended (1990) to remove gender-specific references from the original text (see AAUP, sec. III, The Governing Board, 220).

In 1973 a report issued by the Carnegie Commission on Higher Education, under the direction of Clark Kerr, endorsed the concept of statewide coordinating boards to oversee master planning in their states. A companion report, *Control of the Campus* (Carnegie Foundation 1982), called for a governance framework in which trustees set goals, resolve disputes, "participate in shaping educational priorities," are involved in institutional quality reviews, and "link the campus to the outside world" (Hines 2000, 110). Pressures from militant students during the 1970s also led to proposals to give student leaders a voice in campus governance.

Although actual numbers are difficult to calculate, their appointment as trustees of governing boards contributed indirectly to an increase in board diversity, expanding the participation of women and minority faculty and students in ex officio or voting roles.

This trend was reversed in the 1980s during a period of fiscal retrenchment and environmental turbulence. A contentious dialogue emerged in which faculty and presidents were often at odds about the viability of shared governance and the allocation of scarce resources for their programs with "some high-profile casualties" (Burgan 2004, vii). Mary Burgan, former General Secretary of the AAUP, attributes board-faculty dissension to the influence of market forces on higher-education leadership and escalating declines in state fiscal support. Her observations are consistent with findings from a recent survey of trustees conducted by the *Chronicle of Higher Education* in which only 1.6 percent of respondents indicated that they formally represented the faculty on their boards, 57 percent of respondents agreed with the statement that "tenure for faculty members should be replaced by a system of long-term contracts," and 76.5 percent agreed that "colleges should be held more accountable for what students learn" (*Chronicle* 2007, A21).

The Culture Wars and Trustee Activism

Trustee activism increased in the 1990s as governors appointed like-minded trustees to carry out ideological political agendas, cutting budgets, overseeing curriculum changes, and restricting faculty unionization. Governance restructuring tended to weaken campus decision making as states became more intrusive in board decision making. Among the consequences were the appointment of trustees of public universities with political ties to the party in power, the formation of alternative organizations to hold boards and presidents more accountable for academic standards and student outcomes, and increased difficulty in attracting "strong leadership to highly politicized environments and institutions" (Hines 2000, 133). Gender, race, and ethnicity became corollaries to party affiliation in this overtly contested environment.

Rethinking Board Governance

Having arrived at a phase where traditional academic governance, dominated by alumni, political appointees, and major donors, is being questioned by those inside and outside the universities, it seems imperative that women take more than a casual interest in what is happening and consider how their potential majority on boards can revitalize the governance of higher education. Women's historic role as activists in philanthropy, education, social welfare, and cultural institutions as well as on school and college foundation boards provides them with a strong platform for board leadership. But as Andrea Walton states in her history of women in educational philanthropy, women have historically encountered numerous challenges and limitations "as both donors and recipients" (2005, 16). She reveals their tenacity and skill in capitalizing on their social and intellectual networks to advance their educational causes, ranging as they did from the founding of new colleges and the reform of existing ones to the creation and dissemination of knowledge in professional and academic disciplines. Walton is one of a very few scholars to observe candidly that not only gender has leveraged women's philanthropic role in education, but also race, ethnicity, social class, religion, and professional affiliation.

In what follows, I offer demographic data to support my assertion that the borderlines of gender and race equity overlap and must be addressed simultaneously to correct the imbalance that currently exists and to actively promote a redistribution of power as the basis for substantive change.

Current Demographics of Women Trustees

The AGB estimates that 50,000 women and men currently serve as trustees of higher-education governing boards in the United States. They may be civic or corporate leaders, benefactors, or alumnae/alumni. In the case of public institutions, they are likely to be appointed by governors or state legislatures, or, in a few states, to be elected based on their political affiliation. In the private sector, they are apt to be self-perpetuating (current board members selecting new recruits), generally for specified terms of office. On any master plan, they are at the top of the organizational chart, working directly with the president or chancellor and his or her staff and well insulated from faculty, students, and other campus constituencies. Their powers extend to presidential selection, formulation and pursuit of institutional missions and purposes, oversight of academic programs, the care and feeding of tangible assets, and, in the words of James Freedman, a former Dartmouth College president, care for "the institution's intangible assets, academic freedom, the commitment to excellence, and its ethical standards" (2004, 15, 16). Private boards meet on average three to four times annually; public boards, six to ten times annually. Much of the work that trustees do is conducted through committees: finance, academic affairs, student affairs, trustees, executive, buildings and grounds; and additionally, in the private sector, development, investments, and audit. Except for Historically Black Colleges and Universities (HBCUs), men and women of color fare less favorably than white women in board appointments.

Women on University and College Boards

A comparative analysis of the characteristics of trustees conducted by the AGB in 2004 shows private boards to be on average three times as large as public boards (30.2 members: 10.5 members) with a fairly similar profile in terms of average age (50–69 years), gender (71% men: 29% women), and professional status (51% business-related) (Schwartz and Akins 2004a and 2004b). The AGB also reports that men outnumber women trustees by more than two to one in both the private and public sectors and that the proportion of women trustees is fairly similar: 29 percent women on public boards and 28 percent women on private boards.

The data also show a slowdown in the proportion of women trustees relative to their male counterparts. In the twenty years from 1977 to 1997, women's representation increased from 15 percent to 30 percent (Madsen 1997, 1998). However, between 1997 and 2004, the percentage of women trustees increased by only 1.6 percent on private boards and decreased by 1 percent on public boards. Furthermore, data for private sector trustees is skewed by the fact that, on average, women account for two-thirds (63%) of trustees of women's colleges.[4] Excluding this group, women hold 27 percent of seats on private college boards. Women's participation is often a function of their alumnae status, family or spousal philanthropy, or professional prominence; whereas on public boards their selection is more overtly political—tied to patronage, political affiliation, or in some states, a result of the electoral process. Minority representation is almost 11 percent higher on public than on private boards, with African-Americans representing 21 percent of minority trustees compared to 6 percent Latinos, 2.7 percent Asian and Pacific Islanders, and 2.3 percent Native Americans (Schwartz and Akins 2004a and 2004b). This is an increase of only 1.5 percent on private boards and 5 percent on public boards since 1997 (Madsen 1997, 1998). Women of color comprise only a small number of trustees.[5]

A roundtable conducted at an AGB national conference in 2002 and attended by twenty women trustees elicited comments on the issue of trust, particularly about male trustees who are "high-powered executives and not interested in bringing women along," "good old boys who can't recognize or value new perspectives," or those who "don't always listen to women" (Kaufman 2002). In disaggregating data on board composition, AGB reports that men comprise 81 percent of chairs of private boards and 72 percent of public board chairs. Indicative of status hierarchies in the public sector, women are more likely to chair the boards of community colleges (30.3%) than comprehensive universities (25%) or multicampus systems (13.2%). In terms of race and ethnicity, more than four-fifths of both public and private board chairs are Caucasian. AGB also reports that most chairs are selected by the board, except for system boards, where governors appoint 7.9 percent of the chairs (Schwartz and Akins 2004b, 20).

What Trustees Think: A Survey of Women and Men Trustees

In 2007 the *Chronicle of Higher Education* reported results of a 63-question online survey of trustees from 1,082 institutions (*Chronicle* 2007, A11–21). A total of 1,479 trustees from public and private colleges and universities in all fifty states responded to this survey. The demographic profile of respondents parallels AGB findings: the majority were male (64%), Caucasian (89.5%), alumni of the institutions they served (57%), working in the business sector (50%) or in the professions (22%), and 60 years of age or older (49%). Indicative of the ability of trustees to offer financial support to their institutions, 65.8 percent reported annual incomes exceeding $100,000; 82.5 percent have made unrestricted cash donations; and more than half (51%) have made restricted cash donations and raised money from other individuals or organizations (50.2%) (*Chronicle* 2007). Whereas the "old rule of thumb" estimated trustee giving at 14 percent of a campaign goal, some fundraising consultants now suggest that 40 to 50 percent should come from members of governing boards (Selingo 2007). With capital campaigns now edging upward into the billions of dollars, presidents and trustees in private sector institutions will undoubtedly be looking more closely for new recruits with very deep pockets. And with the expectation of privatization among public universities, governors and their surrogates will also be more inclined to reward loyal supporters with governing board appointments. This is consistent with an earlier survey in which 86 percent of women and 91 percent of men reported being major donors to the institutions on whose boards they serve (Scollay et al. 1996).

The increased emphasis on large donations from trustees can have significant implications for the appointment of women trustees who are alumnae of their institutions and far less likely to have the financial capacity of their male counterparts. Many trustees say that money matters constitute their "biggest challenge." However, indicative of why gender matters, the survey reports that women "worry more" about issues of racial and ethnic diversity, declines in state support, and, in the words of one female trustee in the SUNY system, "a real crisis" in financial accountability and data transparency (June 2007).

Women on Corporate Boards of Directors

Since trustee selection in private universities and colleges is a critical function of board nominating committees, I was particularly interested in the "pool" from which nominees are selected. A recent study by Pusser, Slaughter, and Thomas (2006) provides a complex diagram of the interaction between corporate and university boards, referred to in the literature as board "interlocks." They define these interlocks as "the pattern of multiple board memberships held by individual trustees at the nation's top public and private research universities," with a greater proportion of lay trustees in private universities also serving as corporate directors of Fortune 1000 companies (2006, 748). They also assert that these relationships reinforce social and professional networks that may be tapped into by current board members in cultivating their successors (765).

Although they do not provide gender data on "interlocks," it can be assumed that women would be less likely to be included in these organizational networks, and as a consequence, less apt to be on the radar screen of trustee selection committees or governors' appointments secretaries. Two studies of women in the corporate boardroom raise relevant issues in this context: Do women on corporate boards make a difference? (Kramer, Konrad, and Erkut 2006). And if so, what numbers constitute their "sufficient, appropriate or satisfactory" representation (Thomson et al. 2005, 192)? Kramer and colleagues assert that a "critical mass" of at least three women is needed to move beyond gender tokenism and to address the intersection of race and gender on corporate boards. A woman trustee with whom I spoke and who serves on both college and corporate boards agreed that a critical mass "of at least three women" is necessary to assure that their voices are heard and they can influence the policy process.

Catalyst, which has played an historic role in promoting women's participation in corporate governance, also contends that direct commitment and intervention will be needed for corporate diversity policies to better reflect changing demographics and extend beyond token appointments to corporate boards of women and minorities. An excellent example of the disconnect between board representation and rhetoric can be seen in multinational corporations that are extending their presence in the developing world where the majority of the population are people of color. However, there is no evidence that globalism has precipitated heightened sensitivity to the demographic composition of their own governing boards. Catalyst's data show that, despite ostensible commitments to diversity in a globalized economy, "the glass is less than half full for women in corporate America" (Catalyst 2005). In 2006, women held 14.6 percent of all Fortune 500 company board seats, down from 14.7 percent in 2005, and an increase of only 5 percent since 1995. (Women were 13.6% of the total in 2003 and 9.6% in 1995.) For women of color, Catalyst calls the figures "abysmal," merely 3.1 percent, down from 3.4 percent in 2005. At this rate, it estimates, "it will take women 73 years to reach parity with men in the boardrooms of Fortune 500 companies" (Catalyst 2007). A total of fifty-eight boards have no women directors (a disturbing increase from 2005 when there were fifty-three all-male boards). Catalyst observed in 2005 that women continue to be "significantly underrepresented as chairs of the most powerful board committees, including audit, compensation, and governance, which may exclude them from key leadership, agenda-setting, and decision-making" (2). The comparative data show little forward momentum for women or people of color.

The InterOrganization Network (ION), another nonprofit research organization that seeks to increase the number of women in executive leadership and on corporate boards, asserts that the appointment of more women to the boards of public companies would alter the balance of power on their boards and thereby improve corporate governance (ION 2005). It stands to reason that the same criteria that are being applied in ION's Board of Directors Network could provide a template for those charged with similar responsibilities in higher-education institutions and systems.

The uneven representation of women on university and college governing boards indicates that although the civil rights and women's movements have had an impact on board composition and diversity, the representation of women and minorities in positions of leadership on boards continues to be problematic. Women trustees with whom I spoke about these issues were quite candid about the challenges of exercising power and influence as board members and about their determination to shape the legacy for those women who follow them. In the following section, I report on our conversations.

Women's Voices: Governing Board Experiences

Three arguments are generally advanced in discussing the gender imbalance on boards as well as in leadership generally: the dearth of qualified women in the pipeline, the inefficiency of markets, and family/workplace dichotomies. To learn more about the experiences of women trustees, in 2006 I spoke with women who have served or currently serve as members of either public or private governing boards.[6] My questions focused on their access routes to board appointments, how they construct their identities and professional priorities on boards, the difference that gender makes in establishing their legitimacy, and the new and continuing challenges or "unfinished agendas" that need to be addressed to redress the current gender and race imbalance. The overarching question, and one that relates to the sameness-difference debate in feminist discourse, is whether they believe that gender makes a difference in trustee effectiveness.

Routes to the Boardroom

Mindful of how presidential interaction with trustees is crucial to an understanding of the nomination and selection process, I focused initially on the multiple identities of trustees. They shared several characteristics: they were alumnae with close ties to the institutions or systems they now represented as trustees; they had achieved professional prominence in the corporate sector in finance, banking, media, and marketing or in the nonprofit sector in the arts, education, and health foundations. In public sector institutions, they had strong political connections to the governor's office or possibly to the legislature, were savvy political players who had been vetted by the state or county political committee, and their appointments bore the imprimatur of the party in power. In both the public and private sectors, the majority of these women also served on various college and university foundation boards and could be relied on to contribute generously to their institutions. In the private sector, however, access to resource networks through family, spousal, foundation, or independent sources was a primary factor in their appointments. More than one told me that "there is an expectation that we will make our college the primary beneficiary of our annual giving" and that, if called upon to support a specific project or building program, "we will be able to tap into sources of support through our social networks."

A former trustee of a state governing board, who also served on other boards, stated: "I had been on a lot of boards prior to being a Regent—you know, one thing leads to another, and I think life is kind of a stepping stone. I wasn't consciously seeking these things, and when they came along, I grasped them as a new opportunity." She typified the women with whom I spoke, the majority of whom shared multiple board experiences as directors of corporate and nonprofit boards (including college foundation boards) and as trustees of hospitals, museums, or other colleges or universities. A community college trustee also served as an elected school board member in her county. She explained that when she was appointed, "an all-call went out for people who might be interested in an appointment to the board, and I had been so involved with the college as an alumna and fund-raiser, so I had several people call me and say, please put your name in. So I did, and actually the party chairman called me and said, I would appreciate it if you would pull your name *out* of there because I have some people who have given a lot of money to the party and that we want to appoint and I said, 'No, I'm not doing it.' And so I stayed in and got appointed." She laughed, "He was not happy with me. Oh, well."

All of the women I interviewed were alumnae of the college, university, or system they now represented; two had started their service as alumnae association presidents; and on the public boards, their political activism and prominence in their state or county was a contributing factor. Those who served on trustees' selection committees indicated that nominations came to them from several sources—professional networks, political leaders, alumni recommendations, and external searches for individuals with (mainly) financial expertise. To some extent, this process overlapped with the work of the development officer in the cultivation of potential trustees who were also alumni; served as directors of philanthropic foundations; or were senior executives, managing partners, or corporate directors. Another, who commented that "women trustees would be wonderful assets," acknowledged that she had been trying to get an appointment to a corporate board but "it is very difficult. There are too many gatekeepers." Her comment was reminiscent of Kramer and colleagues (2006), who heard repeatedly that CEOs would rather have on their boards other CEOs who understand the pressures and dynamics of corporate culture. They are concerned that women may be more sympathetic to shareholder activists, and they generally want people in their own image.

Where do the women who serve on university boards gain their experience, and how do they establish their legitimacy? The AGB surveys estimate that more than half (51%) of those appointed to both public and private boards come from the business sector, followed by professionals (22–25%), educators (13%), and other occupations (11–13%) (Schwartz and Akins 2004a and 2004b). Jill Conway, a former president of Smith College, recalled in an autobiographical account of her presidency that when, in the mid-1970s, there were no female senior money managers, "we found Smith fathers and husbands who ran successful money management firms to serve as trustees, assess our portfolio strategy, and watch over our own stable of money managers" (Conway 2001, 72). This is no longer the case on the boards of women's colleges.

As one woman related, "most of the women on the board are graduates, so what you have is this very family orientation, people who love the college, who care about continuing a woman's education." However, she said that "years ago, women who served on private college boards were pretty seasoned volunteers who worked their way up through the alumnae association and volunteer work," but they are now being replaced by women who may also be alumnae but "have risen quite high in corporate and professional ranks." In her view, "it has changed the nature of boards; now we could get women who have these sets of skills. We still love to have men on the board because we like a diverse board." When I asked how these accomplished women were selected, she responded, "In a mysterious way, they're looking for someone with legal training, with architectural training, a lot of times with financial training, so they have [women] CEOs, CFOs, treasurers of companies, women who fill a niche. Geography is also important. Of course, they hope that anyone coming on this board would put that at the very top of their philanthropy." And although more than one of the women I interviewed felt that "women have to prove themselves" to have a voice on boards, those who had shown themselves to be successful fund-raisers for their colleges and in their service on nonprofit or university foundation boards are very much in evidence.

A woman serving on the board of a coeducational college also noted the emphasis on diversity across a range of categories—professional skills and accomplishment, geographic location, gender, and ethnicity, although she did add that "boards in general tend to be dominated by affluent people and people in finance." She thought her appointment to the trustees' nominating committee served an important function in her ability to work toward increasing the number of women on her board and that as a consequence of the increased diversity of her board, it had recently appointed an African-American woman as president. "I don't know that a woman goes out to recruit other women per se, but you may look at candidates and leadership styles in a different way, and that also includes the president." She expressed what seemed to be a universal feeling among alumnae serving on their college boards: "It certainly deepened my commitment to the college, and also let me understand much more clearly what its needs are. It's been a fantastic experience for me because [in my profession] we don't often commit to causes in our lives." Others echoed her sentiments, stating, "It was a big honor to be asked to serve on my undergraduate university's board. And I find myself being able to have a voice, and an equal voice, to feel like I had not only that voice, but the right to be talking about what I think needs to be done."

Sources of Power and Influence

The primary source of power on boards derives directly from service on the executive committee or as board chair. One woman chair of a private university board with whom I spoke asserted rather forcefully: "Boards are there to set policy, not to run the organization. We need to ask the right questions of management, meet the expectations of our primary constituencies, see that donor requirements are being met and that we are on target in fulfilling our mission." A woman who had chaired a system board said that her MBA in accounting provided her with budgetary skills and reported that the CFO of one of the universities in their system "tutored me in the different categories of funding that we considered every year, so I got to be regarded as the expert on funding." Following her service on a joint faculty-administrative-trustee committee to develop more equitable funding formulas and provide newer universities with the resources to build "areas of excellence," she was asked to serve as chair. She added that "one good old boy on the board called me to his law office (in the state capital) and said, 'Now, you've only been on the board two years and I feel you're going to be chair one of these days, but I really think you need a little more seasoning, and if it were I, I would want to—well, I'll be glad to take it this time.' And I said, 'You're a little late because I've already talked to everybody on the board and they all support me.' And that was it. He backed down and I was not only elected, I was re-elected by the [opposing] party then in power." Three other women chairs also had MBA degrees, had held senior corporate vice presidencies, or senior staff positions in government. All of them have significant experience as trustees or directors of corporate or nonprofit boards, strong indicators of the interlocking directorates that characterize the power elite at the pinnacle of governance hierarchies. When I asked women chairs to define their leadership style, they described themselves as collaborative, team players, consensus builders, sounding boards for the president, and as using their position to develop a shared vision of the institution's mission and goals. Those who served on public boards used more political descriptors, such as negotiator, problem solver, activist, and political realist.

The implications of this process are that power and influence are unevenly distributed and that much of the decision making relies on the chair, the president, and senior staff. Whether or not this was a problem for the women with whom I spoke, they each commented on the importance of "trust" in their dealings with each other as well as with the president of their university or college. In the light of the critiques of the demise of shared governance, I did find that they had minimal interaction with faculty.

New Challenges for Women Trustees

In their comments, women trustees indicated that the barriers to women's appointment as trustees related not only to the "give or get" priorities of universities in this competitive fiscal environment, but to the perpetuation of masculine stereotypes that continue to set the standard for effective leadership. Among the issues they raised in this context are the size of capital campaigns in major public and private research universities—now in the billions rather than the millions—with twenty-two universities now in drives to raise $1 billion or more (Glater 2006)—and the expectation that trustees will be among the major donors. Related challenges arise from accountability legislation such as the Sarbanes-Oxley Act of 2002,[7] which has greatly expanded the fiduciary responsibilities of boards and the committees that oversee budgets, audits, and government reporting, and the legal responsibilities of boards in establishing commercial relationships with business and industry. As noted in my analysis of the *Chronicle* trustee survey (2007), women have not been in the forefront of these trends, and to women trustees of public and private universities they represent new borderlines to be navigated. Public college and university trustees are mindful of the political realities of their somewhat tenuous positions: the line item veto powers of governors and legislatures; the contentious nature of collective bargaining contracts with faculty, staff, and graduate students; and the trade-offs that must be made in determining the placement of capital projects, tuition differentials, and graduate and professional schools.

Other challenges relate to the tensions that arise in addressing preferential admissions policies and how this plays out demographically. For example, in one urban university, the governor's appointments secretary asked a woman trustee for her views on remedial education and the admission of underqualified students to the four-year colleges in the system. Another discussed the fact that since 75 percent of their undergraduates are female, the board is considering ways to attract more males to the university through shifting "brand recognition" from feminized fields such as nursing and teaching to engineering, science, and technology.

Why Gender Matters in Educational Leadership

A review of empirical research on gender and leadership supports only small differences in leadership style and effectiveness, with women exceeding men in the use of democratic, relational, and transformational leadership styles (Hoyt 2006;

Kezar 2006). In announcing the appointment of Harvard's first woman president, attention is being given to Faust's collaborative leadership style and her "uncanny ability to administer both well and with a heart" (Rimer and Finder 2007).

The women I spoke with answered emphatically that "Yes, women would be a tremendous asset on boards." A woman on a system-wide board added, "We're so detail-oriented—we make sure that all the i's and t's are dotted and crossed, and that there is something you can look at and say it was successful. Men are wonderful architects, and they will put the whole thing together, and when it's completed, they're bored and they walk away, and the women are left to make sure that it's operational and it succeeds." Another commented, "I've been a leader, and I think that process and consensus building are very important, but I also think men appointees just go to the bottom line." A woman serving on a community college board asserted : "I think that on a community college board, we look for the compassionate ones that are going to reach out to the kids that can't afford the programs and make sure we're doing what we can to help. The men are apt to be more, you know, we're not making money on this program, cut it." Another saw the differences as "a personal thing," stating that "women are more holistic; they look at the big picture. Men are more linear in their thinking—they just, B follows A, and it's just without maybe taking into account some of the peripheral issues that bear on the matter at hand that maybe they would consider unimportant. But intuitively, women see it just a little differently. I became much more aware when I met with women's groups on different campuses who felt that the tenure issues were different for women. They felt they needed a champion, a spokesperson." As one woman put it: "It's engaged me in philanthropy in a way I've never experienced. I've clearly given more than I ever thought I would. I've gained a wonderful set of friends. There's nothing better than a set of friends committed to a common cause, and that's really what a board is at its best. It's people being committed to a common cause in a collegial spirit. To me, it's just one of the most rewarding things I do."

Assertions regarding women's readiness to chair boards were not unanimous, however. One trustee expressed the view that some women may be reluctant to step up to the "ultimate" leadership position, since being board chair is "traditionally sort of a patriarchal kind of role" and for many women "there's a greater comfort level having a man chair the board. Women still have family responsibilities and child care and the husband's job becomes dominant—this is also a challenge." She thought trustee selection was pretty much "gender blind" at her institution—"you look for the best person and what do they bring? What kind of contribution can they make both intellectually and obviously financially? What do they offer that other board members don't? You look for a mix of voices. I think you hope that every trustee brings her talents and skills and not simply because you're wealthy or able to contribute. That you need to also be able to participate in board deliberations. I do think on our board that everyone speaks up and everyone does contribute something." And finally, a woman with significant professional experience who had worked mostly with men throughout her career observed:

> Women tend to be very honest, very straightforward, and very collegial. I mean, women are socialized to talk to each other very easily about a wide range of issues. I think men are socialized somewhat differently. They don't form ties, sort of social networks even in the same way; maybe more through jobs or sports. It seems to be more sort of authority-driven, although that's sort of a crude way of putting it. It's far more subtle than that, you know. Women are really the glue that holds the family together, and that carries over into their professional relationships. I find when I first join an organization that it's more comfortable to make friends with women or to begin to form a network with women, so when I joined the board, I probably felt most comfortable getting to know other women on the board, although what I would try to do—and I think boards in general probably need to think a little bit more about bringing new people in, especially when new people come from a different background or ethnicity. You know, they've been mostly male boards, and you're recruiting women. How do you integrate them into the life of the board?—[I would try to] sit down and talk to someone I didn't know; maybe those conversations first were easiest with the other women on the board.

In other words, mapping the political terrain, identifying the most influential players, analyzing the potential for getting one's voice heard, and anticipating strategies that will gain the most acceptance—these characteristics highlight the political dimension of trusteeship. These women express confidence in their leadership skills and their ability to make a difference on their boards.

Conclusions

The historical context of women's entry into university and college boardrooms reveals the levels of courage, tenacity, and persistence of pioneering women who established colleges and organized professional associations and led the way for the generations that followed. Gaining access and gaining power were not necessarily synonymous, and it would take many decades and a great deal of consciousness raising before women were able to assume more than token positions of leadership. Undoubtedly, the confluence of the civil rights and women's movements in the 1960s and 1970s accelerated that process, and yet women and people of color still comprise a minority of trustees in both the public and private sectors of higher education.

By the late 1980s, concern about the changed political climate portrayed lay trustees as protectors of the autonomy of their institutions from "outside bureaucratic, economic, and political domination" (Kerr and Gade 1989). The "how-to" books and training manuals for would-be leaders are still being published, but the most compelling work addresses the profound impact of environmental changes on higher-education institutions. Questions are being raised about the expertise of part-time lay boards in providing adequate oversight, given the complexity of college and university operations and donor relationships, the validity of traditional hierarchical governance structures, and the corporatization of board decision making.

In their mission statements, policy directives, and other public documents, colleges and universities articulate commitments to equality and diversity. Yet there is only modest evidence that affirmative action has extended to increasing women's participation in senior administrative and governing board appointments. And even though boards have expanded in size in the interests of diversity and resource acquisition, the relative lack of progress in gender and race diversity is palpable. For the past two decades, women have been in the majority of student enrollments, a phenomenon that is being characterized by the media as the "new gender gap." But when one looks more closely at who serves in positions of power and influence on boards of trustees, the composite portrait remains as I described it in *Shattering the Myths* (1999)—overwhelmingly white, predominantly male, affluent, business-connected, middle-aged, active in civic affairs, and serving on multiple boards, both corporate and nonprofit.

Women have been in the majority of undergraduate and graduate degree recipients for the past two decades, but as survey data show, their presence on governing boards appears to have reached a plateau in the past decade. However, it does not take actuarial tables to calculate that in many institutions it will not be long before women comprise the majority of living alumnae. It is also the case that their acquisition of advanced degrees has enabled women to secure professional positions in corporations, law, medicine, and other fields that until the 1970s were virtually closed to them. Is it not appropriate that those who represent the public interests come from this vast pool of leaders and potential leaders? This premise has been doubly reinforced by listening to the voices of women trustees who confirm what many of us know intuitively about women's ability to lead. Indeed, it can also be argued that gender and race equality should extend beyond admissions, recruitment, and promotion criteria to affirmative action in the selection of lay governing boards, not for cosmetic purposes, but in the context of their fiduciary, legal, and policy-making responsibilities and what they convey about an institution's culture, mission, and viability in the academic marketplace.

In their comments, women trustees, some of whom also serve on corporate boards, remark on the need for greater transparency in board governance, agreeing that federal regulations such as Sarbanes-Oxley will increase pressures on all boards (including nonprofit organizations) to make financial and legal expertise higher priorities. Related to this challenge is the whole issue of accountability systems as they relate to executive compensation, tuition-setting, collective bargaining contracts, and capital expenditures. And given the prominence of fund-raising in both public and private higher education, women continue to be at a disadvantage when trustee selection is linked to their ability to contribute sizable amounts of money to support capital campaigns and university endowments.

For women seeking leadership positions, the strategy has long been playing by the rules of the game (whether or not they have had a voice in making those rules) and learning how to maneuver around the barriers that often deter their advancement (Glazer-Raymo 1999). Two problems implicit in diversity and inclusion policies relate to the tendency to consider women "overrepresented" or one of several target groups—race, ethnicity, religion, and profession among them. And while being at the pinnacle of one's career may lead to appointment as trustees, whether on corporate or academic boards, access to the boardroom generally follows a parallel path of privilege and access to senior positions. Indeed, governing boards are viewed as a separate locus of power and authority at the pinnacle of the organization or system—the external social, political, and economic environment and the internal collegiate structure—but relating most closely to the president and his or her staff, who studiously cultivate those who sit on their boards.

The flatter hierarchies I envisioned in 1999 have not materialized in twenty-first-century organizations. If anything, the movement toward entrepreneurial activity (as discussed in chapter 4 by Metcalfe and Slaughter) and top-heavy management (mirroring corporate America) presents new challenges for part-time lay boards of trustees who find it difficult to respond to the multiple demands on their time, expertise, and pocketbooks. If, as Rhode and other feminists argue, gender neutrality is a form of gender bias, greater attention should be given to frameworks that accommodate gender and racial differences and advance both the public interest and women's equality. As a first step in this process, much greater attention should be given to the criteria for trustee selection, with particular emphasis on social and professional networks that celebrate gender, race, and ethnic diversity.

ACKNOWLEDGMENTS

I wish to thank Merrill Schwartz, director of special projects at the Association of Governing Boards for providing access to resources, answering my queries, and facilitating my research for this essay. I also thank Rita Bornstein, Anna Neumann, and Betty Sichel for their astute and perceptive comments on earlier drafts of this chapter, and Diane Dean for her help in its early stages. Portions have been presented at the annual meeting of the Association for the Study of Higher Education in Anaheim (2005) and the Cosmopolitan Club Speakers Series in New York City (2007).

NOTES

1. Analyses of presidential compensation are reported annually by the *Chronicle of Higher Education.* In its most recent issue, *Executive Compensation* (2006), it reports that 112 presidents of four-year public and private institutions had compensation packages of at least $500,000, a 53 percent increase in the number of presidents at that level since the previous year. See also Jaffe (2006) for a detailed account of the presidential–board of trustees' debacle at American University.

2. In May 1981, for a study of the development of the State University of New York, I interviewed Elizabeth Luce Moore at her home in New York City. See also Glazer (1989) for an account of the politics of higher education in New York State.

3. See also Ehrenberg (2004, 281–84) for a state-by-state breakdown of "Statewide Postsecondary Governance Structures." This appendix illustrates the complexity of state governance and the appointment process of trustees. For example, in Michigan, three university boards are popularly elected, ten are gubernatorially appointed, and twenty-nine community college boards are locally elected (284).

4. The Women's College Coalition reports a total membership of 57 women's colleges, one-third of which are denominational colleges with an average enrollment of fewer than 1,000 students.

5. AGB surveys (Schwartz and Akins 2004a and 2004b) report that institutions enrolling more than 50 percent minority students have on average 54 percent minority trustees, compared to mainstream institutions where only 11 percent of trustees are members of minority groups. In a sample of 12 HBCUs, almost three-fourths (73%) of the trustees were African-American; in 14 Hispanic-serving institutions, 24 percent of trustees were Hispanic (2004a).

6. I conducted one-hour interviews, both in person and by telephone, with nine women trustees (three African-American and six Caucasian). My aim was to go beyond the demographic data and listen to the voices of women trustees with at least three years of experience chairing boards or key committees and working directly with presidents of their institutions or systems. I selected women who served on diverse public or private boards located in six different states. The boards included multicampus system, research university, comprehensive university, liberal arts college, and community college boards.

7. The Sarbanes-Oxley Act was enacted in 2002 to regulate publicly held companies in the wake of the Enron scandal. It requires corporations to adopt governance safeguards for auditing, ethical behavior, and internal financial controls. Although tax-exempt colleges and universities are not directly affected by this law, AGB surveys and articles in *Trusteeship* indicate greater attention by trustees to their legal and fiduciary responsibilities (see Michaelson 2005).

REFERENCES

American Association of University Professors (AAUP). 2001. Statement on government of colleges and universities. In *Policy documents and reports,* 9th ed., 217–22. Washington, DC: Author.

American Association of University Women. 2006. *Online museum advocacy and action, 1884–1939.* Retrieved 12/1/2006 from www.aauw.org/museum/advocacy.

Birnbaum, R. 1992. *How academic leadership works: Understanding success and failure in the presidency.* San Francisco: Jossey-Bass.

Bornstein, R. 2003. *Legitimacy in the academic presidency: From entrance to exit.* Westport, CT: American Council on Education/Praeger Publishing.

Burgan, M. 2004. Why governance? Why now? In *Competing conceptions of academic governance,* ed. W. G. Tierney, vii–xiv. Baltimore: Johns Hopkins University Press.

Carnegie Foundation for Policy Studies. 1982. *Control of the campus.* New York: McGraw-Hill.

Catalyst. 2005. Census of women board directors of the Fortune 500. Retrieved 10/24/2006 from www.catalyst.org/knowledge/titles/title.php?page=cen_WBD03.

———. 2007. 2006 Catalyst census of women board directors of the Fortune 500. Retrieved 10/18/2007 from www.catalyst.org/knowledge/titles/title.php?page=can_WBD_06.

Chait, R. P. 2006. When trustees blunder. *Chronicle Review* 52 (24): 17 February, 1–4.

Chait, R. P., T. P. Holland, and B. E. Taylor. 1996. *Improving the performance of governing boards.* Phoenix, AZ: American Council on Education/Oryx Press.

Chamberlain, M. 1991. Women trustees. In *Women of academe,* ed. M. Chamberlain, 333–56. New York: Russell Sage Foundation.

Chronicle of Higher Education. 2007. A Chronicle survey: What trustees think. *Chronicle of Higher Education,* 11 May, A11-A21.

Conway, J. K. 2001. *A woman's education: The road from Coorain leads to Smith College.* New York: Alfred Knopf.

Duderstadt, J. J. 2004. Governing the twenty-first-century university: A view from the bridge. In *Competing conceptions of university governance,* ed. W. G. Tierney, 137–57. Baltimore: Johns Hopkins University Press.

Ehrenberg, R., ed. 2004. *Governing academia.* Ithaca, NY: Cornell University Press.

Executive Compensation. 2006. The million-dollar president, soon to be commonplace? *Chronicle of Higher Education,* 24 November, B3.

Fain, P. 2006. U.S. senator threatens action against American University board. *Chronicle of Higher Education,* 26 May, A33.

Freedman, J. O. 2004. Presidents and trustees. In *Governing academia,* ed. R. Ehrenberg, 9–27. Ithaca, NY: Cornell University Press.

Glater, J. D. 2006. With $4 billion, Columbia raises the fund-raising ante. *New York Times,* 21 May, A13.

Glazer, J. S. 1989. Nelson Rockefeller and the politics of higher education in New York State. *History of Higher Education Annual* 9:87–114.

Glazer-Raymo, J. 1999. Women who lead. In *Shattering the myths: Women in academe,* 140–64. Baltimore: Johns Hopkins University Press.

Hartman, M. S., ed. 1999. *Talking leadership: Conversations with powerful women.* New Brunswick, NJ: Rutgers University Press.

Hines, E. R. 2000. The governance of higher education. In *Higher education: Handbook of theory and research,* Vol. XV, ed. J. C. Smart, 105–55. New York: Agathon Press.

Hoyt, C. L. 2006. Women and leadership. In *Leadership: Theory and practice,* 4th ed., ed. P. G. Northouse, 265–300. Thousand Oaks, CA: Sage.

Ingram, R. T., and W. A. Weary. 2000. *Presidential and board assessment in higher education: Purposes, policies and strategies.* Washington, DC: Association of Governing Boards of Universities and Colleges.

InterOrganization Network (ION). 2005. *Time for a charge: A status report on women directors and executive officers of public companies in seven regions of the United States.* Atlanta: ION. www.boarddirectorsnetwork.org. Accessed January 9, 2007.

Jaffe, H. 2006. Let them eat truffles. *Washingtonian* 41 (April): 76–79, 116–20, 131–33.

June, A. W. 2007. Fiscal reality. *Chronicle of Higher Education,* 11 May, A17–18.

Kaufman, B. 2002. *Women, boards, and leadership.* Association of Governing Boards, National Conference on Trusteeship, roundtable discussions. Boston, April 23.

Keller, G. 2004. A growing quaintness: Traditional governance in the markedly new realm of higher education. In *Competing conceptions of academic governance,* ed. W. G. Tierney, 158–76. Baltimore: Johns Hopkins University Press.

Keohane, N. O. 2006. More power to the president? In *Higher ground: Ethics and leadership in the modern university,* 112–19. Durham, NC: Duke University Press.

Kerr, C., and M. L. Gade. 1989. *The guardians: Boards of trustees of American colleges and universities. What they do and how well they do it.* Washington, DC: Association of Governing Boards of Universities and Colleges.

Kezar, A. 2006. *Rethinking the 'L' word in leadership.* ASHE Higher Education Reports. San Francisco: Jossey-Bass.

Kramer, V. W., A. M. Konrad, and S. Erkut. 2006. *Critical mass on corporate boards: Why three or more women enhance governance.* Report No. WCW 11. Wellesley, MA: Wellesley Centers for Women.

MacTaggart, T. J. 2004. The ambiguous future of public higher education systems. In *Competing conceptions of academic governance,* ed. W. G. Tierney, 104–36. Baltimore: Johns Hopkins University Press.

Madsen, C. 1997. Composition of governing boards in public colleges and universities. Occasional paper no. 36. Washington, DC: Association of Governing Boards of Colleges and Universities.

———. 1998. Composition of governing boards in independent colleges and universities. Occasional paper no. 37. Washington, DC: Association of Governing Boards of Colleges and Universities.

Michaelson, M. 2005. The significance of Sarbanes-Oxley for college and university boards. *Trusteeship* (May-June): 1–6.

Myer, A. N. 1935. *Barnard's beginnings.* Boston and New York: Houghton Mifflin.

Pusser, B., S. Slaughter, and S. Thomas. 2006. Playing the board game: An empirical analysis of university trustee and corporate board interlocks. *Journal of Higher Education* 77 (5): 747–75.

Rhode, D. 2003. *The difference 'difference' makes: Women and leadership.* Stanford, CA: Stanford Law and Politics.

Rimer, S., and A. Finder, 2007. After 371 years, Harvard plans to name first female president. *New York Times,* 10 February, A1, 11.

Schmidt, P. 2003. Government and politics: Happily stuck in a power vacuum. *Chronicle of Higher Education,* 16 May, A23.

Schwartz, M., and L. Akins. 2004a. *Policies, practices, and composition of governing boards of independent colleges and universities.* Washington, DC: Association of Governing Boards.

———. 2004b. *Policies, practices, and composition of governing boards of public colleges and universities.* Washington, DC: Association of Governing Boards.

Scollay, S. J., C. S. Bratt, and A. R. Tickamyer. 1996. Gender and college and university governing boards: Final report of a grant from the Gale Fund. Unpublished report. Lexington, University of Kentucky.

Selingo, J. 2007. Trustees don't expect to give as much money as their colleges ask. *Chronicle of Higher Education,* 11 May, A16–17.

Simmons, R. J. 1999. Ruth J. Simmons in conversation with Alice Kessler-Harris and Cora Kaplan. In *Talking leadership,* ed. M. S. Hartman, 237–55. New Brunswick, NJ: Rutgers University Press.

Talbot, M., and L. K. Rosenberry. 1931. *The history of the American Association of University Women, 1881–1931.* Boston and New York: Houghton Mifflin.

Thomson, P., J. Graham, and T. Lloyd. 2005. *A woman's place is in the boardroom.* Houndmills, Basingstoke, Hampshire: Palgrave Macmillan.

Tierney, W. G. 2004. A perfect storm: Turbulence in higher education. In *Competing conceptions of academic governance: Negotiating the perfect storm,* ed. W. G. Tierney, xv–xxxi. Baltimore: Johns Hopkins University Press.

Walton, A. 2005. *Women and educational philanthropy.* Bloomington: Indiana University Press.

CHAPTER NINE

Female Faculty in the Community College

Approaching Equity in a Low-Status Sector

KATHLEEN M. SHAW, M. KATE CALLAHAN,
AND KIMBERLY LECHASSEUR

Is the community college a good place for women to work? This would appear to be a straightforward question. Comparatively speaking, women make up a higher proportion of the faculty at community colleges than at any other institutional type: women comprise over 50 percent of the faculty at community colleges compared to 36 percent at public four-year colleges and universities (National Center for Education Statistics 2005a, table 4). Women are also more likely to be appointed to leadership positions in these institutions. In 1998, 40 percent of department chairpersons in community colleges were female (Miller and Creswell 1998), and by 2004, women made up a higher proportion of community college presidents than in the four-year sector (27.6% compared to 21%) (American Association of Community Colleges 2004). While differences in male/female faculty salaries persist across all institutional types, they are smallest in community colleges (NCES 2005a, table 8). In short, the community college appears to offer an academic work environment that is uniquely hospitable to women.

Research on the attitudes of community college faculty would seem to bear this out. Several studies point to relatively high levels of satisfaction among women community college faculty. Although not as high as those of men in this sector, female academics in community colleges report being more satisfied than females in the four-year sector (e.g., Hagedorn and Laden 2002; Townsend 1998; Townsend and LaPaglia 2000; Wolf-Wendel et al. 2006). Female community college faculty perceive less discrimination in the workplace than do their four-year counterparts (Huber 1998) and they also believe that community colleges are more conducive to a balanced family life (Austin 2002; Perna 2001). Moreover, Wolf-Wendel, Ward, and

Twombly's recent qualitative work (2006) examining how community college female faculty juggle work and parenthood suggests that this group of women largely chose to work in community colleges because they perceived them to be a more flexible and hospitable environment for women in their child-rearing years than that provided by four-year institutions. It is certainly true that research on female community college faculty is scant, as Wolf-Wendel and her colleagues point out. However, with few exceptions, current research suggests that community colleges provide a work environment that is less discriminatory and more welcoming toward women than in most four-year institutions.

Despite the evidence suggesting that community colleges are generally more manageable workplaces for women, these institutions occupy the lowest rungs of both status and resources when compared with their four-year counterparts. "Status" is a subjective term; an institution's status can vary among different groups or geographical locations. But in general, the status of an institution or educational sector is determined by: (a) the selectivity of the institution; (b) the "quality" of the student population as measured by such factors as high school GPA or graduation rates; and (c) the endowment or available level of resources. For example, Kevin Carey reports that the college rankings developed by *U.S. News and World Report* are based largely on three major categories: fame (peer rankings); wealth (class size, average faculty salary, faculty/student ratio, percentage of full-time faculty); and exclusivity (average student SAT score, acceptance rate, graduation rate) (Carey 2006, 6). Not surprisingly, community colleges rank low in all three categories. Central to their mission is an "open admissions" policy that allows virtually anyone to enroll in some type of course (although many community colleges do have selective admissions policies to particular programs, such as nursing). As a result of this open-door policy, community college students on average do not have high SAT scores (if they take the SATs at all); and they perform poorly in terms of retention and graduation when compared with students in more prestigious institutions. Finally, these institutions receive far fewer resources than any other postsecondary sector (NCES 2006a), and this fact shows up in many of the measures of wealth used by *U.S. News and World Report* and other ranking systems.

Because of their nonselective admissions policies and the modest levels of funding they receive, community colleges educate the most challenging student populations with the fewest resources among all sectors of postsecondary education. What effect do these factors have on the everyday lives of the female academics who are more likely to teach in this sector? What do the lives of community college female faculty look like when viewed from a perspective that considers both resources and status? The purpose of this chapter is to answer these questions by drawing first on available quantitative data that allow a comparative analysis of resource-relevant aspects of the professional lives of female faculty members across sectors, and next by using interviews and observations of twenty-three community college faculty members and administrators to examine the effects of these factors on their ability to do their jobs well and with contentment. By tracing the influence of institutional resources on the quality of life for community college faculty, we attempt to show how professional employment in a low-status institution presents unique challenges for the work life of female faculty situated in community colleges.

Factors Affecting the Work Lives of Community College Female Faculty

As previous studies have suggested, the work lives of female academics in the community college are, by their own account, positively affected by such factors as flexibility of work schedule, ease of the tenure process, and a lack of pressure to publish (Cohen and Brawer 2003; Wolf-Wendel et al. 2006). Yet the women that we interviewed presented a more nuanced and complex analysis of the community college work environment that was fraught with ambivalence. A number of these faculty expressed some level of contentment, and in the same breath listed substantial barriers to a productive, welcoming work life. For example, one full-time female faculty member stated, "I order movies, books, the library is good—I get everything I need," right after explaining that she often teaches in a classroom that has been subdivided in such a way that noise from the other class disturbs her own, and vice versa. Another faculty member, after stating that her office space was shared with ten other adjuncts, quickly rationalized the set-up, saying, "Like I said, everybody is friendly, and it's not a matter of tension or jealousies or anything like that. It's just kind of the way it works out. But it is actually very nice."

Most of the factors affecting the quality of their work life were related to a lack of instructional or other resources. To begin to understand the effects that resources have on the work lives and working conditions of community college female faculty, we examine a number of tangible resource measures below.

Instructional Resources

Several studies (e.g., Wolf-Wendel et al. 2006; Perna 2001) have found that devotion to teaching appears to unite female faculty members in general and female community college faculty members in particular. But if this is true, then it is also

TABLE 9.1
Comparative Statistics: Community Colleges versus All Four-Year Public and Private Nonprofit Institutions (2003)

	Instructional Expenditures per FTE	Academic Support per FTE	% Female Full-Time Faculty	Average Full-Time Faculty Salary	% Faculty Part-Time	% Female Part-Time Faculty	Average Part-Time Faculty Salary
Community College	$3,979	$775	49.6	$52,000	66.7	49.2	$9,000
Four-Year Sector	$7,746	$2,151	35.9	$70,500	33.9	47.1	$13,000

SOURCE: National Center for Education Statistics (2005a, 2005b, 2006a).

true that the conditions under which an individual teaches are of particular importance. It makes sense, therefore, to examine more closely the instructional resources that are available to community college faculty.

Resources are not distributed equally across two-year and four-year sectors of higher education. In fact, instructional expenditure per student increases as institutional selectivity and status increase. For example, community colleges expend far fewer resources than do four-year institutions across a range of indicators. As table 9.1 shows, in the areas most directly related to community college faculty work—teaching and academic support—community colleges spent $3,979 per student on instruction in 2003, compared with $7,746 in public and private four-year institutions. Analyses of resources devoted to academic support services revealed large discrepancies as well—$775 per full-time student in community colleges, compared with $2,151 in four-year institutions (NCES 2006a, table 341). In short, community colleges spend less than half what four-year institutions spend on instructional resources.

These discrepancies become apparent in two specific areas—faculty salaries and the proportion of part-time to full-time faculty employed at the institution. Since women are both more likely to be employed by community colleges *and* more likely to be counted among the adjunct faculty population than in four-year institutions, discrepancies in both of these arenas are critically important aspects of academic work life in community colleges.

FULL-TIME FACULTY SALARY

Data from the 2004 National Study of Postsecondary Faculty (NCES 2005b) reveal that community college faculty earn less money than do their peers in any other sector of nonprofit postsecondary education. As table 9.1 shows, whereas the average faculty salary across all four-year institutions is $70,500, full-time community college faculty earn on average only $52,000.

By definition, part-time faculty receive lower wages than their full-time counterparts. But part-time faculty in community colleges are, once again, disproportionately disadvantaged. As table 9.1 shows, whereas the average part-time faculty member in a four-year institution earns $13,000 per year, community college part-timers, on average, earn only $9,000 per year.

We see additional discrepancies across the sectors when looking at the proportion of faculty that are part-time. Fully two-thirds of community college faculty—66.7 percent—are part-time. In contrast, the average proportion of part-time faculty at four-year institutions is only a third, or 33.9 percent (NCES 2005a). And as table 9.1 shows, while the ranks of part-time (and full-time) faculty are more likely to be male, there is a slightly higher proportion of female part-time faculty members in community colleges than in the four-year sector.

Student Population

Despite the lower levels of instructional resources, community college faculty teach the most challenging students. Disadvantaged and underprepared students are far more likely to attend community colleges, while their more privileged peers attend more prestigious and higher-resourced institutions (NCES 2006b). For example, nearly 65 percent of full-time community college students qualify for federal grants, compared with 37.7 percent of full-time students enrolled in four-year institutions. And whereas more than 80 percent of all students attending four-year colleges and universities are full-time, only 39 percent are full-time in community colleges (NCES 2006b). Forty-two percent of students entering community colleges require at least some kind of remediation, whereas 28 percent of students entering the four-year sector received remediation (NCES 2006b). In short, there is little doubt that community college faculty educate a student population that is more disadvantaged and less well prepared for college-level work than students enrolled in four-year institutions.

Digging Deeper: How Institutional Resource Levels Affect Faculty Work Life

When taken together, these data call into question the relatively rosy picture often portrayed in the research on community college work life for female academics. It is indeed true that community colleges employ a larger percentage of female faculty members than any other sector of higher education. Moreover, leadership opportunities for women appear to be more abundant in this sector as well. But other measures discussed above identify a number of troublesome factors.

Institution-level statistics show that community college faculty work in institutions that have far fewer resources to devote to instruction than any other sector of higher education. They earn less than either full- or part-time faculty at four-year institutions. And a faculty member working in a community college is far more likely to be part-time than at a four-year institution. Even within this clearly disadvantaged sector, women are slightly more likely to inhabit the part-time faculty ranks at community colleges than in any other postsecondary educational sector. They are also more likely to teach disadvantaged and underprepared students. In short, available statistics strongly suggest that community colleges, while generously populated with women, are far from ideal workplaces along a number of dimensions—nearly all of them related to resource levels.

Despite clear documentation that community college faculty members work under a relative disadvantage, we know very little about how resource levels translate into the working conditions of female community college academics. In the next section of this chapter, we attempt to shed light on this subject by presenting qualitative data that provide a faculty perspective from in-depth site visits at two suburban community colleges.

By tracing how resources affect the academic workplace culture, we can develop a better understanding of the quality of life for women who choose to teach in the community college. In comparison to much of the literature on this population that currently exists, our data suggest that female community college faculty members are deeply ambivalent about their workplaces; and when questioned directly, they point to significant areas of dissatisfaction, most of which are related to a unique characteristic of community colleges—a chronic lack of resources.

The data presented below were drawn from a larger ongoing study of how resources affect the quality of undergraduate education across four sectors of public postsecondary education: community colleges, comprehensive four-year universities and colleges, historically black institutions, and large research universities.

In addition to in-depth, semi-structured interviews with twenty faculty members and administrators from two community colleges, we also observed faculty in their classrooms, in their offices, and in the other physical spaces that they typically inhabit.

Institutional and Faculty Profiles

The two community colleges from which our sample of faculty was drawn are located in a state in which significant disparities exist in funding and expenditures across postsecondary educational sectors. Recent analyses of IPEDS (Integrated Postsecondary Educational Data System) data indicate that the state's four-year Research I institutions spend more than $12,000 per FTE student on instructional expenditures, compared to about $5,500 in comprehensive state universities and $4,400 for community colleges. Recent research by Dowd and Grant (2006) reveals that expenditures for community colleges also vary to a degree by funding structures. Revenue variations tend to be larger in states with a local (county, municipal, or school district) finance role, but the difference is a small proportion of total funding and is due in part to higher levels of appropriations in those states.

The state in which the community colleges in this study are located is one that includes local funding; therefore, these institutions are likely to vary to some degree in their total revenue.

And in fact, the amount of money spent for instructional-related expenses per FTE student varies by about $1,200 between the two colleges. According to 2004 IPEDS data, whereas one college spends slightly more than the national average of $4,400 for community colleges—$4,789—the other spends $3,585 per FTE, which is below the average for community colleges. Both colleges spend significantly below the average for institutions in any other postsecondary sector. Both institutions are located in suburban sections of a large northeastern metropolitan area. The colleges are similar in size, enrolling about 10,000 FTEs each. The overall proportion of full-time students receiving financial aid is roughly similar—about 33 percent—but one of the colleges enrolls significantly more African-American students than does the other—3 percent compared with about 16 percent.

The faculty members and administrators that we interviewed at the two community colleges were chosen to represent a broad spectrum of experiences and career goals. Of the twenty that we interviewed, sixteen were female and four were male. They ranged in age from late twenties to early sixties, and all were white. Nine of our subjects were full-time, tenured faculty; four were on the tenure track but not yet tenured; and four were part-time adjuncts. Of these four, two were young females who wished to obtain a full-time tenure-track position; the other two were older and retired from their first careers, content with their part-time status. Finally, we interviewed three college administrators.

Tracing the Influence of Resources on the Lives of Community College Faculty

Many women in academe opt to teach in the community college sector despite low salaries, an ever-shrinking pool of full-time positions, a challenging student population, and few instructional resources. How do resource levels influence the quality of working conditions at community colleges? Below, we identify four distinct but related spheres of faculty work life that are negatively affected by this sector's relative lack of resources: workload, part-time employment, physical space, and support services.

Workload

As noted earlier, an often-stated argument in support of the community college working environment for women is the ability to focus on teaching and student learning. Community colleges are also said to provide more flexibility for women who are parenting, making it a "better" place for these women to work. However, both of these arguments depend, to some degree, on the teaching load and available instructional resources for women who choose to become faculty at community colleges. The ability to truly focus on delivering high-quality instruction to students is highly influenced by the amount of time a teacher is able to devote to the students in her classes. And while flexibility of schedule and the ability to bring one's children into the workplace in emergencies can seem quite appealing to professors who are also mothers, their family life is also heavily influenced by the sheer *amount* of work they are required and expected to do.

Because community colleges spend less than half the resources that four-year institutions do on instructional costs, it comes as no surprise that faculty members at these institutions carry relatively heavy teaching loads. The National Study of Postsecondary Faculty reports that community college faculty spend 18.1 hours per week in the classroom on average, which is almost double the amount of classroom time spent by faculty in four-year institutions (9.4 hours per week) (NCES 2005b). Whereas four-year faculty commit 64 percent of their time to instruction, community college faculty devote fully 85 percent of their time to teaching.

The teaching load for full-time faculty members in the community colleges that we visited were in line with national averages. Most carry a five-course load per semester[1] and are expected to hold at least one office hour per course during each week of the semester. Indeed, we found that community college faculty are sometimes asked to teach as many as six courses. Due to a shortage of faculty at one of the community colleges in our study, a female faculty member confided that the previous semester she had agreed to take on a six-course load, which she described as "scary." She explained:

> Well last semester I taught the six courses, which was an overload. Four is full-time, six is an overload. And you do get a little bit of extra compensation above and beyond for teaching an overload. I was teaching all comp courses, so it means a lot of grading—a lot of paper grading—so it is very, very time-consuming. And to top it all off before [taking the overload] I had enrolled in a computer science class because I want to get myself better with technology; and I thought am I going to be able to handle this taking a class and teaching six classes?

Thus, the heavy course load expected of community college faculty requires so much time—both in class and out of class—that the argument that community colleges provide a more flexible work life warrants serious questions.

For adjunct faculty, the workload can prove to be even more taxing, since adjuncts often work at more than one institution to pay the bills. As one department chair said, "For [the adjuncts that are] rushing around from community college to community college, I think it's really hard for them." Many adjunct faculty we encountered were teaching at more than one institution. According to these faculty, "rushing around" was not only time-consuming, but it also prevented them from establishing relationships with their colleagues. As one part-timer explained, "[The college will] have different adjunct get-togethers and things like that. But, in the regular semester, I'm teaching three classes here and three up at Mason County, so I don't really have time for that, which I'd like to, but I just don't. It's not practical."

In short, the workload for both part-time and full-time community college faculty members is often onerous. Not surprisingly, faculty members in our study consistently asserted that their heavy teaching loads made it more difficult for them to teach well.

Reliance on Adjuncts: The Hidden Costs

Because this sector of postsecondary education is able to devote only a fraction of what most four-year institutions can afford for instruction, community colleges must economize by relying on a steadily increasing part-time workforce. On average, adjunct faculty members make up about two-thirds of the teaching staff at community colleges. Our analyses reveal that such heavy reliance on part-time faculty reduces the quality of faculty work life for the *entire department*—full-timers as well as part-timers.

This phenomenon plays out in several ways. First, despite their best efforts, community colleges cannot fully integrate part-timers into the life of the institution or the academic departments. The two institutions in our study varied in the degree to which they attempted to address this issue. In one community college, a dean manages and interacts with full-time faculty, while her assistant dean manages part-time faculty separately. This degree of segregation makes it difficult for an academic department to assess and address the needs of the faculty in a comprehensive manner. For example, when one full-time female faculty member was asked if there were any meetings that gave faculty members teaching composition an opportunity to focus on their issues as a unit, she replied, "No. As a matter of fact, we now have an assistant dean who only does adjuncts, and then full-time faculty meet with the dean. So to some extent, it's even more separated [than it used to be], although adjuncts were never invited to faculty meetings." By creating a separate administrative structure to address the needs and concerns of the adjunct faculty, this institution makes it more difficult to address the overlapping needs of full-time faculty, adjuncts, and students.

The other community college in our study worked harder to integrate adjunct faculty. For example, in the English department adjuncts are invited to all departmental meetings and are asked to serve on committees as well. There are also several social events that are designed to create camaraderie among the faculty. But the degree to which adjuncts can participate is hampered by the structure of their work life. As one female part-time faculty member said:

> The adjunct faculty is encouraged—not just invited, encouraged—to be on all the committees, all right. The adjunct faculty receive notices and minutes from old meetings, okay. There are Christmas parties and stuff like that which are planned so that the times for the adjunct faculty are most available, they're held then, okay. The beginning of semester departmental meetings, lunch is provided so that there is a mix, and that's when we mix the most, actually. So I mean this has nothing to do with the department attempts. I would say that the secretarial staff, the departmental staff, the chair certainly would like to see a fused faculty, but I think it's the norm. It's just the norm—it's a matter of scheduling.

Despite departmental attempts to ameliorate the disconnect between the two groups of faculty, this faculty member is pointing to a set of very real structural and logistical factors that erect barriers to full participation in the life of the department for adjuncts. Participating on a committee or attending a social event carries with it no financial remuneration; in fact, it may well cost the adjunct faculty member money, since spending more time at one institution reduces the amount of time an adjunct has to teach courses at other institutions. A female part-time faculty member described how she has to choose teaching for pay over participation in faculty meetings:

> It sounds awful, but the adjunct faculty, quite honestly, the pay that adjuncts receive is not very inspiring. And then if they have things on top of that like adjunct in-service . . . if they could pay for that, then I could actually make sure I went to it. Because if I have a choice between teaching another class and earning some money or coming to something I won't get paid for, I have to make that decision for making some money.

As a result, a smaller and smaller full-time cohort of faculty must carry the weight of nearly all departmental and college service duties. This burden is another hidden cost of the low resource levels at community colleges. This trend is certainly not unique to community colleges; institutions from all sectors are relying increasingly on non-tenure-track appointments. However, as we reported above, the situation is far more extreme in the community college sector, which reports that fully two-thirds of its faculty is non-tenure-track (compared with about a third in four-year institutions). Indeed, part-time faculty at these two institutions comprise between 75 and 78 percent of the total faculty.

Not surprisingly, a lack of collegiality across the two types of faculty members marks both institutions in our study. As one full-time female professor puts it, "It is difficult to know all of [the adjuncts] or even recognize them as one of our part-time instructors." This is reiterated by part-time faculty who also felt isolated from full-timers. As one said:

> Well, really, as an adjunct professor, I really thought there wasn't much of [a relationship with full-timers]. To the extent of not really even saying "Hi" to people. It's not really . . . it's kind of a shame. And it's also because, I did kind of see the other side when I was full-time. [Part-timers] are just faces that are in and out. [They] don't necessarily go to an office. I go to the mailroom, so we don't really interact, not much. And I think because even the in-services are separate for the adjuncts and for the full-time, so even that situation would be a chance to interact with the full-timers.

The organizational structure of a department that relies on an exorbitant number of adjunct faculty members is hardly conducive to a collegial workplace or an even distribution of departmental duties. Instead, both full-time and part-time community college faculty members report a disjuncture that diminishes the quality of the workplace.

The Impact of Physical Space on Work Life

While it is not uncommon for faculty members in any type of institution to complain about physical space, the community college faculty members in our study were particularly vociferous in voicing their grievances. In fact, many described physical space as a critically important factor in determining their ability to do their jobs well.

The most obvious problem is the simple lack of adequate space. The state in which the community colleges in this study are located had not made appropriations for physical plant construction or upgrades in over a decade, despite the fact that enrollment has been growing steadily over the last fifteen years. As a result, the growing number of faculty members needed to teach these students often find themselves without adequate office space and teaching in outdated, cramped classrooms. As one female community college professor aptly surmised, "Space is a problem at any place." However, space is particularly limited at institutions such as community colleges, which are often chronically underfunded.

A low-quality physical space or simply a lack of space can obstruct the delivery of in-class instruction. At one of the community colleges in our study, a single classroom building must accommodate all course offerings. There is no room to adjust for either increased class sizes or a greater number of classes. As a result, one classroom is sometimes split into several teaching spaces. One full-time, tenure-track faculty member said that overall, classrooms were sufficient "except when you get in a classroom with a partition." She went on to say that the partitions do not sufficiently block out noise and can be incredibly disruptive to both the professor and students.

Classroom space at the other community college was also heavily criticized. According to one full-time female faculty member, classroom space was "horrible." She explained: "I mean, go up and look at some of these closets that we call classrooms. You can't even get around to have group work, unless I lose an awful lot of weight!" Observations of an array of classrooms at both community colleges confirm these descriptions. Often cramped and outdated, with uncomfortable or inadequate furniture, classroom space at these institutions did not provide high-quality teaching environments.

In addition to classrooms, office space further determines professors' opportunities to meet with students, their access to colleagues, and even their professional identity in some instances. In the two community colleges in our study, even full-time faculty are not guaranteed a private office. At one of the colleges, full-timers are located in semi-private offices where four to five faculty inhabit cubicles within the same larger office. Each cubicle is furnished with a desk, a computer, some bookshelves, and sometimes an extra chair where a visitor might sit. At the other community college, the situation is slightly better in that at least some of the full-time faculty have private offices. But a significant number of the full-timers are expected to share their space with one or more adjuncts.

Generally speaking, the community college faculty members that we interviewed did not find cramped or non-private office space to be conducive to doing their job well. Not only is it difficult to concentrate or to work efficiently when sharing office space, it is also difficult to maintain a professional demeanor when students pay a visit. A full-time English Composition professor in the Liberal Arts department of one of the colleges explained her dissatisfaction:

> I think our office areas are below average when you compare them to other colleges. Sometimes it would be nice to have a little more space where I could even have a group of students, have a group tutoring session. But as it is, barely one student can fit in the office area comfortably. Just the way they are, no matter how neatly you keep it, they seem cramped. I think they come across as unprofessional to students; we look holed away. I've had so many students come in and say, "This is your office? They don't give you a lot of room."

Office space is particularly problematic for part-time faculty. Neither community college provided any part-time faculty with individual offices; all were required to share with at least two or three other faculty members. Conditions were particularly dire in one community college. A tenure-track, full-time professor who spent many years as an adjunct described the office space for part-timers: "[Adjuncts have] shared office space. I think there were sometimes as many as 56 people assigned to the same office, the size of a large walk-in closet—no desk space that you could claim as your own."

The lack of office space makes it extremely difficult for these faculty to meet with students. As one former adjunct faculty member said, "Most of the time, as a part-timer, you met with students either in the classroom, or there's a conference room . . . that you can reserve and most of the time it's available. Otherwise you arrange to meet with the student in the part-time faculty office room, hoping that there'll be some space and some privacy."

Some part-time faculty members circumvent the office space problem by meeting during class or by e-mail: "It's usually during class [that I meet with students]; sometimes it's part, both during and after class. It depends on how many students are in the class. I have to ask some to meet outside of class. That's the other thing that's tricky about adjuncts. We don't have to have office hours, and sometimes we can't have office hours because of our schedules. So I do a lot of that through e-mail these days."

Despite the creativity of community college faculty, the inadequacy of the physical plant presents a chronic barrier to high-quality teaching and student-faculty interactions. Aside from the obvious impact this deficit has on students' ability to persist in these institutions, it is clear that faculty members also suffer from it in distinct ways that compromise their ability to excel in their jobs.

Inadequate Academic Support Services

As was pointed out earlier, community college students are relatively disadvantaged and are often unprepared for college-level work. Fully 42 percent of entering community college students require at least some form of remediation, and many require assistance in multiple subject areas. This situation has been exacerbated by recent state and local efforts to remove remedial students from the four-year sector altogether and to require students who test into pre-college courses to enroll in community colleges, thereby further burdening this sector.[2] The community college student population was described by one faculty member we interviewed in this way: "Well, we have open admissions, so we do have a wide variation. And I believe we have a lot of students with disabilities sometimes that haven't been discovered; they've just been cast off."

Yet on average, community colleges spend about one-third as many resources per full-time student on academic support services as do their four-year counterparts (NCES 2005a). This under-financing of support services such as writing centers, tutoring services, and study skills labs has a significant impact on community college faculty. For example, in both community colleges, the college-level English composition courses are designed to focus on developing higher-order thinking and writing skills. According to both lead coordinators of the English composition programs, ideally, grammar and the mechanics of writing would not be addressed in the non-remedial classroom at all. However, because community college students come in with such a range of skills, many of those who place into college-level writing courses still require significant assistance on mechanical issues such as sentence structure. As one female full-time faculty member said, "I find that I spend more time teaching them the nuts and bolts of writing and organization . . .

I mean, I try to teach them the different rhetorical modes, but because most of the students have no organizational skills, they don't know how to start. They don't take notes."

Yet the degree to which a faculty member must address these issues is directly dependent on the quality and availability of academic support. Both community colleges in our study had a tutoring center of some sort; and both centers had a clear mission to assist students to improve their writing by providing them with guidance, but not with easy answers. Yet the scope and quality of their services varied significantly. One institution had a more extensive center that provided tutoring for a range of subjects, from composition to mathematics to psychology. Although tutoring occurred at a single location on campus, the center's hours were extensive, and it was overseen and staffed by individuals with advanced degrees in relevant subject areas. English composition faculty members at this institution consistently reported that they regularly utilized the center, referring students with a range of mechanical and grammatical problems. In fact, the tutoring center used a computerized tracking system to inform faculty members of which students took advantage of these services. Thus, while these faculty still addressed a range of skills-related issues in their classrooms, due to the extreme diversity of community college students, they assigned the most onerous of these tasks to the tutoring center.

The academic support services at the other community college in our study were far more modest. The Writing Center is open only from 9 a.m. to 3 p.m. Monday through Friday, with no evening or weekend hours. It is staffed by only two full-time tutors. Faculty at this institution realize the limitations of the tutoring center; and as a result, they seldom rely on it for support. When one faculty member was asked if she ever refers students to the Writing Center, she replied in the negative, stating: "Our Writing Center needs to be opened more hours. We have eight o'clock classes. Yet there is not a computer on this campus that is open to students before eight o'clock so a student whose computer was eaten by his dog the night before has no way to get something ready for his eight o'clock class except to come to class late." Another faculty member responded with more detail, stating:

> When you are trying to explain something to someone who is having a lot of trouble with a certain punctuation or problem, the only way for them to get it is to have someone sit down with them one on one. And when I have 100 students, it is just not possible. I mean, I want to do it for all of them, but I can't. And so I think one thing that is really missing is I would love to be able to require all of my students to have one hour of tutoring a week. And then I could fill out a form and say I want you to

work on run-ons; I want you to work on apostrophes. I think they could really benefit from that, but we don't have the resources. If I made it a requirement, it would totally overwhelm our writing center.

Due to both their open admissions policies and the recent emergence of state policies designed to isolate remedial students in the two-year sector, community college faculty members are presented with what is arguably the most difficult teaching assignment in the postsecondary arena—to reach an extraordinarily broad range of students, some of whom arrive with significant deficiencies. The faculty we interviewed provide potent examples of the ways in which their ability to do their jobs well—in this case, to ensure that students master both the mechanical and critical thinking skills they need to succeed in college—is significantly dependent on the scope and quality of the academic support services available to students. While faculty at both institutions found themselves teaching more basic-level skills than they would like or deem appropriate even in a college-level course, the community college that devoted more resources to academic support services did relieve some of this pressure. Yet even under the best of circumstances, teaching in a community college is challenging and often frustrating.

Conclusions: Approaching Equity in a Low-Status Sector

Community colleges are the most female of postsecondary education institutions. There is a higher proportion of both part-time and full-time women faculty in these institutions than in any others; and they are generally considered to be hospitable to the female faculty who inhabit them. Women report a relatively high level of satisfaction in the community college workplace, citing flexibility and a relative lack of sexism as attractive aspects of this sector. While they are still less satisfied than their male counterparts, there is less disparity on satisfaction measures in community colleges than in any other sector of higher education. Gender-related salary disparities are lowest in this sector, and the proportion of female full-time faculty and senior administrators is higher here than in public and private four-year institutions. In many ways, female community college faculty members are approaching equity with their male counterparts.

But the question of what equity means when achieved in a low-status, low-resourced sector is one that cannot be ignored. In this chapter, we have closely examined the workplace conditions under which community college faculty—so many of whom are female—labor. Admittedly, none of the factors that we explored is explicitly "gendered." That is, the parameters of the community college academic workplace described by the faculty that we interviewed did not apply specifically, or disproportionately, to women. But because so many women inhabit this lowest-resourced, lowest-status sector of postsecondary education, understanding the work life of community college faculty members necessarily means that we must develop a deeper understanding of the workplace conditions in the institutions that employ more female academics than any other.

The bottom line is this: the low levels of resources in community colleges negatively affect the work life of faculty in these institutions in a myriad of related ways. Some are rather straightforward—community college faculty members are paid less than their four-year counterparts, whether full-time or part-time; their institutions spend far less for instructional and academic support services than do four-year institutions; and they are increasingly reliant on an expanding pool of part-time faculty.

Yet a careful tracing of the ways in which resource levels affect the quality of the academic workplace reveals additional insights. A lack of resources means a heavier workload. It means smaller, cramped office space and inadequate classrooms. It means a diminished capacity to create a collegial environment due to the growing number of part-time faculty. This, in turn, places an increasing burden on the remaining full-time faculty, who are expected to carry nearly all of the service and administrative duties of a department or college. And it means the absence of the comprehensive academic support services that both students and faculty members need to insure that high-quality learning is occurring.

In the face of these analyses, it is difficult to assert that the community college offers an environment to women that is conducive to a satisfying work life. Reports of relatively high levels of satisfaction from female community college faculty members must be tempered with a careful, realistic assessment of how the chronic underfunding of this sector of postsecondary education impedes its ability to offer these women even the most basic elements of an adequate workplace. This is not to dismiss or discount the body of research that reports high levels of satisfaction among female community college faculty members; rather, this study points to the importance of in-depth qualitative work that pays careful attention to the entirety of the workplace environment. While it may indeed be true that community colleges provide a set of circumstances that are relatively hospitable to women, these benefits must be carefully weighed against the real disadvantages of laboring in a postsecondary sector that remains at the bottom of the resource and status ladder.

We know from the important work of Slaughter and Leslie (1997) that *within* institutions, female-dominated fields such as social work and education receive fewer resources than more male-dominated departments such as engineering or physics, as colleges and universities act increasingly like entrepreneurial businesses. This phenomenon is not unique to the postsecondary education arena; so-called "feminine" work has been devalued for nearly as long as it has existed (Reskin and Padavic 1994). Moreover, if we are to take the results of the study presented in this chapter seriously, this phenomenon is particularly acute when one looks *across* postsecondary sectors as well—that is, the institutions that employ (and teach) the most women are exactly those that receive the fewest resources. This financial inequality is so longstanding and so entrenched that women who labor in community colleges are unlikely to see real improvements in their working conditions any time soon.

NOTES

1. In one of the community colleges, full-time English composition faculty teach a 4/4 load. However, they are the only faculty in the institution with a reduced load. All others teach a 5/5 load.

2. Recent examples include Massachusetts, California, and the City University of New York.

REFERENCES

American Association of Community Colleges. 2004. About community colleges. www.aacc .nche.edu/Template.cfm?section=About community colleges. Accessed August 21, 2006.

Austin, A. E. 2002. Preparing the next generation of faculty: Graduate school as socialization to the academic career. *Journal of Higher Education* 73 (1): 94–122.

Carey, K. 2006. *College rankings reformed: The case for a new order in higher education.* Washington, DC: Education Sector.

Cohen, A. M., and F. B. Brawer. 2003. *The American community college,* 4th ed. San Francisco: Jossey-Bass.

Dowd, A., and J. Grant. 2006. Equity and efficiency of community college appropriations: The role of local financing. Working paper.

Hagedorn, L. S., and B. V. Laden. 2002. Exploring the climate for women as community college faculty. *New Directions for Community Colleges* 118:69–78.

Huber, M. T. 1998. *Community college faculty attitudes and trends, 1997.* Palo Alto, CA: National Center for Postsecondary Improvement, Stanford University.

Miller, M. T., and J. W. Creswell. 1998. Beliefs and values of women in community college leadership. *Community College Journal of Research and Practice* 22 (3): 229–38.

National Center for Education Statistics (NCES). 2005a. *2004 National study of postsecondary faculty (NSOPF: 04): Background characteristics, work activities, and compensation of instruc-*

tional faculty and staff: Fall 2003. Washington, DC: U.S. Department of Education Institute of Education Sciences. NCES 2006–176.

———. 2005b. *2004 National study of postsecondary faculty (NSOPF: 04): Report on faculty and instructional staff in fall 2003.* Washington, DC: U.S. Department of Education Institute of Education Sciences. NCES 2005–172.

———. 2006a. *Digest of education statistics: 2005.* Washington, DC: U.S. Department of Education Institute of Education Sciences.

———. 2006b. *The condition of education.* Washington, DC: U.S. Department of Education Institute of Education Sciences.

Perna, L. W. 2001. The relationship between family responsibilities and employment status among college and university faculty. *Journal of Higher Education* 72:584–611.

———. 2003. The status of women and minorities among community college faculty. *Research in Higher Education* 44 (2): 231–40.

Reskin, Barbara, and Irene Padavic. 1994. *Women and men at work.* Thousand Oaks, CA: Pine Forge Press.

Scott, M., T. Bailey, and G. Kienzl. 2006. Relative success? Determinants of college graduation rates in public and private colleges in the United States. *Research in Higher Education* 47:249–79.

Slaughter, S., and L. L. Leslie. 1997. *Academic capitalism: Politics, policies, and the entrepreneurial university.* Baltimore: Johns Hopkins University Press.

Townsend, B. K. 1998. Female faculty: Satisfaction with employment in the community college. *Community College Journal of Research and Practice* 22:655–62.

Townsend, B. K., and N. LaPaglia. 2000. Are we marginalized within academe? Perceptions of two-year college faculty. *Community College Journal of Research and Practice* 22 (7): 655–61.

Wolf-Wendel, Lisa, Kelly Ward, and Susan Twombly. 2006. Faculty life at community colleges: The perspectives of women with children. *Community College Review* 34 (4):255–81.

CHAPTER TEN

Women of Color in Academe

Experiences of the Often Invisible

CAROLINE SOTELLO VIERNES TURNER

Information on the experiences of women of color in academe can be invisible, buried within studies that report results under categories such as "faculty of color" or "women."[1] Women of color fit both racial/ethnic and gender categories,[2] inhabit multiple social identities, and experience multiple marginality; moreover, their stories are often masked within these contexts (Turner 2002; 2007). This chapter presents a perspective on the status of women of color in the professoriat and in senior-level administrative positions based on evidence emerging from my personal reflections as a Latina/Filipina scholar and from the perspectives of other women of color on their workplace experiences derived from interviews, focus groups, and literature reviews.

In order to present perspectives of women of color in academe, I first describe my own experience and then draw on narrative data from studies I conducted or co-authored of faculty, predominantly in research universities (Turner and Myers 2000; Townsend and Turner 2000; Turner 2000; Turner 2002), and senior-level administrators (Turner 2007; Turner and Kappes in press).[3] As part of the discussion on faculty women of color, I also present information from a current study emerging from focus groups conducted with faculty women of color examining their perspectives on the effect, if any, of the *Grutter v. Bollinger*[4] decision (2003) on their careers and the recruitment of others.

Within the higher education literature, exclusion and the "glass ceiling" phenomenon are well documented as affecting all women (Glazer-Raymo 1999). Allen and colleagues (1991, 190) note that "women from underrepresented populations face barriers due to historical, cultural, and social factors that have shaped their experience and development in American society. . . . Pervasive racist and sexist attitudes continue to limit educational opportunities for women of color." References to some of the extant literature, in conjunction with demographic data on women of color students, faculty, and academic leaders, provide a national context for the narratives presented. Numerical data provide evidence of varied student educational attainment for women of color and their lack of representation as faculty and administrators. In fact, their representation decreases significantly at the level of full professor and senior administrator (American Council on Education 2007; *Chronicle of Higher Education Annual Almanac* 2006). Such data point to the continued failure of higher education to serve its publics. Relevant data within each section of this chapter address the situation for women of color in various academic roles.

Why is it important to examine the perspectives of women of color emerging from narrative studies as well as to provide these data in the context of numerical data and relevant literature? The invisibility of women of color as students and teachers and in leadership positions creates a void in the learning experience of all students. Without adequate pools of women of color candidates for academic positions, college and university departments lose out on the perspectives they bring to the learning process. As noted by Smith, Turner, Osei-Kofi, and Richards (2004, 133), diverse faculties (and administrations) are necessary in an era of increased diversity of student bodies, along with "the need to prepare students for a diverse society." The lack of women of color in high academic positions sends a message that women of color cannot succeed in these positions and, most unfortunately, that our institutions cannot benefit from their participation. This situation becomes a disincentive for women students of color who might consider an academic or administrative career in higher education.

Living in an increasingly diverse society and a competitive global world, the importance of nurturing cross-cultural communities is crucial. Who you are shapes the questions you ask, the issues that interest you, and your approach to solving problems. The life experiences and backgrounds that women of color bring to academia contribute to the development of a wider range of scholarly perspectives and the creation of an enriched intellectual campus climate.[5] These experiences also contribute to the development of a welcoming campus environment and can dispel stereotypes through cross-racial interactions inside and outside of the classroom. It is my hope that this discussion can assist those who are striving to improve the representation of women of color in all areas and levels of academe. I begin this dialogue with my own experiences as a woman of color student and faculty member.

Author Perspective

Picking tomatoes and cutting apricots with my family in California,
I played games and scenarios in my mind to keep me otherwise
occupied. I never dreamed of becoming a professor or even going to
college. I grew up doing field work and now, as a qualitative
researcher, I find it amusing that I still find myself doing field work.

I became a researcher with a focus on access and equity in higher education because I knew how important those issues are to my home community. I am a woman of color from a "no collar" laborer class. I grew up as part of a large immigrant family living and working on farm labor camps in the agricultural fields of rural California. I, along with my six sisters and my brother, was born in California and graduated from high school. We are a female-enriched household. Graduating from high school was an accomplishment for farm labor families then—and unfortunately, even now.

In many ways, my educational accomplishments and those of my family provide examples of how the educational system works to educate underrepresented and low-income groups in American society. And indeed, narratives shared by many women of color with whom I have spoken point to an educational pathway fraught with challenges due to race/ethnic, social class, and gender bias. Their stories, reflective of my personal experience in many ways, provide important insights into the quality of life for those who have typically been denied access to mainstream higher education institutions and cultures.

As a freshman in college in the early 1960s, I was an alien in a world vastly different from the one in which I was raised. I learned that while my family was highly respected in our community, in academe they were seen as failing to earn money and therefore perceived and treated as marginal. For instance, during a discussion in my dormitory, one classmate asked: "Why are people poor?" The response was that people were poor because they were lazy. Everyone there nodded in agreement, to which I interjected: "But my father works all day, sunup to sundown, every day. He is not lazy and we are poor." Everyone looked at me, but no one responded; they just walked away.

Where does such ignorance come from? Too many times, it is not unlearned in college. Chances to learn and understand do exist, but for real change to take place, individuals must have opportunities to interact with others from different backgrounds, and they must also be open to the incorporation of new and unfamiliar ways of thinking. This was only one of many such encounters I experienced as an undergraduate student, as a graduate student, and as a faculty member.

I recall a personal example of how multiple social identities may shape one's opportunities in higher education. When I was first exploring graduate school options, an admissions advisor discouraged me from applying to a master's level program in business, stating that I would not "fit in." I was a woman, a minority, a single parent. I had a background in the public sector, and I had some but not enough mathematics. This would make it nearly impossible for me to succeed, since others in the program fit a more typical profile. Although all of this may be the case when looked at from a conventional perspective, it did not occur to the admissions officer that this might not be the only appropriate entry point for every student enrolling in the program. It was merely accepted as the way things were and should remain. I remember being struck by the many ways I could be defined as not "fitting" and therefore not encouraged—and, more than likely, not admitted. I was so easily "defined out" rather than "defined in."

I have received mentoring from individual faculty and administrators throughout my career. These individuals had confidence in my capabilities and selected and supported me in leadership positions that would lead to national and international spotlights. Today, I find myself as a scholar-advocate, conducting research to illuminate access and equity issues for women and men of color who are underrepresented as well as marginalized in higher education. In my research I have found that the dynamics of defining out diversity exist not only at the point of student admissions but also at the points of hiring and promotion of faculty and administrators. As I work to improve the quality of life for people of color in higher-education institutions, I combine research with service. My writing is for scholarly audiences and for practitioners who want to stimulate organizational change and to make a difference by increasing the numbers of faculty and administrators of color, especially women, at all levels on their campuses. I am frequently called to advise college and university presidents, provosts, and faculty across the nation as they pursue their goals to diversify their campuses. Some of this work has been highlighted in the *Chronicle of Higher Education* (2006). At times, graduate students, faculty of color, and academic administrators come up to me and say that my work provides validation and support for the work in which they are engaged. These interactions confer needed energy, revitalization, and life meaning for my work. Closely aligning the tasks of faculty research, teaching, and service has helped to sustain my persistence in the field.

While progress has been made in diversifying the academy, data show that I am one of only 957 Hispanic women full professors in the United States and one of

1,611 Asian women full professors (*Chronicle* 2006). The total Hispanic women full professors (957) and Asian women full professors (1,611) represent approximately 2.4 percent and 4.1 percent, respectively, of the total women full professors (39,366) and 0.6 percent and 0.9 percent, respectively, of all full professors, men and women (166,415). In addition, there are 1,916 African-American women full professors and only 154 American Indian women full professors. These numbers underscore the almost invisible presence of women of color who are full professors, a matter of concern in the context of faculty governance and the implementation of tenure and promotion policies. These policies represent an extreme challenge for women of color, given the propensity of higher education to reproduce itself through the hiring process and to appoint and promote those more like themselves (Konrad and Pfeffer 1991; Light 1994; Mickelson and Oliver 1991).[6]

In addition, the doctorate is a necessary credential for tenure-track positions in most fields. Yet, according to recent data, few women of color enroll in college, and even if they do enroll, they are not well represented among those being awarded the doctoral degree (*Chronicle of Higher Education Almanac* 2006). Of those awarded the doctorate, how many are prepared to successfully compete for faculty positions? A study examining the socialization of women doctoral students (Turner and Thompson 1993) found that minority women had fewer opportunities for professional socialization experiences such as research and teaching assistantships, coauthorship of papers with a faculty member, presentations at professional conferences, and introductions by faculty to a network of influential academics who could provide support for them in gaining entry-level positions. In order to gain additional insights into the quality of faculty life[7] and the leadership experiences of women of color, in the next sections I present narrative data from research I conducted with women of color faculty and campus presidents.

Women of Color in the Professoriat: Lived Contradictions

I am struck by my lived contradiction: To be a professor is to be an *anglo*; to be a *Latina* is not to be an *anglo*. So how can I be both a Latina and a professor? To be a Latina professor, I conclude, means to be unlike *and* like me. *Que locura!* What madness! . . . As Latina professors, we are newcomers to a world defined and controlled by discourses that do not address our realities, that do not affirm our intellectual contributions, that do not seriously examine our worlds. Can I be both Latina and professor without compromise? (Alemán 1995)

In reflecting on her experiences as an African-American law student and junior faculty member, Patricia Williams (1991, 55–56) describes vividly her "feelings of exaggerated visibility and invisibility" as products of not being "part of the larger cultural picture." Unfortunately, as Essien (2003, 64) reports, "there has been no appreciable change in the quality of life of the minority law professor," also citing Barbara Bernier to say that "the politics of a 'society of one' continue to concern me as I watch the dearth of hiring not only of people of color but of women as well." Morrobel-Sosa (2005) describes the invisibility she felt despite her multiple identities as a "woman, immigrant, Latina, of color, chemist, faculty, and administrator." And in her report on women chemistry faculty, Nelson (2005) shows that "underrepresented minority (URM) women faculty are almost non-existent in science and engineering departments at research universities, and that while women's representation in science and engineering doctoral attainment has significantly increased in recent years, the corresponding faculties are still overwhelmingly dominated by White men" (1–2). (See also Stage and Hubbard, chapter 5 in this book, on women baccalaureates in the STEM fields).

The interlocking effects of gender, race, and ethnicity compound the pressures of the workplace environment for faculty women of color. Situations in which a woman of color might experience marginality are multiplied, depending on her outsider status in various contexts. Often it is difficult to tell whether race or gender stereotyping is operating. One woman told me that "dealing with the senior (mostly white) males in my department has been a huge challenge . . . I don't know if they tend to discount my contributions because I'm new, female, Latina, young, or what. Perhaps [it's] a combination of all of the above." Promotion processes are especially problematic for faculty women of color. Often they report having been told they did not fit the profile of someone to be promoted or having been bypassed in the process and advised to try for promotion at another institution. An Asian-American faculty member describes being defined out of consideration for an administrative position because of her race and gender:

> A [university administrative] position opened up and there were a lot of names mentioned—-I felt that if I were a white male, my name would have been out there. I mean, I am sure of that. But it never was and, you know . . . there is no question in my mind that race and gender influenced that.

Five themes emerged from our interviews with faculty women of color (Turner and Myers 2000): (1) feeling isolated and under-respected; (2) salience of race over gender; (3) being underemployed and overused by departments and/or institutions; (4) being torn between family, community, and career; and (5) being challenged by students.[8] Each of these themes is further explicated below.

One woman of color expressed her feelings of isolation and the added pressure to perform, stating:

> I have to think about the fact that black females or any female in the field of [name] that has been predominantly a white male profession has a problem. Many [white] females in the college complain about the fact that up until recently . . . we had never had a full professor in [department name]. It's changing, but it's not changing fast. And then you add to that being the black female who has to be superwoman.

Seen as a sign of under-respect, a new hire describes her dean as focused more on slots filled than on expertise or potential programmatic contributions:

> This one dean was writing down all the federal slots that I would fit in as far as hiring . . . And he says, "Okay, you're a woman, you're over fifty-five, you're an American Indian," and then he looks at me and grins. He said, "Do you have a handicap?" These schools have to fulfill these guidelines, and in getting me they can check a lot of boxes.

This situation creates great discomfort for minority women faculty because they feel diminished in their professional capacities. They want to be recognized for their academic credentials, not for their race or gender:

> I'm the department chair in the [science] department and I meet with a lot of people who don't know me—you know, prospective students and their parents. And I know that their first reaction to me is that I'm an Asian American woman, not that I'm a scientist or that I'm competent.

With regard to the salience of race over gender, women faculty of color participating in the Turner and Myers study indicate that despite shared gender discrimination, they feel they cannot always expect support from their white female colleagues. An American Indian woman notes: "Even the white females they've hired still have a problem with minority students and minority perspectives. This is particularly true in [discipline]. It is really dominated by Western European notions." She confirms Montero-Sieburth's observation that "being female does not necessarily guarantee the sympathy of mainstream women toward them nor does it offer entry into mainstream academic domains" and that Latina professors must overcome more obstacles to gain support for academic advancement because they are further removed from the academic old-boys network than Latino or white female counterparts (1996, 84).

Although there is some evidence of mentorship across and within racial/ethnic and gender groups, scarce resources such as tenured faculty positions and chairs of Chicano studies programs can pit Latinas against Latinos. In a similar vein, hooks (1989) states that scholars writing about black intellectual life focus solely on the lives and works of black men, ignoring and devaluing the scholarship of black women intellectuals.

Unlike white male and female faculty members, women of color say that issues of gender and diversity are channeled to them. For example, an American Indian woman explains the situation for her as a woman faculty of color:

> Issues of pedagogy and cultural diversity and gender are not the province of just women or just faculty of color. I think that happens too often and that puts the faculty of color person or woman on the spot, to kind of convince or persuade—be this change agent . . . The faculty members feel the added pressure, but are caught in a 'Catch-22' because minority issues are also important to them.

Her observation is confirmed by Mitchell (1994), who notes that the small numbers of faculty women of color compels them to serve simultaneously as role models for their profession, race/ethnicity, and gender. A Latina woman also said: "When you are one of three or four Latinos and being a woman, almost every committee wants you to be on it. It gives you opportunities at the same time . . . you are expected to do a lot of things not expected of other faculty." And due to their scarcity, faculty women of color face greater service and out-of-class instructional loads. Other faculty study respondents describe these experiences:

> When I first arrived, I was overwhelmed by the amount of students, mostly women of color, who came to me to ask for guidance [from all over campus] feeling like most other faculty did not acknowledge their existence. It is difficult to balance this with the research and publication pressures, and course preparation.

Another states:

> It is hard to say no, especially on minority issues, when there are so few people . . . I realize how few people are available [to address these issues] . . . I sit on 53 doctoral committees. Doctoral students take a lot of time for the dissertation process . . . I'll wind up spending all my time correcting dissertations and not doing my own writing.

Many faculty women of color speak about being psychologically divided between home and career and/or between community and career. They seemingly have two choices: sacrifice family and community commitments for several years to focus almost exclusively on their careers, or honor non-work commitments, an essential part of their identity, at the risk of not earning tenure. Although policies to accommodate faculty needs for maternity and family leave and childcare are becoming common, little attention has been paid in the academy to minority faculty's desire to contribute actively to their racial or ethnic community (for further discussion, see Townsend and Turner 2000; Turner and Myers 2000; Turner 2002; Turner 2004).

Finally, women faculty of color report that they are more likely to have their authority challenged by students than are white male professors,[9] and as three women faculty state:

> If a white male professor says something that's wrong in class, my observation is that even if the students perceive that it's wrong, they may say something outside of class, but they hesitate to challenge a 50+ white male professor. They feel quite comfortable challenging an African American woman in class.

> Regarding interaction with students, there's a different expectation for us when we walk in as a minority, [the students] automatically assume that we know less than our colleagues in the same department . . . It doesn't matter whether it's undergraduate level or graduate level . . . They challenge females more . . . So, I wear dark, tailored suits and I am very well prepared. They don't hire us unless we're prepared anyway, but students think we are here because of our color.

> I think gender is an issue for some students. Some students want to be more familiar with a woman. Some students don't trust the authority of a woman of color in the classroom.

These women are called upon by students to serve not only as educators but as mentors, mothers, and counselors; and these demands are compounded by those placed upon them by colleagues, administrators, and people in their personal lives at some cost to their emotional well-being. Ng (1997, 367) stresses that educators must "break the conspiracy of silence that has ensured the perpetuation of racism, sexism, and other forms of marginalization and exclusion in the university" and to counteract some of the negative outcomes of these inequitable workloads.

Preliminary data from focus groups conducted with faculty women of color[10] to assess their interpretations of the *Grutter v. Bollinger* decision and to examine their perception of the impact of this decision on their work lives show that the five themes derived from previously collected interview data remain major issues (Turner and Myers 2000; Turner 2006b). Even today, faculty women of color describe the situation on their campuses as alienating, isolating, and discouraging.

They report little awareness of institutional efforts to diversify student populations or the faculty and say that nothing much has changed for them since *Grutter v. Bollinger*. There is a perception that once search committees have made attempts to diversify the applicant pool, no further efforts are required to hire and retain diverse faculty. Women of color faculty also experience a lack of resources to support their research or to facilitate collaborative research and mentoring opportunities. And even if resources do exist, they are not made aware of these, nor is there a central clearinghouse that disseminates information regarding such initiatives. They also describe continually having to overcome undergraduate student resistance to being taught by a woman of color. Despite the challenges described by women faculty of color, several are successful; and of these, some eventually seek positions of academic leadership, including a campus presidency. Each of the women of color presidents presented below began their academic careers as faculty and moved through the ranks as new challenges presented themselves.

Women of Color in the Campus Presidency

Given that academic administrators often begin their careers as faculty, the low numbers of women of color receiving doctorates and achieving the rank of full professor can be viewed as predictive of their low representation as deans, provosts, and college presidents. However, the low representation of women of color should also be viewed in the historical context of a legacy of exclusion, substandard educational facilities, and few opportunities for students. Wilson (1989, 85) refers to the limited presence of women of color in senior administration as "rooted in the history of America," describing the "lack of educational opportunities that existed for racial minorities in the nineteenth and early twentieth centuries and the fact that women were expected to raise families, not to become educated and have careers" (87). He recognizes that "affirmative action and court decisions were the primary levers that forced open the doors of mostly White male institutions to people of color" (93) and that higher education's demographic composition tends to reproduce itself through its hiring practices. Konrad and Pfeffer's (1991) research on the hiring of women administrators in 821 institutions of higher education provides compelling evidence that newly hired administrators reproduce the race, ethnicity, and gender of their predecessors, regardless of the composition of the labor pool. The present status of women of color as presidents appears to indicate that these patterns continue to prevail.

The profile of women presidents in the current American Council on Education survey of 2,148 male and female presidents reveals that between 1986 and 2006, the proportion of women presidents more than doubled, from 10 percent to 23 percent of those surveyed (ACE 2007, 15). However, the rate of increase for presidents of color was smaller, from 8 percent in 1986 to 14 percent in 2006. The authors of this report state that the "demographic profile of the typical college or university president is slowly changing but continues to be primarily white (86.4%) and male (77%)" (ACE 2007, 9). When disaggregated by race/ethnicity, 6.6 percent of women presidents are Hispanic, 1.0 percent are Asian American, 1.5 percent are American Indian, 8.1 percent are African American, and 81.1 percent are white (72, Appendix C). They conclude that "the imperative of rapidly changing economic, demographic, and political conditions suggests the need for adaptability and diversity in educational institutions and their leaders" (58). Taking institutional type into consideration, Harvey and Anderson (2005) also report that of 200 women presidents of public four-year institutions in 2004, 18 (9%) are African American, 8 (4%) are Hispanic, 2 (1%) are American Indian, 1 (0.5%) is Asian American, and 171 (85.5%) are white.

Racial and ethnic stereotyping, gender bias, and cultural differences that lead to feelings of dissonance and contradiction in the workplace are the primary themes that cut across the literature focusing on Hispanic, American Indian, Asian-American, and African-American women in positions of academic administrative leadership. While these themes are reflective of the experiences of women faculty of color, it is also important to closely examine the lives of women of color in senior administration in order to gain insight into the barriers and facilitators of their success. As described above, the demographics for women of color in presidential positions reflect a continuing problem of gross underrepresentation. A brief review of published work documenting the experiences of these women of color further illuminates the challenges they have faced. Scholars writing about the experience of Latinas[11] in higher-education leadership note the challenge of racial, ethnic, and gender stereotyping but concentrate most of their discussion on cultural differences leading to feelings of dissonance and contradiction in the workplace. Nieves-Squires describes cultural differences that can lead to tension for Hispanas in academe, stating that "challenging someone's statements, trying to change another person's opinion, or debating issues can be viewed as a sign of disrespect" (1991, 2). Hansen (1997) cites Latina administrators who speak about learning how to function in two distinct sociocultural environments either by drawing on their identity and upholding institutional values (dualism) or by drawing on their identity and working toward the social transformation of their institution (negotiation).

Warner's study of American Indian[12] women administrators in higher education concludes with an exploration of circumstances in which they perceive dissonance in their work environment because "cultural expectations within tribal communities are significantly different from cultural expectations of a formal organization" (1995, 1). According to Swisher and Benally, "in many Indigenous cultures, humility is a value . . . so it is inappropriate for individuals . . . to bring attention to her/his deeds or accomplishments" (1998, xiii). Krumm (1997), underscoring the connection between culture and leadership, reports that tribal college leadership is inseparable from culture. Her study participants described their preferred leadership styles as high in supportiveness, which is reflective of their cultural values, although situations often compelled them to use a more directive leadership style.

Asian Americans, representing twenty nations and sixty ethnic groups, give some indication of the diversity of people of color in the United States. However, this diversity is severely underrepresented among academic leaders (Escueta and O'Brien 1991; Hune 1998; Hune and Chan 1997). Cho (1996) describes the absence of Asian Pacific American (APA) women at the executive and managerial levels in higher education as a manifestation of "academic caste," accent discrimination, and sexual/racial harassment. Hune (1998) refers to cultural differences that may hinder APA women's mobility, citing being polite and deferential, seeking consensus, and generally being viewed as demonstrating a lack of leadership, confidence, or originality. Ideta and Cooper also comment that "Asian women leaders seem to live in the confines of paradoxes. As Asian females they struggle in organizations which define leaders as primarily male and White. . . . Behaviors which are typical of leaders (displays of power, authority, and fortitude) are considered atypical for women and doubly atypical for Asian women . . . expected to be compliant and subservient in their behavior" (1999, 141).

Several challenges impede the progress of African-American women into senior level administrative positions on predominantly white campuses. These relate to racial and gender stereotypes, pressures to conform to the majority culture, and difficulties in overcoming biases as the "first" to grasp the higher rungs of the academic ladder (Davis 1994; Farris 1999; Harvey 1999; Jackson 2004; King 1999; McDemmond 1999; Moses 1989). Despite the challenges for administrative advancement described by these women and also reflected in my study of the career trajectories of three women of color presidents (Turner 2007), the good news is that these women have become campus leaders. My extensive research on women of color presidents has shown that women such as Juliet Garcia, president of the University of Texas at Brownsville/Texas Southmost College; Karen Swisher, president of Haskell Indian Nations University; and Rose Tseng, chancellor of the University of Hawaii at Hilo are quite successful in influencing changes in learning environments that foster the development of all students, including women of color. They describe their use of local, national, and international resources to create structural opportunities, developing new baccalaureate degree programs, articulation agreements with community colleges, and external funding to strengthen their programs.

Garcia describes her satisfaction when she sees the impact that her efforts have had on students:

> The best experience [as president] is the kind of quiet moments when you see what happens to people. . . . One young lady came from Matamoros, couldn't speak any English, and went through our program for intensive English. . . . She [ended] up with a bachelor's degree in physics, went off and got a master's degree—this is all in between having children with her family—and is now working on her doctorate.

Garcia, Swisher, and Tseng all relate the importance of their social and professional interconnections with others as key to their success, and they mentor other women of color who aspire to positions in academic administration. Their advice to women of color calls for trusting one's instincts, "being centered and knowing exactly who you are," having the courage to fail, and treating others as you want to be treated. They say that being oneself gets easier the longer you are in a top-level position. Garcia discusses the importance of fitting into the institution as critical to her success: "There's a good match every once in a while, and some of the energy that you need for a job comes from being at the right place and doing what your soul tells you you're supposed to be doing."

Garcia also describes the attempts of women of color to minimize feelings of dissonance and maximize congruence in the workplace or to conceal their real identities in attempts to fit in to the majority culture, stating: "I have to tell you that I thought at first that I had to become like someone else. I had to look like, or act like, or talk like the models that were here before us. And if I could just dress like, look like, talk like them, whoever they were, then I had a chance for that type of position."

However, acknowledging who we are and how that affects our approaches to research and to our leadership styles may result in a more viable work environment for women of color now and in the future. Although the socialization process for doctoral students, faculty, and administrators is strong, these women argue that women should not lose their identities in their efforts to fit in. Also, as demonstrated here, the background one brings to academia need not take a back seat but can be placed in the foreground of one's work (Turner 2000). By breaking through glass ceilings and supporting colleagues, we can define ourselves in and challenge those assumptions that erected barriers in the first place and that created workplace environments of dissonance and contradiction for women of color. We can work toward the creation of inclusive campus climates based on discourses that address our realities, affirm our intellectual contributions, and make us visible.

Rewards and Satisfactions: Contributing to Reshaping the Academy

While some women of color students, faculty, and academic leaders have achieved success, much more work needs to be done not only to support their continued success and to bring their accomplishments to light but also to stem the loss of talent represented by the overall lack of women of color in academe. Although their numbers are growing, they continue to be viewed as "the minority" and to make history as "firsts." For example, although Ruth Simmons is not the first African-American woman president, in July 2001 she became the first African-American woman to lead an Ivy League institution, Brown University.

Interviews and conversations with women of color faculty and presidents reveal that although they are confronted by unique pressures, the satisfactions that attracted them to higher education sustain their participation. The three presidents I have cited each began her career as a faculty member, experiencing the intellectual challenge; the freedom to pursue research interests; and the ability to make contributions, to create new knowledge, and to promote gender, racial, and ethnic understanding. The personal rewards most commonly articulated by the faculty and presidents that I interviewed were their satisfaction with teaching, supportive working relationships, and a sense of accomplishment. In addition, both women of color faculty and presidents speak about the value of mentoring and networking experiences in their career development and their desire to make a difference, reshaping the academy to further accommodate and incorporate women of color at all levels and in all fields. Their descriptions of why they stay as well as the barriers they have had to overcome are the basis for my recommendations for more inclusive campus communities.

If women of color with requisite educational achievements, academic rank, and prior leadership experiences are not encouraged to pursue advanced degrees and academic positions, their invisibility as doctoral students, faculty, deans, and presidents will persist. The contributing factors for success cited by study respondents and in the literature point to the critical role of colleges and universities in the education, recruitment, and mentoring process.

Institutional racial, ethnic, and gender composition may matter to prospective faculty women of color who are considering new employment opportunities because the more diverse the population, the greater the probability of establishing mentoring and networking relationships with individuals who may understand their unique experiences. Certainly, individual mentoring and the validation of their potential have enabled women of color to persevere. Each of the three presidents told me about the importance of maintaining close relationships with other women of color, seeking advice on issues that concern them, mentoring, and networking.

Another critical element to the success of women of color is being selected for increasingly responsible and visible positions where they can demonstrate their talents. Cuadraz provides this insight: "We know that without structural opportunities, moments of validation are stripped of their transformative force and left to dwell in the realm of memory" (2006, 104). The coupling of individual validation with institutional opportunity is critical to professional and personal growth. Such support promotes a comfort level that can increase productivity at work and persistence on campus.

Overall, academe must be more focused on providing structural opportunities to ensure the development of diverse talents for all women of color, providing pathways for their upward mobility. These opportunities can include appointments as chairs of influential committees, visible interim positions, endowed chairs, or named professorships; support to participate in professional leadership development programs; and access to resources that facilitate collaborations across fields. Colleges and universities can facilitate opportunities for faculty women of color by hosting academic and networking activities, creating faculty learning communities on and off campus, and offering institutional support to women of color for cross-cultural and cross-gender research teams and for national or regional conferences.

Deans and department chairs can address the service burden of faculty women of color by formally monitoring their research and service workload, compensating them through redistribution/reassignment of responsibilities. Rewarding such commitments in evaluations for tenure and promotion is central to addressing issues related to service. Gregory (1995) recommends the transformation of tenure and promotion criteria by exploring ways to expand the definition of scholarly activity and to place more importance on teaching, service, and curriculum development activities. Baez (2000) stresses that scholars must condemn higher education practices and norms that produce conflict through differential reward systems for faculty of color, especially for minority scholars dedicated to race-based service. He contends that "service, though significantly presenting obstacles to the promotion and retention of faculty of color, actually may set the stage for a critical agency that resists and redefines academic structures that hinder faculty success" (2000, 363). If service is seen as addressing social justice issues, it can be a source of pride and validation for many minority faculty. It gives them much-needed connection with communities of color within and outside the academy as a whole, which can translate into supportive networks for the individual providing the service.

Doing work that closely aligns oneself to communities of color and gender may provide a way to maintain one's sense of self. Delgado-Gaitan describes this process as a kind of dance: "My life has been a 'TINKLING' dance in which I have hopped between two clanking bamboo sticks, skillfully avoiding getting a foot severed as I jumped in and out. I have searched to find the space that is a synthesis of my worlds . . . the 'borderland' or meeting ground that synthesizes my identity, experience, feelings, beliefs, and dreams" (1997, 37).

Barbara Townsend and Caroline Turner recommend three steps that institutional leaders can take to address the challenges and conflicts of family, work, and community commitments described by faculty women of color in community colleges, as a means of recruiting and sustaining them in their institutions: (1) identify and acknowledge institutional norms and policies that place women faculty of color at a disadvantage resulting from their family and community commitments; (2) promote the development of norms that support community and family involvement; and (3) include women of color in the identification of the challenges, conflicts, and their solutions (Townsend and Turner 2000).

Most women of color contend that a healthy, supportive, rewarding, inclusive environment is good for everyone. One crucial component in producing such an environment is to increase the representation of women of color across the campus as undergraduates and graduate students, administrators, and faculty at all ranks. As Harvey (1999) and others observe, it is critically important to develop a campus culture that values and welcomes the contributions made by women of color to the academic enterprise, acknowledging that their inclusion contributes to the academy as a whole. Cole (2000) emphasizes this point, stating that valuing diversity—in the people, the ideas, the theories, the perspectives and experiences, and the pedagogy in American higher education—is crucial to a quality education.

When asked about the future of women of color in senior administration, one of our study participants makes a statement applicable to the future of women of color in this and other academic positions:

> I think it is promising . . . First, however, women of color must have opportunities to come up successfully through the ranks across all disciplines of the professoriat. Then

they and their institutions must see that they have opportunities for line experience leading faculty in academic departments on up. It will take an enlightened system for all of this to happen. (Turner and Kappes in press)

Education can play a critical role in helping people to realize their dreams and to develop their talents to the fullest, contributing to the sustainability of a diverse and democratic society. As evidenced by the numbers of women of color in academe, however small, progress has been made in promoting and recognizing the achievements of women of color. However, giant leaps are needed to significantly increase their presence at all levels of higher education. Yes, there are bright spots reflected in the success stories for women of color, but we need overall brilliance. Women of color need the support of their home institutions as they progress toward the doctorate, toward full professorships, and toward senior level administrative positions.

The overall conclusion to be made from the demographic and narrative data on women of color faculty presented in this chapter, which are also reflective of their low representation as students and academic administrators, is that parity for women of color remains an unfinished agenda in higher education. Themes emerging from a study published in 2000 (Turner and Myers) are also articulated in a current study on the status of women faculty of color post–*Grutter v. Bollinger* (Turner 2006b). To briefly reiterate, narratives from women faculty of color in ongoing research document their continued isolation; the salience of race over gender in the workplace; their underemployment and overuse by departments and/or institutions; their challenge to balance needs of family, community, and career; and their challenges by students in the classroom. Unfortunately, alienation and discouragement resulting in large part from such workplace experiences continue to be expressed by women faculty of color. In a sense, the presence of faculty women of color can be viewed as an indicator of higher education's commitment and receptivity to the multiple voices that comprise their diverse constituency. These are continuing challenges faced by higher education.

Given the level of debate regarding affirmative action and challenges to its continuation, the impact on efforts to increase student and faculty racial/ethnic diversity has become more critical. In *Grutter v. Bollinger* (2003), the Supreme Court ruled on the use of race in student admissions in higher education. While supporting the merits of a diverse student body as a "national compelling interest," the court also established boundaries such as the use of "tailored" approaches to achieve diversity in the student body and specified a window of "twenty-five years" within which this goal must be achieved. Such challenges, as previously described, have implications not only for student diversity but also for efforts to diversify the faculty and academic administration.

In facing these new and continuing challenges to increase the recruitment, retention, and development of women of color faculty and administrators at all institutional types and in all fields/disciplines, higher education institutions can view this challenge as an opportunity to renew their diversity mission in preparing the next generation of women of color as students, faculty, and administrative leaders.

NOTES

1. The terms "woman or man of color," "students of color," "faculty of color," and "minority" refer to persons of African-American, American Indian, Asian-American, and Latino origin. I understand that "people of color" aren't a monolithic group and recognize that whites are also members of a distinct racial category. And by using the individual racial and ethnic categories I do not intend to imply that all persons so designated experience anything in a uniform way. Rather, these categories are used in order to present existing data distinguishing between these groups, to identify some common themes, and to make overall statements about the varying experiences of the identified groups. Many categories of diversity exist; this chapter focuses on the experience of women of color faculty teaching primarily at research universities and women of color presidents who are located mainly in four-year baccalaureate institutions.

2. Several scholars have concluded that race, ethnicity, and gender are interlocking sources of marginalization in higher education (Aronson and Swanson 1991; Carter, Pearson, and Shavlik 1987; Collins 1989; hooks 1989). See also *Through My Lens* (Aparicio 1999), a video depiction of the intersection of race and gender in higher education and of the impact of race, gender, and culture on one's career.

3. Unless otherwise noted, quotations from faculty women of color draw on interviews with women in the social sciences, natural sciences, humanities, and education for a study conducted by Turner and Myers (2000). Campus presidents quoted are from public baccalaureate degree–granting universities.

4. On June 23, 2003, the U.S. Supreme Court ruled in *Grutter v. Bollinger* that diversity is a compelling interest in higher education and that race is one of a number of factors that can be taken into account to achieve the educational benefits that flow from a diverse student body. The Court found that the individualized, whole-file review used in the University of Michigan Law School's admissions policy is narrowly tailored to achieve the educational benefits of diversity. The Court also stated that the Law School's goal of attaining a critical mass of underrepresented minority students does not transform its program into a quota.

5. See the video *Shattering the silences* (Nelson and Pellett 1997) for a portrayal of the lives of eight scholars of color in the humanities and social sciences, illustrating how they transformed and were transformed by their respective disciplines and institutions. These scholars bring new research questions and fresh perspectives to the academic enterprise. See also Turner 2000 for a discussion by a professor of organismic biology at the University of California of how

her interest in topics concerning her community helped to bring new issues into the world of scientific scholarship.

6. In a letter to the author, a white male endowed professor writes, "I have no doubt whatsoever that discrimination is 'alive and well' in the academy and that, at whatever level of conscious or subconscious behavior, it serves to thwart minority hires and (all the more insidiously, I believe) their retention . . . [but in addition] the shortfall in the pipeline is still daunting."

7. There is a body of literature citing the barriers that women of color must overcome to succeed as faculty (see, e.g., Alemán 1995; Hune 1998; Ladson-Billings 1997; Rains 1999; Turner 2002; Turner and Myers 2000).

8. Even though common themes are noted in this essay, it is important to acknowledge that all women of color are not the same and that institutions should not expect them to behave as such. Furthermore, women of color have a range of interests and ways in which they choose to contribute to the academy.

9. One white male professor quoted in Ladson-Billings' "Silences as Weapons: Challenges of a Black Professor Teaching White Students" (1996, 79) states that students perceive him as objective, scholarly, and disinterested when teaching issues related to class, race, and gender. On the other hand, minority females teaching in these areas are often seen as self-interested, bitter, and espousing political agendas.

10. These faculty are employed at large public research institutions in states with high minority populations. This study, funded by the Ford Foundation, was conducted to assess university institutional interpretations of the 2003 *Grutter v. Bollinger* decision and to examine the perceived impact of these interpretations on campus policy and practices related to faculty diversification. The project included both survey and interview methodology. Fourteen large public institutions in states with high minority populations were chosen as study sites. Within each institution, four categories of employees were recruited as participants for the interview process: general counsels, affirmative action officers, provosts, and women of color faculty of all ranks.

11. Hispanics can be of Cuban, Mexican, Mexican-American, Puerto Rican, South or Central American, or other Spanish ancestry or descent (Nieves-Squires 1991). Data analyses project 32 million women of Mexican origin by 2050, 8 percent of U.S. population (Cuadraz 2005). U.S. citizens or residents of Mexican descent are defined as Chicana/o. Chicana and Latina are terms employed by feminists to increase gender inclusivity for women of Spanish-speaking descent.

12. When referring to studies about American Indians, tribal affiliations and their respective cultures and traditions must be taken into consideration.

REFERENCES

Alemán, A. M. 1995. Actuando. In *The leaning ivory tower: Latino professors in American universities,* ed. R. Padilla and R. Chavez, 67–76. Albany: State University of New York Press.

Allen, W., E. Epps, E. Guillory, S. Suh, M. Bonus-Hammarth, and M. Stassen. 1991. Outsiders within: Race, gender, and faculty status in U.S. higher education. In *The racial crisis in Amer-*

ican higher education, ed. P. Altbach and K. Lomotey, 189–220. Albany: State University of New York Press.

American Council on Education (ACE). 2007. *The American college president,* 2007 edition. Washington, DC: American Council on Education, Center for Policy Analysis.

Aparicio, F. R. 1999. *Through My Lens:* A video project about women of color faculty at the University of Michigan. *Feminist Studies* 25: 119–30.

Aronson, A. L., and D. L. Swanson. 1991. Graduate women on the brink: Writing as "outsiders within." *Women's Studies Quarterly* 19 (3–4): 56–74.

Baez, B. 2000. Race-related service and faculty of color: Conceptualizing critical agency in academe. *Higher Education* 39:363–91.

Carter, D., C. Pearson, and D. Shavlik. 1987. Double jeopardy: Women of color in higher education. *Educational Record* 68 (4): 98–103.

Cho, S. 1996. Confronting the myths: Asian Pacific American faculty in higher education. *Ninth Annual APAHE Conference Proceedings,* 31–56. San Francisco: Asian Pacific Americans in Higher Education.

Chronicle of Higher Education Annual Almanac. 2006. The nation: Faculty and staff. *Chronicle of Higher Education,* 26 August.

Cole, J. 2000. Social change requires academic women's leadership. *Women in Higher Education* 9 (6): 1–2.

Collins, P. H. 1989. The social construction of Black feminist thought. *Signs: Journal of Women in Culture and Society* 11 (41): 745–73.

Cuadraz, G. H. 2005. Chicanas in higher education: Three decades of literature and thought. *Journal of Hispanic Higher Education* 4 (1): 215–34.

———. 2006. Myths and the "politics of exceptionality": Interpreting Chicana/o narratives of achievement. *Oral History Review* 33 (1): 83–105.

Davis, J. D. 1994. *Coloring the halls of ivy: Leadership and diversity in the academy.* Bolton, MA: Anker.

Delgado-Gaitan, C. 1997. Dismantling borders. In *Learning from our lives: Women, research, and autobiography in education,* ed. A. Neumann and P. Peterson, 37–51. New York: Teachers College Press.

Escueta, E., and E. O'Brien. 1991. *Asian Americans in higher education: Trends and issues,* American Council on Education Research Briefs, vol. 2, no. 4. Washington, DC: American Council on Education, Division of Policy Analysis and Research.

Essien, V. 2003. Visible and invisible barriers to the incorporation of faculty of color in predominantly white law schools. *Journal of Black Studies* 34 (1): 63–71.

Farris, V. 1999. Succeeding as a female African American president of a predominantly white college. In *Grass roots and glass ceilings: African American administrators in predominantly white colleges and universities,* ed. W. B. Harvey, 57–69. Albany: State University of New York Press.

Glazer-Raymo, J. (1999). *Shattering the myths: Women in academe.* Baltimore: Johns Hopkins University Press.

Gregory, S. 1995. *Black women in the academy: The secrets to success and achievement.* New York: University Press of America.

Grutter v. Bollinger et al. (02–241). 2003. 539 U.S. 306.

Hansen, V. L. 1997. *Voices of Latina administrators in higher education: Salient factors in achieving success and implications for a model of leadership development for Latinas.* Ph.D. diss., Claremont Graduate School and San Diego State University. UMI Microform 9805058. Ann Arbor, MI: UMI Company.

Harvey, W. B., ed. 1999. *Grass roots and glass ceilings: African American administrators in predominantly white colleges and universities.* Albany: State University of New York Press.

Harvey, W. B., and E. L. Anderson. 2005. *Minorities in higher education: Twenty-first annual status report 2003–2004.* Washington, DC: American Council on Education.

hooks, bell. 1989. *Talking back.* Boston: South End Press.

Hune, S. 1998. *Asian Pacific American women in higher education: Claiming visibility and voice.* Washington, DC: Association of American Colleges and Universities.

Hune, S., and K. S. Chan. 1997. Special focus: Asian Pacific American demographic and educational trends. In *Minorities in higher education: Fifteenth Annual Status Report,* ed. D. J. Carter and R. Wilson, 39–67. Washington, DC: American Council on Education.

Ideta, L., and J. Cooper. 1999. Asian women leaders of higher education: Stories of strength and self discovery. In *Everyday knowledge and uncommon truths: Women of the academy,* ed. L. Christian-Smith and K. Kellor, 129–46. Oxford: Westview Press.

Jackson, J. F. L. 2004. Engaging, retaining, and advancing African Americans in executive-level positions: A descriptive and trend analysis of academic administrators in higher and post-secondary education. *Journal of Negro Education.* Retrieved 1/25/2006 from www.find articles.com/p/articles/mi_qa/3626/is_200401/ai_n9401821/print.

King, R. C. 1999. Succeeding against the odds in higher education: Advancing society by overcoming obstacles due to race and gender. In *Grass roots and glass ceilings: African American administrators in predominantly white colleges and universities,* ed. W. B. Harvey, 9–37. Albany: State University of New York Press.

Konrad, A. M., and J. Pfeffer. 1991. Understanding the hiring of women and minorities in educational institutions. *Sociology of Education* 64:141–57.

Krumm, B. 1997. Leadership reflections of women tribal college presidents. *Tribal College: Journal of American Indian Higher Education* 9:24–28.

Ladson-Billings, G. 1996. Silences as weapons: Challenges of a black professor teaching white students. *Theory into Practice* 35 (2): 79–85.

———. 1997. For colored girls who have considered suicide when the academy's not enough: Reflections of an African American woman scholar. In *Learning from our lives: Women, research, and autobiography in education,* ed. A. Neumann and P. Peterson, 52–70. New York: Teachers College Press.

Light, P. 1994. Diversity in the faculty "not like us": Moving barriers to minority recruitment. *Journal of Policy Analysis and Management* 13 (1): 163–86.

McDemmond, M. 1999. On the outside looking in. In *Grass roots and glass ceilings: African American administrators in predominantly white colleges and universities,* ed. W. B. Harvey, 71–82. Albany: State University of New York Press.

Mickelson, R. A., and M. L. Oliver. 1991. Making the short list: Black candidates and the faculty recruitment process. In *The racial crisis in American higher education,* ed. P. G. Altbach and K. Lomotey, 149–66. Albany: State University of New York Press.

Mitchell, J. 1994. Visible, vulnerable, and viable: Emerging perspectives of a minority professor. In *Teaching and learning in the college classroom,* ed. K. Feldman and M. Paulsen, 383–90. Needham Heights, MA: Simon and Schuster Custom Publishing.

Montero-Sieburth, M. 1996. Beyond affirmative action: An inquiry into the experiences on Latinas in academia. *New England Journal of Public Policy* 2:65–98.

Morrobel-Sosa, A. 2005. Minding the canary in the academy: A case for inclusive transformational leadership. *On Campus with Women* 34, 4:1. www.aacu.org/ocww/volume34_4/national.cfm. Accessed July 19, 2006.

Moses, Y. T. 1989. *Black women in academe: Issues and strategies.* Washington, DC: Association of American Colleges and Universities.

Nelson, D. J. 2005. *A national analysis of diversity in science and engineering faculties at research universities.* Norman, OK. http://cheminfo.chem.ou.edu/faculty/djn/diversity/briefings/DiversityReportFinal.pdf. Accessed February 17, 2007.

Nelson, S., and G. Pellett, producers. 1997. *Shattering the silences: Minority professors break into the ivory tower.* Public Broadcasting Service.

Ng, R. 2000. A woman out of control: Deconstructing sexism and racism in the university. In *Women in higher education: A feminist perspective*, ed. J. Glazer-Raymo, B. K. Townsend, and B. Ropers-Huilman, 360–70. Boston: Pearson Custom Publishing.

Nieves-Squires, S. 1991. *Hispanic women: Making their presence on campus less tenuous.* Washington, DC: Association of American Colleges and Universities.

Rains, F. 1999. Dancing on the sharp edge of the sword: Women faculty of color in white academe. In *Everyday knowledge and uncommon truths: Women of the academy*, ed. L. Christian-Smith and K. Kellor, 147–73. Oxford: Westview Press.

Smith, D. G., C. S. Turner, N. Osei-Kofi, and S. Richards. 2004. Interrupting the usual: Successful strategies for hiring diverse faculty. *Journal of Higher Education* 75 (2): 133–60.

Swisher, K. G., and A. Benally, eds. 1998. *Native North American firsts.* Detroit, MI: Gale.

Townsend, B., and C. Turner. 2000. Reshaping the academy to accommodate conflicts of commitment: Then what? Presented at the Shaping a National Agenda for Women in Higher Education conference. Minneapolis, MN, March 27, 2000.

Turner, C. S. 2000. New faces, new knowledge. *Academe* 86 (5): 34–37.

———. 2002. Women of color in academe: Living with multiple marginality. In *The faculty in the New Millennium,* ed. James Fairweather. *Journal of Higher Education* 73 (1): 74–93.

———. 2004. Writing instead of sleeping: Conflicts of commitment. *On campus with women: From where I sit* 33 (2). Washington, D.C.: American Association of Colleges and Universities. Available at www.aacu.org/ocww.

———. 2006a. Before starting a faculty search, take a good look at the search committee. *Chronicle of Higher Education,* 29 September, B32, B34.

———. 2006b. Report on preliminary findings: Diversification of the academy post-*Grutter* for the Women of Color Research Collective (WoCRC) Advisory Board Meeting at the American Council on Education Third Summit for Women of Color in Higher Education: Making our Mark, Making a Difference. November 6, Long Beach, California.

———. 2007. Pathways to the presidency: Biographical sketches of women of color firsts. *Harvard Educational Review* 77 (1): 1–38.

Turner, C. S., and J. Kappes. In press. Preparing women of color for leadership: Perspectives on the American Council on Education (ACE) fellows program. In *Women scholars, learners, and leaders,* ed. D. R. Dean. Sterling, VA: Stylus.

Turner, C. S., and S. L. Myers Jr. 2000. *Faculty of color in academe: Bittersweet success.* Needham Heights, MA: Allyn and Bacon.

Turner, C. S., and J. R. Thompson. 1993. Socialization experiences of minority and majority women doctoral students: Implications for faculty recruitment and retention. *Review of Higher Education* 16 (3): 355–70.

Warner, L. S. 1995. A study of American Indian females in higher education administration. *Initiatives* 56 (4): 11–17.

Williams, P. J. 1991. *The alchemy of race and rights: Diary of a law professor.* Cambridge: Harvard University Press.

Wilson, R. 1989. Women of color in academic administration: Trends, progress, and barriers. *Sex Roles* 21 (1/2): 85–97.

CHAPTER ELEVEN

Choice and Discourse in Faculty Careers

Feminist Perspectives on Work and Family

KELLY WARD AND LISA WOLF-WENDEL

Since 2002, we have been actively involved in a research project that looks at the interface of work and family for junior women faculty. Initially, the project included interviews with 120 women at four different types of institutions (research universities, regional/comprehensives, liberal arts colleges, and community colleges) and from a variety of disciplines. We have written up the findings from these interviews from multiple perspectives. We looked at the unique context of research universities and how women faculty members manage work and family in this setting (Ward and Wolf-Wendel 2004). We also conducted an in-depth analysis of the work/family policy context at research universities (Ward and Wolf-Wendel 2005). We examined how work and family demands vary by institutional type (Wolf-Wendel and Ward 2006a) as well as the policy perspectives that emerge from different institutional types (Wolf-Wendel and Ward 2006b). Most recently, we analyzed the data by looking specifically at community college faculty (Ward, Wolf-Wendel, and Twombly 2007) and at comprehensive college faculty (Wolf-Wendel and Ward 2006b). Collectively, this work has been mostly descriptive and relies on organizational theory, institutional culture, and individual perspectives to provide foundations for analysis. In an ongoing attempt to more fully understand work and family, we also interviewed department chairs, senior faculty, and junior faculty (male and female) with and without children within given departmental contexts. The findings from our research are part of an evolving literature about faculty life and about institutional policy contexts related to work and family.

One of the assumptions we held as we embarked on this research project is that women faculty members manage the combination of work and family. The roles of faculty and mother are not impossible to reconcile, and there are many successful examples of women who do both well. We saw this as an important story to tell, because the findings of "peril" and "doom" were so prevalent in prior research literature (e.g., Aisenberg and Harrington 1988; Armenti 2004; Bassett 2005; Mason, Goulden, and Wolfinger 2005), and we wanted to show that it was possible for women to achieve success in the roles of professor and mother simultaneously. We wanted to find women who were combining work and family to see how they made these roles work and how they could serve as models for other women to follow.

The purpose of this chapter is to offer new and different ways to look at some of the underlying findings that emerged throughout our research. As is the case in most research projects, there are the findings that emerge and present themselves readily for analysis (as we have done in the above-cited articles), and then there are the findings that are not as easily analyzed and that often get overlooked. This chapter is about the latter type of findings—findings that present themselves more as hunches or questions that seemingly defy explanation. In this chapter we delve more deeply into the findings related to the concept of *choice* that has been a major part of the "story line" of our study and also the concept of *discourse* as it manifests itself in how the women in our research talk about their campuses and the current policies on these campuses. These two concepts, we believe, are related to greater understanding of larger issues surrounding gender equity on college and university campuses today.

The concept of choice is foundational to our research in personal and professional ways. Life is about choices, and choices have consequences, both negative and positive. As women faculty members in the middle stages of our careers, we have each achieved some degree of professional and personal success, leading us to think about the choices we have made to get to this point in our lives. Where, how, and whether we work were choices we made. Where, how, and whether to have a family were choices we made. What did we choose? We each chose to go to graduate school and pursue doctorates. We chose to become professors of higher education at research universities. We chose to marry, and we chose to have more than one child. We have chosen to operate in the public realm of work and the private realm of family, and we are making it work. The birthday cakes and Halloween costumes might not be homemade, and we might turn down invitations to travel abroad for work—these are just a few of the choices we have made—but when we think about our lives, we conclude that we are happy and that we have made good choices. Our fortunate circumstances, which are strikingly parallel to one another, have led us to seek out other faculty women with young children to find out how they have made their lives work. What choices have other women faculty made? What have been the consequences of those choices? How have the institutions where they work been helpful to them (or hindered them) in making choices?

Answering these questions has been the focus of our research agenda for the last five years—and we have learned a lot about ourselves and about other women faculty across the country. What we have learned from this research project has been enlightening. The findings show that many women faculty with young children are managing their multiple roles admirably. For example, we learned that the roles of parent and professor can be congruent rather than inconsistent with one another. We also learned that being a parent can lead to being a better professor, certainly a more efficient one. Similarly, being a professor can mean being a better parent, at least a more patient one.

The women in the study, furthermore, talked about the *joy* of being a parent and the *joy* of being a professor. They explained that when they got home from work, in addition to working the second shift (e.g., cooking, cleaning, childcare), their family life was gratifying. Going home offered reprieve from the endless amounts of work, the ambiguity of tenure, and the high-stakes nature of achieving success. Going to work was also a source of satisfaction. Going to work made these women temporarily forget about the endless amounts of work at home, the ambiguity of being a parent, and the high-stakes nature of success as a parent. Balancing multiple roles seems to offer these women a sense of perspective—tenure is important, but so are other parts of life, and vice versa. We learned that time is a precious commodity and that women faculty members with young children make the choices they can and try not to let their work, their family, or themselves down. Certainly, the challenge of not being able to do things perfectly was present, but few had time to wallow in it or succumb to it.

Interestingly, we found that women faculty members were deliberate in choosing where they wanted to work, cognizant of wanting to combine work and family in a meaningful way. Many saw prestigious research universities and their increasingly high tenure demands as incongruent with the demands of parenthood. Thus, they opted for less prestigious institutions or places they perceived to have more "reasonable" tenure expectations. In addition, the women we interviewed achieved their personal and professional goals, often without the assistance of institutional policies or guidance from others. Work and family policies on most campuses included in the study either didn't exist, weren't considered useful, or weren't talked about. We concluded from our prior research that women faculty with young children find ways to make their choices work, despite the lack of institutional support and assistance. We have also concluded from our research that we needed additional understanding about the concept of choice. In particular, we wanted to know what goes into shaping these choices and how the campus discourse around work and family shaped these choices.

Because the concepts of choice and discourse surround so much of our work, both personally and professionally, they call for more in-depth analysis and are the focus of the remainder of this chapter. The research on women's progress in higher education, especially within the faculty ranks, demonstrates that despite the freedom for women to make choices, there is not gender equality in the consequences of such choices. Women are underrepresented among the ranks of faculty at the most prestigious colleges and universities (*Chronicle of Higher Education Almanac* 2006). Women's underrepresentation is particularly pronounced at the senior ranks (Mason, Goulden, and Wolfinger 2005; Perna 2001). Women faculty members are less likely than other women professionals to have children or be married (Baker 2002; Cooney and Uhlenberg 1989). Promotion and tenure patterns for women faculty with young children are not as positive as they are for men (with or without children) (Grant, Kennelly, and Ward 2000; Mason, Goulden, and Wolfinger 2005; Perna 2001). All of these phenomena can, in part, be explained by the choices women make.

Undoubtedly women have made progress in their quest for representation and equality in the academic ranks. Our point in citing the above literature is to show that in spite of the progress women have made, there is still some way to go to achieve gender equity in higher education. While we certainly need to look at the progress women have made as faculty members, looking at representation alone is insufficient. It is easy to look at incoming cohorts of faculty and see the strides women have made, since many of these cohorts are comprised of equal parts men and women. However, further analysis of these cohorts by discipline shows gross inequities by gender. Women are still severely underrepresented in many disciplines. Oversimplified pipeline perspectives on these data suggest that the women who are incoming today will rectify the inequities that have existed in the past. Faculty cohort analysis, however, shows that such a perspective is short-sighted and that women do not advance at the same rate as their male counterparts (Goulden 2006). Any examination of gender in the academic workplace needs to take into account academic culture and tradition.

Glazer-Raymo's groundbreaking work, *Shattering the Myths* (1999), calls for thinking about gender equity in ways that recognize the micro and macro inequities that exist in higher education. Even though there are more women present in nearly every aspect of higher education today, this progress does not signify widespread change about gender in the academy. Her analysis makes clear that the greater presence of women faculty (with or without children) does not mean that policies and practices related to gender equity will change. It is within this context that women make choices about their work and their careers.

To examine the concepts of choice and discourse, we turn to two strands of feminist theory—liberal feminism and poststructural feminism—to aid our analysis. The goal of this analysis is to attempt to make sense of what it means to make choices about work and family amidst a policy discourse that prefers silence. The ultimate goal of such an analysis is not an exercise unto itself, but it is instead a way to help steer conversations about policy, to offer individual women different ways to think about their choices, and to enable faculty leaders and administrators to think more broadly about the work and family discourse in higher education. The ultimate goal is to create environments that are more equitable.

We use liberal feminism and feminist poststructuralism to consider the concepts of choice and discourse from our previous research. *Choice* is a term we use that captures how women faculty members approach their work and the decisions they make to work in particular contexts. Choice is also pertinent for how people talk about the policy context at their institutions and whether they make use of such policies to assist them in balancing academic work and motherhood. Choice is a foundational premise to feminist thought; in particular, it is a basic element of the liberal feminist perspective.

Discourse is another term we use to organize our thinking about work and family. We use this word to capture how work and family is talked about within the policy arena of higher education. The term *discourse* helps us make sense of the language people use to talk about work and family (and the policy context, in particular), recognizing that the language used is reflective of the historical positions and traditional notions about women in the workplace and women as mothers. Discourse shapes the language people use in addition to shaping what people talk about (or not) and how they talk about it (Chalaby 1996). In order to think more critically about the concepts of choice and discourse, we use the theoretical perspectives of liberal feminism and poststructural feminism.

We chose these two perspectives because much of the progress women have made in higher education is a credit to a *liberal feminist framework* and because the *feminist poststructural lens* is helpful as one thinks about some of the constraints women still face as they seek to accomplish the dual roles of mother and professor. Furthermore, we have found looking at our project from these two feminist lenses useful as we explore "hunches" and findings that do not resonate with existing research findings and/or that defy ready explanation.

Feminist Perspectives: Liberal Feminism and Feminist Poststructuralism

Liberal feminism is grounded in the enlightenment principle that women are entitled to the same "natural rights" as men—a belief that underlies the contemporary notion of equal opportunity (Acker 1987) and that responds to restrictions on women's full participation in the public sphere. For liberal feminism to be realized, women should be "free and equal" to participate in society, unencumbered by traditionally defined gender roles, and should be afforded full participation in the workforce. Liberal feminism posits that men and women are created equal and that policies and practices ought to level the playing field for both genders to compete on an equal footing (Donovan 2000).

Feminist poststructuralism is "a mode of knowledge production that uses poststructuralist theories of language, subjectivity, social processes and institutions to understand existing power relations and to identify areas and strategies for change" (Weedon 1997, 40). Feminist poststructuralism focuses on understanding gender and gender differences in relationship to societal structures. Feminist poststructural analysis emphasizes understanding gender and gender differences through the lens of discourse and the power relationships that are manifested through discourse. Such a perspective allows for the examination of women's experiences and shows how these experiences relate to social practices and the power relations that support and structure them (Weedon 1997). Poststructural feminism focuses on language, meaning, power, difference, and subjectivity (Allan, Estler, and Iverson 2004; Ropers-Huilman 1998; Scott 1988; Weedon 1997). A core element of a feminist poststructural theoretical position is change—this is a framework that questions the status quo and seeks to address inequitable social systems and divisions of labor from the perspective of gender (Weedon 1997). The poststructural feminist perspective is particularly useful to us because it helps us to think about our research as a vehicle to change higher education.

It is important to note that this chapter draws more distinct divisions between liberal feminism and poststructural feminism than might otherwise be necessary. The two strands of feminism are not dichotomous concepts—but rather, can reinforce one another. Nonetheless, for the sake of helping us to delve deeper into the issues of choice and discourse and to make sense of these concepts, we draw relatively sharp distinctions between the two theoretical frameworks. Furthermore, we understand that women's lives cannot be fully understood through purely theoretical positions—lives and choices are complicated. Still, part of understanding complex issues is breaking them down to their most simple components and then building them back up again to demonstrate their richness. We hope that our dissection of the concepts and the theories allow us to do just that.

Choice

From a liberal feminist perspective, the ultimate freedom granted to women is choice. In the context of feminism, choice is often associated with reproductive rights, but it is also foundational to employment rights (Acker 1987). In essence, we have liberal feminists to thank for opening the door to the professoriat and other aspects of employment that excluded women. Policies and practices that made higher education, from undergraduate to the professoriat, more open and accessible to women are due to the work of liberal feminists.

We first thought about choice and women faculty while sitting at a conference several years ago. At a research presentation about the contingent academic labor market, a colleague indicated that working as a part-time faculty member was a "good choice" for women because it allowed them to accommodate their desire to combine work and family. Certainly, the overrepresentation of women among part-time academic appointments provides some evidence of such personal choices. However, we recall feeling uncomfortable with this conclusion. If full-time academic work and societal expectations about work and family were "more reasonable" or were less gendered, would women be opting for positions with less security, lower pay, fewer (or no) benefits, and less prestige? We asked then—and now—what if women were choosing this track as a result of systemic discrimination rather than just as an individual choice?

Deciding to work part-time has long-term economic implications. Choosing to work part-time also has implications for keeping women faculty on the margins of the academic workplace. Part-time workers do not contribute to the collective organizational good in the same way as do full-time employees (Hertz 2004). Given the tradition of shared governance in higher education, part-time work has unique implications based on the limited involvement of part-time faculty members in decision making. Adding to these implications is recent research that shows that once in the contingent labor force, it is very difficult to transition to the full-time tenure-track ("real") academic workforce (Schuster and Finkelstein 2006). The choices one makes initially about an academic career can lead to a permanent— and potentially unintended—professional consequence. While our research did not explicitly look at women who chose to work part-time, we see parallels between the choice to work part-time as a way to manage work and family demands and the choice to work in a particular institutional setting based on the perception that it is more compatible with work and family demands.

A major theme from the first phase of our research project is related to where women choose to work, mindful of a desire to combine work and family. Many women indicated that they opted to work at teaching-oriented colleges to support their desire to have children. From a liberal feminist perspective, we see the notion of free will in operation. Women can and do opt to work in different types of environments based on the kinds of work and life they prefer. The supposition under liberal feminist theory is that women can (and do) choose to work in whatever type of institution they want and should be free to do so. Certainly, there were women in our study who ended up working in a particular institution because it was their only offer or option or because their values as an academic were compatible with particular institutional missions (e.g., working at liberal arts colleges, given a passion for teaching). However, more often we heard women in the interviews discuss making a purposeful choice to work at a community college, liberal arts college, or comprehensive institution because these contexts were viewed as more compatible with a desire to have a child than the research university context.

After earning doctorates at major research universities—the primary broker of the doctorate in U.S. higher education—many of the women in the study were clear that they did not want to work in that type of setting because they wanted to "have a life." This finding resonates with other research (e.g., Austin 2002) that suggests that graduate students see faculty in their departments leading stressful and hectic lives, which serves as a deterrent to working at a research university. What we found is that this mindset can lead to the choice not to work in the research university setting. Again, the supposition here, using a liberal feminist view, is that choice is a "free and equal" one. There is also a supposition that all of these academic institutions are gender neutral and that women and men can move freely in and out of these environments as a matter of choice. While this is one way to look at choice and one we used following the lead of the data, it left us wanting. We felt there was more to the concept of choice than simply choosing to work at a less-prestigious institution because it was a "good choice" for combining work and family.

Rational choice theories that are aligned with a liberal view assume that actors (in this case, women faculty) are "primarily motivated by the rewards and costs of their actions and the likely profit they can make. . . . Within assumptions of rational choice, one has a list of options and carefully selects the most appropriate within the ordinary constraints that exist of, say, time, money or sufficient information" (Hughes 2002, 85). This concept of choice conveys a strong image of human agency. From a liberal feminist perspective, choosing where to work relative to work and family is the ultimate right associated with freedom of choice. However, we believe that the notion of choice is not that simple, because it ignores the constrained structures of choice and the constrained structures of higher education organizations for women. The hegemonic culture of the workplace assumes and depends upon an infrastructure in which individuals sequence their lives according to jobs and career demands and in which individuals sacrifice excessive individualism (read: have a baby) to be team players (Hertz 2004).

Hughes argues that choice is illusory in nature. "One may feel autonomous and free to choose, but the power of regulatory discourses mean that such choice is 'forced' and of false appearance" (2002, 101). It is here that we transition to a feminist poststructural standpoint as a means to understanding choice as a function of social and hegemonic structures and related ideologies (Jones 1997). A poststructural view of choice enters into the findings of our study in two ways: first, early gender socialization shapes people's ideas about what they can do and where they can do it; and second, research universities socialize people to have certain expectations of an academic career. As a result of these socialization experiences, we conclude, individuals choose not to work in research universities because they believe them to be incompatible with achieving work and family balance. Moreover, prospective women faculty members are steered away from choosing research universities because these settings are characterized as "greedy institutions," where only the ideal worker can succeed (Coser 1974; Williams 1999; Wilson 2004).

The finding that women choose not to work in major research universities for fear of not being able to balance work with other aspects of life (including family) is of major concern. Higher education as an enterprise should be worried about this opting out of working at research universities, for such decisions can negatively affect the diversity of perspectives present at these institutions (Wilson 2004). Research universities stand to lose significant female talent if these settings are viewed as incompatible with having a family. It should be of great concern to research universities that women of high caliber and quality, such as those in our study, are opting to work in different types of institutions based on the perception of unreasonable work norms.

From a liberal feminist perspective, choice is a matter of individual human agency (i.e., "I choose to work at a community college because it is a good setting for me to combine a personal life that includes family"). And certainly, women should be free to make such choices. The findings of our study are replete with such examples of women acting upon personal agency. A feminist poststructural perspective of choice, however, sees the operation of agency taking place in contexts shaped by discourses of work and family that influence perceptions of what is acceptable and desirable behavior for a successful faculty member. We believe that choice is problematized in the poststructural sense in that perceptions of the academic hierarchy may lead people to make decisions based on structures of tradition that have historically excluded women—and in particular, women with children. Such a view makes agency a matter of discursive consequence as opposed to a matter of the consequence of free will.

Discourse

We now shift to the concept of discourse, because it is not possible to look at the choices people make without considering the milieu in which these choices are made. Indeed, choice is a foundational concept necessary, but not sufficient, to create equality in higher education. Choice cannot be separated from context, which cannot be separated from the dominant discourses that shape particular contexts. Discourse is often used synonymously with the term *language,* given its linguistic origins (Chalaby 1996). However, the sociological use of the term is more encompassing, since it looks at the social context that surrounds the use of language (Chalaby 1996). We use the term *discourse* to make sense of the ways people talk about (or don't) work and family in the higher-education context.

In particular, the concept of discourse is helpful to us as we make sense of what we found about the postsecondary policy context. We note that there are dominant discourses about motherhood and about women's roles in society that undoubtedly inform the personal choices women make. These discourses affect all women as well as represent and shape the socially acceptable norms of women's existence outside of work, which in turn shape how women think about work (Acker 1987; Blair-Loy 2003; Donovan 2000). Without intent to minimize these discourses, we focus our analysis here exclusively on academic workplace norms and discourses. These were the most salient influences on the women we interviewed—in part because we were focusing on the academic side of their lives. As such, the discourses we discuss focus on issues of tenure, academic policy, and academic culture.

In our research, we found that people make choices—for example, the choice about where to work—based on what they believed to be prevailing discourses about what it takes to be a successful academic. We also found that the women in the study made choices about whether to use particular work/family policies based on dominant discourses about what it takes to be a successful academic and how one should act if one is serious about her position. The postsecondary policy discourse is shaped by prevailing campus norms about what is expected in order to be successful and what is deemed by campus culture as acceptable.

Viewed from the perspective of liberal feminism, the policy discourse on a given campus recognizes the need to have work/family policies. The assumption is that if the policies are available, they will be used by those who need them. The presence of a policy can be equated with the ability to use the policy. The very creation of the Family and Medical Leave Act (FMLA)—legislation that provides for people, both men and women, to take time off for having a child and for dependent care (young and old) without fear of losing their job—created an ideal that says job security is important for those with family medical needs. The FMLA does not provide financial remuneration for those who take leave; it simply protects employees from unfair dismissal in the event of a family-related life event like having a child. FMLA is in effect at all the colleges and universities in the study (and the majority of campuses in the U.S.) and is the primary source of parental leave policy on most campuses. On many campuses FMLA is the only leave option associated with work and family.

Other work/family policies, such as those that stop the tenure clock or modify duties in response to the birth or adoption of a child, were created as mechanisms to provide equality of opportunity for men and women, given the demands of being a new parent that can coincide with the demands of the tenure clock. Such policies, which are typically open to both men and women, recognize that having a child can negatively affect work productivity during the finite probationary period that is so crucial to ongoing success of a faculty member and the award of tenure. Throughout the past twenty years, college campuses have seen an increase in the availability of such policies in an effort to enable faculty to balance workplace and family demands (Smith and Waltman 2006).

In an era where academic credibility is often challenged and tenure is threatened, it is difficult to protect the sanctity of tenure while simultaneously arguing for its alteration. Many of the suggestions for work and family policies call for maintaining tenure, while making changes to the tenure *process* to make it less strict and rigid. Regardless, any changes to the tenure process can be quite threatening to the status quo, given the history and current status of tenure and the important role tenure plays in protecting academic freedom.

One of the challenges to creating policies around work and family during the tenure-track years is the sacrosanct nature of the tenure process. Dominant discourses associated with what it means to be an academic are shaped by the history and development of the institution of tenure in higher education. Tenure is the ultimate academic totem (Tierney and Bensimon 1996). Indeed, the tenure process has remained largely unchanged since its inception: a person earns her doctorate, starts her academic career as an assistant professor, and typically, after a five or six year probationary period, she applies for promotion and tenure. Success in an academic career calls for adhering to this timeline. The academic career is imbued with "ideal worker" norms that call for faculty to be married to their career (Hochschild 1975). Dominant discourses surrounding academic work are based on work norms that call for primary devotion. The structure of the tenure process came of age when the profession was organized according to traditional familial norms that placed men in the workplace and women at home with children (Ward and Bensimon 2003). For women to take family leave or to stop their tenure clock calls for interrupting the traditional career ladder and its prescribed order, leaving one to ask: How do I maintain my legitimacy as a faculty member and become a parent?

Our research and other studies suggest that faculty skirt issues associated with work and family policies by using bias avoidance strategies (Colbeck and Drago 2005). This means employing such strategies as having a baby in the summer or returning to work as soon after birth as possible without missing any (or very little) work or, in extreme cases, not having a baby at all. The goal of such strategies is to avoid bias by eliminating the need to call upon the campus for support. Of course, using such strategies assumes situations where a woman can plan her due date to coincide with the academic calendar and where the baby arrives on time and without complications.

Bias avoidance is rooted in fear. Faculty members, women in particular, are fearful that if they use policies they will face negative repercussions. This fear is rooted in dominant discourses associated with tenure and academic culture. It is also triggered by the need for women to maintain legitimacy as faculty members. Women as "outsiders in the sacred grove" still occupy a tenuous place in the academic hierarchy (Aisenberg and Harrington 1988; Cooper and Stevens 2002). Taking leave or stopping the tenure clock is an action that can compromise legitimacy. Dominant discourses prevail and dictate what the tenure process "should" look like, and these discourses do not allow for stopping the clock or taking a leave without fear.

The findings from our research demonstrate that many women were hesitant to utilize family leave policies even if such policies existed. We found that an increasing number of institutions have created tenure stop-clock policies and/or provided some type of maternity leave, yet many of the women we spoke with did not even know these policies existed or were reluctant to use them. Many believed that there was a "cost" associated with use of such policies and therefore chose not to use them.

Using policies is viewed as a risky proposition and one that is best avoided in order to show commitment to the academic career. Women go to great lengths to avoid the perception that they need help or are not dedicated to their careers (Colbeck and Drago 2005). The academic policy discourse shapes not just the presence of the leave, but also how people approach the utilization of policy.

Based on interviews with department chairs and other colleagues in given departments, we found that entire departments remain silent around the use of family leave. Department chairs adopt a reactive stance when it comes to working with women faculty members having a child. None of the department chairs we talked to approached faculty who were pregnant to see what they (or the institution) could do to be helpful. It was incumbent on the woman herself to ask for assistance. Even department chairs who were progressive in their thinking about what they thought should be available to accommodate women having children (e.g., paid leave, semester leave) did not bring up such options. There was an air of silence around policy utilization—a silence that was perpetuated by faculty members and their department chairs.

What are we to make of such organizational silence? We attribute this orientation to separatist notions of what counts as public and what counts as private. The premise of "separateness" (Ferree 1990) firmly establishes work as a public concern and issues associated with family as private ones. Traditional theories of sex role separation align private concerns with women and public concerns with men. In an organizational context, this separatism leads to silence and invisibility for issues associated with the female sphere (i.e., the private, family sphere) (Ashcraft and Mumby 2004).

A feminist poststructural analysis of the policy environment looks at discourses of work and family and discourses of faculty work to help explain the silence, fear, and lack of use surrounding work and family policy. The presence of a policy is a matter of language—the policies are presented in faculty handbooks as stand-alone documents that one opts to use or not use. However, the findings from our study make clear that opting to use a policy is shaped by more than the text of the message (i.e., the actual policy). Instead, policy utilization is shaped by the dominant discourses about what it means to be a successful faculty member. The presence of a policy is a matter of language; the use of the policy is a matter of discourse. The utilization of policy is shaped by power relationships (Mills 1997), and these power relationships render entire departments silent when it comes to work and family policy.

We do not think this silence is deliberate or intentionally divisive. We repeatedly heard well-meaning comments like this one, "It goes without saying that we wouldn't discriminate against someone because of their gender or their parental status." But, we ask, if it goes without saying, does that mean that there isn't bias? Department chairs received no training on these issues: the upper administration didn't talk about them. Departmental colleagues may engage in social pleasantries that involve asking others about their families, but this is not an issue that has been deemed worthy of discussion in the general departmental context. As a result, the whole notion of having a family is silenced, in part, because it is separate from what is defined as work (Ferree 1990). From a poststructural feminist standpoint, silence is interpreted as part of the discourse (Ropers-Huilman 1998), a discourse that is based on gendered norms that separate work and family.

The discourse of successful academia is imbued with ideal worker norms that lead women to make certain kinds of decisions (e.g., to not take a leave, to delay having a baby, to work in particular settings) based on what they believe the dominant discourse is telling them is the "right" way to act in order to fit existing norms. These norms are communicated through the dominant discourse, and they clearly (though not always verbally or in writing) indicate that it is not okay to be different or to deviate from a traditional path to be a successful professor. Gee (1999, 21) explains that discourse leads people to "build identities and activities not just through language but by using language together with other 'stuff' that isn't language." These identities are built based on assumptions about the right way to act in a particular setting. He uses the example of gang members and how the discourse (language, symbols) of what it means to be a gang member dictates how people act, based on what they believe is required to be recognized as a gang member: "If you want to get recognized as a street-gang member of a certain sort, you have to speak in the 'right' way, but you have to act and dress in the 'right' way as well. You also have to engage (or, at least, behave as if you are engaging) in characteristic ways of thinking, acting, interacting, valuing, feeling, and believing" (1999, 21). This example illustrates that the discourse of gangs expects people to behave in a certain way if they want to belong. The academic discourse related to tenure is similar, and those wanting membership (i.e., tenure) are expected to act in certain ways.

We heard repeatedly throughout our interviews about how certain kinds of behaviors were expected if a faculty member is to succeed (to belong, to join the "gang"). For example, a senior faculty member talking about combining work and family had this to say: "I don't know why anyone would do it [have a family] when so clearly what is required to be successful as a faculty member is total dedication, especially when trying to get tenure. It's not a job that is designed so that people do other things beyond focus on the discipline." Another faculty member had a related thought to share: "I recommend for faculty to get established first, to get tenure, before thinking about having a child. It's what I did, and if anyone ever asks me, that is what I tell them they should do." We believe that comments like these contribute to an overall culture that creates a discourse that says "Don't ask, don't tell." These comments show how dominant discourses around what it means to be a dedicated and successful academic both reflect and produce culture. A feminist poststructural view can help reveal the underlying messages and assumptions of language, power, and meaning inherent in such comments, with a focus on how these messages are shaped by gendered positions.

Power is also an important element in this equation. The woman faculty member, often without tenure and new to the profession (given typical age at hire and biological clock issues), may not know what is a culturally appropriate request. She is in a position of lesser power in the organization and therefore, understandably, feels that she cannot control the situation and doesn't have the right to impose her needs on others. Typically, we found that there were not a lot of senior colleagues who could or would offer assistance in explaining how to negotiate for work and family needs, because they either did not have children or policies didn't exist when they did. And even the sympathetic colleague or department chair didn't have the tools to be able to tell the woman professor how to navigate this issue. There were few precedents to guide the way. This creates a situation where you have a person with little power who has no one to turn to for the answers—so they all decide not to talk about it or acknowledge the concerns. Those with power (department chairs, senior colleagues) control the discourse and dictate—through their use of language (and silence), actions, interactions, reactions, ways of thinking, and behaviors—what they recognize as legitimate (Gee 1999). In such a context, those without power are left to interpret, infer, and respond based on what they think is socially recognized.

So What? Now What?

The intent of this chapter is not to talk about issues associated with work and family from a theoretical perspective as an intellectual exercise only. Instead, our intent is to use theory as a way to think differently about some of the dilemmas that face the current work and family policy environment. The dilemma of having a family leave policy but then not having it utilized is important to understand, because we do not want to see policies go away due to underutilization. Instead, what we want to see is an uncovering of some of the assumptions that surround the creation and implementation of particular policies and to explore, theoretically and practically, why people don't use policy and what we can do about it. We believe that looking at dominant academic discourses using different theoretical lenses can lead to expanded understanding and more pointed action.

The findings from our research related to choice suggest that the "ideal worker" norms of the research university sector, in particular, are steering talented and well-qualified faculty away from this sector. That is, they are choosing to work in different types of institutions based on the perception that liberal arts colleges, community colleges, and comprehensives are more compatible with having a family. Looking at this phenomenon of choice from liberal and poststructural feminist perspectives helps us to think differently about constrained choice. Our intent is not to steer all faculty into the research university. Instead, we want colleges and universities to be self-reflective about ideal worker norms and what impact they might have on creating and maintaining a qualified and diverse faculty pool. If this were to occur, then those who choose to work in the research sector can do so without fear of bias and inferiority because they don't (or won't) subscribe to norms and a discourse that communicates that to succeed requires a dedication to the work place that excludes other interests and other aspects of life.

In terms of the future, what might improve the lives of faculty members with children as well as the institutions where they work? We suggest that institutions consider adopting the following "family-friendly" policies to help tenure-track faculty respond favorably to work and family demands:

- Offer paid family leave for family-related concerns for men and women distinct from sick, vacation, or short-term disability leave.
- Allow faculty members to go on a "modified duty" status, where they continue to engage in service or research obligations, but are relieved from teaching responsibilities for a term. Courses taught by faculty members on modified duty would be cancelled or taught by someone else. Similarly, consider allowing faculty members to "cover" their courses in other creative ways, such as banking the courses (teaching an overload in a different semester); team teaching courses with another professor (or adjunct or graduate teaching assistant); or offering courses in alternative formats (on-line, condensed formats, etc.).
- Stop the tenure clock for faculty with primary or co-primary caregiving responsibilities. The latest such policies are automatic and do not require the faculty to request that the clock be stopped.

- Offer part-time tenure-track options.
- Maintain affordable and accessible childcare on campus and/or provide on-campus referral for childcare services.
- Provide affordable and comprehensive health insurance coverage for faculty members and their families.

A recent prescription for campuses in creating work-family policies utilizes an integrative model in which a series of policies is adopted that can be used alone or in combination with one another as needed by employees. Such a model recognizes the way people work and supports the coherence faculty want with regard to work and home life.

One practice that we believe holds promise and is worthy of additional consideration is that of an entitlement policy rather than a discretionary one (Smith and Waltman 2006). Entitlement policies, such as the one recently adopted at Princeton University, automatically stop the tenure clock if a faculty member has a child. The University of Kansas created a similar policy in which faculty, both male and female, are granted an automatic one-year extension of the tenure clock if they have a child. Bryn Mawr College also offers all tenure-track assistant faculty members a leave once they successfully complete their third-year review. While this last policy is not designed specifically with family needs in mind, it is a helpful means of providing much-needed support and time for those on the tenure track and was found to be particularly useful in de-stigmatizing the use of leaves for not-yet-tenured professors.

Having an entitlement policy such as those at the University of Kansas, Princeton, and Bryn Mawr has the potential to create a different or alternative discourse that results in new practices, where the assumption is that taking additional time on the tenure clock to meet family-related needs is not reflective of academic qualification. Entitlement policies stand in contrast to discretionary policies that require faculty members to ask their department chair to use the policy. The latter approach puts exclusive power in the hands of the department chair as he or she decides on a case-by-case basis what "deal" faculty will get when they have a child. Such an arrangement has the potential to create unfair use of policies and is also subject to changes if there is turnover in departmental administration.

Each of these policy perspectives (entitlement and discretionary) has its pros and cons, and we do not mean to suggest an overly simplistic response to what is a complex problem. What we do want to suggest is that faculty and administrators work together to look at different policy arrangements and to look at them from a perspective that can reveal underlying assumptions and power relationships. We also want to suggest that faculty and administrators think about the assumptions and expectations that are communicated both subtly and openly about what it means to be a faculty member.

An important first step to reshaping dominant discourses about academic culture is engaging in discourse itself. Campus conversations about promotion and tenure expectations, work-family policy utilization, and workplace culture are important in beginning to create new discourses about faculty roles and rewards. Our work has led us to the conclusion that there is a "don't ask, don't tell" mindset when it comes to the policy discourse. Metaphorically, it is time for all members of the campus community to "come out of the closet" and bring light to issues associated with work and family for faculty. New discourses cannot be created if prevailing ones are not discussed.

The discourse surrounding ideal worker norms is pervasive in research and writing about the academy and faculty work. The good news is that new discourses can be created to reflect meaningful practices about work and family. Asking tough questions about assumptions embedded in workplace discourses and their impact on the choices junior faculty make has the potential to help us think about academic work in new and different ways—ways that can promote a faculty life marked by dedication, commitment, competence, and personal choices.

REFERENCES

Acker, S. 1987. Feminist theory and the study of gender and education. *International Review of Education* 33 (4): 419–35.

Aisenberg, N., and M. Harrington. 1988. *Women of academe: Outsiders in the sacred grove.* Amherst: University of Massachusetts Press.

Allan, E. J., S. E. Estler, and S. V. Iverson. 2004. Working the ruins: Feminist poststructural perspectives and higher education research. Presented at the Annual Meeting of the Association for the Study of Higher Education, Kansas City, Missouri, November.

Armenti, C. 2004. May babies and post-tenure babies: Maternal decisions of women professors. *Review of Higher Education* 27: 211–31.

Ashcraft, K. L., and D. K. Mumby. 2004. *Reworking gender: A feminist communicology of organization.* Thousand Oaks, CA: Sage.

Austin, A. E. 2002. Preparing the next generation of faculty: Graduate school as socialization to the academic career. *Journal of Higher Education* 73 (1): 94–122.

Baker, J. G. 2002. Women in the workforce. *Monthly Labor Review.* Retrieved 6/26/2006 from www.findarticles.com/p/articles/mi_m1153/is_8_125/ai_95263056#.

Bassett, R. H. 2005. *Parenting and professing: Balancing family work with an academic career.* Nashville, TN: Vanderbilt University Press.

Blair-Loy, M. 2003. *Competing devotions: Career and family among women executives.* Cambridge, MA: Harvard University Press.

Chalaby, J. K. 1996. Beyond the prison-house of language: Discourse as a sociological concept. *British Journal of Sociology* 47 (4): 684–98.

Chronicle of Higher Education Annual Almanac. 2006. Retrieved 1/27/2006 from http://chronicle .com/free/almanac/2005/nation/nation_index.htm.

Colbeck, C. L., and R. Drago. 2005. Accept, avoid, resist: Faculty members' responses to bias against caregiving . . . and how departments can help. *Change* 37 (6): 10–17.

Cooney, T. M., and P. Uhlenberg. 1989. Family-building patterns of professional women: A comparison of lawyers, physicians, and postsecondary teachers. *Journal of Marriage and the Family* 51:749–58.

Cooper, J. E., and D. D. Stevens. 2002. *Tenure in the sacred grove: Issues and strategies for women and minority faculty.* Albany: State University of New York Press.

Coser, L. A. 1974. *Greedy institutions: Patterns of undivided commitment.* New York: Free Press.

Donovan, J. 2000. *Feminist theory: The intellectual traditions,* 3rd ed. New York: Continuum.

Ferree, M. M. 1990. Beyond separate spheres: Feminism and family research. *Journal of Marriage and the Family* 52 (4): 866–84.

Gee, J. P. 1999. *Discourse analysis: An introduction to theory and method,* 2nd ed. New York: Routledge.

Glazer-Raymo, J. 1999. *Shattering the myths: Women in academe.* Baltimore: Johns Hopkins University Press.

Goulden, M. 2006. The family friendly tipping point? Feminization and academic culture. Presented at the Association for the Study of Higher Education, Anaheim, California, November.

Grant, L., I. Kennelly, and K. B. Ward. 2000. Revisiting the gender, marriage and parenthood puzzle in scientific careers. *Women's Studies Quarterly* 28: 62–85.

Hertz, R. 2004. The contemporary myth of choice. *Annals of the American Academy* 596: 232–44.

Hochschild, A. R. 1975. Inside the clockwork of male careers. In *Women and the power to change,* ed. F. Howe, 47–80. New York: McGraw-Hill.

Hughes, C. 2002. *Key concepts in feminist theory and research.* London and Thousand Oaks, CA: Sage Publications.

Jones, A. 1997. Teaching post-structuralist feminist theory in education: Student resistances. *Gender and Education* 9 (3): 261–69.

Mason, M. A., M. Goulden, and N. H. Wolfinger. 2005. Babies matter: Pushing the gender equity revolution forward. *The balancing act: Gendered perspectives in faculty roles and work lives,* ed. S. Bracken, J. K. Allen, and D. Dean, 9–30. Sterling, VA: Stylus Publishing.

Mills, S. 1997. *Discourse.* London: Routledge Press.

Perna, L. W. 2001. The relationship between family responsibilities and employment status among college and university faculty. *Journal of Higher Education* 72 (5): 584–611.

Ropers-Huilman, B. 1998. *Feminist teaching in theory and practice: Situating power and knowledge in poststructural classrooms.* New York: Teachers College Press.

Schuster, J. H., and M. J. Finkelstein. 2006. *The American faculty: The restructuring of academic work and careers.* Baltimore: Johns Hopkins University Press.

Scott, J. W. 1988. Deconstructing equality-versus-difference: Or, the uses of poststructuralist theory for feminism. *Feminist Studies* 14 (1): 32–50.

Smith, G. C., and J. A. Waltman. 2006. *Designing and implementing family-friendly policies in higher education.* Ann Arbor: Center for the Education of Women, University of Michigan.

Tierney, W. G., and E. M. Bensimon. 1996. *Promotion and tenure: Community and socialization in academe.* Albany: State University of New York Press.

Ward, K., and E. M. Bensimon. 2003. Engendering socialization. In *Women in higher education: An encyclopedia,* ed. K. Renn and A. Martínez Alemán, 431–35. Santa Barbara, CA: ABC-CLIO.

Ward, K., and L. Wolf-Wendel. 2004. Academic motherhood: Managing complex roles in research universities. *Review of Higher Education* 27 (2): 233–57.

———. 2005. Work and family perspectives from research university faculty. In *The challenge of balancing faculty careers and family work,* ed. J. Curtis, 67–80. San Francisco: Jossey-Bass.

Ward, K. A., L. E. Wolf-Wendel, and S. B. Twombly. 2007. Faculty life at community colleges: The perspective of women with children. *Community College Review* 34 (4): 255–81.

Weedon, C. 1997. *Feminist practice and poststructuralist theory,* 2nd ed. Malden, MA: Blackwell Publishing.

Williams, J. 1999. *Unbending gender: Why work and family conflict and what to do about it.* New York: Oxford University Press.

Wilson R. 2004. Where the elite teach, it's still a man's world. *Chronicle of Higher Education,* 3 December, A8.

Wolf-Wendel, L. E., and K. A. Ward. 2006a. Academic life and motherhood: Variations by institutional type. *Higher Education* 52 (3): 487–521.

———. 2006b. Faculty life at comprehensive universities: Between a rock and a hard place. *Journal of the Professoriate* 1 (2): 1–21.

Epilogue

JUDITH GLAZER-RAYMO

The essays in this book reveal the complexities and the contradictions of women's professional lives. The authors have contextualized their research in many ways—in the stories related to them by women faculty, administrators, and trustees; in their feminist critical analyses of institutional and public policies; and in the evolving relationships between universities and the academic marketplace. For many decades those in positions of leadership have tended to reify higher-education institutions, maintaining artificial boundaries and borderlines and the hierarchies that sustain them. Thirty-six years have elapsed since passage of the omnibus Higher Education Act of 1972 that extended equal employment protection, affirmative action, and anti-bias laws to women in postsecondary institutions and that increased their access as students, faculty, and administrators. As the authors of the preceding chapters demonstrate, women have learned how to use their agency to expand their presence, to create new knowledge in their disciplines, and to gain senior-level positions. However, they have not yet been able to have much impact on the existing organizational structures, whether they are two-year or four-year colleges, master's level or doctoral-granting universities. And there is a great deal of evidence that the corporate outlook of higher education will continue unabated in the future, challenging women even further in their quest for resources on a par with their male colleagues. The narratives and the data contained in these essays affirm that, although significant progress has been made by women in the academy, higher education remains one part of a much larger social canvas that is increasingly susceptible to external forces. This epilogue brings together the many insights and recommendations made by the contributing scholars in an effort to focus attention on the new and continuing challenges that confront women in academia and to propose steps for promoting a new vision for substantive change.

The themes that cut across the preceding chapters shed light on the complex and multifaceted nature of gender and gendered experiences in higher education.

They are embedded in the multiple identities of the authors as well as their inter-viewees, and as Ropers-Huilman, Turner, and Ward and Wolf-Wendel explicate in their research, enable them to "delve more deeply" into their own experiences and the issues of gender, race, ethnicity, work, family, and colleagueship. The liberal feminist perspective, often denigrated as "essentialist" due to its emphasis on en-lightenment values of gender equality, continues to demonstrate its usefulness in providing the tools for comparative data analysis that, in the case of higher educa-tion, serve to highlight the persistence of gender disparities across a range of criti-cal areas affecting women (see, for example, Ward and Wolf-Wendel, and Stage and Hubbard in this volume).

However, as Metcalfe and Slaughter assert in their discussion of third-wave feminism in chapter 4, gender may also be experienced as fluid and relational, illu-minating women's experiences as multifaceted, contradictory, and complex. Third-wave feminism, informed by cultural theory, interdisciplinary academic scholarship, and autobiography, originated in the late 1990s in anthologies that articulated both its similarities and its differences from second-wave feminism. In this intergenerational text, the authors listen to the voices of women faculty, ad-ministrators, and trustees from a spectrum of professional backgrounds, demo-graphic differences, and orientations, eliciting nuanced feminist standpoints grounded in the social sciences. By using various feminist standpoints, they pro-vide a framework for tackling unfinished agendas and the challenges that continue to test women's resolve. The adoption of generational metaphors or "waves" can serve as the basis for discovering the multiple meanings of women's lives and con-ceptualizing a collective vision for the future. To do that, it is necessary to address the new and continuing challenges faced by women in higher education.

New and Continuing Challenges

Eight sets of challenges are articulated by the contributing scholars: (1) the ways in which women construct their identities to incorporate multiple and changing expectations of their roles; and, related to this challenge, (2) how women negotiate their career choices in balancing work, family, and community commitments; (3) how women faculty also negotiate their identities as teachers, scholars, and good citizens of their academic communities; (4) the inequalities of gender that inter-sect with race, ethnicity, and social class, in which gender stereotypes and race and gender bias heighten feelings of dissonance and isolation; (5) market-like behavior of institutions as manifested in academic capitalist knowledge/learning regimes and administrative structures that mirror corporate America; and, related to the competition of the marketplace, (6) the growth of dual employment systems for faculty; (7) the academic pipeline for women in the STEM fields; and (8) the ungendering of public policy intensifying in this decade with the appointment of a conservative judiciary, the abrogation of civil rights and women's rights, and the unraveling of time-honored legal precedents.

Constructing Multiple Identities

Ropers-Huilman uses autobiography to frame her analysis of how women construct their identities "as leaders, family members, ethnic community members, members of various disciplines, and academic citizens." She provides four vignettes that capture vividly the dilemmas she has faced in negotiating her multiple roles as doctoral student, faculty member, parent, and feminist scholar, asserting that this "dance of identities" both facilitates and impedes expectations of productivity associated with her faculty roles and her feminist affiliation within the academy. Both Ropers-Huilman and Turner heighten awareness of the salience of race, ethnicity, and social class over gender in constructing their personal and professional identities. The role of agency in identity formation is also revealed by Terosky, Phifer, and Neumann in their interviews with mid-career women faculty who feel themselves being pulled away from their scholarly learning to serve in roles not of their own choosing under the supposition that outreach and service will allow them to pursue their scholarly learning in other ways.

Work-Family Roles and the Concept of Choice

Ward and Wolf-Wendel also explore identity construction in their interviews with women faculty who have chosen to combine faculty careers and parenting roles. They reflect on the purposeful choices women make in selecting the appropriate workplace for their lifestyle, the consequences of these choices, and the policy contexts that influence their ability to balance work and family roles. They find that "the ideal worker norm" of the research university is counterproductive, acting as a deterrent to diversity and as a disincentive for women who do family work. In her book *Unbending Gender: Why Family and Work Conflict and What to Do About It* (2000), Joan Williams calls for a paradigmatic shift from the ideal worker norm in order to restructure the relationship of the market and family work, stating that "after thirty years of feminist activism, it is time to acknowledge that work patterns of many women are not the same as men's" (2000, 272). Given that reality, Ward and Wolf-Wendel find institutional discretionary policies either non-existent or not very useful. They cite untenured women faculty's reluctance to make use of the Family and Medical Leave Act, which grants eligible employees up to twelve work weeks of unpaid leave during any twelve-month period for birth and care of a newborn child, care of an immediate family member, or for serious medical conditions.

The U.S. Department of Labor estimates that 76 million workers were eligible for the FMLA Act's provisions during 2005, but only 6 million made use of the policy. A study released by Harvard and McGill Universities of 173 countries found that the United States does less than other countries in helping workers balance work and family: 169 countries guarantee paid maternal leave; 98 offer 14 or more weeks of paid leave. "Although in a number of countries many women work in the informal sector, where these government guarantees do not always apply, the fact remains that the U.S. guarantees no paid leave for mothers in any segment of the work force, leaving it in the company of only 3 other nations: Liberia, Papua New Guinea, and Swaziland" (Institute of Health and Social Policy 2007, 1–2).[1] Ward and Wolf-Wendel propose a number of family-friendly entitlement policies that address work-family demands for women on the tenure track, citing baccalaureate colleges and research universities that have taken positive steps toward accommodating women faculty of child-bearing age.

Negotiating Faculty Roles of Teaching, Scholarship, Research Management, and Community Service

Barriers to women's advancement have been characterized as glass ceilings that restrict their ability to move into senior-level positions of power and authority. Terosky, Phifer, and Neumann put a novel twist on this metaphor in their essay, arguing persuasively that these barriers are more like Plexiglas than glass—durable and virtually shatterproof—and that to make the problem even more complex, these ceilings constitute only one element of Plexiglas rooms that are "gleaming, invisible, and sharply resistant to intrusion." Thus, in constructing the identities of mid-career women faculty, they raise important questions about how the labyrinthine structure of the research university becomes entwined with women's professional work, and in so doing, develops into a maze that pulls women away from the production of knowledge through research and teaching that initially drew them to academic life. As more women enter the faculty workforce, the challenge is how to remove these barriers that may otherwise discourage them from pursuing academic careers. They question the illusory nature of the academic reward system that expects mid-career women faculty in research universities to undertake "unstrategized work for which they may be unprepared and unsupported," resulting in a loss of scholarly learning for knowledge production in their fields.

Alemán focuses on women's identification with undergraduate teaching, questioning the absence of gender as an "organizing, conceptual, and functional principle" in discussions of faculty productivity. As a consequence, she observes that assessments of productivity and teaching effectiveness as "output variables" privilege masculine activities and have a negative impact on the reward system for women faculty. She would replace the production model that is one part research and one part teaching with a construct that recognizes the gendered economy of teaching and learning.

Equity, Diversity, and Social Justice

In her essay, Turner considers the impact of race/ethnicity, social class, and gender inequality on women of color faculty and administrators. Through her interviews, she seeks commonalities in the diverse experiences of women of color faculty and presidents. Instead, she finds more differences than similarities not only in their career trajectories but also in the challenges they have faced in establishing their identities. The overriding challenge that has not been adequately addressed, she argues, is the "often invisible" visibility of women of color in leadership positions. The data show quite clearly that power and influence are unevenly distributed at all levels of academic hierarchies, with the possible exception of private women's colleges and HBCUs. And although the Equal Pay Act has been in effect since 1963 and was extended to higher education in 1972, the data also show that women earn less than men across institutional types and levels of control.

The picture is better for women in community colleges, which, as Shaw, Callahan, and LeChasseur observe, remain the least prestigious sector of higher education and have the highest proportion of contingent faculty, even though they educate 50 percent of all undergraduates. And a baccalaureate degree does not guarantee equity since, as the Institute for Women's Policy Research reports, "The ratio of women's to men's median annual earnings was 77.0 in 2005 (the latest available data) for full-time, full-year workers, statistically the same as in 2004 (76.6) and virtually unchanged since 2001 (76.3)" (IWPR 2007). Earlier, the IWPR estimated that if part-time and part-year workers are included, the ratio would be much lower, "as women are more likely than men to work these reduced schedules in order to manage child-rearing and caregiving work" (IWPR 2005).

Bornstein and Turner both comment on the "mixed trends" revealed by data on the college presidency, where women are more likely to head two-year or baccalau-

reate colleges than other types of institutions, and white males are still in the majority in a system that structurally and culturally privileges men. Turner also expresses the dissonance and contradictions that women of color experience and the
salience of race over gender that pervades the campus culture in white-majority
institutions. The pervasiveness of gender bias reaches into the highest levels of academia, and as Bornstein states, in this "diverse, global, market-driven high-
technology era" organizational biases and structures continue to limit women's
options. Gendered expectations perpetuate playing by the rules of the game,
adapting to institutional norms, avoiding (in Bornstein's words) "overt displays of
femininity" and downplaying any interest in women's issues and feminism. These
inequities also extend to governing boards that sustain only token representation
where race, gender, social class, and sexual orientation serve as deterrents to
increasing women's participation.

Academic Capitalist Knowledge/Learning Regimes

In their case study, Metcalfe and Slaughter focus on the need for women to position themselves strategically in public research universities in which the "academic
production process" is no longer "buffered by the state," exposing faculty to the va-
garies of the marketplace. They raise issues implicit in Stage and Hubbard's research regarding the redistribution of resources to research universities that they
characterize as academic capitalist knowledge/learning regimes in which departments close to high-end markets gain the lion's share of resources and "the public
good is redefined as what is good for economic development." Reminiscent of
Alemán's observations on faculty productivity as a function of two competing gendered economies and two contradictory intellectual paradigms, Metcalfe and
Slaughter show how male faculty in one research university are recapturing their
historic privilege by shifting to new prestige systems that marginalize women faculty. This restructuring not only affects the nature of faculty work; it also assigns a
higher value to entrepreneurial activity across institutional types: research universities, private baccalaureate colleges, and two-year community colleges (Slaughter
and Rhoades 2004, 205).

In this competitive climate, where higher education and other institutions are
being privatized and deregulated, the dilemma for women faculty is how to achieve
a balance between their teaching and their research, meet state and institutional
demands for productivity, achieve a balance between their research agenda and
their teaching, and maintain an equal footing with their male colleagues. As several

authors suggest, unworkable assumptions are built into reward structures that are increasingly gendered and in which the psychic and intellectual costs are high.

Dual Employment Systems

Academic organizations with an interest in faculty employment have drawn attention to how an emergent dual employment system is solidifying glass ceilings and sticky floors, creating insurmountable barriers for those now entering the professoriat. This trend has significant implications for women now in the doctoral pipeline as the professoriat is reconfigured into a largely part-time and non-tenure-track system. Early warning signals of the erosion of tenure began in the 1980s as privatization, deregulation, and the free market–dominated public policy making. Efforts to reverse this trend in the 1990s were countered by arguments about budget shortfalls and the need for greater flexibility in meeting market needs. At the same time, universities engaged in bidding wars for "star" professors in high-profile, high-status fields such as economics, business, and the natural sciences.

No longer a transitory phase of the academic labor market, the traditional faculty reward system is undergoing paradigmatic changes that are already having a significant impact on the academy (Glazer-Raymo 2001). As Shaw, Callahan, and LeChasseur point out in their chapter, women enjoy a higher status in the community college but are also more likely to be teaching in substandard facilities, experiencing heavier workloads, and having part-time/adjunct or non-tenure-track positions. The dual systems of tenurable/nontenurable faculty also raise questions about the role and viability of the research doctorate. In the sciences and psychology, for example, an increasing number of Ph.D. recipients are moving directly into the industrial workplace. Meanwhile, the part-time untenured workforce is becoming a larger presence in two-year, four-year, and doctoral universities. Since this contingent workforce has few if any departmental responsibilities, full-time faculty bear the burden for upholding academic standards, student advisement, and committee service. From the standpoint of women faculty now coming through the academic pipeline in greater numbers, this eventuality is ominous. As Ward and Wolf-Wendel report in their chapter, efforts to reform the benefit structure by resolving family-work concerns, supporting subsidized childcare, and closing the gender gap have had mixed results.

Women and Science

Events at Harvard in 2006 portrayed the gender dynamics of faculty in unmasking the rhetoric of a university president. The discourse on women's aptitude for science and mathematics gained national media attention, striking a vital chord among women from a diversity of backgrounds and mobilizing feminists around the issue of whether women can "do science." In their chapter, Stage and Hubbard go well beyond the rhetoric in their analysis of data on women baccalaureates who obtained doctorates in the STEM fields, showing quite clearly that, when data are disaggregated by institutional type and level of control, there are both "expected" and "unexpected" producers of women Ph.D.s in science, mathematics, and engineering. Their findings are rather sobering, and one wonders why research universities have the lowest percentage of women baccalaureates earning doctorates in comparison with their male cohorts. On the other hand, HBCUs, women's colleges, and less selective comprehensive universities are producing successful women graduates in these fields. Their findings also raise questions about how women undergraduates construct their identities and what motivates them to pursue challenging careers in the STEM fields. Stage and Hubbard build on Alemán's arguments, stressing the importance of the teaching mission and classroom experiences to the success of these students.

Ungendering Public Policy

In *Shattering the Myths,* I called for a new feminist agenda framed around the resolution of issues of economic and social justice. This agenda may have then appeared to be within reach but is now proving more elusive. In terms of social justice, voter approval of referenda to end affirmative action in the states of California, Washington, and Michigan will be followed in November 2008 by similar challenges in at least five other states. Women's rights and civil rights are being sidelined in this context, making it appropriate and timely to reiterate support for the values that undergird equity, diversity, and social justice.

The ripple effect of these reversals manifests itself in the Supreme Court's 5–4 decision in the case of *Ledbetter v. Goodyear,* in which the majority opinion written by Justice Alito declared that "a 45-year-old doctrine excusing people whose 'unique circumstances' prevented them from meeting court filing deadlines was now 'illegitimate'" (Greenhouse 2007, 1). Greenhouse observes in her analysis of this decision that this is the second precedent to fall in the Roberts court, but "it surely will not be the last. . . . So the question is not whether the Roberts court will overturn more precedents, but how often, by what standard, and in what terms" (2007, 2).[2]

In 2004, the National Women's Law Center warned that women's hard-earned gains since the 1960s were in danger of "slip-sliding away" under a barrage of anti-choice, anti–civil rights, anti–women's rights, and anti–gay rights legislation in the states, in the Congress, in the executive branch, and in the courts (NWLC 2004). Organizations that monitor the external environment, including the NWLC, the American Association of University Women (AAUW), and the National Coalition for Women and Girls in Education (NCWGE), continue to express their concern about an increasingly polarized judiciary, a lack of vigorous enforcement of protective laws and regulations, and policies that raise questions about institutional guarantees of free speech and academic freedom.

Whereas much of the literature constructs higher-education policies and practices in gender-neutral terms, the essays in this text seek to deconstruct the masculine norms around which faculty and administrative work has been structured. As Williams cogently observes: "Gender is a system of meaning so pervasive and inescapable that it shapes our identity" (2000, 198). Gender matters even when it is not articulated, and in a more stratified higher-education system, women will find it necessary to be more strategic in articulating their priorities.

Looking toward the Future

In her dance of identities, Ropers-Huilman asks whether it is realistic to think that women can really change social institutions or whether we will have to continue performing our rites of passage and professional roles with fewer attempts to mask our individual differences. As a former college president, Rita Bornstein suggests that academic leaders will need to re-create themselves and their institutions into more nimble, flexible, and responsive entities that can compete effectively in the global marketplace. The challenge for women presidents, deans, and trustees will be to establish their legitimacy in organizations that sustain gendered perspectives and expectations of those at the helm. And although Bornstein and Ropers-Huilman perform very different roles as professor or president, each in her own orbit is executing a form of leadership that is relational, adaptable, and collaborative. Bornstein proposes strategies to overcome gender stereotypes by identifying those leadership qualities that derive from women's experiences, and in this context her views are aligned with the women of color presidents interviewed by Turner, each of whom has sought to eliminate cultural and structural barriers that threatened their advancement, and who personify a diversity of leadership styles and strengths.

The fact that several women scholars have recently been elevated to the presidency of leading institutions indicates that governing boards and their constituencies may be ready to support women in leadership positions. This trend occurs at a time when Representative Nancy Pelosi (D-CA) has become the first woman to serve as Speaker of the House of Representatives, Senator Hillary Clinton (D-NY) is considered a serious contender for the presidency of the United States, 16 women serve in the U.S. Senate, 71 in the House of Representatives, 9 as governors, and 1,734 as state legislators (CAWP 2006).

Women college and university presidents and women trustees are now in a unique position to mobilize their resources in addressing the challenges that continue to confront women faculty, reversing some of the more troubling trends that threaten to diminish the status of the professoriat, and eliminating structural barriers that exclude or diminish women's participation, whether these relate to subsidized childcare, tenure and promotion policies, named chairs, or access to entrepreneurial initiatives. As Terosky and her colleagues state in their analyses of the multiple responsibilities faced by women faculty at mid-career, academic leaders and policymakers need to pay closer attention to the "institutional positioning of women's knowledge construction efforts" and to assure that service and administrative demands do not impede women's scholarly learning.

In formulating recommendations for the future, these authors stress the importance of structured mentoring of women students, faculty, and mid-level administrators; the development of women's networks that foster collaboration, teamwork, and consensus-building techniques; the modification of work-family policies; the removal of impediments to legitimacy for women of color, gay women, and women who have pursued nontraditional paths to senior administrative and faculty positions; and a moratorium on rhetoric that perpetuates racial, ethnic, and gender stereotyping and bias.

The essays included in this volume convey solid evidence that structural, attitudinal, and cultural barriers to gender equality may have lessened in the past decade but that the nature of the problems has intensified in a globally competitive marketplace. The forward momentum that has propelled women to their current status can be maintained through a combination of collaborative activism and executive leadership that is fluid, dynamic, and cognizant of the need for maintaining the leverage women have gained and using it to create a more equitable society.

NOTES

1. The United States is also the only industrialized nation that has not ratified two United Nations human rights treaties: the Convention on the Elimination of All Forms of Discrimination Against Women (CEDAW), adopted by the UN General Assembly in 1979, and the Convention on the Rights of the Child (UNCRC), adopted by that body in 1989. CEDAW, which has 185 co-signers among the nation-states, provides an international standard for women's equality and women's rights while UNCRC, with 193 co-signers among the nation-states, seeks to protect the civil, economic, political, and cultural rights of children to age eighteen. Periodic efforts to gain political support for these treaties in the U.S. Congress have met with conservative resistance, presenting human rights advocates with new and continuing challenges in obtaining their ratification.

2. In *Alberto Gonzales v. Leroy Carhart et al.* (No. 05–380) and *Gonzales v. Planned Parenthood et al.* (No. 1382), the Supreme Court ruled 5–4 to uphold the federal Partial Birth Abortion Act (April 18, 2007).

REFERENCES

Center for American Women in Politics (CAWP). 2006. *Facts and findings.* Eagleton Center for American Women in Politics. Rutgers University, The State University of New Jersey. Retrieved on 4/5/2007 from www.cawp.rutgers.edu.

Glazer-Raymo, J. 2001. The fragmented paradigm: Women, tenure, and schools of education. In *Faculty work in schools of education: Rethinking roles and rewards for the twenty-first century,* ed. W. G. Tierney, 169–88. Albany: State University of New York Press.

Greenhouse, L. 2007. Supreme Court memo: Precedents begin to fall for Roberts Court. *New York Times,* 21 June, A1.

Institute for Women's Policy Research (IWPR). 2005. The gender wage ratio: Women's and men's earnings. *Fact Sheet.* Retrieved on 9/15/2005 from www.iwpr.org.

———. 2007. The gender wage ratio: Women's and men's earnings. *Fact Sheet.* Retrieved on 6/20/2007 from www.iwpr.org.

Institute of Health and Social Policy. 2007. *Work, family, and equity index: How does the U.S. measure up?* 1–15. Montreal, QC: McGill University. Retrieved from www.Mcgill.ca/files/tbsp/WFEIFinal2007.pdf.

National Women's Law Center (NWLC). 2004. *Slip-sliding away: The erosion of hard-won gains for women under the Bush administration and an agenda for moving forward.* Washington, DC: Author.

Slaughter, S., and G. Rhoades. 2004. *Academic capitalism and the new economy: Markets, state, and higher education.* Baltimore: Johns Hopkins University Press.

Williams, J. 2000. *Unbending gender: Why family and work conflict and what to do about it.* New York: Oxford University Press.

ANA M. MARTÍNEZ ALEMÁN is an associate professor of education at Boston College. Her empirical studies have included investigations of women's friendships as learning relationships, the impact of gender and race on teaching and learning, and the ideal of community in higher education and the challenge of multiculturalism. Her research and publications focus on the impact of gender, race, and ethnicity on American higher education. She is a recipient of the National Academy of Education Spencer Postdoctoral Scholar Development Program, the Five College Women's Studies Research Center Fellowship, and the Ford Foundation's Bridging Project in International Studies. She is the editor of *Educational Policy,* co-editor (with Kristen Renn) of *Women in Higher Education: An Encyclopedia* (2002), and author of articles in scholarly journals.

RITA BORNSTEIN is President Emerita and Cornell Professor of Philanthropy and Leadership Development at Rollins College, where she served as president from 1990 to 2004. Previously, she was vice president at the University of Miami. She has served on the boards of the American Council on Education and the National Association of Independent Colleges, and has chaired the board of the Council for Advancement and Support of Education. She was also a member of the Association of Governing Board's Task Force on the State of the Presidency in American Higher Education. She consults, speaks, and writes on issues related to leadership, governance, and fund-raising. Her publications include *Legitimacy in the Academic Presidency: From Entrance to Exit* (2004).

M. KATE CALLAHAN is a research associate at Temple University. She is currently working on a study, funded by the Lumina Foundation, of how resource allocation in U.S. higher education affects educational quality across sectors. She recently defended her dissertation, "Relative Advantage: Honors Programs and Stratification in American Higher Education." Research interests include stratification and inequities in American education.

JUDITH GLAZER-RAYMO is a lecturer and fellow of the Higher and Postsecondary Education Program at Teachers College, Columbia University, and professor of education emerita at Long Island University. Her recent books include *Shattering the Myths: Women in Academe* (1999); *Professionalizing Graduate Education: The Master's Degree in the Marketplace* (2005); and *Women in Higher Education: A Feminist Perspective* (co-edited with Becky Ropers-Huilman and Barbara K. Townsend, 2000). She is also the author of book chapters, articles, and review essays on gender equity, social justice, higher-education policy, and the professionalization of graduate education. She has been the recipient of the Research Achievement award and the Leadership award from the Association for the Study of Higher Education (ASHE), the Willystine Goodsell award from the American Educational Research Association (AERA), and the Trustees Award for Scholarly Achievement from LIU.

STEVEN HUBBARD is a clinical assistant professor and program coordinator for the M.A. Program in Higher Education at New York University. He recently defended his Ph.D. dissertation, "Identifying Factors that Influence Student-Centered Teaching in the Undergraduate Classroom." His research interests include student learning, assessment, faculty development, and LGBT students. Before coming to NYU, he worked for ten years in student affairs at the University of Iowa and Hamline University.

KIMBERLY LECHASSEUR is a doctoral student in the Urban Education Program at Temple University. She holds an A.B. in psychology from the College of the Holy Cross. She is currently working with Kathleen Shaw on her study of how resource allocation in American higher education affects educational quality across and within sectors. Her research interests include the political sociology of education reform and issues of access and equity in the United States. Her dissertation research will examine the ways in which local intermediary organizations redistribute power in educational reforms for out-of-school youth.

AMY SCOTT METCALFE is an assistant professor in the Department of Educational Studies at the University of British Columbia in the Adult and Higher Education program area. Her research has focused on the role of intermediating organizations in the university-industry-government relationship and academic capitalism in the United States and Canada. She is currently associate editor of the *Canadian Journal of Higher Education*.

ANNA NEUMANN is a professor of Higher Education at Teachers College, Columbia University. Her publications include *Learning from Our Lives: Women, Research, and Autobiography in Education,* co-edited with P. Peterson (1997); *Redesigning Collegiate Leadership: Teams and Teamwork in Higher Education,* co-authored with E. Bensimon (1993); *Qualitative Research in Higher Education: Experiencing Alternative Perspectives and Approaches,* with C. Conrad, J. Haworth, and P. Scott (1993); and *Making Sense of Administrative Leadership: The 'L' Word in Higher Education,* with E. Bensimon and R. Birnbaum (1989). Currently in process is *Professing to Learn: Creating Tenured Lives and Careers in the American Research University,* a Spencer Foundation–funded research study on mid-career faculty's scholarly lives.

TAMSYN PHIFER is an advanced doctoral student in Higher and Postsecondary Education at Teachers College, Columbia University. She has worked in student and academic affairs at Coe College, Cooper Union, and Teachers College, Columbia University.

BECKY ROPERS-HUILMAN is a professor of higher education at the University of Minnesota. Until 2007, she held a faculty position at Louisiana State University. Her research interests focus on diversity and inclusivity in higher education, especially in terms of social change and activism. While the majority of her work relates to women in higher education, recent scholarship considers students' efforts as they participate in social and organizational change through their involvement on college campuses. Her books include *Feminist Teaching in Theory and Practice: Situating Power and Knowledge in Poststructural Classrooms* (1998); *Women in Higher Education: A Feminist Perspective* (2000), co-edited with J. Glazer-Raymo and B. K. Townsend; and *Gendered Futures in Higher Education: Critical Perspectives for Change* (2003).

KATHLEEN M. SHAW is Deputy Secretary for Postsecondary and Higher Education in the Pennsylvania Department of Education. She is on leave from Temple University, where she served as a faculty member in the Urban Education Program and most recently as chair of the Department of Educational Leadership and Policy Studies. Her work focuses on issues of access, equity, and stratification in higher education, with emphasis on how large-scale federal and state policy affects higher education policy and practice. Her publications include *Putting Poor People to Work: How the Work-First Ideology Eroded College Access for the Poor* (2006). She also serves as a senior research associate at the Community College Research Center, Teachers College, Columbia University, and was a guest editor of "Community Colleges: New Environments, New

Directions," *Annals of the American Academy of Political and Social Science* (2003). Her current research project, funded by the Lumina Foundation, examines how different levels of resource allocation across sectors of higher education affect educational quality.

SHEILA SLAUGHTER is Louise McBee Professor of Higher Education, Institute of Higher Education, University of Georgia. Her research areas are political economy of higher education, science and technology policy, academic freedom, and women in higher education. She is the co-author of *Academic Capitalism and the New Economy: Markets, State, and Higher Education* (2004) with G. Rhoades, and co-author of *Academic Capitalism: Politics, Policies, and the Entrepreneurial University* (1997) with L. Leslie. Her most recent grants are "Virtual Values: Information Technology, Distance Learning, and Higher Education" (National Science Foundation) with J. Croissant and G. Rhoades; and "University Trustees and Conflict of Interest" (National Institutes of Health).

FRANCES K. STAGE is a professor of Administration, Leadership, and Technology at New York University. She was previously professor and associate dean of the College of Education at Indiana University and a National Science Foundation Senior Fellow. Her research includes student development and student achievement in mathematics and science. Recent books include *Answering Critical Questions Using Quantitative Data* (2007); *Theoretical Perspectives on College Students* (2004); *Research in the College Context: Approaches and Methods* (2003) with K. Manning; *Creating Learning Centered Classrooms* (1998) with Muller, Kinzie, and Simmons; and *Enhancing the Multicultural Campus Environment* (1992) with K. Manning.

AIMEE LAPOINTE TEROSKY is adjunct assistant professor of the Higher and Postsecondary Education Program at Teachers College, Columbia University, and dean of Anderson Middle School (Public School 334, Manhattan). She was a teaching consultant for Columbia University's Center for New Media Teaching and Learning and New York University's Center for Teaching Excellence. Her dissertation, "Taking Teaching Seriously: A Study of University Professors and their Undergraduate Teaching," won the 2005 Bobby Wright Dissertation of the Year Award from the Association for the Study of Higher Education (ASHE).

CAROLINE SOTELLO VIERNES TURNER is a professor of Educational Leadership and Policy Studies and Lincoln Professor of Ethics and Education at Arizona State University. Her research interests are in the areas of educational access, equity, leadership, and faculty gender and racial/ethnic diversity. Her publications include *Diversifying the Faculty: A Guidebook for Search Commit-*

tees and *Faculty of Color in Academe: Bittersweet Success* (with S. L. Myers, Jr.). She has been an American Council on Education Fellow; is co-founder of Keeping Our Faculties, a national program on recruitment and retention of faculty of color; and has conducted studies of faculty of color, Latina/o faculty in theological education, and women of color university presidents.

KELLY WARD is an associate professor of higher education at Washington State University. She conducts research on faculty development, campus and community engagement, work and family policies in higher education, and faculty involvement in student development. Her expertise in work and family stems from two Sloan Foundation projects, investigating how tenure-track faculty manage work and family responsibilities and departmental contexts that support or hinder their development. She is co-author of *The Department Chair's Role in Developing New Faculty into Teachers and Scholars* (2000) and *Putting Students First: How Colleges Develop Students Purposefully* (2006); and author of *Faculty Service and the Scholarship of Engagement*, and book chapters and articles on work and family.

LISA WOLF-WENDEL, a professor of higher education at the University of Kansas, is a graduate of Claremont Graduate School. Her research focuses on equity issues of women and people of color in higher education, exploring the characteristics of programs, policies, or institutions deemed exemplary in responding to diversity issues in higher education. Her research projects include a study of faculty of color and the academic labor market, and faculty and work/family balance. She recently published a book, *The Two Body Problem: Dual Career Couple Hiring Practices in Higher Education* (2003).